WORK AND CARING
FOR THE ELDERLY

WORK AND CARING FOR THE ELDERLY

International Perspectives

edited by

Viola M. Lechner, D.S.W.

Margaret B. Neal, Ph.D.

USA	Publishing Office:	BRUNNER/MAZEL
		A member of the Taylor & Francis Group
		325 Chestnut Street
		Philadelphia, PA 19106
		Tel: (215) 625-8900
		Fax: (215) 625-2940
	Distribution Center:	BRUNNER/MAZEL
		A member of the Taylor & Francis Group
		47 Runway Road, Suite G
		Levittown, PA 19057
		Tel: (215) 269-0400
		Fax: (215) 269-0363
UK		BRUNNER/MAZEL
		A member of the Taylor & Francis Group
		1 Gunpowder Square
		London EC4A 3DE
		Tel: +44 171 583 0490
		Fax: +44 171 583 0581

WORK AND CARING FOR THE ELDERLY: International Perspectives

1 2 3 4 5 6 7 8 9 0

Printed by Braun-Brumfield, Ann Arbor, MI, 1999. Cover design by Joe Kolb.

A CIP catalog record for this book is available from the British Library.
   The paper in this publication meets the requirements of the ANSI Standard Z39.48–1984 (Permanence of Paper).

Library of Congress Cataloging-in-Publication Data available from publisher.

ISBN 0-87630-996-1 (case)
ISBN 0-87630-997-x (paper)

CONTENTS

Contributors   xi

Preface   xiii

Chapter **1**   *Viola M. Lechner and Margaret B. Neal*

Introduction   1

Background Data on Countries Examined   *1*
Definition of Terms: Who Are the Frail Elderly and
   What Is Elder Care?   *5*
Limitations of the Data   *6*
Plan of the Book   *6*
References   *7*

I. MOST DEVELOPED COUNTRIES

Chapter **2**   *Anne Martin-Matthews*

**Canada and the Changing Profile of Health and
Social Services: Implications for Employment and
Caregiving**   11

Introduction   *11*
Canada: The Demographic Context   *11*
The Canadian Aging Research Network   *12*
The "Costs" of Caring   *13*
Working and Caregiving over Time:
   Some Preliminary Findings   *15*
Public Policy: Entitlement and Need   *15*
What Employees Want and Need   *19*
Future Developments   *21*
Notes   *24*
References   *25*

Chapter **3**   *Monika Reichert and Gerhard Naegele*

**Elder Care and the Workplace in Germany: An Issue
for the Future?**   29

Introduction   *29*
Extent of the Work-Family Problem in Germany   *29*
Policies, Benefits, and Programs and Services to Assist
   Employed Caregivers and Elders   *32*
Strengths and Weaknesses of Supports for
   Employed Caregivers   *38*
Factors Contributing to Future Policies and Services for
   Employed Caregivers   *38*
Recommendations with Regard to Elder Care and
   the Workplace   *41*
Future Trends   *43*
References   *44*

Chapter **4**   *Judith Phillips*

Developing a Caregivers' Strategy in Britain   47

Introduction: The Extent of Work-Family Problems   *47*
Types of Policies and Programs to Assist Employed
   Caregivers   *49*
Factors Contributing to Britain's Configuration of
   Supports   *54*
Strengths and Weaknesses   *59*
Future Change   *62*
References   *65*

Chapter **5**   *Jenny Brodsky and Brenda Morginstin*

**Balance of Familial and State Responsibility for the
Elderly and Their Caregivers in Israel**   68

Introduction   *68*
Work-Family Issues   *69*
Supports for Employed Caregivers and Elders   *73*
Future Trends: Issues and Problems   *80*
Note   *81*
References   *82*

Chapter **6**   *Masako Ishii-Kuntz*

Japan and Its Planning Toward Family Caregiving   84

Introduction   *84*
Work and Family Concerns   *85*
Supports for Employed Caregivers   *88*
Factors Contributing to Supports for Employed Caregivers
   and Elders   *94*
Future Trends   *98*
References   *99*

Chapter **7**   *Lars Andersson*

Sweden and the Futile Struggle to Avoid Institutions   101

Introduction   *101*
Work-Family Issues   *102*
Supports for Employed Caregivers: Description and
   Evaluation   *103*
Supports for Older Persons: Description and Evaluation   *107*
Contributing Factors   *108*
Future Trends   *115*
Note   *117*
References   *117*

Chapter **8**   *Viola M. Lechner and Margaret B. Neal*

**The Mix of Public and Private Programs in the
United States: Implications for Employed Caregivers**   120

Introduction   *120*
Managing Work and Care of Older Persons   *120*
Supports for Employed Caregivers: Description and
   Evaluation   *122*
Factors Contributing to Supports for Employed
   Caregivers   *130*
Future Trends   *135*
References   *137*

II. MORE DEVELOPED COUNTRIES

Chapter **9**   *Ursula Karsch and Corina Karsch*

**Migration and Urbanization in Brazil: Implications for
Work and Elder Care**   143

Introduction   *143*
Work-Family Problems   *144*
Supports for Employed Caregivers and Elders   *147*
Strengths and Weaknesses of Supports   *151*
Factors Contributing to Limited Supports for Employed
   Caregivers and Elders   *152*
Future Trends   *156*
References   *157*

Chapter **10**   *Raquel Bialik*

**Urbanization in Mexico Affects Traditional Family
Caregiving of the Elderly**   160

Introduction   *160*
Work-Family Problems   *160*
Supports for Employed Caregivers and Elders   *163*
Strengths and Weaknesses of Supports   *166*
Factors Contributing to Strengths and Weaknesses of
   Supports   *168*
Future Trends   *171*
References   *172*

III. LESS DEVELOPED COUNTRIES

Chapter **11**   *Iris Chi*

China and the Family Unit: Implications for Employed Caregivers   177

Introduction   *177*
The Components of the Welfare System in Urban China   *179*
Employment-Based Welfare   *179*
Responses to Managing Work and Informal Care of
   Frail Elders   *182*
Family Caregiving Values   *190*
Future Trends   *191*
References   *192*

Chapter **12**   *Caroline Njuki*

Poverty and Economic Development: Implications for Work and Elder Care in Uganda   194

Introduction   *194*
Work and Family Issues   *196*
Supports for Employed Caregivers and for Elders   *199*
Evaluation of Supports for Employed Caregivers and
   Elders   *202*
Factors Contributing to Lack of Services for Employed
   Caregivers and for Elders   *203*
Summary   *208*
Future Trends   *208*
References   *209*

Chapter **13**   *Viola M. Lechner*

Final Thoughts   211

Managing Work and Elder Care   *211*
Supports for Employed Caregivers and Elders   *215*

Future Trends 220
Conditions That Foster the Development of Supports for
   Employed Caregivers and Elders 223
Recommendations 229
Concluding Comments 231
References 232
Index 233

CONTRIBUTORS

Lars Andersson, Ph.D.
Section of Social Gerontology
Stockholm Gerontology Research Center
Stockholm, Sweden

Raquel Bialik, M.A., Consultant
Technological Universities
Ministry of Education
Mexico City, Mexico

Jenny Brodsky, Ph.D.
Research Program on Aging
JDC-Brookdale Institute of Gerontology and Human Development
Jerusalem, Israel

Iris Chi, Ph.D.
Social Work and Social Administration
University of Hong Kong
Hong Kong

Masako Ishii-Kuntz, Ph.D.
University of California Tokyo Study Center
Tokyo, Japan

Ursula Karsch, Ph.D.
Pontificia Universidade Catolica De Sao Paulo
Sao Paulo, Brazil

Corina Karsch, M.A.
Johnsons & Johnsons do Brazil
Sao Paulo, Brazil

Anne Martin-Matthews, Ph.D.
School of Social Work and Family Studies and
Dean, Research and Graduate Studies
Faculty of Arts, University of British Columbia
Vancouver, British Columbia, Canada

Brenda Morginstin, Ph.D.
Division of Research in Long-Term Benefits
National Insurance Institute
Jerusalem, Israel

Gerhard Naegele, Ph.D.
Institute for Gerontology
Dortmund, Germany

Caroline Njuki, Ph.D.
World Young Women's Christian Association
Geneva, Switzerland

Judith Phillips, Ph.D.
Department of Applied Social Studies
University of Keele
Keele Staffordshire, United Kingdom

Monika Reichert, Ph.D.
Institute for Gerontology
Dortmund, Germany

PREFACE

Whose responsibility is it to care for the dependent members of a society, such as frail elders? Historically, different countries' approaches to the care of dependents, including frail elders, have varied dramatically. In some countries, governmental support is relied on nearly exclusively; in others, families shoulder the whole responsibility. In the remaining countries, responsibility is shared, to varying degrees, between the public and private sectors, including work organizations as well as families.

A number of factors—economic, political, sociocultural, demographic, and others—have influenced the degree of responsibility assigned to the state, family, workplace, or private agencies. Today, in developed and developing countries alike, widespread demographic, social, and economic changes are occurring. Families throughout the world are experiencing unprecedented changes in their domestic and employment responsibilities. In developed and in most developing countries, women are becoming as economically active as men. Along with their growing employment commitments, families are facing increasing responsibilities for the care of frail elders due to the growth in the numbers and proportion of elderly in all countries' populations, and especially the growth among the very old. These elders are most likely to need assistance, such as with shopping, transportation, and personal grooming, as well as with necessary medical, nursing, social, financial, and legal services.

Throughout the world, women have been the traditional caregivers for dependents. As a result, the increased labor force participation of women has raised questions about the continued ability of families to assist their frail elders. Moreover, although individuals' work and home lives traditionally have been viewed as separate spheres, there is growing recognition of the interrelationship between work and family, with each sphere having important "spillover" effects, both positive and negative, on the other. Receiving the greatest amount of attention has been the negative spillover from family to work; that is, the impact of family caregiving responsibilities on employees' productivity at work. In response, some work organizations in developed countries have implemented policies, benefits, and services designed to help their employees better manage their dual work and family roles so as to minimize negative effects on the workplace. Recently, however, many work organizations have begun to restructure themselves in order to remain competitive in the global economy. Reorganizations have resulted in increases in the number of part-time and temporary workers. These workers generally receive few, if any, benefits and often receive lower wages than full-time permanent workers.

Similarly, at the same time that families' work and care responsibilities are expanding, governments throughout the world are carefully examining their role in the provision of social welfare programs, especially health and retirement benefits for the growing numbers of older people. In many developed countries, where governments typically have funded public social welfare programs, the governments are reducing their expenditures on such programs. Such cutbacks not only affect the elders, but also their families. In developing countries, where public funds are, by definition, extremely limited, governments are reluctant to initiate public social welfare programs due to the costs involved.

Within this context of changing families, governments, and work organizations, this book examines various countries' supports to elders and the working families who care for frail elders. In particular, this book investigates how 11 geographically dispersed countries in various stages of economic development are responding to the changing needs and demands of individuals who are employed and, at the same time, caring informally for elderly family members who need assistance in their daily lives.

In the future, countries worldwide will need to find cost-effective and fair ways to care for their growing numbers of older people, especially those who are frail and need considerable help. Formal care (e.g., professional home care services, adult day care, institutional care) can be very expensive. Informal care by family members is the least expensive care, but it can result in stress for the caregivers, negatively impacting not only themselves but also their employers (due to lost productivity) and their elders. So that families engaged both in paid work and in caring for their elders will not be overburdened, governments, work organizations, and for-profit and not-for-profit health and social service agencies will need to find solutions to support these families.

It is our hope that, by presenting the various approaches used in these countries and the factors leading to the development of the approaches, this book will heighten awareness of the possible options for addressing the work–elder care dilemma. As such, it is targeted to a broad audience of policy makers, social service providers, researchers, educators, and students in all countries who wish to find ways to promote more support to people who are employed and also care informally for frail elders. In particular, we hope that the knowledge gained from this book will help concerned decision makers in all countries—governmental representatives, business leaders, union leaders, and advocacy and political interest groups alike—develop cost-effective, humane public and workplace approaches for assisting employed women and men who also are informal caregivers of elders.

Thanks are due to many individuals and organizations for the assistance they provided in the development and preparation of this book. First and foremost, we wish to express our most sincere appreciation to the authors of each of the chapters. They persevered through numerous drafts and requests for revisions through the years that it took to bring the book to fruition. Moreover, English is not the native language of most of these authors; for them to write their chapters required special skill and effort. Second, Elaine Pirrone and Bernadette Capelle at Taylor and Francis worked with us from the proposal phase through the acquisition of the first drafts of the chapters. Thaisa Tiglao provided valuable editorial advice and assistance, and saw the book through its final stages. We thank each of them for their help. Third, we wish to acknowledge our respective employers, the Department of Sociology, Anthropology, and Social Work at St. John's University and the Institute on Aging and the Department of Urban Studies and Planning of the College of Urban and Public Affairs at Portland State University. They provided us with access to necessary equipment (e.g., telephones, computers, fax machines, copy machines, e-mail), office space, and supplies. Fourth, a special thanks to Li Feng, a graduate assistant at St. John's University, for carefully transcribing numerous edits of chapter drafts. Fifth, we thank our husbands, Sandy Lechner and David Leckey, for their emotional support as we shifted time and energy from our lives at home to complete this book in addition to our regular teaching and research responsibilities at work. Finally, we are grateful to the many family caregivers and managers of work organizations who have so generously shared their experiences and thoughts with us in the research we have conducted over the years on work and elder care in the United States. It is our hope that, ultimately, family caregivers throughout the world will benefit from policies developed as a result of the perspectives and options presented in this book.

Viola M. Lechner
Margaret B. Neal

CHAPTER

Introduction

The first section of this chapter sets the stage by presenting cross-country comparisons of the extent of the work–elder care problem. Employment trends are examined, as are trends in population aging and other intercountry differences and similarities. Also presented is a description of the range of approaches to support individuals who are engaged in paid work and who also are caregivers to frail elders. The subsequent sections of this chapter describe the overall plan of the book, define terms that are used throughout the book, and discuss limitations in data presented related to work and elder care issues.

☐ Background Data on Countries Examined

In this book, the ways in which 11 diverse countries are responding to the work–elder care dilemma are examined. The 11 countries selected were chosen to obtain diversity by amount of income, degree of economic development, and geographic location. The countries are arbitrarily categorized according to their level of economic and social development: most developed, more developed, and less developed. The 11 countries are: (1) the most developed—Canada, Germany, Great Britain, Israel, Japan, Sweden, and the United States; (2) the more developed—Brazil and Mexico; and (3) the less developed—China and Uganda. Altogether, these countries comprise one third of the world's population. Some of the other ways in which these countries vary are highlighted below.

Employment Trends

Throughout the world, the primary caregivers of dependent persons typically are women. For this reason, women's increased participation in the labor force is an important phenomenon to note. In particular, this phenomenon has raised concerns about families' abilities to continue to care for their elders. Table 1-1, in the first two columns, reveals that women in all 11 countries increasingly are working outside the home. In 1995, the percentage of the labor force comprised of women neared that of men in Uganda (48%), Sweden (48%), the United States (46%), Canada (45%), and

TABLE 1-1. Employment and aging trends

Countries	% Females in Labor Force[a] 1980	% Females in Labor Force[a] 1995	% Women 40–60 Economically Active in 1995[b] 1995	% Increase 60+ Population 1996–2025[c]	% 75+ Population[c] 1996	% 75+ Population[c] 2025
Most developed						
Canada	40	45	71.4	111	5.3	9.6
Germany	40	42	63.1	59	6.4	11.0
Great Britain	39	43	70.2	42	7.2	10.5
Israel	34	40	58.8	99	4.1	5.9
Japan	38	41	67.5	51	5.8	14.9
Sweden	44	48	89.7	41	8.5	11.6
United States	42	46	72.8	88	5.7	7.9
More developed						
Brazil	28	35	43.0	164	1.4	3.8
Mexico	27	31	35.8	198	1.6	3.6
Less developed						
China	43	45	74.2	152	1.9	4.9
Uganda	48	48	89.9	37	0.5	0.6

[a]From *World Development Report.* Copyright 1997 by the World Bank. Oxford: Oxford University Press.
[b]From *Working Papers: Economically Active Population: 1950–2010,* Vols. II, III, IV. Copyright 1997 by the International Labour Office (ILO).
[c]From *Global Aging into the 21st Century.* Copyright 1996 by the U.S. Bureau of the Census. U.S. Department of Commerce. (Wallchart is available from the National Institute on Aging, Washington, DC.)

China (45%). It is interesting to note that Ugandan women were as economically active in 1980 as they were in 1995. Such high female labor force participation rates are common throughout African countries. Although the proportions of women in the Mexican and Brazilian labor forces lag behind those found in the other nine countries, Table 1-1 shows steady increases in each country from 1989 to 1995.

The third column of Table 1-1 shows the rate of labor force participation among all women age 40 to 60 (the typical age of most caregivers) in each of the countries. These rates were fairly high in most countries, ranging from 63% in Germany to almost 90% in Sweden and Uganda. Not surprisingly, the rates of participation among Brazilian and Mexican women were lower, at 43% and almost 36%, respectively.

Population Aging Trends

In all 11 countries, the proportion of persons age 60 years and over is projected to increase from 1996 to 2025, as shown in the remaining columns of Table 1-1. Countries differ, however, in degree and nature of the aging of their populations. First, the greatest growth in persons age 60 and over will occur in the developing countries of Mexico (198%), Brazil (164%), and China (152%). Worldwide, the elderly population is growing fastest in developing nations (Kinsella & Taeuber, 1993). A second important difference among the 11 countries is that the greatest increase in persons 75 years of age and over will occur in the most developed countries, especially Japan (15%) and Sweden (11.6%). With advanced age, many elders will need assistance from others with such tasks as shopping, transportation, personal grooming, and obtaining needed medical, social, and financial services.

The demographic projections in Uganda differ from those for many developing nations; Uganda's aged population will increase only 37%. One explanation for this lower increase is the country's high poverty rate, which limits the country's ability to provide a safe and healthy environment for its citizens. Another explanation is the number of premature deaths from AIDS, which reduces the number of persons who would have lived into their senior years.

Other Intercountry Differences

Not only do the 11 countries differ in their female employment patterns and population aging trends, they differ in population size and in their level of economic and social development. As shown in the first few columns of Table 1-2, the countries range in population size from over 1 billion (in China) to only 6 million (in Israel). Populations in Israel and Uganda are still growing fairly modestly, at slightly over 3% for the period 1990 to 1995; immigration accounts for the increases in Israel, while Uganda's continuing high fertility rate (6.7%) contributes to its growth. The remaining countries are growing more slowly, with the slowest growth (0.3%) in Japan and Great Britain.

Countries vary greatly in their amount of wealth. As shown in Table 1-2, middle columns, Uganda's per capita income was only $240 in 1995, compared to almost $27,000 in the United States and $40,000 in Japan. Table 1-2 also shows the amount of change in gross domestic product (GDP) for each of the 11 countries during two time periods: 1980 to 1990 and 1990 to 1995. The GDP is a measure of the total cost of all the goods and services produced in a given year; as such, it is an important indicator of economic growth. The countries varied greatly in terms of the amount of change they experienced in GDP. For the years 1990 to 1995, China's change in GDP was the highest, at 12.8%, and Sweden's was the lowest at, −0.1%; Israel's was in the middle, at

TABLE 1-2. Social and economic indicators

Countries	Population Size (millions) 1995	Population Growth[a] (%) 1990–1995	Fertility Rate (%) 1995	GNP Per Capita (dollars) 1995	Poverty[b] (%) 1981–1995	Adult Illiteracy (%) 1995	Infant Mortality Rate[c] 1995	GDP Growth[a] (%) 1980–1990	GDP Growth[a] (%) 1990–1995	Urban Population % Population 1995	Urban Population % Growth[a] 1980–1995
Most developed											
Canada	30	1.3	1.7	19,380		h	6	3.4	1.8	77	1.4
Germany	82	0.6	1.2	27,510		h	6	2.2	—	87	0.6
Great Britain	59	0.3	1.7	18,700		h	6	3.2	1.4	90	0.3
Israel	6	3.5	2.4	15,920		—	8	3.5	6.4	—	—
Japan	125	0.3	1.5	39,640		h	4	4.0	1.0	78	0.6
Sweden	9	0.6	1.7	23,750		h	4	2.3	-0.1	83	0.4
United States	263	1.0	2.1	26,980		h	8	3.0	2.6	76	1.2
More developed											
Brazil	159	1.5	2.4	3,650	28.7	17	44	2.7	2.7	78	3.0
Mexico	92	1.9	3.0	3,320	14.9	10	33	1.0	1.1	75	3.1
Less developed											
China	1,200	1.1	1.9	620	29.4	19	34	10.2	12.8	30	4.2
Uganda	19	3.2	6.7	240	50.0	38	98	3.1	6.6	12	5.2

Note. h, According to the United Nations Educational, Scientific, and Cultural Organization, (UNESCO), illiteracy rate is less than 5%. GDP, gross domestic product. GNP, gross national product. From *World Development Report.* Copyright 1997 by the World Bank.
[a]Average annual growth rate in percent.
[b]Defined as living on less than $1 per day.
[c]Infant mortality rate is per 1,000 live births.

4

6.4%. Countries' GDP can vary a fair amount from year to year, as reflected in the differences between the two time periods. Countries with the highest economic growth are in a better position to improve the quality of life of all citizens; in part, through employment opportunities and the provision of social welfare programs.

The middle columns of Table 1-2 reveal intercountry differences on several social indicators: poverty, illiteracy, and infant mortality rates. Many people in developing countries live on less than one dollar a day: 50% of Ugandans, 29.4% of Chinese, 28.7% of Brazilians, and 14.9% of Mexicans. In these same countries, the proportion of the population that was illiterate in 1995 ranged from 10% to 38% while, in developed countries, the illiteracy rate was less than 5%. The last columns show that, in all of the countries except China and Uganda, over 75% of the population lived in urban areas in 1995. The urban populations in China and Uganda, however, are growing steadily at 5.2% and 4.2%, respectively, per year.

Supports for Employed Caregivers and Elders

The 11 countries, as described separately in each of the next 11 chapters, have differing levels of government, workplace, union, and not-for-profit and for-profit agency involvement in helping employees manage their dual work and elder care roles. These various approaches include policies, benefits, and services that directly or indirectly help employed caregivers (Lechner & Creedon, 1994; Neal, Chapman, Ingersoll-Dayton, & Emlen, 1993). Direct responses refer to those policies and services that directly benefit employed persons (e.g., flexible work schedules). Indirect responses are those policies and services that are available to older people (e.g., home care assistance) rather than to caregivers. Services that help the elderly also can help employed caregivers better manage their dual responsibilities of work and caregiving. For example, when home care services are in place, it may be easier for employed caregivers to work without interruptions or worries about frail elders. The particular configuration of policies, benefits, and services that exists in each country has an impact on employed caregivers, their older relatives, the workplace, and the society itself.

☐ Definition of Terms: Who Are the Frail Elderly and What Is Elder Care?

For the purposes of this book, by *frail elders*, we mean those persons over a particular age, typically 60 or 65, who require assistance with tasks of everyday living. When help is provided informally (i.e., by family members or friends), it is considered *elder care*. Frail elders may or may not be living with the caregiver. Assistance to the elder may be necessary because of a variety of reasons, such as physical or mental disease or impairment, social isolation, or lack of necessary skills, such as the ability to speak the language of the dominant culture. Help may be needed because of a gradual worsening of a condition (e.g., incremental loss of vision, hearing, strength, or short-term memory) or as a result of a sudden or acute illness, incident, or event. Examples of the latter would include the experience of a stroke or a fall by the elder, the elder wandering off and becoming lost in what should be familiar surroundings, or the loss of a spouse or other primary caregiver.

The caregiving assistance that may be provided includes a broad range of responsibilities, from less to more emotionally, physically, or time intensive. More intensive forms of assistance typically involve help with *activities of daily living* (ADLs), such as helping with bathing, dressing, getting in and out of a chair or bed, toileting, or eating (Katz, Ford, & Moskowitz, 1963). Elder care also includes help with *instrumental activities of daily living* (IADLs). Such assistance includes, for example, shopping for or with the elder, cooking, housekeeping, transporting the elder to various appointments, making telephone calls to obtain needed goods or services, managing the elder's legal or financial affairs, and managing medications (Lawton & Brody, 1969). Regular telephone calls to check on the elder's safety and well-being also may be considered a part of elder care (Neal et al., 1993), including those made by caregivers who live at some or even a great distance from the elder. Long-distance caregiving may involve periodic travel to the elder's place of residence and the making of long-distance telephone calls for purposes of management of care, help with expenses, providing advice and information, managing legal and financial affairs, as well as all of the other above-mentioned types of assistance (Wagner, 1997).

☐ Limitations of the Data

The data presented in each of the 11 country-specific chapters were derived from a variety of sources, including the authors' own research, the published work of other scholars and organizations, government documents, and personal communications with key informants. Research on managing work and elder care is fairly limited, especially in the developing countries. And, even among the developed countries, only one—Germany—has conducted an in-depth, national work and family study with a randomly selected sample. Various relevant studies have been conducted in Canada, Great Britain, the United States, Israel, Japan, and Sweden; however, most have been either regional, nonrandom studies of employed caregivers or national studies of only informal caregivers or only employees. The national studies of caregivers generally elicit very limited data related to the managing of work and family duties, and those of employees may suffer from response bias (i.e., surveys concerning employees and their family responsibilities may not be completed by employees who do not have such responsibilities). For their chapters in this book, the authors from China, Uganda, and Mexico conducted small-scale, regional studies of employed caregivers. These studies represent the first of their kind in those countries and, although limited in scope, they provide preliminary data and are useful for identifying potential trends for further study.

Where possible, findings are presented concerning within-country variations among employees who are caregivers, particularly variations due to race or ethnicity. Other potential sources of variations exist, such as economic status, educational attainment, and geographic location, for countries with large or diverse geographical areas. The data on within-country variations, however, are extremely limited; there is a great need for research in this area.

☐ Plan of the Book

The following 11 chapters address issues related to work and elder care in the countries selected. The authors for each country-specific chapter were selected based on two criteria: residence in the country being discussed and expertise in social policies that affect the elderly, employees, or both population groups. The authors of each chapter examine the following questions with regard to their country:

1. What is the extent of the work-family problem in the country, particularly with respect to the care of elderly family members?
2. What types of policies, benefits, and programs or services (governmental, employment-based, union-initiated, not-for-profit and for-profit, and so forth) exist to assist employed persons with caregiving responsibilities for frail elders? What is the relative weight or importance of public versus private support?
3. What are the strengths and weaknesses of the country's particular configuration package?
4. What factors have contributed the most to this particular configuration of policies and services, including historical, demographic, sociocultural, political, economic, and other relevant factors?
5. What changes in workplace, government, and not-for-profit and for-profit responses are foreseen in the near future? Why?

The book's final chapter summarizes the key findings regarding the 11 countries' work–elder care situation and solutions. It then synthesizes these findings to identify the necessary and sufficient conditions for the initiation of work–elder care assistance.

The chapters in this book reveal that some countries have fairly generous policies, benefits, and programs, while other countries have very few supports available. Reasons for these differences are examined, with close attention given to the necessary and sufficient conditions that support the more generous approaches.

☐ References

International Labour Office. (1997). *Working papers: Economically active population: 1950–2010: Vol. II. Africa.* Geneva, Switzerland: Author.

International Labour Office. (1997). *Working papers: Economically active population: 1950–2010: Vol. III. Latin American and the Caribbean.* Geneva, Switzerland: Author.

International Labour Office. (1997). *Working papers: Economically active population: 1950–2010: Vol. IV. Northern America, Europe, Oceania.* Geneva, Switzerland: Author.

Katz, S., Ford, A. B., & Moskowitz, R. W. (1963). Studies of illness in the aged. The Index of ADL: A standardized measure of biological and psychosocial function. *Journal of the American Medical Association, 185,* 914–919.

Kinsella, K., & Taeuber, C. (1992). *An aging world. II* (International Population Reports P95/92-3, U.S. Bureau of the Census). Washington, DC: U.S. Government Printing Office.

Lawton, M., & Brody, E. (1969). Assessment of older people: Self-maintaining and instrumental activities of daily living. *Gerontologist, 9,* 179–186.

Lechner, V., & Creedon, M. (1994). *Managing work and family life.* New York: Springer.

Neal, M., Chapman, N., Ingersoll-Dayton, B., & Emlen, A. C. (1993). *Balancing work and caregiving for children, adults, and elders.* Newbury Park, CA: Sage.

U.S. Bureau of the Census, Department of Commerce. (1996, December). *Global aging into the 21st century.* Washington, DC: Author. (Wallchart is available from the National Institute on Aging, Washington, DC)

Wagner, D. (1997). *Long distance caregiving: Getting by with a little help from their friends.* Washington, DC: National Council on the Aging.

I

MOST DEVELOPED COUNTRIES

CHAPTER

Anne Martin-Matthews

Canada and the Changing Profile of Health and Social Services: Implications for Employment and Caregiving

☐ Introduction

As in many industrialized countries, the national policy context within which employees provide assistance to—and receive assistance from—their elderly relatives is rapidly changing in Canada. While some of these changes relate to the aging of the population and the rise in female labor force participation, the urgency of fiscal constraints in the provision of publicly funded programs and services largely has been the impetus for changes in health policies and in the broad formal system of care (Havens, 1995). This chapter will examine the character and implications of care to elderly family members by employed caregivers, set against the backdrop of a rapidly changing health and economic security system.

☐ Canada: The Demographic Context

At the time of the 1996 census, 12% of Canada's population of 30 million people was over the age of 65. However, there is considerable variation in the composition and distribution of the population by region and province; of the 10 Canadian provinces and two territories, for example, several have aged populations in excess of 13% (Manitoba and Saskatchewan), while others have substantially lower proportions (Al-

The data reported in this chapter were collected as part of a study of Work and Family, conducted by the Work and Eldercare Research Group of the Canadian Aging Research Network (CARNET), based at the University of Guelph, Ontario, from 1991 to 1996. The project was funded by the Canadian Ministry of Science and Technology through its Networks of Centres of Excellence Program.

berta at 9.9% and the Yukon and Northwest Territories each with less than 5%) (McPherson, 1998). By the year 2011, approximately 14% of the Canadian population (an estimated 5 million people) will be age 65 and over (Moore & Rosenberg, 1997).

☐ The Canadian Aging Research Network

Many of the findings reported in this chapter derive from the research activities of the Work and Eldercare Research Group of the Canadian Aging Research Network (CARNET). Between 1991 and 1995, the Research Group[1] surveyed over 8,500 employees from across regions of the country in a series of studies designed to examine the prevalence of "elder care"[2] among Canadian workers, the impact of such responsibilities on employees' abilities to balance their work and family lives, and the efficacy of selected workplace and community initiatives in enabling employees to balance employment and care of elderly family members. In order to examine how the patterns of balance between work and elder care may change over time, data also were collected from 685 of these workers at two points in time, and from 250 of them at three points over a 3-year interval.

The CARNET Work and Eldercare Studies began with a very broad view of the levels of involvement of employees in the lives of their elderly relatives, proceeding from there with various refinements on what might be called elder care (Martin-Matthews & Campbell, 1995). Data were collected on 18 tasks with which these employees may have helped an elderly relative at least once in the 6 months preceding data collection.

If an individual indicated that help had been provided with any one of these activities, he or she was defined, for purposes of the study, as involved in elder care. The most frequent types of assistance were with transportation, shopping, filling out forms, and home maintenance. The CARNET studies further distinguished between the provision of personal and instrumental care. *Personal care* involves providing help with any one of what gerontologists call the activities of daily living (ADLs), which include bathing, feeding, toileting, dressing, or administering medications. *Instrumental care* involves helping with the instrumental activities of daily living (IADLs), such as transportation, shopping, laundry, finances, and arranging services. In this chapter, the types of assistance which employees provide are therefore categorized either in terms of instrumental or personal care, although those who provide personal care usually also assist with instrumental tasks.

Using these criteria, CARNET researchers estimated that approximately 45% of the employees who were surveyed had some measure of involvement in assisting elderly relatives. For most employees, this involved modest to moderate levels of help with IADLs. However, for about 12% of the employees, assistance to elderly relatives included the potentially more demanding responsibilities associated with the provision of personal care.

Approximately half the employees with elder care responsibilities also had some responsibilities for dependent children.[3] However, the term *serial caregiving* is now generally understood to be a more appropriate description of the caring responsibilities of most individuals. Typically, caregiving evolves through the life span "in a temporal unfolding rather than providing care to several groups at one time" (Centre on Aging and the Caregivers Association of British Columbia, 1995, pp. 17–18). Analysis of data from the nationally representative sample of the 1990 General Social Survey of Canada suggests that "being caught in the middle" in terms of simultaneous caregiving responsibilities to parents and dependent children, and responsibilities to employment is not a typical experience (Rosenthal, Martin-Matthews, & Matthews, 1996; Stone, 1994). Therefore, the comparatively high proportion of employees with dual responsibilities for both child care and elder care, as found in the CARNET studies, may reflect a self-selection bias in the sample due to the particular salience of these combined caregiving roles for employees in this unusual situation.

Analyses of data from the General Social Survey of Canada indicate that "over one-third of the population with full-time jobs and with a high level of parent-care responsibility in 1990 consisted of men" (Stone, 1994, p. 11). In the CARNET studies, men and women were almost equally likely to provide instrumental care. However, men were only half as likely as women (7% vs. 14%) to be involved in the provision of personal care (Martin-Matthews & Campbell, 1995). Some researchers have suggested that the predominance of women as caregivers is a function of the fact that women also predominate among the recipients of care. Mothers or mothers-in-law were by far the most common recipients of care in our studies, accounting for about three quarters of those to whom assistance was provided.

Factors which predict the involvement of employed men in caregiving roles to elderly family members also have been examined in the CARNET studies (Campbell, 1997). For this analysis, the various caring "tasks" that comprise the CARNET measure of elder care were categorized in terms of those which could be deemed "traditionally male" tasks (e.g., yard maintenance), more gender neutral tasks (e.g., transportation), and typically "nontraditional" tasks for men (e.g., personal care). Overall, Campbell found that, although certain factors predict men's involvement independent of the type of task (e.g., distance and sibling network composition), the gendered nature of the task was important in determining how other factors (such as filial obligation, parent status, education, and income) influence the provision of care by men.

Differences also exist in the amount of care provided by men and by women. Arber and Ginn (1990) suggested that the provision of 5 hours of assistance per week distinguishes "caregivers" from "helpers." Among the employees surveyed by CARNET, 13% of the women and 8% of the men provided 5 or more hours of care on average per week. While the majority of employed caregivers assisted only one elderly relative (60%), almost a third (32%) helped two, and 8% assisted three or four.

☐ The "Costs" of Caring

Statistics Canada data indicated a 100% increase over the past 10 years in absenteeism for personal or family reasons. "Some 37% of that increase is attributed to time spent caring for an elderly relative" (Ontario Women's Directorate & Ontario Ministry of Community and Social Services [OWD & OMCSS], 1991, p. 18). In examining the factors associated with employees' involvement in the provision of care to elderly family members, the CARNET studies sought to distinguish between shorter term job costs, longer term career costs, and personal costs.[4] These costs have been discussed in general elsewhere (Gottlieb, Kelloway, & Fraboni, 1994), by types of care (Martin-Matthews & Rosenthal, 1993) and by gender (Martin-Matthews & Campbell, 1995), and only are summarized here. Personal care is associated with a greater impact than is instrumental care for both women and men. This pattern holds for virtually all types of job, career, and personal costs.

There are some gender differences. Women are more likely than men to use sick days in order to meet their family obligations and are more likely to miss work-related social events. Men are generally more likely than women to report interrupted workdays. A major gender difference is evident in relation to promotion, with women almost twice as likely to report lost opportunities for promotion because of providing informal care. Regardless of the type of care provided, women also are significantly more likely than men to report most of the caregiver costs examined. However, the long-term consequences associated with not seeking promotion or advancement are particularly pronounced for women involved in the provision of personal care (Martin-Matthews & Campbell, 1995). As noted by McDaniel (1993), the inequities associated with the combination of employment and elder care (in particular, personal elder care) "render women less able to be competitive for the best opportunities that society can offer" (p. 140). Employers who claim a commitment to maximizing career advancement opportunities for women, and yet express no interest in issues of work and elder care, are deluding themselves. While much CARNET research documents the apparently greater "costs" to women than to men of their "caring" roles, another line of inquiry undertaken by CARNET researchers sought to understand the reasons for the relationship between work-family conflict and adverse job outcomes. Research by Gignac, Kelloway, and Gottlieb (1996) advanced the hypothesis that work-family conflict will mediate the relationship between elder care involvement and job-related outcomes. They argued that employees' elder care responsibilities will not have a direct adverse impact on their work life; rather, these responsibilities will predict outcomes in the job domain only to the extent that they engender work-family conflict. In testing this hypothesis, work-family conflict is analyzed in bidirectional terms and as separate on two components: work interference with family (WIF) and family interference with work (FIW). The results confirm the hypothesis and suggest that the nature and amount of employees' caregiving responsibilities do not adequately predict employees' workplace performance or job satisfaction. The greater the work-family conflict experienced by employed caregivers, the more likely they are to report reduced job satisfaction, increased job costs, and absenteeism. Gignac et al. (1996, p. 537) suggested that "one implication of these results is that organizational or community interventions that prevent or limit the extent to which eldercare involvement intrudes on work may substantially reduce the adverse workplace consequences experienced by caregivers."

An interesting gender-related finding of the research by Gignac et al. (1996) is that the hypothesis was not supported in analyses specific to female employees. That is, not only did women report significantly more FIW and WIF than did men, it also was the case that caregiving responsibilities directly predicted FIW among women. The authors speculated that these findings reflect differences in the nature and quantity of the elder care performed by women and by men.

Other CARNET studies, however, speak to the importance of focusing not only on the direction of work-family conflict but also on the source of the conflict. Gottlieb, Kelloway and Martin-Matthews (1996) studied the contribution of demographic, job-related, social support, and caregiving variables to the prediction of work-family conflict, stress, and job satisfaction among a sample of nurses providing child care or elder care. The argument was that both WIF and FIW can have two bases: time-based conflict, whereby the time demands of one sphere interfere with role performance in the other; and strain-based conflict, whereby strain arising from the demands of one role spill over to performance in the other role. The results overall underscore the value of distinguishing between time-based and strain-based conflict, although they suggest the need for further examination of the actual situations that lead to each type of conflict.

☐ Working and Caregiving over Time: Some Preliminary Findings

Over a 3-year period, 33% of a group of employees with the "structural potential" (Rosenthal et al., 1996) for elder care (in that they had elderly relatives) moved from nonactive into active caring roles. This suggests that estimations of the proportion of employees providing elder care at one point in time potentially can be quite misleading if used to project involvement. Similarly, the implications of involvement in elder care can change over time. Comparisons of two waves of CARNET data collection found that employees with elder care responsibilities reported significantly lower levels of stress; of job, career, and personal costs; and of the perception of FIW at "time two" than they had at "time one." It may be that these employees developed ways of coping with their responsibilities or that they or their elderly relatives were able to access other kinds of supportive services. In either case, these findings suggest that the needs of working caregivers do indeed change over time.

For some, continuing employment has a "role enhancing" quality in relation to caregiving (Martin-Matthews & Keefe, 1995, p. 132) and actually facilitates the caregiving role by acting as a buffer against, or respite from, the stresses and demands of caregiving. It is estimated that approximately 9% of caregivers leave paid employment in order to provide care for an elderly person (Canadian Study of Health and Aging, 1994). Almost 12% of current employees indicated that they have left past employment because of family obligations, and slightly over 14% reported that they have considered leaving their current employers for this reason (MacBride-King, 1990).

However, it is important to recognize that the provision of elder care need not be inherently stressful or have an impact in terms of the workplace. The Canadian data suggest that many elder care tasks may be manageable outside of work hours or may be accommodated largely through the introduction of more flexible job arrangements such as flextime, telecommuting, and job sharing. Involvement in elder care therefore is not inherently associated with negative job impact. The nature and degree of impact depends instead on the moderating influences of coping, availability of services, policies, and demands (Gignac et al., 1996).

☐ Public Policy: Entitlement and Need

The focus above in this chapter has been on the character of the elder care provided by employees and its consequences. However, as Stone (1994) has noted, "job/family conflict results from the interplay between work-related sources of stress and supports, family stresses and supports, and the extent to which community-based resources . . . effectively meet individual and family needs" (p. 35). Table 2-1 lists the supports available in Canada for employees with caregiving responsibilities.

A key element of public policy is the issue of whether eligibility is based on entitlement or on need (McDaniel, 1993, p. 128). Under entitlement, recipients of benefits (e.g., health services or pensions) are entitled to these benefits as a function of some universal criterion, such as age. When eligibility is based on need, some assessment of means is necessary in order to receive benefits. This distinction between need and entitlement is fundamental to public policy in Canada. Its impact on the lives of em-

TABLE 2-1. Canadian supports for employees with elder care responsibilities

Government Initiatives	Nongovernmental Organization Initiatives	Union Initiatives	Workplace Initiatives
For employed caregivers Federal and provincial dependent tax credits Canada/Quebec Pension Plan (drop out provisions) Indirectly, for older persons Old Age Security Guaranteed Income Supplement Various provincial income supplements Medicare (provincial jurisdictions) Drug assistance plans (provincial) Integrated homemaker programs (provincial) Home care (subsidized) Housing-related programs (i.e., home conversion) Widow's Pension Act (provincial) Spouse's/Widowed Spouse's Allowance	For employed caregivers Case management Work-family vendors Caregiver support networks Provincial caregiver associations Indirectly, for older persons Private home care services Day care Nursing homes Self-help organizations	Political and work organization influence Federal and provincial lobbying Union-management negotiations Services Assistance programs for members Sensitivity training for union negotiators and other staff	Policies: Work scheduling Parental and family leave (usually paid)[a,b] Sick, vacation, personal leave (usually paid)[a] Medical leave (usually paid)[a,b] Flextime, compressed work week[a] Part-time work, job sharing[a] Flexplace[a] Relocation policies Policies: Corporate culture Top-level management support Management sensitivity training[a] Work and family task forces[a] Benefits: Income assistance Canada/Quebec Pension Plan[b] Health coverage[a] Employer pension benefits[a] Services Educational materials, seminars[a] Counseling and support[a] Resource and referral[a] Case management services[a] On-site care center and other direct services[a] Employee assistance program (EAP)[a]

[a]Voluntary.
[b]Government mandated.
[c]Government encouraged.

ployed caregivers is felt primarily in terms of policies addressing health and community care, and income security. These are discussed below.

Health and Community Care

Since 1972, Canada has had a national medical insurance program. Working cooperatively, federal and provincial governments "have ensured that medical and hospital care remain free. It is a principle engraved on the Canadian soul: the sick will not face financial ruin" (Janigan, 1995, p. 10).

As a result, "the values and principles of the Canada Health Act [especially the principle of universality] are inherently definers of the Canadian psyche" (Havens, 1995, p. 260) and "entrenched in the Canadian ethos" (Béland & Shapiro, 1995, p. 157). Having a national medical insurance program takes an enormous psychological and economic burden off individual sick people and their families, and thus has significant implications for the provision of elder care. However, two features of national health policy potentially disadvantage caregivers.

First, the national health insurance schemes have a very strong "medical and an institutional focus within the health care system . . . , the two most expensive forms of care" (Chappell, 1988, p. 74). Community-based programs are not covered by a comprehensive national insurance and have tended to develop as add-ons to the cost of existing institutional and medical care. CARNET studies indicate that employed caregivers rely on community-based services to supplement their caring roles, so the lack of uniform patterns of availability and accessibility of such services is problematic, especially for long-distance caregivers (Hallman & Joseph, 1995).

Potentially greater problems lie ahead, however. Canada now ranks fourth among the Group of Seven nations (after the United States, Germany, and France) in terms of the percentage of its gross domestic product (GDP) that is spent on health care. With 9.1% of GDP spent on health care (Coutts, 1998), on a per capita basis, Canada has the second most expensive health care system in the world. In fact, Canada spends more on health care per capita than any industrialized country that has national health insurance (Chappell, 1994, p. 3).

In recent years, the federal government, in strident efforts at deficit reduction, has cut by one third the monies it transfers annually to the provinces for health care, postsecondary education, and welfare. Approaches to cost control of the Canadian health care system have varied from province to province, but they have several common elements, including caps on payments to individual physicians and the removal of certain items (such as cataract surgery) from the list of insured services. As Havens (1996, p. 44) has noted, "Administrative consolidation and program integration have given way in most provinces . . . to a decentralization of policy and eventually of funding to smaller geographical aggregates or regions. . . . [In the process] health care system policy-makers have chosen to focus almost exclusively on reducing costs to government while deferring questions about alternative programs or services and innovations relative to staffing ratios and mixes of staff."

These changes in Canadian health care policy and delivery stand to have an enormous potential impact on Canada's elderly and those who care for them. Family care not only is recognized as an essential component of care to the elderly, but "indeed has become a cornerstone in the rhetoric of reform for health care in Canada. This recognition comes at a time of perceived fiscal crisis . . . [and] . . . is being used as part of the argument for re-shaping universal health insurance" (Chappell, 1994, p. 7).

However, as cutbacks have occurred, and delays in health services have resulted, caregivers increasingly have come to recognize that community-based social services are "neither abundant nor readily accessible" in Canada. "Cut-backs to hospital and institutional services are apparent, but the corresponding financial support for the extension and strengthening of community care is not evident" (National Council on Aging [NACA], 1995, p. 14). Ideally, community and alternative services should be in place before hospitals are closed down, but this is not happening. The growing need for support agencies "has emerged in a period of relatively slow economic growth, of spending constraint, during a decline in the belief in state intervention. So adaptations to this new reality have been slow in coming" (Underwood & DeMont, 1991, p. 33). As a result, there is evidence of a growing lack of appropriate follow-up care for patients discharged from hospitals (NACA, 1995). Another negative effect is an increase in the burden of care borne by informal caregivers, who already assume about 80% of seniors' care needs (Chappell, Strain, & Blandford, 1986).

However, in a reversal of recent trends, spending on health care in Canada is expected to increase by almost 4% in 1999, with almost all provincial governments within Canada increasing health care spending (Coutts, 1998). These increases will come after years of restraint, which have led to hospital closures across the country, shortages of many types of health care personnel in nonurban areas in particular, shortages of nursing staff throughout the country, and emerging concerns about the prospect of "passive privatization" with a shift of health care costs from public to private spheres. The latest figures (Coutts, 1998) suggest that the rate of growth of private sector care in Canada has slowed during the 1990s, with the current proportion being approximately 70% public and 30% private spending on health care in Canada.

Income Security Policies and Programs

National data on both employed and unemployed Canadians between the ages of 35 and 64 indicate that less than 3% provide monthly financial help to elderly parents and less than 5% do so yearly (Rosenthal et al., 1996). One potential explanation for the low financial contribution of adult children lies in the degree of income security that elderly Canadians recently have enjoyed. At present, Canada has a three-tier income security system for those over age 65: Old Age Security providing a fixed benefit every month; the Canada/Quebec Pension Plan, which provides benefits to those who were contributors while in the labor force; and the third tier of employer pension plans and registered retirement savings plans. The elimination in 1989 of universal access to Old Age Security represented a fundamental shift in philosophy from access based on entitlement to access based on need, and this shift would become even more pronounced if a revised income security system, known as the "Seniors' Benefit," is implemented, as proposed, in 2001.

In terms of the third tier of income support, among employed persons age 45 and over, only 53% of men and 42% of women are covered by employer pension plans (Schellenberg, 1994). Public policy in Canada is shifting more and more to individual responsibility by offering tax incentives for retirement savings, while making few reforms to the public pension system (McDaniel, 1993, p. 129). These reforms also stand to substantially alter the context within which employees in Canada provide assistance to elderly relatives. Reductions in health services, delisting of procedures for coverage by medical insurance, longer waiting lists, and alterations in income security programs together reflect a pattern of increasing emphasis on individuals within families assuming more substantial and active roles as providers of care for elderly relatives.

☐ What Employees Want and Need

As health care and income security policies change in Canada, it is important to con-sider what employees feel they need in order to optimize their work-family balance. For the most part, employees identified comparatively inexpensive options such as education programs and seminars and literature (OWD & OMCSS, 1991). Flexible working hours have been described as "perhaps one of the most valuable benefits a company can offer to employees who are combining a job with eldercare" (OWD & OMCSS, 1991, p. 47). The CARNET surveys corroborate this. Flexible hours ranked second only to "time off/no pay" as the employee benefit utilized by most respon-dents (24% had utilized flextime, 33% had taken time off with no pay). Employees also expressed a preference for compressed workweeks, personal days with pay, and part-time work (particularly if it did not result in a reduction in benefits) as ways of helping to balance their work and family responsibilities.

Some employed caregivers may be reluctant to make their needs known to their employers. To invoke the need versus entitlement dichotomy presented above, em-ployees know well that, whatever their needs, in most workplaces, they are entitled to very little. Typically, it is viewed as the responsibility of the employee to take care of individual need. Even where employees have access to benefits, they may be reluctant to use them. Many employees who participated in the CARNET studies indicated that, in the current economic climate, they would endure all manner of work interfer-ence with their family life before they would attempt to access benefits to which they were entitled, because of their fear that doing so might draw them to the attention of supervisors or that they might be viewed as "disloyal" to the company.

Even though a report to the Minister of Employment and Immigration over a dec-ade ago recommended the development of a "major . . . National Policy on Care for the Elderly which would focus on the growing support needs of workers with elderly dependents" (Canada Employment and Immigration Advisory Council [CEIAC], 1987, p. vii), this has not come to pass (National Advisory Council on Aging [NACA], 1990). Despite the lack of national policy, however, much of the initiative to date has come from the public sector.

The federal government has provided leadership in Canada in terms of programs designed to meet the needs of caregivers, primarily in the form of labor legislation. Most statutory or collective agreement provisions dealing with family responsibilities tend to focus on leaves of absence (Lero & Johnson, 1990). Family-related leaves vary by type and duration of leave, and also by jurisdiction. The power to regulate labor matters is shared by federal, provincial, and territorial governments. Government documents refer to legislative provisions which grant short-term leave of not more than a few days, typically unpaid, for attending to family obligations other than those relating to the birth or adoption of a child (Lero & Johnson, 1990).

The federal government also has taken a leadership role in the implementation of work-at-home programs and major initiatives within the federal public service. At the provincial level, there are several initiatives involving payment for care, although all are tied to social welfare assistance and have very stringent criteria for eligibility (Martin-Matthews & Keefe, 1995). Financial compensation for family members who provide informal care to elderly relatives frequently has been discussed but rarely has been implemented in Canada (NACA, 1990). One exception is the Nova Scotia Home Life Support Program, which financially compensates family members for care of the elderly. Financially compensated caregivers tend to be younger females who live in

nonurban areas and coreside with the care receiver. The greater proportion of financially compensated caregivers in nonurban areas is likely influenced both by the limited availability of home help services in these areas and by the high rates of unemployment and underemployment in these areas, which create a surplus pool of labor
that is available to provide elder care services at minimal costs (Keefe & Fancey, 1997).

The few private sector initiatives that have been introduced include child care and
elder care information services; handbooks, which explain how to apply for and manage flexible work arrangements; special training for managers; job share registries;
quarterly work and family newsletters; compressed workweeks; and flexible work
arrangements. One company, which implemented such programs emphasizing employees' entitlement to these resources, noted that the number of job shares had more
than tripled in 3 years to over 850 in 1994, and the Eldercare line (a service that offers
health and social service referrals to the caller) had rung 800 times in 2 years (Gaetz,
1994). Other options implemented by Canadian employers include regular part-time
employment, leave programs, work-at-home arrangements, telecommuting, flexible
benefits, and "supportive manager" training (Smith, 1994); people care days; and elder care referral services (Totta, 1994).

Often, however, "employers recognize the problems in the abstract but see themselves as having limited responsibility which in actual fact is true" (Kamerman, 1991,
p. 13). Many employers believe that "employees must separate their work life from
their family life and that any problems experienced at home should be taken care of
by the employee" (CEIAC, 1987, p. 24). Nevertheless, Canadian corporations are
showing a growing recognition of the potential value of family supportive programs.
In one survey of 300 organizations, five benefits surfaced as most likely to show an increase within the next 10 years: flexible benefits, employer-sponsored day care, flextime, employee assistance plans, and maternity and paternity leave. Interestingly, all
of these practices have applications to the integration of paid work and family life
(Stone, 1994, p. 32). Although it can be argued that flexible working hours and special
family-related leaves are "somewhat prevalent" among Canadian corporations, most
workplace policies continue to be informal arrangements with requests handled on an
ad hoc basis (Stone, 1994, p. 32).

Indeed, many Canadian employers feel that they meet social obligations to their
employees by means of the corporate tax burden in Canada rather than through specific workplace-based policies. These taxes pay for the "social safety net" of national
health insurance and income security. Matching employee contributions to pensions,
for many employers, represents a "tax on payroll," which they find burdensome
enough without extending their responsibilities further (Paris, 1989). In addition, recent employment growth in Canada primarily has taken place in small companies. In
these work environments, employees are less likely to be unionized or to receive pension plan coverage, and are more likely to face termination by permanent lay offs and
to receive lower wages on average (McDonald & Chen, 1994).

In order to promote greater involvement of the private sector in workplace-based
initiatives, several potential "solutions" have been advanced. These involve defining
the "problem" in a way that goes beyond the "women and work" issue, thereby
ostensibly engaging a larger constituency in support (Kamerman, 1991). The Canadian situation suggests that many employers will develop work and family programs
to meet the competition from other companies in their field. It is no accident that
much of the private sector initiative in relation to work-family balance comes from
Canada's major financial institutions, all highly competitive and each with a predominantly female labor force.

Of all the possible workplace responses to these issues, the two which have received particular attention in the literature are management attitudes and flexible work arrangements. The issue of the role of managers and supervisor attitudes toward flexible work arrangements and the work-family balance has been an emerging thrust of the CARNET research agenda to date (Barham, 1995; Barham & Gottlieb, 1994; Barham, Gottlieb, & Kelloway, 1993, 1994; Gottlieb, Kelloway, & Barnham, 1998).

One CARNET study (Barham, 1995; Barham & Gottlieb, 1994; Barham et al., 1993) examined the ways in which managers' expectations about the effects of flexible work arrangements influence the likelihood of their using these arrangements themselves and their granting of them to a subordinate. Flexible work arrangements also may be categorized in terms of whether they involve retention of full-time employment or a reduction in hours of work. In general, managers reported more negative effects of the use of reduced hours arrangements than for full-time flexible arrangements. Over 80% of managers endorsed the options of flextime, work-at-home arrangements, and reduced hours. Fewer than 60% endorsed the options of job sharing and unpaid leave. Overall, the managers overwhelmingly favored flextime as their preferred way of trying to address issues of WIF and FIW among subordinates. Only a small minority of managers chose job sharing and unpaid leaves in such situations.

Managers generally viewed elder care as being less demanding on employed adult children than child care is on employed parents. They perceived the degree of responsibility to provide care as lower for adult children than for parents, and also believed the elderly generally are more able to care for themselves than are dependent children. "Overall, eldercare seems to be a less acceptable reason than childcare for making special workplace arrangements" (Barham & Gottlieb, 1994, p. 15). In terms of specific flexible work arrangements, managers generally were more likely to consider the option of reduced hours for child care than for elder care.

☐ Future Developments

Canada is in the process of conducting a thorough review of its federally funded social programs, which include income security for the elderly. Health care programs and policies, under the aegis of the provinces, are very much in flux. While there is some hope that reforms actually will benefit the elderly and those who care for them through a channeling of funds away from hospitals and institutions and to more preventative and community-based programs (Béland & Shapiro, 1994), it is becoming increasingly evident that "reform" means merely cost cutting.

It is projected that labor force dependency ratios will rise to 1.6 or 1.7 by the year 2036; this means that there will be 160 to 170 Canadians outside the labor force for every 100 people in it. Other, more conservative, estimates put the number at 140 (Schellenberg, 1994). Not only does this have implications for the funding of universally accessed social programs so important to the Canadian psyche, but also for the responsibilities faced by those Canadians in the labor force. One recent estimate suggests that, into the next century, some 70% of employees will have responsibilities for care of older family members (MacDonald, 1996).

Another area of emerging need in Canada involves the aging of persons who are developmentally disabled and with special needs. Much of the research on work and family balance has focused on the two ends of the family life cycle: on employees caring for children and on those caring for elders. Employees who provide care to dependent adults aged 18 to 64 with special needs, either in the form of physical and mental disabilities or with chronic illnesses, with few exceptions, have been ignored in the literature on the balance of work and family responsibilities. (Irwin & Lero, 1997). Recent analyses of CARNET data (Livingstone, Tindale, & Martin-Matthews, 1998) indicate that caregivers to this population include both parents and siblings with labor force attachments. The substantially longer duration of the provision of dependent adult care, in comparison to duration of either child care or care of elderly relatives, reflects the need for policies and practices, in both the public sphere and in the workplace, to address the unique aspects of this situation. Such analyses and comparisons, however, are complicated by the finding in the CARNET data that fully 80% of employees providing care for dependent adults also were providing care to children or to elders. With the increased longevity and aging of the population of adults with special needs occurring at the same time as Canada's constraining of health and social care costs, and the associated closing of community based facilities serving the needs of this population, this is very much an issue of concern to families, service providers, employers, and policy makers in this country.

In a country like Canada, with a geographically dispersed population and a northern climate, the challenges are many. Proximity can be an important determinant in the extent and nature of participation in the family work of parent care. Fully a quarter of all Canadians live in rural areas, many of which have concentrations of the aged well beyond the national average (Joseph & Martin-Matthews, 1994).

One CARNET study specifically examined the geographical context within which employed caregivers provide assistance to elderly relatives, specifically in terms of the spatial arrangement of the employed caregiver's home, their workplace, and the care recipient's home (the "locational triangle"). Joseph and Hallman (1996) found that the spatial arrangement of home, workplace, and the elderly relative has a discernable impact on levels of perceived stress and interference with both work and family life. They further found that "while travel time to work has a consistent and logical impact on various measures and symptoms of work-family balance . . . , our results point toward the greater importance . . . of travel time to elder as a variable within the locational triangle" (p. 409). In policy terms, Joseph and Hallman argued that the variability in travel time between employed caregiver and dependent elder serves to emphasize one of the many differences between elder care and child care. They concluded that workplace policies designed to balance work and family responsibilities will need, among other things, to be sensitive to the distinctive demands that may be placed on long-distance caregivers.

The issue of "minority caregivers" also is an important factor to consider in examining work and elder care issues. Canada has had a policy of family reunification in immigration, which has resulted in an increase in the number of elders from ethnocultural minorities. Approximately 17% of the elderly were born outside of Canada (Norland, 1994) and almost a quarter of the elderly population speaks neither English nor French (McPherson, 1998). This reflects "high rates of immigration from Europe and China in the early 1900s and from developing regions of the world after the 1980s" (McPherson, 1998, p. 117). Language barriers, religious and cultural differences, and economic dependency conspire to reduce the access of elders (and their caregivers) from ethnocultural minorities to community-based health and social services. Canada's First Nations include just over 1 million people who "claim a single or multiple origin including Indian, Métis, and Inuit" (McPherson, 1998, p. 42). They are among the least visible and most deprived groups in North America, with elderly members of First Nations typically worse off than other elderly persons in Canadian society. These disadvantages are reflected in annual incomes frequently below the poverty line, high rates of disability, chronic poor health, reduced life expectancy, and lack of access to health care facilities (McPherson, 1998; Wister & Moore, 1997). Virtually nothing is known about the dynamics of elder care in First Nations communities; outside these communities, First Nations people "have remained both culturally and physically isolated" (McPherson, 1998, p. 43).

Several CARNET researchers have explored the relationship between ethnicity and the provision of assistance to older relatives. Keefe, Rosenthal, and Béland (1996) found that, while ethnicity is related to the amount of assistance provided, structural factors (such as living arrangement, gender, and age) are stronger predictors of the level of assistance than are culturally relevant expectations of filial obligation and ethnic group identification. Their findings suggested important avenues for further exploration of issues of ethnicity and elder care.

Another important contextual issue in the balancing of employment and care of elderly relatives in Canada is the legal recognition of the statutory obligations of adult children to elderly parents. Under the Family Law Acts in most Canadian provinces, adult children have an obligation to support a parent who can prove need and "who has cared for or provided support for the child" (Canadian Press, 1996; Snell, 1990). While this section of the Family Law Act has existed in various forms since 1921, it has been "rarely ever used" (Carey, 1995, p. A1). It has been suggested that the law did not need to be invoked until now, because of the clear role that government played in helping to support the economically vulnerable.

Attempts to enforce filial obligation laws seldom have been an effective means of gaining support for the elderly when the support is not given willingly (Snell, 1990). Recently, however, the Ontario Court of Appeal upheld a lower court ruling ordering three adult children to provide monthly support to their 60-year-old mother. This case may well illustrate that, "as the welfare state begins to be restructured or crumble, we may see more jurisdictions calling on these statutory obligations. . . . Now, the suggestion is that families must once again take on these responsibilities" (Glossop, as cited by Carey, 1995, p. A9). Indeed, some analysts have observed that, as baby boomers age and governments cut back on the social safety net, "going after children could become a way of saving the public purse" (Carey, 1995, p. A1).

Fundamental to any process of reform is a change in attitude. Almost 10 years ago, Canadian first ministers (the prime minister and provincial premiers) mandated the development of comprehensive strategies to facilitate the integration of work and family responsibilities. They recognized that "changes were needed in Canadian attitudes, programs, services and legislation if workers with dependents were to be ensured the same range of opportunities and treatment as workers without dependents" (Lero & Johnson, 1990, p. 1). These changes have yet to occur in Canada. Nevertheless, as Lero and Johnson (1994, p. ii) noted, "a coordinated response [in] changes to policies, programs and workplace practices that would facilitate the harmonization of paid work and family responsibilities . . . seems warranted in light of current trends, global economic restructuring, and recession, and the very real limits that are being placed on health and social welfare spending."

Summary

Canadian employees are actively involved in the provision of care to elderly relatives, especially in terms of assistance involving the IADLs. Research conducted by CARNET has revealed short-term job costs, longer term career costs, and personal costs associated with elder care, especially when the assistance involves ADLs. This is true for both women and men, and for a wide variety of occupations, although more so for women.

Most research focuses on the direction and nature of work-family conflict, but the source of the conflict also is important. Canadian data underscore the value of distinguishing between time-based conflict (involving interference with role performance between two spheres) and strain-based conflict (involving spillover arising from the demands of one role) when analyzing elder care.

In terms of policies and programs designed to meet the needs of employed caregivers, the federal government has taken leadership in Canada in implementing work-at-home options. Financial compensation for family members who provide informal care is provided in some provinces, but under quite restricted guidelines. While private sector initiatives (particularly, flexible working hours) do exist, most workplace practices involve informal arrangements between managers and subordinates. The CARNET data suggest that managers typically perceive elder care to be a less acceptable reason than child care for making special workplace arrangements.

If workplace-based initiatives are to become widespread in Canada, numerous challenges must be overcome: the geographical dispersion of the population, the northern climate, the concentrations of the aged in rural areas, the increasing ethnocultural diversity of the elderly population, and the language barriers which limit the access of almost a quarter of the elderly population to linguistically and culturally appropriate services. In time, the increasing legal recognition of the statutory obligations of adult children to elderly parents, together with changes in the delivery of national health care and income security programs, may well become important sources of impetus driving the development of workplace-based initiatives.

☐ Notes

1. The members of the Work and Eldercare Research Group were as follows. From the University of Guelph, Guelph, Ontario, were Anne Martin-Matthews, Research Group leader (Department of Family Studies), Benjamin H. Gottlieb (Psychology), Alun E. Joseph (Geography), E. Kevin Kelloway (Psychology), and K. Victor Ujimoto (Sociology). Other members are Carolyn J. Rosenthal (Gerontology and Sociology, McMaster University, Hamilton, Ontario); Victor W. Marshall (Centre for Studies of Aging, University of Toronto); François Béland (GRIS, Université de Montréal, Quebec); Ingrid Connidis (Sociology, University of Western Ontario, London, Ontario); Nancy Guberman (Social Work, Université de Québec à Montréal). Monique M. A. Gignac and Lisa Barham completed postdoctoral fellowships; Lisa Barham, Lori D. Campbell, Bonnie C. Hallman, and Janice M. Keefe completed their doctoral studies based on the CARNET project, and Christina L. Levins completed her master's degree. CARNET-related presentations and publications by several of these researchers are noted in this chapter, and appear in the literature.

2. Although the term *elder care* is used in this chapter, elsewhere (Martin-Matthews, 1996), I have indicated my concerns about the potentially pejorative nature of this concept and the ways in which it implies inappropriate parallels to child care. Martin-Matthews and Campbell (1995) described a series of factors which distinguish child care from elder care. These include the trajectory and duration of care, the presumption of dependency of the care receiver, the role of reciprocity, the autonomous decision making of the care receiver, and the potential involvement of formal community services.

3. Care for dependent family members between the ages of 19 and 64 rarely has been addressed in the literature on work and family balance (Levins & Martin-Matthews, 1995). In nearly half of these cases, care was provided by an employee to a parent not yet age 65.

4. In terms of job costs or effects, employees were asked whether, in the 6 months preceding data collection, they had experienced any of the following as a result of having to meet their family responsibilities: having to use sick days when they personally were not sick, arriving late for work or having to depart early from work, being absent from work for 3 or more consecutive days, having to use vacation time to attend to family obligations, experiencing interrupted workdays (e.g., because of telephone calls concerning family matters), or being unable to work their desired shift.

Career costs were measured by asking whether, in the 6 months preceding the study, employees' family care responsibilities had occasioned them to miss business meetings or training sessions, decline business travel, miss job-related social events, decline extra work projects, decline or not seek a promotion, or experience difficulty with a manager or supervisor.

Personal costs were assessed by asking employees whether, in the 6 months preceding data collection, their family care responsibilities had resulted in a reduction in time available for volunteer work, leisure activities, continuing education, socializing with friends, housework, or sleep.

☐ References

Arber, S., & Ginn, J. (1990). The meaning of informal care: Gender and the contribution of elderly people. *Ageing and Society, 10,* 429–454.

Barham, L. (1995). *Managers as gatekeepers: Factors affecting managers' willingness to grant alternative work arrangements.* Unpublished doctoral dissertation, University of Guelph, Guelph, Ontario, Canada.

Barham, L., & Gottlieb, B. H. (1994, October). *Managers' decisions to grant flexible work arrangements and beliefs about childcare and eldercare: Replication and extension in a male-dominated workplace.* Paper presented at the annual meeting of the Canadian Association on Gerontology, Winnipeg, Manitoba, Canada.

Barham, L., Gottlieb, B., & Kelloway, E. K. (1993, June). *But will my manager understand? Managers' reactions to employees' caregiving responsibilities.* Paper presented at the Canadian Aging Research Network (CARNET) Colloquium, Toronto.

Barham, L., Gottlieb, B., & Kelloway, E. K. (1994, June). *What's to be gained and what's to be lost? Anticipated risks and rewards of flexible work arrangements.* Presentation at the CARNET Colloquium, Toronto.

Béland, F., & Shapiro, E. (1994). Ten provinces in search of a long term care policy. In V. W. Marshall & B. D. McPherson (Eds.), *Aging: Canadian perspectives* (pp. 245–261). Peterborough, Ontario, Canada: Broadview Press.

Béland, F., & Shapiro, E. (1995). Policy issues in care for the elderly in Canada. [Editorial]. *Canadian Journal on Aging, 14,* 153–158.

Campbell, L. D. (1997). *Sons who care: Exploring men's involvement in filial care.* Unpublished doctoral dissertation, University of Guelph. Guelph, Ontario, Canada.

(CEIAC) Canada Employment and Immigration Advisory Council. (1987). *Workers with family responsibilities in a changing society: Who cares* (Publication No. WH-6–174E) Ottawa, Ontario, Canada: The Council.

Canadian Aging Research Network. (1996). *Work and Eldercare Research Group: Final report.* Toronto: University of Toronto, Centre for Studies of Aging.

Canadian Press. (1996, January 24). Mother wins court fight for adult children to support her. *The Vancouver Sun,* p. A5.

Canadian Study of Health and Aging. (1994). Patterns of caring for persons with dementia in Canada. *Canadian Journal on Aging, 13,* 470–487.

Carey, E. (1995, September 17). Can kids be forced to support parents? *The Sunday Star* (Toronto), pp. A1, A9.

Centre on Aging and the Caregivers Association of British Columbia. (1995). *Informal caregivers to adults in British Columbia: Joint report*. Victoria, British Columbia, Canada: University of Victoria.

Chappell, N. L. (1988). Long term care in Canada. In E. Rathbone-McCuan & B. Havens (Eds.), *North America elders: United States and Canadian perspectives* (pp. 89–108). New York: Greenwood Press.

Chappell, N. L. (1994, October). *Health care reform: Will it be better or worse for families?* Opening plenary address, annual meetings of the Canadian Association on Gerontology, Winnipeg, Manitoba, Canada.

Chappell, N. L., Strain, L. A., & Blandford, A. (1986). *Aging and health care: A social perspective*. Toronto: Holt, Rinehart and Winston.

Coutts, J. (1998, November 20). Health-care spending in Canada to hit $80-billion. *The Globe and Mail* (Toronto), p. A5.

Gaetz, C. G. R. (1994, March). Work and family challenges: A corporate response. In *The work and family challenge: Issues and options*. Symposium conducted at the meeting of the Conference Board of Canada, Toronto.

Gignac, M. A. M., Kelloway, E. K., & Gottlieb, B. H. (1996). The impact of caregiving on employment: A mediational model of work-family conflict, *Canadian Journal on Aging 15*, 525–541.

Gignac, M. A. M., Martin-Matthews, A., & Rosenthal, C. J. (1995, November). *Upsetting the balance: The impact of caregiving crises on employed caregivers*. Paper presented at the annual meeting of the Gerontological Society of America, Los Angeles.

Gottlieb, B. H., Kelloway E. K., & Barham E. (1998). *Flexible work arrangements: Managing the work-family boundary*. Chichester, England: John Wiley and Sons.

Gottlieb, B. H., Kelloway, E. K., & Fraboni, M. (1994). Aspects of eldercare that place employees at risk. *The Gerontologist 34*, 815–821.

Gottlieb, B. H., Kelloway, E. K., & Martin-Matthews, A. (1996). Predictors of work-family conflict, stress, and job satisfaction among nurses. *Canadian Journal of Nursing Research 28*, 99–117.

Hallman, B. C., & Joseph, A. E. (1995). *A woman's place: Gendered geographies of eldercare provision*. Unpublished manuscript, University of Guelph, Guelph, Ontario, Canada.

Havens, B. (1995). Long term care diversity within the care continuum. *Canadian Journal on Aging 14*, 245–262.

Havens, B., & Bray, D. (1996). International comparisons of long-term care: Canada, with specific reference to Manitoba. *Canadian Journal on Aging 15*(Suppl. 1), 33–44.

Health and Welfare Canada. (1993, February). *Health expenditures in Canada fact sheets*. Ottawa: Planning and Information Branch.

Irwin, S. H., & Lero, D. S. (1997). *In our own way: Child care barriers to full workforce participation experienced by parents of children with special needs*. Cape Breton, Nova Scotia, Canada: Breton Books.

Janigan, M. (1995, July 31). A prescription for medicare. *Maclean's: Canada's Weekly Newsmagazine*, pp. 10–18.

Joseph, A. E., & Hallman, B. C. (1996). Caught in the triangle: The influence of home, work and elder location on work-family balance. *Canadian Journal on Aging 15*, 393–412.

Joseph, A. E., & Martin-Matthews, A. (1994). Growing old in aging communities. In V. W. Marshall & B. D. McPherson (Eds.), *Aging: Canadian Perspectives* (pp. 20–35). Peterborough, Ontario, Canada: Broadview Press.

Kamerman, S. B. (1991). The meanings of research findings for policies relating to the balancing of work and family obligations: Building bridges between research and policy making. In *Conference proceedings* (pp. 43–49). Ottawa: The Canadian Centre for Management Development.

Keefe, J. M., & Fancey, P. (1997). Financial compensation or home help services: Examining differences among program recipients. *Canadian Journal on Aging 1*, 254–278.

Keefe, J. M., Rosenthal, C., & Béland, F. (1996). *The impact of ethnicity on helping for older relatives: Findings from a sample of employed Canadians*. Unpublished manuscript, Mount Saint Vincent University, Halifax, Nova Scotia, Canada.

Lero, D. S., & Johnson, K. L. (1990). *Integrating work and family responsibilities: A review of work-place policies and programs in Canada.* Ottawa: Population Studies Division, Statistics Canada.

Lero, D. S., & Johnson, K. L. (1994). *110 Canadian statistics on work and family* (Catalogue No. 94-E-204) Ottawa: Canadian Advisory Council on the Status of Women.

Levins, C. L., & Martin-Matthews, A. (1995). *Fighting to be recognized in work and family research: Employees caring for dependent adults.* Unpublished manuscript, University of Guelph, Guelph, Ontario, Canada.

Livingstone, S. R., Tindale, J. A., & Martin-Matthews, A. (1998, October). *Balancing work and family: Perspectives of employed individuals providing care to adults with special needs.* Paper presented at the annual scientific and educational meetings of the Canadian Association on Gerontology, Halifax, Nova Scotia.

MacBride-King, J. L. (1990). *Work and family: Employment challenge of the 90's.* (Report No. 59–90). Ottawa: The Conference Board of Canada, Compensation Research Centre.

MacDonald, G. (1996, January 30). Who is looking after elderly parents? *The Globe and Mail* (Toronto).

Martin-Matthews, A. (1996). Why I dislike the term "eldercare." *Transition 26*(3), 16. Ottawa: Vanier Institute of the Family.

Martin-Matthews, A., & Campbell, L. D. (1995). Gender roles, employment and informal care. In S. Arber & J. Ginn (Eds.), *Connecting gender and ageing: Sociological reflections* (pp. 129–143). Buckingham, England: Open University Press.

Martin-Matthews, A., & Keefe, J. M. (1995). Work and care of elderly people: A Canadian perspective. In J. Phillips (Ed.), *Working carers: International perspectives on working and caring for older people* (pp. 116–138) Aldershot, England: Avebury.

Martin-Matthews, A., & Rosenthal, C. J. (1993). Balancing work and family in an aging society: The Canadian experience. In G. L. Maddox & M. P. Lawton (Eds.), *Annual review of gerontology and geriatrics: Focus on kinship, aging and social change* (pp. 96–119). New York: Springer.

McDaniel, S. A. (1993). Caring and sharing: Demographic aging, family and the state. In J. Hendricks & C. J. Rosenthal (Eds.), *The remainder of their days: Domestic policy and older families in the United States and Canada* (pp. 121–143). New York: Garland.

McDonald, L., & Chen, M. Y. T. (1994). The youth freeze and the retirement bulge: Older workers and the impending labour shortage. In V. W. Marshall & B. D. McPherson (Eds.), *Aging: Canadian perspectives* (pp. 113–139). Peterborough, Ontario, Canada: Broadview Press.

McPherson, B. D. (1998). *Aging as a social process* (3rd ed.). Toronto: Harcourt Brace.

Moore, E., & Rosenberg, M. (1997). *Growing old in Canada: Demographic and geographic perspectives.* Ottawa: Statistics Canada.

National Advisory Council on Aging. (1990). *The NACA position on informal caregiving: Support and enhancement* (Catalogue No. 71–1/1–9-1990). Ottawa: Ministry of Supply and Services.

National Advisory Council on Aging. (1995). *The NACA position on community services in health care for seniors: Progress and challenges.* Ottawa: Minister of Supply and Services.

Norland, J. (1994). *Profile of Canada's seniors.* Ottawa: Statistics Canada.

Ontario Women's Directorate, & Ontario Ministry of Community and Social Services. (1991). *Work and family: The crucial balance.* Toronto: Author.

Paris, H. (1989). *The corporate response to workers with family responsibilities.* (Report No. 43–89). Ottawa: The Conference Board of Canada.

Rosenthal, C. J., Martin-Matthews, A., & Matthews, S. H. (1996). Caught in the middle? Occupancy in multiple roles and help to parents in a national probability sample of Canadian adults. *Journal of Gerontology: Social Sciences, 51* (B), S274–S283.

Schellenberg, G. (1994). *The road to retirement: Demographic and economic changes in the 90s.* Ottawa: Canada Council on Social Development, Centre for International Statistics.

Smith, P. (1994, May). *Work/family Issues: Changing the organizational structure.* Paper presented to the conference, The National Work and Family Challenge: Issues and Options, cosponsored by the Conference Board of Canada and the Canada Committee for the International Year of the Family, Vancouver, British Columbia, Canada.

Snell, J. G. (1990). Filial responsibility laws in Canada: An historical study. *Canadian Journal on Aging, 9,* 268–277.

Stone, L. O. (1994). *Dimensions of job-family tension* (Catalogue No. 89–540E). Ottawa: Statistics Canada.

Totta, J. M. (1994, May 10). *Workplace equality: An integrated approach to "measuring up."* Paper presented to the conference, The National Work and Family Challenge: Issues and Options, cosponsored by the Conference Board of Canada and the Canada Committee for the International Year of the Family, Vancouver, British Columbia, Canada.

Underwood, N., & DeMont, J. (1991, August 19). Mid life panic. *Maclean's: Canada's Weekly Newsmagazine*, pp. 30–33.

Wister, A., & Moore, C. (1997). First Nations elders in Canada: Issues, problems and successes in health care policy. In A. W. and G. Gutman (Eds.), *Health systems and aging in selected Pacific Rim countries: Cultural diversity and change* (pp. 83–104). Vancouver, British Columbia, Canada: Simon Fraser University, Gerontology Research Centre.

CHAPTER

Monika Reichert
Gerhard Naegele

Elder Care and the Workplace in Germany: An Issue for the Future?

☐ Introduction

The purpose of this chapter is to document the current situation and sociopolitical debate with regard to work and elder care in Germany. It is structured as follows. First, referring to a study on elder care and the workplace conducted in 1994 by the Institute of Gerontology in Dortmund, Germany, on behalf of the Ministry of Family and Senior Citizens (Beck, Dallinger, Naegele, & Reichert, 1997), the authors outline the key characteristics of German employed caregivers. In this context, special emphasis is given to differences between caregivers in the former East and West Germany. Second, the types of policies and programs that exist in Germany to assist employed caregivers of elders are presented. Third, the strengths and weaknesses of these responses by the social partners (employers, trade unions, community services, and federal government) are noted. To point out the importance of work and elder care as an issue of the future, the fourth section describes the most important demographic, social, economic, and political changes that can be observed in Germany. The final part of the chapter discusses what has to be done by the different social partners in Germany to support a reconciliation of work and care.

☐ Extent of the Work-Family Problem in Germany

According to a representative survey by Infratest Sozialforschung from 1991 to 1992, about 3.2 million Germans (4.1% of the population) living in private households need some kind of regular help and assistance (Infratest Sozialforschung, 1992). About 1.1 million (1.4% of the population) require intensive and regular care; that is, they need help more than once a week with activities of daily living, such as eating, grooming, and ambulating. Of this total, 190,000 need assistance around the clock, 468,000 require help daily, and 465,000 need assistance a few times a week. Another 2.1 million persons (2.7% of the population) need general care; that is, they need help in performing instrumental activities of daily living, such as help with shopping, housecleaning,

29

and sociocommunication. Also taking into consideration the 500,000 persons who receive care in institutions, in all, approximately 3.7 million Germans depend on help from others (Infratest Sozialforschung, 1992).

Of special interest for the subject of this chapter is the question of who provides these enormous amounts of care in private households. In all, 2 million persons have been identified as primary caregivers for the disabled or the elderly in need of care. Among those caregivers who look after someone 65 years of age and older (856,000 persons), 45% (380,000 persons) combine paid work and caregiving duties. Of the 45% engaged in paid work and caregiving, 7% are employed less than 15 hours per week, 10% work between 15 and 35 hours, and 27% work at least 35 hours per week.

The major findings from the 1994 study by the Institute of Gerontology (Beck et al., 1997) and the Infratest Sozialforschung (1993) are summarized below:

1. A typical employee with caregiving responsibilities for a frail elder is a close female family member, married, between 40 and 55 years old.
2. The extent to which employed caregivers have to be available for the dependent elderly person varies. While 20% of caregiving employees claim that they have to be available all the time, 48% are engaged in caregiving duties a couple of hours every day, 20% a few times a week, 9% once a week, and 1% twice a month.
3. The caregiver's employment status depends on the kind and amount of care needed by the elder: The higher the level of care, the less likely the caregiver is able to work.
4. Thirty-three percent of caregivers who provide either personal or general elder care were not employed when they started caregiving, 7% gave up employment, 9% reduced the hours they work per week, and 38% did not change their working situation at all (none of these categories applies to another 13%). Of special relevance is the fact that 16% of caregivers gave up employment or restricted their working hours in order to deal with the competing demands of work and care. Among only those caregivers who provide personal care, 25% were not able to continue working the way they used to do, 11% gave up their jobs, and 14% reduced the hours they worked per week.
5. For both men and women, rearranging work schedules is the most frequently reported strategy to combine work and care.
6. Important variables which have an influence on the employment status of working caregivers are, in particular, age, gender, marital status, living arrangements (sharing or not sharing the same household with the elderly person), and occupational status. Basically, being in a higher age group, female, married, of lower occupational status, or sharing the same household with the elderly relative reduces the likelihood of combining work and elder care.
7. Important variables that can influence the consequences of combining caregiving and employment are level of care needed by the elder person and extent of perceived burden. The higher the level of care needed by the elderly or the higher the extent of burden experienced by the caregiver, the more likely the caregiver is to reduce working hours or to quit work.
8. Only 25% of employed caregivers are supported by community services, such as daily in-home services, day care centers, or institutions for short-term care.

Findings from the Beck et al. (1997) study illustrate that, when caregivers try to balance domestic life, caring responsibilities, and work, they often suffer psychological, interpersonal, social, financial, and practical stress. Thirty-nine percent of employees providing care for an elder feel strongly burdened and 19% feel very strongly burdened. Although no exact data are available, case studies with employed caregivers confirm that the reasons for this high level of stress are poor physical and mental health status (e.g., back problems, headaches, apathy, tiredness, depression), reduced free time and social contacts, financial burdens, and, last but not least, work-related problems. In particular, the caregivers who were interviewed complained that they very often (1) are unable to work effectively; (2) experience work interruptions or have to miss work altogether; (3) have financial losses, for example, due to unpaid time off; (4) miss business meetings and training opportunities; and (5) forgo promotions.

Ethnic Issues

The surveys reviewed above do not include data on the foreign population living in Germany, particularly, the "guest workers" from Turkey, Spain, Italy, Greece, and the former Yugoslavia. Very little is known about these groups of employed caregivers and their elders (Gerling & Naegele, 1998). One reason for this lack of information is that the number of ethnic elderly in need of support is still relatively small. Another reason is that researchers and policy makers in Germany have not recognized the significance of the problem.

In situations where care and support is needed by older "guest workers," evidence suggests that their family members are very willing to provide this care and that the elders themselves prefer family care (Gerling & Naegele, 1998). Changes in the various ethnic groups' family structures and social networks, crowded living conditions, and increases in the labor force participation rates of foreign women, however, challenge the provision of family care (Gerling & Naegele, 1998). Therefore, balancing work and the care of frail elders will be an important future issue for ethnic minorities in Germany.

Differences Between Former East and West German Employed Caregivers

Interesting results emerge when the Infratest Sozialforschung (1993) data are considered separately for the former German Democratic Republic (East Germany) and West Germany. The different political, socioeconomic, and sociocultural conditions before the unification in 1990 still have an influence on the amount of hours worked per week, the consequences of care for employment, and the use of caregiving services, as described below.

First, former East and West German employed caregivers differed on the amount of hours worked per week. While only 14% of caregivers providing personal care for an elder worked more than 35 hours per week in West Germany, 32% of these caregivers worked more than 35 hours per week in East Germany. Second, the groups differed on the consequences of care for employment. A much higher percentage of East German employees as compared with West German employees (52% vs. 32%) did not change their work situation at all after they took over caregiving responsibilities (general or personal care) for an elderly person. Furthermore, while 40% of the caregivers in West Germany engaged in either personal or general elder care were not employed before they had to fulfill caregiving duties, only 17% of caregivers in East Germany were not employed prior to caregiving. Third, the groups differed on their use of community services. While, in West Germany, only 19% of employees who are informal caregivers to elders used community services, 37% did so in East Germany. This is not a question of availability of services, as is illustrated by the following data. About 64% of West German caregivers, compared to 60% of East German caregivers, had community services located near their homes.

Several possible reasons can explain the differences between East and West German employed caregivers. Because of the traditionally high labor force participation rate of East German women, they always had had to manage the arrangement of work and family obligations, and had been accustomed to taking on multiple roles. Also, most women in East Germany have a strong commitment toward work because it is (or, at least, it was) part of a normal biography to be continuously employed without interruptions. Hardly any East German women are "only" housewives, mothers, or caregivers. Moreover, particularly now, in the face of high unemployment rates, many East German women fear that they will not be able to reenter the workforce should they leave their job. Finally, financial reasons force many East German women to keep working full time, although they might want to stop working or to work part time.

One important reason for the stronger use of community services in East Germany is the long tradition of calling on community services in the former German Democratic Republic. Being a communist country, the state took care of the individual by providing him or her with services and institutions of all kinds. The use of these "offers" not only was expected but also was explicitly reinforced. Therefore, to this day, for most East Germans, it is completely normal to rely on professional help.

☐ Policies, Benefits, and Programs and Services to Assist Employed Caregivers and Elders

The following section reviews the reactions and attitudes of German companies, trade unions, community services, and the federal government to existing policies, benefits, and programs relevant to employed caregivers.

Companies

Elder care–related problems have not been widely recognized among German employers (Bäcker, 1994a, 1994b; Naegele, 1994). In fact, issues associated with combining work and informal elder care have been ignored in the past, and hardly any action has been taken to support employees with elder care responsibilities. Bäcker and Stolz-Willig (1997) suggested several possibilities for the lack of company support. First, although many employers are aware of the importance of the problems surrounding elder care, they claim that the number of employees who also are caregivers is still relatively low or that only a few of those concerned are making their situation known and demanding new regulations. However, up to now, no German employer has formally assessed its employees' elder care–related needs.

Second, according to the opinion of some employers, employees' elder care responsibilities are not viewed as a workplace issue. Employers see managing work and elder care as a private matter, and the responsibility to support employed caregivers is attributed to public welfare. This especially is the case since the implementation of the Long-Term Care Insurance (Pflegeversicherungsgesetz) (see below). Therefore, employers feel that, in any case, it is not the company's task to provide support for these employees.

Third, employers have strong concerns about the perceived costs of offering elder care policies and programs, especially during the present economic situation. In other words, in recessionary times, many employers deem these kinds of benefits and services to be unnecessary expenses. On the other hand, employers also reported that they have not noticed that an insufficient strategy to arrange work and elder care has produced any costs for their company. Fourth, some employers have no information about the subject. They simply are not aware of the impact that elder care can have on the workplace.

Against the backdrop of these reasons, the lack of programs and policies, which aim especially at helping employees with caregiving duties for the elderly, is not surprising. If at all, such measures can be found only in very large, international companies such as Bayer, IBM, Siemens, or Mercedes Benz (Bäcker & Stolz-Willig, 1997). The programs and policies that these companies offer mainly refer to provisions covering part-time work and breaks from work. Specifically, these policies comprise (a) a career break for up to 12 months (Mercedes Benz, Siemens) with a guaranteed return to the same job, or (b) compassionate leave from the job for up to 2 or 3 years, or (c) flexible working hours and part-time work (Bayer, Mercedes Benz, IBM, Siemens). Financial assistance to compensate for the loss of wages during compassionate leave is offered only by Bayer. Under the influence of the provisions governing the Long-Term Care Insurance, it is generally felt that companies would be overstretching their boundaries if they were to take on tasks falling within the public domain.

So, how do most German companies handle the problems of balancing work and elder care? First, there are informal arrangements worked out between individual employees and personnel managers. Second, family-oriented provisions, such as part-time work, flextime, shift arrangements, short-term release from work, and the use of overtime are gaining some ground in companies. Although these family-oriented regulations essentially have been designed to solve problems associated with child rearing, employees with elder care duties also can use them. The limited responses from most German companies are, in part, related to their orientation of the role model of an average male worker, which does not consider employees' family duties. Moreover, the attitude of most German employers is still characterized by a "structural thoughtlessness" (*"strukturelle Rücksichtslosigkeit"*). It refers to the fact that working hours (defined as the number of hours worked in gainful employment as well as the distribution of working hours per day) does not take into consideration employees' personal and family demands (Kaufmann, 1995).

In order to make flexibility of working time a successful measure, the requirements of the workplace in terms of time have to be coordinated with people's wishes in regard to utilization of time (Parsons, 1994). This involves, on the one hand, the possibility of reducing work hours on an individual basis and, at the same time, making them flexible. On the other hand, it also involves the option to cease work for a certain length of time without being penalized. But, the difficulty in this context is that the relationship between the requirements of the workplace and those of employees is much more likely to be one of conflict than one that is harmonious. Up to now, many of the new working time regulations in Germany, which can be categorized under the heading "flexibilization," threaten to have a negative effect on employed caregivers. For example, where family duties, such as care for the elderly are concerned, the duration, scheduling, and distribution of annual or monthly working hours are oriented more toward company profit making than toward the needs of employed caregivers.

It should also be noted that employed caregivers very often hesitate to use measures or policies that have the potential to help them better manage employment and caregiving duties (Bäcker & Stolz-Willig, 1997; Schneekloth, 1996). The main reasons for this disuse are that employees with caregiving responsibilities for the elderly very often

- do not define themselves as caregivers. Most caregivers believe they should provide care for family members and consider it their duty to do so. In consequence, employed caregivers look for a private solution to their work-family conflicts and do not express a need for special programs and services at the workplace.
- do not use existing programs and policies because they fear disadvantages, like losing the job or being classed as "overburdened." These kinds of fear are especially relevant in times of high unemployment rates.
- do not feel addressed by existing programs and policies (such as unpaid leave and flextime), because they do not fit their needs or they are not entitled to use them because "care" is defined very narrowly.
- simply do not know about existing programs and services, mainly due to an inadequate or irregular information policy of the company.

It remains to be seen whether it will be possible to overcome these barriers in the future. Important steps to do so are presented in detail in the last section of the chapter. In brief, these comprise forcing more employers to implement policies and measures that support employed caregivers and raising the consciousness among employees that elder care is a workplace issue. In this context, the trade unions are of special importance.

Trade Unions

In Germany, one third of all employees who are in dependent employment (10 million out of 31 million) are members of a trade union. German trade unions are decentralized, but united in a umbrella association, and they are organized according to different sectors. The biggest trade unions are the IG Metall (the union for employees in the steel industry, with 2.7 million members) and the ÖTV (the union for employees who work in the public sector, with 1.7 million members). Every union is independent and can make its own collective agreements, which usually are negotiated for whole sectors of industry, either nationally or regionally. With regard to important matters (e.g., reducing working hours), usually one union starts the negotiation with employers of their sectors. If a successful agreement is made, other unions might take this example and do the same. In general, however, collective agreements set legally binding minimum terms and conditions only for the sectors covered.

Although trade unions claim to be the representative of all (male and female) workers, the needs and wishes of women (they comprise 30% of all members), particularly of those confronted with the double burden of work and family duties, were not on the sociopolitical agenda of unions for a long time (Bäcker, 1994b; Bäcker & Stolz-Willig, 1997). In fact, flexible (and, therefore, possibly family friendly) work schedules were even combated.

Nevertheless, after years of holding back in this area, around the mid-1980s, the trade unions began regulating individual working hours, which deviate from the rigid pattern of standard working hours. This step was taken in order to eradicate the many disadvantages traditionally linked with jobs having such hours, and to grant rights to the employees holding these jobs. Included are part-time work (equal treatment vis-à-vis full-time work, the right to reduced work hours with the option of returning to full-time work, preferential treatment in filling full-time posts, and so forth) and the possibility of a temporary break from one's occupation with the option of returning. It should be noted that, as mentioned earlier with regard to companies, the problems surrounding elder care played only a secondary part when these work time regulations were designed. This may be linked to the fact that, in the view of trade unions, the number of employees with elder care duties is still relatively low. Also, many women employees who also are caregivers give up their jobs prematurely, something which continues to be supported through early retirement campaigns.

At any rate, there are increasing numbers of collective agreements (e.g., in the paper and plastics processing industries) and work agreements (particularly in large-scale enterprises in the chemical and metal-producing and -working industries) that expressly acknowledge care obligations as grounds for claims for reduced work hours (part-time work) and release from work. Formalized agreements, which confer such rights, meet with opposition from employers and establishments that would prefer to continue with models and agreements, which are limited to individual cases. Thus, there still is a long way to go before one will find a blanket regulation in Germany encompassing both small- and medium-sized enterprises and sectors employing primarily women.

Community Services

With regard to community services, there are no systematic programs and policies that support employed caregivers (Naegele, 1995; Naegele & Reichert, 1997). Certainly, the extension of day and short-term care centers and better community care systems for the elderly, which were influenced primarily by the implementation of the Long-Term Care Insurance, slowly have improved the situation of employed caregivers indirectly. The services, however, remain inadequate in terms of quantity and quality. In addition, most services continue to be available according to their own time structures and not according to the needs of employed caregivers. For instance, caregivers who work nonstandard hours or on the weekends, as is typical for employees in the service sector where many women in Germany are employed, have little likelihood of finding professional support.

Government

In Germany, public policy statements in relation to caregivers generally are vague and unfocused, because social policy focuses on the older dependent person rather than on the caregiver. However, to some extent, the needs of caregivers are recognized in the Long-Term Care Insurance Law that came into force in Germany in 1994. As a fifth pillar of the Social Security System (the other four pillars are Health, Unemployment, Pension, and Accident Insurance), Long-Term Care Insurance has the following aims: (1) covering the financial risks that may accompany long-term care and disability, (2) promoting home responsibility family care instead of residential care, (3) improving the quality of life of care recipients and caregivers, (4) improving the financial situation of local authorities, (5) promoting prevention and rehabilitation, and, last but not least, (6) promoting the implementation of a highly qualified professional care system (Reichert, 1997; Rothgang, 1997a, 1997b; Schulte, 1996).

The German Long-Term Care Insurance follows the traditional Bismarck model of social insurance, which is based on a pay-as-you-go principle. It is a mandatory insurance scheme covering the whole population. All those who are (compulsorily or voluntarily) insured under the statutory sickness insurance scheme are obliged to pay compulsory contributions to the new insurance for long-term care scheme. Pensioners also have to be insured.

Long-Term Care Insurance is administered by care funds. It is financed by contributions made by employers, employees, and pensioners. Fifty percent of the contribution is made by the insured person and 50% by the employer, or, in the case of pensioners, by the pension insurance funds. Initially, employers refused to pay more costs of labor. They were compensated by a reduction in the cost of paid holidays: One of Germany's public holidays was abolished and, therefore, the equivalent of one day's paid holiday was lost to employees. This way of "handling" the problem shifted most of the cost to employees, an aspect that also is new in the history of the German Social Insurance System.

To understand the attitude of German employers, and those of the political groups that are linked to them, with regard to the introduction of Long-Term Care Insurance, one has to know that reducing labor-related costs has been a very popular political goal for many years in Germany. This reaction is embedded in the belief that reducing the costs of labor might, first, have a positive effect on the labor market and, second, increase the international competitiveness of companies. Therefore, only a compromise, which shifted nearly all the costs of Long-Term Care Insurance away from the employers to the employees and pensioners, made employers and their advocates in Parliament able to agree to the new Long-Term Care Insurance.

With regard to caregivers, Long-Term Care Insurance offers several innovations. First, to facilitate home care, persons in need of care who are entitled to receive benefits from the insurance can choose between benefits in kind and benefits in cash. If the care receiver chooses benefits in kind, professional care services will help the care receiver to perform physical or instrumental activities of daily living. A choice of benefits in cash enables the care receiver to pay informal caregivers (as a rule, family members) privately. Both types of benefits can be helpful for employed caregivers: The support of professional helpers (benefits in kind) might enable them to stay in the workforce, while the benefits in cash might compensate, at least to a certain extent, for income losses due to a reduction of working hours. Second, Long-Term Care Insurance also pays contributions to the pension funds on behalf of the caregiver in case he or she is not employed at all or is employed less than 30 hours a week. A prerequisite is that the caregiver must be providing care for at least 14 hours a week. In this way, the insurance contributes to the financial security of persons who care for a disabled or older person. Third, Long-Term Care Insurance has led to an extension of special services and institutions to support home care, which indirectly supports employed caregivers. Services and institutions that support home care include day or night care, short-term care (up to 4 weeks per year), funds for modifying homes for persons with disabilities, and funds for technical care aids and appliances, such as wheelchairs.

There is, however, another side of the coin. The first two innovations might also serve as incentives for employed caregivers to give up work completely and become "full-time" caregivers, without realizing that some employment-related factors are potential buffers against the stress associated with caregiving. These factors are, for example, social support from and social contacts with coworkers, the "respite function" of the workplace, and having one's own income. Therefore, leaving the workforce can be very burdensome which, in turn, might negatively influence the relation-

TABLE 3-1. German supports for employees with elder care responsibilities

Government Initiatives	Nongovernmental Organization Initiatives	Union Initiatives	Workplace Initiatives
For employed caregivers Some benefits of the long-term care insurance Tax credit Indirectly, for older persons Long-Term Care Insurance Health insurance	Indirectly, for older persons Home care, day and night care Short-term care Nursing homes	Collective and work agreements that acknowledge care obligations	Policies: Work scheduling Parental and family leave (usually unpaid)[a] Sick, vacation, personal leave (usually paid)[b] Flextime, compressed work week[a] Part-time work, job sharing[a] Flexplace[a] Services Counseling and support[a]

[a]Voluntary.
[b]Government mandated.
[c]Government encouraged.

ship with the elder needing support. Also, last but not least, it must be kept in mind that, especially, middle-aged or older women who have been out of the workforce for a long period of time because of caregiving duties will find it increasingly difficult to find suitable work. Given this potential "double effect" of Long-Term Care Insurance for employed caregivers, it will be interesting to see just how employed caregivers will be affected in the future.

Two other governmental initiatives for a better arrangement of work and family duties also should be mentioned. First, there is the so-called "2. Equality Law" (2. Gleichberechtigungsgesetz), which explicitly urges public employers to allow highly qualified employees as well as those with executive functions to choose part-time work or to take a career break because of family reasons (Presse- und Informationsamt der Bundesregierung, 1994). However, this law seems to be only declamatorical; it hardly ever is used by employees. Second, German parents can take a government-mandated paid leave from work for up to 10 days a year if they have to look after a sick child who is younger than 12 years of age (Bäcker, Bispinck, Hofemann, & Naegele, 1999). Regarding the care of older people no such legal claim exists.

Table 3-1 summarizes the benefits, policies, and services for employed caregivers and their elders.

☐ Strengths and Weaknesses of Supports for Employed Caregivers

The comments made thus far with regard to programs and policies to support employed caregivers show that both strengths and weaknesses characterize the existing configuration package. A strength certainly is that Germany, as a so-called welfare state, has developed a network of services and institutions, and now even legislation, in favor of persons in need of care and, to some extent, their caregivers.

However, the expectation that the state is to be responsible for the individual which, in this case, for employees with caregiving duties, has served as a barrier for most companies to provide active support. From the companies' perspective, dealing with social issues is not their responsibility. Therefore, only work schedule flexibility is seen as an appropriate and possible corporate initiative for employed caregivers; offering other measures (e.g., counseling or information, extended leave) that also would be helpful is not considered. Thus, responsibility for helping employed caregivers has shifted from one protagonist (companies) to the other (government). Similarly, inadequate cooperation also can be observed between companies and community services and between trade unions and companies. This lack of sharing of responsibility for the support of working caregivers among the various sectors constitutes the main weakness of the configuration of supports in Germany.

☐ Factors Contributing to Future Policies and Services for Employed Caregivers

There is no doubt that German employers, trade unions, community services, and policy makers will need to become more engaged with regard to elder care and workplace issues. Like many other industrial countries, Germany is facing revolutionary and interrelated demographic, social, economic, and political changes (Reichert, 1996).

Demographic Changes

Growing Number of Dependent Elderly.   Because of gains in longevity due to scientific and technological advances, healthier lifestyles, and better health care, the German population is aging. While 20% (16.5 million) of the population in 1994 were 60 years of age or older, this percentage will rise to 25% in 2020 (17.2 million) and to 35% in 2030 (26 million) (Deutscher Bundestag, 1994). Not only are more and more people becoming older, but it is the segment of the oldest old (those 80 years of age and older), which is growing the fastest (Sommer, 1994)—from proportionately 3.99% (3.2 million) of the population in 1995 to 6.7% in 2020 (4.5 million), and 6.22% in 2030 (4.3 million).

Because the likelihood of chronic disease, dementia, and functional limitations increases with age, the number of older persons needing support and care also will rise dramatically (Deutscher Bundestag, 1994). Against the background of the demographic trends mentioned above, the number of older persons needing care in 2040 has been estimated to be 2.232 million (that is 3% of an estimated population of 72.413 million), of these, 1.419 million will be living in private households and another 813.000 in institutions (1.95%, respectively, 1.12% of the population (Rückert, 1997).

Declining Number of Younger Persons.   Due to a declining birth rate (births per 1,000) and decreasing fertility rate (number of children per woman), the number of younger persons who may be potential caregivers is decreasing; this means that the proportion of caregivers to care receivers is becoming more unfavorable (Kuratorium Deutsche Altershilfe [KDA], 1992; Rosenkranz & Schneider, 1997). Nevertheless, it is necessary to state that family care of the elderly in Germany has not diminished but, in fact, has grown. Today, German families tend to provide their elderly relatives with more assistance for a longer duration of time—the extent of elder care has nearly doubled since the 1950s (Bengtson & Schütze, 1992).

Social Changes

Feminization of the Workforce.   An increase in the participation of women, the traditional care providers, in the paid work force also can be observed in Germany (Klauder, 1992). According to the available statistics, this not only applies to young women, but also to middle-aged women. For example, in 1995 about 75% of German women age 45 to 50 years and 68% of those age 50 to 55 were employed (Greiner, 1996), and there is no doubt that these figures have increased since then.

At least two main factors are responsible for this development. First, because of higher educational and occupational qualifications, women nowadays assign a high priority to their professional life. In the wake of this trend, the aspirations, values, and attitudes of women toward family tasks also have changed (Backes, 1992; Naegele, 1994). Women want equal opportunities and equal rights in all aspects of social and work life; they do not want to take on the sole responsibility for caring for children, or elderly or disabled family members. Rather, it seems—and the increased rate of maternal participation in the labor force is one indicator—that women wish to combine their working and caring roles.

Second, for many women, working is an economic necessity; this especially is true for female-headed families. But, also in two-parent families, women very often have to contribute to the family income, either to maintain or improve their standard of living. Therefore, many women choose to stay in the workforce without long interruptions, and it can be expected that the workforce in the near future will be comprised of almost as many women as men.

Changing Family Patterns.   Changing family patterns are another trend of social change. Among the most important are rising numbers of single households, divorces, remarriages, and single-parent families (Deutscher Bundestag, 1994). For example, on the one hand, divorces and remarriages among the older population indicate that adult children may have responsibility for a greater number of parents, including stepparents and parents-in-law. On the other hand, divorces among the younger generation result in more single-parent households, leaving more adults without a spouse's assistance on which to draw for care of children, and disabled or elderly persons.

Increased Migration.   Especially due to the changing labor market needs, increased migration of younger persons can be expected in the future. In Germany, the authors are observing a migration of younger people from the former German Democratic Republic to the western part of the country in search of better living and working conditions. Additionally, in the near future, it can be expected that the mobility of the workforce within the European Union also will increase. Consequently, families will be living at greater distances from each other, again reducing the availability of younger caregivers who could support older and disabled family members.

Economic Changes

Smaller Workforce.   Although Germany has to fight against high unemployment at present, all available predictions point to the fact that there will be a labor shortage from the year 2010 onward, due to demographic reasons (Naegele, 1992, 1994; Rürup, 1994). The main reason for this development will be the decline of the population and, in connection with this, a decline in the number of new entrants into the labor force. To guarantee economic growth and competitiveness in the future, this expected labor shortage will need to be compensated for by attracting and keeping valued employees. In this context, efforts will have to be made to encourage women to (re)enter the labor market and to encourage aging male and female workers to delay their retirement. Members of these two groups are those most likely to be affected by caregiving responsibilities. Therefore, the implementation of measures to support employed caregivers also has purely economic motivations.

Transition of Labor Market.   The labor market in Germany is in a state of transition, with consequent fragmentation and restructuring. This transition is characterized by a general move toward more external and internal flexibility in the labor market. Whereas external flexibility implies increased mobility of the workforce (see above), internal flexibility refers to a move away from the traditional model of work (e.g., 40-hour week, full-time, throughout life) to more "atypical" work practices such as part-time employment, job sharing, and working at home. It is obvious that these changes in the labor market have an enormous impact on issues related to informal care. Depending on the kind and amount of help that employees with caregiving responsibilities get from others, such flexibility has the potential to make balancing employment and care either more difficult or easier.

Political Changes

Withdrawal of the State.   The German Basic Law (which roughly equates to the Constitution in other countries) defines Germany as a "social constitutional state" (*sozialer rechtsstaat*)—a state in which the government has the sociopolitical duty to ensure as much equality for people as possible, especially in matters of social security, education, and health. Due to budgetary constraints and increasing pressure to reduce public expenditure, a withdrawal of the welfare state can be observed in Germany during the past decade. Mainly in order to save costs and to reduce welfare dependency, more emphasis has been placed on welfare policy that puts more responsibility on the individual. This development has affected the care system for children, the disabled, and needy elderly persons. For example, with regard to the care of dependent elderly, special emphasis is put on community-based care, which is less expensive than nursing home care. However, community-based care also requires the willingness of families or other informal helpers to become caregivers, a fact that is promoted by the German government in many ways (e.g., the benefits of the Long-Term Care Insurance).

"Individualistic" Gender Regime.   As a reaction to the above-mentioned social changes (in particular, the feminization of the workforce and changing family patterns), Germany is moving away from the "familistic" to an "individualistic" regime. In an "individualistic" gender regime, the state promotes equal opportunities for women in all aspects of life, including their financial independence from men, and shared responsibility between men and women with regard to child rearing and care for other family members.

In conclusion, all these developments point to the fact that more and more women, and also men, will not be able or willing to give up employment because of caregiving duties. Moreover, this is not desirable from a labor market perspective. Further, it is neither realistic nor desirable to make elder care a task that primarily has to be carried out by the society with the support of professional helpers. First, there are not now, nor will there be in the future, enough personnel resources to provide exclusively community-based care. Second, it probably cannot be financed either. Third, and perhaps most important, available data show that most persons concerned will want to put family solidarity into practice and balance work and elder care of their own free will (Halsig, 1995; Schütze & Lang, 1992). It follows that there are many important reasons to be more interested in recognizing the balancing of employment and caregiving as one of the big social challenges of the future, with respect not only to the world of labor but also to social policy in general.

☐ Recommendations with Regard to Elder Care and the Workplace

All social partners—employers, trade unions, community services, the government, and caregivers—will need to take different forms of action to face the challenges ahead. These actions, which hopefully will be realized in the future, are described below (see also Beck et al., 1997; Naegele, 1994):

Companies and Employers' Associations.   These organizations play the most central role in facilitating a better arrangement of work and caregiving. To realize their two main aims (i.e., keeping valued employees with caregiving duties on the job and maximizing the employees' ability to be productive), German companies will have to become much more active with regard to implementation of certain measures. To be successful, these measures should meet the following requirements (Reichert, 1994, pp. 9–11):

- Since the needs of employed caregivers vary according to the degree of dependency of the person for whom they care for, a variety of services and programs are necessary. While some employees find different flex-time models helpful, others may need only counseling and/or information. However, both groups should have the opportunity to turn to their employer for assistance, although attention to the corporate culture must be given when implementing programs. Because every company is more or less different with regard to the characteristics of its employees (e.g., gender and age distribution) and its employees' needs, the options should be planned accordingly.
- Programs and services must take into consideration the special circumstances which are characteristic of elder care. Programs helpful for arranging work and childcare do not necessarily meet the needs of employees with eldercare duties.
- Unit managers and front-line supervisors, who are those most directly faced with the problems of employed caregivers, can play an important role in the informal process of assistance to those concerned. Consequently, managers need to be trained to deal with eldercare problems and to be familiar with company programs and policies and potential barriers to their effective use.
- One way to motivate employed caregivers to use existing programs is to offer these programs as a part of a full range of services a company provides to help all of its employees—male and female, full time and part time, management and non-management—in different situations of which eldercare is just one kind. Creation of such a "supportive and family friendly workplace environment" would make it easier for employees to talk about problems at work and to ask for assistance. Also, it would prevent potential users of corporate services from feeling stigmatized and "different" from other employees.

It goes without saying that employers must raise the awareness of the situation of employed caregivers among their colleagues and in the community in general. In this context, it would be helpful if companies would strengthen links to professional care services (see above). This would help to make better use of already existing resources and to identify gaps that need attention.

Trade unions.   In general, trade unions in Germany must become stronger advocates for employees with caregiving duties by supporting existing workplace initiatives and, even more importantly, by negotiating better employment opportunities and working conditions for these employees. For example, to achieve "real" flexibility for employed caregivers (see above), one important task in this context is the reorientation and improvement of the existing framework of conditions in collective agreements. Further, trade unions can (1) raise awareness among their own members and promote the recognition that care issues should be treated holistically, (2) monitor their members' needs and expectations, (3) initiate their own elder care policies and programs, and (4) lobby for more community-based services.

Community Service.   Professional caregiving services and institutions also have an important role when it comes to the balancing of work and elder care. Community services can assist employed caregivers—and, at the same time, care receivers—in many ways. For example, they can (1) show more flexibility regarding the "time needs" of employed caregivers, (2) provide direct services for employees with caregiving duties (e.g., support groups, information, and referral), and (3) collaborate with employers in the provision of services (e.g., conducting lunchtime seminars at the workplace for caregivers).

Government.   The implementation of programs and policies for a good balance of employment and elder care is very much influenced by actions the government does or does not take. The former German Democratic Republic is a good example of this phenomenon. Important steps for the German government to take in order to reconcile work and elder care on the sociopolitical and economic agenda include: (1) raise awareness for the issue within the society, also with regard to greater equality of opportunity between men and women; (2) provide a good example in the public sector; (3) facilitate and, whenever necessary, mandate more family-friendly workplaces; (4) offer financial incentives (e.g., tax relief) advice and material support to companies that are introducing, or have introduced, family-friendly workplace programs, (5) support research on the subject; and, finally (6) subsidize services which aim to help employees with caregiving duties and encourage the use of these services.

Caregivers.   To improve their situation at home and at the workplace, employees with caregiving obligations should not carry their burden in silence. On the contrary, they should (1) realize and communicate their needs; and (2) identify themselves as members of a specific and important sociopolitical target group, and make caregiving for the elderly not only an individual, but a societal, problem. One group that also can help to improve the situation of employed caregivers has not been mentioned above—researchers. There is no doubt that more research is needed with regard to the subject of elder care and the workplace in Germany. Especially lacking are "hard" data concerning (a) the prevalence rate and the real needs of employed caregivers within companies and (b) the economic impact of caring on employers. Furthermore, evaluation research of existing elder care programs should be undertaken. It is only through such evaluation efforts that the effectiveness and cost efficiency of these programs and services can be known.

☐ Future Trends

After describing what should happen in the future with regard to elder care and the workplace, the question of what is likely to happen in the short- to mid-term perspective will be discussed. The authors have to admit that, at present, they are more pessimistic than optimistic. Concerning the majority of companies, it seems that an awareness of this issue will emerge only when companies more strongly feel the negative consequences of caregiving on the workplace or of a labor shortage (Bäcker & Stolz-Willig, 1997). As long as there are no "hard" data available which would document the financial losses companies have when they do not support their employees who have problems outside the workplace, and as long as there are enough available workers in the labor market who can replace caregivers who temporarily or permanently leave the workforce, employers will act with reservation when it comes to implementing family-friendly measures. In addition, companies are trying to minimize labor-related costs whenever possible—the discussion above with regard to costs of the Long-Term Care Insurance showed that clearly.

Radical changes also are unlikely to occur in the near future with respect to the trade union involvement. This is because the fight against unemployment is of higher priority now than actions that would support employed caregivers of the elderly. Regarding professional caregiving services, quicker reaction is possible. Against the backdrop of the recently implemented Long-Term Care Insurance, more and more services, especially private ones, have come into the market. The growing competition among them might lead to an adjustment of their offerings in favor of employed caregivers.

How the German government will react to the problem of work and elder care remains a question. The government seems to have acknowledged that the reconciliation of employment and elder care is an important issue. However, having already introduced Long-Term Care Insurance, the authors believe the government will be very cautious in undertaking further actions, due to the enormous financial burden already weighing on the welfare state.

So, are the recommended actions mentioned above unrealistic and, as a result, will they be ignored in the future? The authors think not. An indispensable prerequisite for action, however, is that all social partners in Germany—employers, trade unions, community services, government, and caregivers—will realize, first, their responsibility for developing initiatives to support employed caregivers in partnership with the other actors and, second, the advantages to be realized by all when employees are able to successfully balance employment and elder care.

☐ References

Bäcker, G. (1994a, November). *Berufstätigkeit und Pflege bedürftiger Erwachsener: Die Probleme für Arbeitgeber und Arbeitnehmer* [Employment and care for adults in need of care: Possible problems for employers and employees]. Paper presented at the conference, Working and Caring: Developments at the Workplace for Family Carers of Disabled and Elderly Persons, Bonn.

Bäcker, G. (1994b, November). *Zur Rolle der Gewerkschaften* [The role of trade unions]. Paper presented at the conference, Working and Caring: Developments at the Workplace for Family Carers of Disabled and Elderly Persons, Bonn.

Bäcker, G., & Stolz-Willig, B. (1997). *Betriebliche Maßnahmen zur Unterstützung pflegender Arbeitnehmerinnen und Arbeitnehmer* [Corporate policies and programs to support employed caregivers]. Stuttgart: Kohlhammer.

Bäcker, G., Bispinck, R., Hofemann, K., & Naegele, G. (1999). *Sozialpolitik und soziale Lage* [Social policy and social condition]. Cologne: Bund.

Backes, G. (1992). Frauen zwischen "alten" und "neuen" Alter(n)srisiken [Women between "old" and "new" risks in old age]. In G. Naegele & H. Tews (Eds.), *Lebenslagen im Strukturwandel des Alters* (pp. 170–187). Opladen, Germany: Westdeutscher Verlag.

Beck, B., Dallinger, U., Naegele, G., & Reichert, M. (1997). *Vereinbarkeit von Erwerbstätigkeit und Pflege* [Balancing work and elder care]. Stuttgart: Kohlhammer.

Beck-Gernsheim, E. (1993). Familie und Alter: Neue Herausforderungen, Chancen und Konflikte [Families and old age: New challenges, changes and conflicts]. In G. Naegele & H. Tews (Eds.), *Lebenslagen im Strukturwandel des Alters* (pp. 158–169). Opladen, Germany: Westdeutscher Verlag.

Bengtson, V., & Schütze, Y. (1992). Altern und Generationsbeziehungen: Aussichten für das kommende Jahrhundert [Aging and intergenerational relationships: Perspectives for the next century]. In P. Baltes & J. Mittelstral (Eds.), *Zukunft des Alterns und gesellschaftliche Entwicklung* (pp. 492–517). Berlin: de Gruyter.

Deutscher Bundestag. (1994). *Zwischenbericht der Enquete-Kommission Demographischer Wandel. Herausforderungen unserer älter werdenden Gesellschaft an den einzelnen und die Politik* [Interim report of the Enquete Commission Demographical Change: Challenges of an aging society for the individual and for politics]. Zur Sache, Themen parlamentarischer Beratung 4, Bundesdruckerei, Bonn.

Gerling, V., & Naegele, G. (1998, November). *Old people from ethnic minorities in the Federal Republic of Germany*. Poster presented at the 51st annual meeting of the Gerontological Society of America, Philadelphia.

Greiner, J. (1996). Erste Ergebnisse des Mikrozensus April 1995 [Results of the Mikrozensus April 1995]. *Wirtschaft und Statistik, 5,* 305–312.

Halsig, N. (1995). Hauptpflegepersonen in der Familie: Eine Analyse ihrer situativen Bedingungen, Belastungen und Hilfsmöglichkeiten [Family caregivers: An analysis of their situation, the extent of burden they suffer and possibilities for support]. *Zeitschrift für Gerontopsychologie und -psychiatrie, 8,* 247–262

Helfrich, T., & Dodson, J. (1992). Eldercare. An issue for corporate America. *Journal of Case Management, 1,* 26–28.

Infratest Sozialforschung. (1992). *Hilfe- und Pflegebedürftige in privaten Haushalten* [Persons in need of care in private households]. Schnellbericht zur Repräsentativerhebung im Rahmen des Forschungsprojekts, Möglichkeiten und Grenzen der selbständigen Lebensführung, Infratest Sozialforschung, Munich.

Infratest Sozialforschung. (1993). *Hilfe- und Pflegebedürftige mit Hauptpflegeperson* [Persons in need of care and their caregivers]. Sekundäranalyse in Tabellenform. Infratest Sozialforschung, Munich.

Kaufmann, F. (1995). *Zukunft der Familie im vereinten Deutschland* [The future of the family in a united Germany]. Munich: Beck.

Klauder, W. (1992). Wirtschaftliche und gesellschaftliche Bedeutung der Frauenerwerbstätigkeit heute und morgen [Economical and social relevance of women's employment today and tomorrow]. *Zeitschrift für Bevölkerungswissenschaft, 18,* 435–463.

Kuratorium Deutsche Altershilfe. (1992). *Pflegende Angehörige zwischen Pflege und Beruf—Wie Unternehmen helfen können [Working caregivers—How companies can provide support]. Presse- und Informationsdienst, Folge 1/1992, Cologne.*

Naegele, G. (1992). *Zwischen Arbeit und Rente* [Between employment and retirement]. Augsburg: Maro.

Naegele, G. (1994, November). *Vereinbarkeit von Berufstätigkeit und Pflege hilfebedürftiger Erwachsener—Dimensionen und Handlungsperspektiven im betrieblichen Kontext* [Balancing work and elder care—Dimensions and perspectives in the context of companies]. Paper presented at the conference, Working and Caring: Developments at the Workplace for Family Carers of Disabled and Elderly Persons, Bonn.

Naegele, G. (1995). Demographischer und sozialstruktureller Alterswandel—Anforderungen an soziale Dienste in der Altenarbeit und -hilfe [Demographical and structural changes with regard to aging—Requirements for social services for elderly persons]. *Sozialer Fortschritt, 5,* 118–125.

Naegele, G., & Reichert, M. (1997). Krankheit, Alter und Pflege als Problem in der Familie [Illness, old age and care in the family]. In L. Vaskovics & H. Lipinski (Eds.), *Familiale Lebenswelten und Bildungsarbeit* (Vol. 2) (pp. 139–182). Opladen, Germany: Leske & Budrich.

Parsons, D. (1994, November). *Work organisation*. Paper presented at the conference, Working and Caring: Developments at the Workplace for Family Carers of Disabled and Elderly Persons, Bonn.

Presse- und Informationsamt der Bundesregierung. (1994). Abbau der Benachteiligung von Frauen—2. Gleichberechtigungsgesetz in Kraft getreten [Reducing the discrimination of women—2. Equality Law in force]. *Sozialpolitische Umschau, 416,* 18–20.

Reichert, M. (1994, November). *Programs and services to help balancing work and eldercare: Experience from the United States.* Paper presented at the conference, Working and Caring: Developments at the Workplace for Family Carers of Disabled and Elderly Persons, Bonn.

Reichert, M. (1996). *Care and employment: Future issues for research?* Discussion paper for the European Foundation for the Improvement of Living and Working Conditions, Dublin.

Reichert, M. (1997, August). *The Long-Term Care Insurance in Germany: First experiences.* Paper presented at the World Congress of Gerontology, Adelaide, Australia.

Rosenkranz, D., & Schneider, N. (1997). Familialer Wandel und Pflege älterer Menschen—Auswirkungen der Generationendynamik [Changing families structures and care for the elderly—Effects on the dynamics between the generations]. *Sozialer Fortschritt, 6–7,* 145–150.

Rothgang, H. (1997a). Die Wirkung der Pflegeversicherung. Analyse von Effekten des Pflegeversicherungsgesetzes [The effects of the Long-Term Care Insurance. An analysis]. *Archiv für Wissenschaft und Praxis der sozialen Arbeit, 3,* 191–219.

Rothgang, H. (1997b). *Ziele und Wirkungen der Pflegeversicherung* [Aims and effects of the Long-Term Care Insurance]. Eine ökonomische Analyse. Frankfurt: Campus.

Rückert, W. (1997). *Von Mensch zu Mensch. Hilfe und Pflege im Alter* [From human being to human being. Help and care in old age]. Studieneinheit 18 des Funkkollegs Altern, Studienbrief 7, Deutsches Institut für Fernstudienforschung, University of Tübingen, Germany.

Rürup, B. (1994, November). *Demographische Entwicklung: Auswirkungen auf den Arbeitsmarkt und die Pflegeproblematik [Demographical development: Effects on the labor market and on care]. Paper presented at the conference, Working and Caring: Developments at the Workplace for Family Carers of Disabled and Elderly Persons, Bonn.*

Schneekloth, U. (1996). Determining the long term care needs of individuals living in private households. In R. Eisen & F. Sloan (Eds.), *Long-term care: Economic issues and policy solutions* (pp. 171–180). Boston: Kluwer Academic.

Schulte, B. (1996). Social protection for dependence in old age: The case of Germany. In R. Eisen & F. Sloan (Eds.), *Long-term care: Economic issues and policy solutions* (pp. 149–170). Boston: Kluwer Academic.

Schütze, Y. & Lang, F. (1992). Verantwortung für alte Eltern—Eine neue Phase im Lebensverlauf [Responsibility for aging parents—A new phase in the life course]. *Familie und Recht, 6,* 336–341.

Sommer, B. (1994). Entwicklung der Bevölkerung bis 2040. Ergebnisse der achten koordinierten Bevölkerungsvorausberechnung [Development of the population until 2040: Results of the eighth coordinated prediction]. *Wirtschaft und Statistik, 7,* 497–503.

Judith Phillips

Developing a Caregivers' Strategy in Britain

☐ Introduction: The Extent of Work-Family Problems

Studies carried out in Britain indicate that approximately 6% of the workforce combine work and care for an adult and many more expect to take on this role in the next 5 years (Whatmore, 1989). Although the number of working caregivers is small, the implications of simultaneously managing work and caregiving are likely to dramatically increase in the future with the increase in population over the age of 80 predicted to require care from working families. Consequently, this issue has been placed on the agenda of employers, government, trade unions, and organizations for caregivers. This chapter discusses the extent of the work-family problem in Britain, reviews the policies and programs to assist working caregivers, and discusses the effectiveness of a configuration of public-private provision. Finally, future trends are projected.

The effects of caregiving on employment vary in a number of ways for caregivers inside and outside of the labor market. Research in Britain focuses on three elements: labor force participation, income, and workplace-based issues. Differences are found in all these areas depending on gender, age, and marital status of the caregiver; whether they are sole caregivers; whether they are providing care from within or outside the household; and the intensity of caring in terms of the practical tasks and hours of care provided.

There are two principal avenues to explore data relating to caregivers in the labor force: participation rates in caregiving by employment studies and participation rates in employment by studies of caregiving. Both categories are drawn on in this analysis. Taking the first category, Joshi (1995) reported that one in seven of the workforce in 1990 were involved in caregiving. In The latter category, 80% of men caregivers and 60% of female caregivers are employed (Joshi, 1995).

Gender is a significant factor in the relationship between caregiving and labor force participation. Evidence from the 1985 and 1990 General Household Survey (GHS)—an annual cross section sample of individuals living in households in the United Kingdom—shows that caregivers are less likely to have paid work, and this is particularly true for women (Evandrou & Winter, 1992). In the Women's Employment Survey (Martin & Roberts, 1984), 19% of women providing care reported that caregiving affected their employment experience, and 79%, not in the workforce at that time, said that caregiving prevented them from seeking employment. Women also were more likely to have left a job to take on a caregiving role than men (Martin & Roberts, 1984). A lack of recent work experience excludes some women from reentering the workforce (Twigg & Atkin, 1994).

Caregiving has a greater impact on employment if the dependent person is a coresident and if more than 20 hours of care are required (McLaughlin, 1994). Caregivers facing severe restrictions in employment are those who provide care on their own and those who care for spouses (Parker, 1990). Caregivers between the ages of 45 and 59 are likely to be heavily committed to caring for other adults and, in many cases, also for children. Such distinctions are important when analyzing the different situations of men and women in the workplace. Class is also a contributory factor. Arber and Ginn (1993), in their analysis of the 1990 GHS data, found that the middle classes were able to care "at a distance" by being able to purchase care in the formal sector. Full participation in the labor force, however, may not necessarily be enabled by the use of formal complementary services. Evidence in relation to day care suggests that this can restrict employment, as paid work often has to fit around the provision of day care because of uncertain transport arrangements and limited hours of availability (Twigg & Atkin, 1994).

Restricted labor force participation will have an effect on the caregivers' own experiences in old age. *Third age caregivers* (defined as people age 50 to 74) in one study were found to have spent a smaller proportion of their adult life in employment compared to noncaregivers and, in many cases, had taken early retirement (Askham, Grundy, & Tinker, 1992). Caregiving is often a long-term experience: The 1985 GH Survey found that 42% of caregivers reported having cared for someone for 1 to 4 years, and 20% cared for someone at least 10 years (Evandrou, 1992). Participation in the workforce can be affected for long periods of time with consequent impact on income. Caregivers' average earnings are below those of noncaregivers; this differential is most marked for sole caregivers (Evandrou & Winter, 1992). Extra expenses involved in caregiving also will affect the economic position of many families (Glendinning, 1988).

Relinquishing employment to provide care full time is not compensated through the British Social Security System. The Invalid Care Allowance, the main caregivers' benefit, is targeted at those giving more than 35 hours of care a week. Hence, it does not facilitate participation by caregivers in the labor market; furthermore, it is perceived as insufficient to live on (Baldwin, 1995).

Workplace-Based Studies

The extent to which caring impacts on the workplace is documented in a growing number of research studies conducted in situ, as "elder care" has become an increasing concern for industry and commerce.

Assessing the numbers of caregivers through workplace-based routes has led to a variety of estimates of employees who have caregiving responsibilities for an older person. The variance in prevalence across studies can be explained by the differing definitions of "caregiver" and "caregiving" that have been used and the range of response rates achieved. The characteristics of employed caregivers reflect those of caregivers who are not in the workforce in relation to age, marital status, and gender. Increasingly, male caregivers are being identified in the workplace; two recent Help the

Aged United Kingdom studies (Help the Aged, 1994) and a study of Scottish employers (Gilhooly & Redpath, 1997) found that 30% of caregivers were male. The same studies also suggest that the average age of caregivers is decreasing.

The commitment to care, both in terms of time and task, among working caregivers is great. The National Caregivers Survey reported that 68% of caregivers spent all of their nonpaid working time in caring; in Avon Cosmetics, 3% of the employed caregivers spent over 40 hours and 2% between 20 and 40 hours a week in caregiving. In a study in Fife, Scotland, 11% of working caregivers said they spent virtually all of their free time in caring (Ramsey, 1994). Greater time commitment to the provision of personal care was evident among women, coresident caregivers, and those living or working in close proximity to the dependent adult (Phillips, 1994; Ramsey, 1994). The Help the Aged study of Avon Cosmetics found that only 7% of employees were living with the older person, but 77% lived within a half hour of traveling time. Caregiving activities were described as keeping an eye on older relatives, providing transportation, companionship, shopping, and help with household tasks. Accommodating such tasks around normal work hours has caused disruption to the workday for many caregivers.

In all of the surveys carried out at the workplace, over half the caregivers perceived caregiving to currently affect their work and predicted this would continue in the years ahead. Such estimates are likely to be conservative, as survey respondents are more likely to have considered the issues; many others have not thought about caregiving, although they potentially may face such a situation in the near future. The negative consequences of caregiving range from losing concentration, tiredness at work, having to take time off, arriving late, and departing early. Many have to use work resources, such as the telephone, to arrange care services and hospital appointments. Taking time off is reported by 40% of employees in both Help the Aged studies (Oxfordshire County Council and Avon Cosmetics Ltd), and 25% mention arriving late and leaving work early. Similar percentages are found in smaller scale studies of medium-sized employers (Graveling, 1989; Phillips, 1991). On the individual level, such problems leave caregivers feeling guilty, worried about their job security, and not wanting to burden colleagues. Also, opportunities for promotion, training, and career enhancement frequently cannot be fully exploited due to caregiving responsibilities, as evidenced in the following comments: "Because I'm tired my judgement suffers, enjoyment of life is lost, I feel resentful and sorry for myself." "I am simply embarrassed at having to dash off." "I couldn't consider relocation with my former department and had to accept a new job offer at the same site or leave the company" (Whatmore, 1989).

These comments and others made by caregivers reveal the less tangible and hidden problems of combining work and caregiving, such as depression, emotional stress, anxiety, financial strain, and the use of vacation time to care for others. Ways of coping with such difficulties include working part time, changing jobs, and, most frequently, adjusting work schedules to accommodate caregiving. Because such consequences affect productivity, some employers have responded by introducing various workplace measures to assist caregivers.

☐ Types of Policies and Programs to Assist Employed Caregivers

Very few policies and programs have been developed that specifically target employed caregivers of older people on a national, regional, or local level. Instead, caregivers often are the indirect beneficiaries of child care policies implemented at the workplace or of the services provided to dependent older people in the community. Table 4-1 summarizes the various supports available to employed caregivers and elders.

Employer-Led Initiatives

Companies are largely unaware of the number of caregivers within their workplace and of their needs; consequently, this issue is not addressed, and corporate policy tends to be reactive rather than proactive. The few employers who have responded generally are large companies with large female populations. Reasons for their responses are (1) to attract and retain female staff, and (2) to a smaller extent, a result of demand from the workplace.

The most popular response from employers has been to develop a range of flexible policies: flextime, allowing flexibility in the start and end of the work day; flexible leave, allowing short breaks of unpaid leave which can be taken in an emergency situation; job sharing; part-time employment; a reduction in work time; and teleworking and homeworking (Phillips, 1995). Many of these policies are open to all employees, not just caregivers, and, hence, can reduce any stigma for caregivers. For example, one employer, the Royal Bank of Scotland, offers a Career Break, available for a maximum of 5 years. Any employee may take up to three breaks of varying duration, provided the 5-year period is not exceeded in total (Berry-Lound, 1997). Such possibilities are few and far between, but do offer a workable model.

One of the growing areas of flexibility in Britain among larger employers concerns the location of work. Both homeworking and teleworking allow employees to work at home or from an alternative site. Homeworking is particularly advantageous if the caregiver is coresident with the person requiring attention. One company in the United Kingdom, the Rank Xerox, found that it reduced overhead by an average of £17,000 per person per annum compared with the £1,800 it cost to set up each employee as a teleworker (Gooch, 1990).

The provision of services at the workplace is not extensive in the United Kingdom. There are a few examples where employees are provided with elder care guides, have access to a telephone hotline, or have workplace-sponsored counseling available. On-site caregiver support groups also exist, although these appear to be time limited. Direct service provision for care recipients is just beginning in Britain. The provision of company-sponsored on-site day care for dependent people is under consideration by three large employers. Other companies provide free lunches, visiting schemes (employers pay a care attendant to look after the dependent elder while the caregiver goes out), and access to social activities at the workplace for ex-employees, many of whom may be caregivers. Long established philanthropic employers also have residential care facilities available for ex-employees and employees (Phillips, 1995). Long-term care insurance and compensation for lost income are not widely available in Britain, but currently are being widely discussed by employers. Some employers participate in insurance policies for nursing or home care, contributing to the administrative costs for up to 5 years, although this is not representative of most companies in the United Kingdom (Phillips, 1995).

Some companies recognize that individually tailored solutions are the only way to assist caregivers in special circumstances. Many such policies are largely informal, with changes in work patterns at the discretion of the managing director (Gilhooly & Redpath, 1997).

TABLE 4-1. British supports for employees with elder care responsibilities

Government Initiatives	Nongovernmental Organization Initiatives	Union Initiatives	Workplace Initiatives
For employed caregivers and for caregivers in general Attendance allowance Research For older persons Social work services, care management National Health Service health care, Social Security Home care, day and respite care Community nursing	Elder care guides, telephone hotline Caregivers' support groups, research Services for older people (e.g., day care, respite care, hospice care)	Union and management negotiations Lobbying on community care Carers Charter	Policies: Work scheduling Flexible leave and career breaks Job sharing and flexible work Review of employees' needs Teleworking and homeworking Sick leave, holiday leave Policies: Corporate culture Residential care management training Benefits: Income assistance Long-term care insurance Services Telephone hotline Elder care guides and leaflets Workplace-sponsored counseling On-site day care

For any of these policies and programs to be effective, the corporate culture has to be sensitive to the needs of the workforce. Although few programs have been evaluated over a period of time, in all studies to date, the key ingredient in the success of such initiatives has been the awareness, understanding, and support of the line manager. Traditional employment values remain resistant to change (i.e., women's role in the workforce). Overcoming this type of corporate culture is essential for the development of this area of welfare. Management training in relation to child care has developed in some companies in the banking, construction, and retail sectors in Britain, but the needs of caregivers of dependent adults are diverse and require specific training and different attitudes from managers (Rossi, 1996).

Union Response

The contribution of the trade unions in supporting initiatives for working caregivers is vital, and the Trade Union Council's production of a Carers Charter goes some way toward establishing this as an area of concern. The charter is endorsed by organizations that represent caregivers such as the Carers National Association. As Carpenter (1994) noted, "It throws the weight of the trade union movement behind the demand for a new deal for carers, including access to flexible working packages, protection of pay, training and other benefits, and a statutory right to special leave" (p. 132).

Trade unions' role in negotiating flexible working practices also promotes opportunities for working caregivers, although this has been a slow process. Trade union influence has been reduced through legislation introduced by the conservative government to weaken and divide the unions following a series of strikes during a time called "The Winter of Discontent," 1978–1979. Such legislation abolishing closed shops, introducing mandatory ballots of members for strike action, making secondary picketing illegal, and holding unions accountable has reduced the negotiating and bargaining power of unions. Trade unions' role in Britain, however, has worked voluntarily to legitimize the elder care and work issue through education of its members and monitoring the situation of caregivers in several workplaces as well as lobbying for community care changes.

National and Local Government Initiatives

One specific policy objective of the National Health Service and Community Care Act (1990) was the empowerment of caregivers. Although the majority of formal provision to assist caregivers stems from the public sector, there are few policies specifically aimed at working caregivers. The National Health Service and local social services provide the context in which needs are assessed and services provided, although caregivers are not placed in a distinct category. The lack of overt policy making stems from the ambiguous relationship caregivers have with social services (Twigg, 1989). In general, public services contribute little specifically to maintain the caregivers in employment.

In theory, all informal caregivers should be supported by a range of statutory services, but discrimination is apparent in relation to gender and race. The ideological view that it is the woman's place to care often is translated into less support services to a female caregiver than a male caregiver (Jones, 1992). Similarly, minority ethnic elders are denied access to services through lack of culturally appropriate information and experiences of racism deterring them from applying (Ahmed & Atkin, 1996).

Caregivers often are beneficiaries of initiatives aimed at the care recipient, for example, day care, respite care, home care adaptations and aids, and community nursing. However, provision of services, such as home care, is targeted mostly at those living alone and "unsupported," and thus does not assist all caregivers. In 1994, 31% of individuals living alone over the age of 65 received home help, compared to 8% of those living with others, and such figures have remained constant over the past decade (GHS, 1995). Residential and nursing home care also are provided by social and health care services and are subject to national means testing. However, with privatization, additional costs of such services are falling on relatives. Even where a service, such as hospital care, is free at the point of delivery, the inflexibility of the system, particularly around the time of discharge, can create problems for working caregivers (Twigg, 1992). Several studies highlight the breakdown in liaison between health and social care at time of discharge, the pressure for a quick discharge, often at an inconvenient time in the day for a working caregiver, and the lack of continuity between hospital and home in terms of formal support (Phillips & Waterson, 1997; Twigg & Atkin, 1994). This is partly the result of two different funding systems in operation and a lack of clear professional responsibility between health care and social services (Phillips & Waterson, 1997).

There are some signs of enlightenment, however, within the policy arena with the implementation of the Carers (Recognition and Services) Act in 1995. This legislation enables caregivers to seek assessment of their own needs separate from those of the older person. However, there is no statutory obligation to provide services to address those needs. Caregivers also have to provide or intend to provide "a substantial amount of care on a regular basis" (i.e., over 20 hours per week). Providing more than 20 hours of care per week is extremely substantial for those who are employed; therefore, this act will benefit only a small percentage of employed caregivers. Social workers, in carrying out assessments of caregivers' needs, should be more responsive to the concerns of caregivers in relation to their employment situation. Working caregivers may face competing demands and anxieties not only in the caring relationship, but in relation to their workplace, particularly if their manager is unsympathetic to their situation (Phillips, 1991). These problems need to be taken into account in any assessment and strategies created to assist caregivers in their role as employees as well as caregivers.

Private Sector Developments

Unlike the United States, there has been little growth in Britain in private sector vendors assisting employers with employees' caregiving concerns. The current emphasis on privatization of welfare, however, may spearhead this development. The private sector has developed initiatives by providing information to employers and placing the issue on the corporate agenda. Help the Aged, a not-for-profit organization, for example, is in the process of developing a nonemergency information Senior Care Service for employees across Britain (Berry-Lound, 1997). Most services, specifically those for caregivers, are found in the private sector. With one or two exceptions, however, they tend to be small-scale local innovations, for example, caregiver support groups operated through local churches.

There is no evidence to suggest that policies and services of local government are more effective than those initiated by the private sector, and it is too early to compare government initiatives with those developed by employers, as little evaluative work has been carried out in this area (Phillips, 1995). The extent to which employers develop a response to the needs of their employees often is conditional on what they believe the public sector should provide. Employers regard provision of services as the domain and duty of the welfare state rather than their responsibility. The difficulty is that often neither side has the primary objective of meeting the needs of working care-givers, and the consequent response falls short of what is required. There is no discussion of the role of employers in community care debates, although it is increasingly important to develop services in partnership. It has been argued that "the role of the state is central to the development of comprehensive and gender equitable policies on family care. However, the role of employer in implementing policies and responding to local demands and needs would seem to be vital, if secondary to that of the state" (Moss, 1996, p. 26).

☐ Factors Contributing to Britain's Configuration of Supports

Demographic Trends

Two important demographic trends in Britain over the past 30 years have had major implications for older people and caregivers who attempt to combine caregiving with paid employment: the increase in the relative size of the elderly population as a percentage of the population as a whole, and the aging of the elderly population itself.

In the United Kingdom, in 1991 one in five of the population was over age 60. The relative size of the elderly population in Britain has increased more than threefold since the start of the century, while in the past 30 years, the proportion of those people age 85 and older has more than doubled. By 2026, projections suggest that those age 65 and older will be twice as numerous as in 1961, while the size of the population age 85 and older will have increased fivefold (Allen & Perkins, 1995).

It is the aging of the older population, however, that is most significant. Those over age 75 account for just under half (1991 figures) of the elderly population. This represents an increase of 8% in the past 30 years (Great Britain). For the United Kingdom, as a whole, those age 75 and older are projected to account for 8% of the total population by the year 2021. These demographic facts take on added significance when placed in the context of the health and social care needs of older people: The propensity for utilization increases with age. In relation to disability, of the 6.2 million disabled people in Britain, 69% were over 60 years of age, with two thirds of those at the highest level of disability being over age 70 (Turner, 1995).

The need for health and social care is met primarily by the family. Despite changing family structures, high levels of divorce relative to other European countries, reconstituted families, and an increase in single parenthood, women in the family still provide the bulk of caregiving, particularly, emotional support and practical support such as shopping, cooking, and cleaning. Of the 6.8 million caregivers in Britain, 3.9 million are men (Office of Population, Census and Surveys [OPCS], 1990). These figures disguise different patterns of caregiving; men are more likely to perform only episodic tasks, such as financial assistance, whereas women are more likely to take on the major responsibilities of caregiving and to be sole caregivers.

Cultural Values

Cultural values also contribute to the development of initiatives to support caregivers in the workplace. In Britain, attitudes toward the nuclear family govern the pattern of care for older people. Under normal circumstances, the caregiving functions in the family fall on women in the family (Dalley, 1996). Public sector policies often reinforce this position.

Secondly, the ethos of public sector welfare is strong in Britain, and older people expect the welfare contract between themselves and the state in terms of service provision to be upheld, particularly in old age. The major shift to private sector welfare over the past decade, based on ability to pay, is viewed by some as reneging on "the welfare contract." Private workplace-based welfare for caregivers and older people, therefore, is not familiar or expected in most British workplaces.

Further, social policy is based on the distinction of family and work being separate, with family matters seen as private and as not concerning the employer. Both organizational culture and work structure reflect this and mitigate against the development of "family-friendly" initiatives. A traditional model of work of a full-time employee, working from school to retirement without family caregiving responsibilities, particularly for older adults, persists despite changes in family and work patterns (Lewis & Lewis, 1996).

Employment and Work Culture

A further contributory factor is change within the labor market and the increasing number of women (re)entering employment. Paid employment has become increasingly important as women need to be in full-time employment to contribute to the family income. An analysis of the Family Expenditure Study in Britain (Ward, Dale, & Joshi, 1996) revealed that this was an important factor in keeping families out of poverty. Occupational pensions, too, are essential to generate independence in later life. Women's aspirations regarding work and its environment are changing. More women are expecting equal opportunities in social and working life and wish to achieve financial independence from their partner; at the same time, they are likely to want to fulfill family tasks both in relation to children and older parents (Lewis, 1996).

The changing work environment in the 1980s in Britain, namely more part-time, shift work, or short-term contracts, enabled many women to enter and reenter the workforce. The movement of women into paid employment, however, has not reduced their care responsibilities, with many actually having increased care commitments in addition to their employment (Joshi, 1995). The situation has been different for men: Their lack of access to part-time jobs and, often, their reluctance to take such work which affects promotion and career advancement, has meant that, as caregiving increases, employment falls (Parker & Lawton, 1990).

Changes in the nature of employment toward part-time, temporary, and short-term contractual work have resulted in increased job insecurity for employees and fewer workplace-based benefits. This has created problems for the growing number of men and women who wish to balance both roles. There is evidence to suggest that, when men in conventional jobs want time off for elder care, they have to rely on the kindness of the employer rather than adapt their work around caregiving duties (Twigg & Atkin, 1994).

Along with broad national changes in the labor market are more local employer-based factors, which have led to the current British configuration of policies and benefits.

Workplace Factors

Limited exploration of the reasons for offering family-friendly policies has been undertaken. However, several factors can be identified in the development of employee benefits in this area: paternalism, management industrial strategy, company image, labor market pressure (e.g., attracting and retaining staff), and trade union pressure (Mann & Anstee, 1989).

Companies have ideas of how they should treat employees, and Britain has many firms with a long history of providing employees with "cradle to grave" welfare. Although today this often is not an independent factor but, instead, part of a business strategy, some employers are committed to a paternalistic approach. Company image, both to its staff and customers, also has been found an influential factor (Princess Royal Trust for Carers, 1995). Gilhooly and Redpath (1997) reported that companies which regard workplace arrangements as part of "health promotion" were described to be flexible, responsive, and sympathetic. These arrangements are more a shift to "hard-headed individualism helping employees care for themselves" (Pickard, 1992, p. 163), combined with a concern for productivity and employers' rights to a minimum standard of performance, rather than an intrinsic concern for the employee (Phillips, 1995).

There are two specific business arguments associated with the issues of working and caring: the loss of staff and avoidable costs of production. Many businesses face the loss of committed and knowledgeable staff if no developments are put in place in the workplace to support those with caregiving responsibilities. The costs of replacing caregivers forced to leave work are considerable. Failing to support caregivers who remain at work also is costly. The impact on workplace performance and productivity for caregivers who remain at work has been a decisive factor in the development of workplace initiatives. Effects of tiredness, feelings of guilt, physical problems, isolation from other noncaregiver colleagues, and feelings of lack of support from public services, caused through combining both roles, have an effect on the caregivers' ability to concentrate and, consequently, pose problems for work performance.

Few attempts have been made to detail the costs to British employers of the resultant problems of absenteeism, the use of work resources for care provision, lack of energy, and reduced quality of work. The costs to the organization of not developing initiatives to address these problems is thought to be considerable, particularly as more women are entering employment. In the Carers in Employment Survey (Princess Royal Trust for Carers, 1995), competing for and retaining key staff was cited as one of the main motives for introducing caregiver-friendly policies. Flexible work schedules made it easier to recruit and retain staff. Appropriate support also enabled companies to maximize the potential of individuals.

Combining work and care can have positive advantages for both employer and employee. Lazcko and Noden (1992) found evidence that caregivers brought acquired interpersonal and managerial skills, as well as patience and a sense of responsibility for others, to the workplace.

Given the reasons why businesses should invest in initiatives to support employee caregivers, why has this form of welfare not taken off? The Caregivers in Employment Study in 1995 found that implementation of policies to support caregivers was not widespread among British business. Companies that have shown interest in the issue of caregivers at work and have developed elder care services have a tradition of paternalism and philanthropy (Rossi, 1995). "Larger companies in the private sector are more likely to offer long-term leave without pay, long-term leave with job security, and geographical transfer. Where employees were more likely to be 'brains' than 'hands' and where work was complex, companies report greater flexibility, responsiveness and sympathy to the needs of caregiving employees" (Gilhooly & Redpath, 1997, p. 13). They also tend to have high levels of female employees. The public sector, for example, has taken some lead in this area. On the whole, however, the issue of working caregivers has not been extensively recognized as a problem for companies (Rossi, 1996).

There are several reasons why employers have not responded. First, to convince employers of the need for support, the background data presented emphasized the catastrophe of rising numbers of older people and the crises businesses would face with impending labor shortages; hence, the need to support caregivers to remain in the workforce. Labor shortages have not become a reality on the forecast scale, however, so this argument has not succeeded. Few employers have implemented policies and practices in response, particularly as many businesses face economic restructuring. Broader employment trends in a period of cutback has impeded research in this area, as many companies do not see the imperative of developing what they term as costly "fringe benefits" during recession and see little legitimacy in the research. What research also has failed to do is to portray a viable economic argument for making a response. There is no concrete evidence of a lack of competitiveness linked to caregiving difficulties.

Second, an unsympathetic response from management has deterred further disclosure of the problem (Whatmore, 1989); this has meant limited awareness of the issues. When problems do arise they often are dealt with on an individual basis (Phillips, 1994; Rossi, 1995), and line managers are given discretionary roles in which they can feel uncomfortable (Lewis & Taylor, 1996). Third, there is an attitude in Britain that family life is a private concern. Caregivers are reluctant to share concerns in the workplace because they fear they will lose their job. Where programs have been introduced, there is some evidence to show low usage of these workplace supports (Princess Royal Trust for Carers, 1995).

Fourth, the level of public provision largely determines how employers perceive their role in the provision of welfare services (Rossi, 1996). Many employers are reluctant to stray into areas where they think government should provide services, such as home and respite care for older people, even if local provision is inadequate. Health care insurance and occupational pensions are the main areas where large employers have a role alongside the public sector. Only a minority of employers see elder care as a company responsibility (Gilhooly & Redpath, 1997). Recent research, however, shows that some employers are aware of the inadequacies of current public provision which, in turn, is influencing their decision to provide assistance to employee caregivers (Rossi, 1996).

Government

Government attempts to control and curb the cost of an increasing older population requiring care pushed community care to the forefront of the policy agenda. The ideology of the New Right in Britain promoted the traditional nuclear family, in which women are dependent on men and responsible for the care in the family. Commentators of the New Right (Morgan, 1994) argue that feminization of the workforce has adverse effects on the ability of couples to maintain families. Morgan argues that women have exchanged rearing and caring for children for employment. In 1990, over 80% of middle and upper management women in top companies surveyed had no children

(Morgan, 1994). This has been a strong argument used in social policy over the past 18 years, with the dependency of women reinforced through community care legislation, which places the care of older people primarily in the hands of the family.

Since 1997, the new Labour government wants to promote equal opportunities, particularly at the workplace. Equal opportunities not only concern gender, but also race and age, and it is in this direction that arguments for change are succeeding. The role of the public sector as a model employer in this area is important, and a limited number of examples are available. For example, Oxfordshire County Council provides major public services, such as social and educational services, planning, and roads to a population of approximately 600,000. Women working part-time constitute half of the workforce of 16,000. In acknowledging that many of their employees have elder care responsibilities, the council has introduced a number of benefits and policies, such as career breaks, unpaid leave, flextime, flexplace, job sharing, and unpaid leave (Berry-Lound, 1997). Oxfordshire also has adopted a Carers Charter—a 10-point plan for caregivers providing a clear statement of what needs to be done to enable and support caregivers in leading an independent life.

The government has been cautious to impose what it sees as costly legislation on companies. Although in Gilhooly and Redpath's (1997) study, 86% of companies reported that legislation would cause them to introduce services for caregivers, the cost to the government of implementing and policing such legislation would be enormous. The government also is reluctant to interfere with business in areas of social welfare, as legislation would be costly for business as well as government. Initiatives affecting caregivers have been driven through changes to the public sector. Two major developments in social policy have impacted on the situation of caregivers in the workplace and on the development of initiatives to assist caregivers: first, the privatization of welfare and commensurate reduction in state services, and, second, the increasing emphasis on informal networks to support the care of older people.

The National Health Service and Community Care Act (1990) introduced far-reaching changes in promoting a mixed economy of welfare, but at the expense of sustaining and developing an adequate public sector, particularly in residential care. Along with cutbacks in the public sector, most local authorities have imposed fees for formerly free services. The new legislation introduced the internal or quasi-market budgets into the National Health Service and the purchaser-provider split into social services. In both cases, the intention is for the state to become the primary funder or purchaser, with services being provided by a mixture of private, not-for-profit, and public agencies competing with each other. In contrast to a free market, the purchase of services is not necessarily through money but through voucher or budget, and the choices often are made by a third party, such as a doctor or social worker (Means & Smith, 1994). Consequently, since 1993, there has been wide contracting out of services for older people. Although the residential care sector (providing institutional care) is now mainly privatized, private sector community care services (provided to people in their own homes) are still underdeveloped.

Trade Unions

The role and attitude of trade unions have been important in the configuration of workplace programs. There has been a lack of trade union interest in work-family issues, with no research activity generated. There are several reasons for this. During the past decade of financial restraint and cutbacks at the workplace, trade unions have been engaged in what they see as more important issues, such as securing employment rights and negotiating contracts. During the past 17 years, the power of the trade unions has been weakened through government legislation (as described above). Consequently, unions are in a less strong position to demand action.

Private and Not-For-Profit Groups

There is a diversity in private and not-for-profit service provision in Britain, ranging from small local caregiver support groups to large national organizations, such as Age Concern, Help the Aged, Crossroads, and the Carers National Association. This latter organization is campaigning for better services, changes in legislation, benefits, and tax concessions that will help caregivers combine employment with their caring duties. Historically, although independent from the state, these private and not-for-profit groups developed services which supplemented and supported those provided by the state. However, as the contract culture pervades the welfare arena, the role of the voluntary sector has been depleted, falling victim to cutbacks in public funding. Throughout 1991 and 1992, for example, not-for-profit organizations in Britain lost almost £30 million in local authority funding (Reading, 1996). This had a devastating impact on a large number of small organizations that served the needs of caregivers and has meant that such groups have lost their capacity to innovate and experiment with new ideas and to promote change. In some cases, local organizations are being asked to become alternative providers of the state (Lewis, 1996).

☐ Strengths and Weaknesses

Caregivers have a variety of needs for which no single sector or service alone is appropriate. Services are uncoordinated between the public and private sectors, and, even within the public sector, service provision is fragmented between a health care and social care divide. The barriers to a "seamless service" are financial, organizational, and cultural. Service organizers have few resources to be creative in meeting the needs of caregivers, and services often have been organized inflexibly and bureaucratically. Distrust between medical and social professionals has led to difficulties in collaboration. Separate budgets also operate in the two systems, creating different assessment processes. In order to alleviate such problems, a system of care management was introduced in Britain in 1990, giving older people and their caregivers access to a care manager who has a coordinating role (Phillips & Penhale, 1996).

Government Initiatives

The government increasingly is driving the issue of work and care both in the workplace and in the community. In 1998, the National Carers Strategy was launched with employment and care a significant area of attention. Although not unique in Europe, the lead from government in this area, along with other family-friendly initiatives, a Royal Commission on Long Term Care, Welfare to Work program, and Better Government for Older People initiative indicates commitment to grappling with issues of ageing, caregiving, and workplace responses.

Ethnic Issues

There is no research on the effects of working and caring among ethnic minority groups in Britain. In relation to caregiving, the statement that Blacks "look after their own" is a common misperception (Ahmed & Atkin, 1996). A third of Afro-Caribbean older people, for example, live alone. Many families are also divided by distance, through immigration policy and geographical dispersal of kin in Britain. Long-distance caring is an issue for such caregivers which, in turn, has an impact on work as longer periods of time have to be taken away from the workplace to respond to the needs of the person requiring care, who may live in another country.

Policy does not reflect the diversity of ethnic minority groups in Britain with services designed around the White norm (Twigg, 1992). Atkin (1998) illustrated that structural barriers to service delivery and the racism of frontline practitioners have been significant issues. The inappropriateness of formal responses in the community therefore have resulted in deterring many ethnic minority groups from seeking help. A greater reliance on informal practices in the community and the workplace may be occurring if caregivers are successfully juggling work and care. However, no studies have been carried out to explore these issues.

Employer Initiatives

There are a number of weaknesses in employer-led initiatives. Most programs are concentrated in large companies, whereas most companies in Britain are family-run, small businesses or firms of a medium size. Also, most initiatives tend to be concentrated in the public sector, which has a high number of female employees, and most often are developed on the initiative of one person, for example, a director who has personal experience of caregiving (Phillips, 1995). The long-term sustainability of initiatives therefore can depend on a few key people. There has been little evaluation of what succeeds, the utilization rate, and whom the schemes benefit most. In some cases, schemes, such as part-time work, may lead to greater gender inequality in the workplace.

Many programs are not available to the total workforce, but are concentrated on particular sections, job type, and level. The Institute of Manpower Studies found that some focus exclusively on female employees (Metcalf, 1990). In the same study, clerical, administrative and sales staff were more likely to have flexible working conditions than managers, professionals, or manual staff. Career breaks often were more open to managers than to manual staff.

Configuration of Programs

One of the major weaknesses in the configuration of welfare is that local authorities and employers are developing initiatives in isolation. Most progress has been ad hoc and on a company basis, rather than working in partnership with the state and local community services (Phillips, 1995). Moreover, private sector employers look to see what the public sector and government are providing, and some do not see it as their responsibility.

Public knowledge of corporate welfare is limited, and current research on solutions to the problems has been slow to develop in Britain. Most studies are descriptive and document the types of services offered; few have built in evaluative research, particularly, research on utilization rates of the services and benefits. One of the difficulties facing many researchers is gaining access to accurate estimates of the prevalence of caregivers and of services and benefits. Even where this is achieved, comparisons between studies are complicated by differing definitions of caregivers, poor response rates, and the current focus on a narrow range of employment types; namely, large public and private organizations in the service industries rather than small- or medium-sized companies (Phillips, 1995).

Research

There also is the issue of the general lack of comparative methodology. Only one study—the Help the Aged *Seniorcare Surveys* (1994)—uses the same methodology in its comparison of two companies. Apart from different definitions and methods of collecting data (e.g., focus groups or questionnaires), different areas of concern are covered. There also is little comparison between groups and little disaggregation of caregivers, (e.g., between men and women who use services).

There also is a lack of basic data. In 1994 the Carers in Employment group conducted a survey to gauge current best practice in meeting the needs of caregivers among U.K. employers. The sample consisted of 23 organizations which had engaged in "family-friendly" employment practices. Twenty-one out of the 23 organizations had no idea of how many caregivers they had in their workforce. In a study of 12 U.K. employers, only three had consulted employees with regard to their needs (Rossi, 1995). In a Scottish study, 91% of the 319 companies had not previously considered the issue of elder care (Gilhooly & Redpath, 1997). None of the U.K. participants monitored the utilization of their policies and services. There is little widespread knowledge about what companies are doing or who is eligible for such initiatives, even among companies that carry out or participate in surveys. Although such exercises are important for a given company, their findings are of questionable value for all companies and different sectors. All studies to date have been conducted in large organizations employing over 50 people. The small- and medium-sized companies predominant in this country have not been surveyed. All that these studies tell us is something about caregivers in those large corporations where researchers have gained access and where employers can afford to respond to caregivers' needs as well as financially support a menu of strategies. Particular problems faced by caregivers in smaller employment bases, where more informal solutions to caregivers' problems may have been adopted, are unknown.

There also is a lack of evaluative research on the strategies, particularly from the caregivers' perspective. Very little is known about which different measures suit which caregivers, and how urban and rural solutions differ. There is a need to explore what "informal" measures already exist, how successful they are perceived to be, and how further measures can be implemented in the workplace, as well as how sustainable policies are for both the employer and employee. One of the obstacles cited to the monitoring of flexible work, career breaks, and leave of various types is that employees do not have to provide reasons for why they are utilizing a particular scheme. In addition, where surveys or audits are carried out, response rates are low and variable, ranging between 29% (National Carers Survey) and 68% (Fife, Scotland). This can be explained, in part, by the difficulties in using a survey instrument, which is introduced through the company, leaving many employees worried about confidentiality. Estimates of prevalence and utilization, therefore, are difficult to substantiate.

Further problems arise in establishing the causal relationship between employment and care. It is difficult to disentangle the relationship, for example, because those who quit work to become caregivers may have lower labor force attachment. Similarly, caring is not a static process: It can be sporadic or continuing, and there is a need to monitor different periods of caregiving within a life course perspective. This points to the need for longitudinal data. In Britain, it is difficult to track down how companies respond and how effective is their response. On the caregivers' side, it has been difficult to see what influenced their decision to relinquish care or work given current methodology. The British Household Panel Survey, a longitudinal study, will address some of these problems as it tracks those with prolonged caregiving responsibilities from child care to adult care, as well as sudden bursts of caring; it also should capture those who have left the workplace in order to care.

The lack of a theoretical framework also hinders much of this work. Similarly, research methods need to be replicable, crosscultural, longitudinal, evaluative, and prospective, rather than retrospective. There is a need to move from the descriptive to more rigorous investigation and analysis.

☐ Future Change

Britain appears to be in an embryonic stage in the development of a response to problems of work-family balance. Given the current economic situation, any immediate and short-term improvements will be taken by larger companies, which will continue to offer benefits as long as there is an economic imperative to do so. Increasing, flexibility has been identified, by employees and employers alike, as an important strategy to pursue. With technological developments in the workplace, different ways of working and increased flexibility regarding location and timing of work will become possible. Companies that have developed good practice in these areas are promoting themselves as model employers and are using the media to publicize their developments. Raising awareness in this way provides some optimism that, in the future, employers will become interested in and respond to such issues. A study of 275 employers who were members of Opportunity 2000 reported that flexible work arrangements, available for all staff, were widespread, with part-time work available in 71% of companies, flexible hours in 60%, and job sharing in 58% (Princess Royal Trust for Carers, 1995).

A key factor in future development, however, will involve the work-family issue from the periphery to the core of the organization (Lewis & Lewis, 1996). Some companies realize this is a central issue for business and have incorporated strategies within their business plan, but attitudes also need to change, and this is a much slower process. Little progress is forecast among smaller companies and family-run businesses. There are a few examples of consortia and other models, which could enable smaller companies to assist caregivers in the workplace. It is not likely, however, that multinational companies' attitudes in this area will transcend national boundaries (Rossi, 1996). Different and often complex legal, financial, and cultural barriers between countries may be seen by employers to hinder transferability of support initiatives between countries.

In the British context, it is difficult to envisage employers taking on the major role as provider to caregivers. However, they can be expected to place the issues facing working caregivers on the employment agenda and consider them alongside workplace practices. Although costs are important, "ultimately these decisions reflect moral and social values" (Stevenson, 1994, p. 98) as to whether business should be responsible in providing assistance and enabling caregivers to continue working, and whether caregivers have a right to expect employers to assist them. There is a need for a widespread debate on informal care, the role of women, and whether and how employers should provide for caregivers in the workplace.

Despite a change in government leadership, the cutbacks, rationalization, and reorganization will continue to take place within social and health care services. It is unlikely that caregivers will be significantly rewarded by these changes; instead, they will be shouldering increased responsibility for older relatives. There are no current moves afoot to expand the system of allowances to caregivers or to provide them with Social Security credits and contributions to their pension schemes when they drop out of employment to care for an older person. At a local level, the assessment of caregivers and the introduction of care management does provide a framework to assist caregivers, and more local governments are raising awareness of the issues caregivers face at work and are providing information and advice as well as working with caregivers' organizations.

Future Implications of the European Union for Britain

Issues of work and care "touch on policy and programme remits of several work areas such as working conditions, employment social protection and social exclusion" (Anderson, forthcoming). There is no legal basis for action on care and work at the European Union (EU) level, and influence can be exerted only through other programs and policies, such as that on equal opportunities for men and women. Current influence from the EU is focused on a reduction in the numbers of hours worked in a week. Future issues include training and research opportunities across countries as well as other issues related to conditions of employment. The Labour government in Britain has adopted a much more open approach to European initiatives, and it is expected that the EU directives may have a more sympathetic response in Britain than in previous years.

There is optimism on the European front, with the EU addressing issues, such as the rights and entitlements of workers, through a number of directives. Such directives will assist working caregivers in terms of entitlement to leave, working time, representation in the workplace, and equal pay (European Commission, 1997). It is unlikely, however, that legislation will be introduced, since this has not been an effective tool in the past to implement equal opportunities, although Gilhooly and Redpath (1997) found that most companies said they would respond to legislation and increased demand from employees.

Private, not-for-profit, and caregivers' oganizations, particularly those with interests in aging and disability, are increasingly lobbying at the local, national, and European levels, exerting pressure for change on Social Security, community care, and working conditions. Providing advice to government and supporting such activities with caregivers' days will increase and strengthen the cause of working caregivers. There also are some plans by caregivers and private sector organizations to directly provide services in the workplace, and this may be the way forward.

Despite many helpful services and policies, the community and employers working in partnership is essential, and the success of initiatives to assist caregivers will depend on this.

Future Research Agendas

In addition to addressing the methodological weaknesses of studies to date (See Strengths and Weaknesses above), there are other important issues on the research agenda. Future research needs to highlight broader issues of work culture. There is a call from women's organizations for wider research into how employers respond to women and men in their workplace, and how and what models can be introduced without reinforcing gender stereotypes and sex segregation in the workplace. Flexible working, for example, may be detrimental to women in terms of their entitlement to occupational pensions. Similarly, further work needs to address attitudes at all levels within companies in relation to such stereotypes and to caregiving in general. It is important to recognize men's involvement in caring so that it is not just women who are seen as the caregivers and, therefore, as having "the problem."

Broad changes in society will have an impact on the kinds of research undertaken in the next decade. Ethnicity is an increasing factor in British multicultural society. Almost a half million people of pensionable age living in Britain were born elsewhere, mainly of Asian and Afro-Caribbean decent. A four- to fivefold increase is forecast by the end of the decade. This has implications for family caregiving, as stereotypical notions of intergenerational ties and reciprocity of older people being cared for by their sons and daughters in exchange for child care are changing, and traditional services are seen as inappropriate and inaccessible. The British welfare state traditionally has not met the needs of older people from such groups, yet a response will be needed to meet the needs of family caregivers who have to continue to work. There is an urgent need for research into the strategies employed by small businesses to accommodate caregivers and into particular problems and solutions faced by those from ethnic minorities.

Different family patterns also are emerging. Men are playing an increasing role in caregiving as behavior and attitudes change. As family patterns change, for example, gay and bisexual men are providing assistance to each other (Pringle, 1995), thus increasing men's involvement in different kinds of care exchange. How this will impact on the workplace requires exploration.

Not all research should be aimed at the labor market. The quality of care given at home and the effects of work on caregiving from the older person's perspective must be researched. Particularly, little is known about the quality of care provided by men and the impact of new technology in the workplace and at home to assist caregivers and older people. Technology may benefit caregivers in rural areas, a location that has been a neglected dimension in most research. Paid caregivers in the workforce, such as nurses, social workers, and home help aides, also need particular attention as low status and low pay in this sector maintains the low regard and attention given to caregiving in general.

The linking of public, not-for-profit, and private care systems together is important in the development of initiatives, and further research is required on how this can be achieved. One question that remains unanswered is the kind of public services that caregivers find useful to keep them in employment. There is a need to improve the perception of public sector welfare, particularly the view of residential care, if caregivers are to be assisted. It also is vital to know the conditions under which welfare becomes acceptable.

Increasing research activity in Britain in relation to caring and work has highlighted the lack of basic data in this area. To redress the balance, research must move from the descriptive to the analytical and conceptual level. There is an onus on researchers to develop appropriate methodology to achieve this and to develop research agendas that are beneficial to employers, caregivers, and policy makers in health care and social care systems. As Britain moves into a new millennium with increasing uncertainties in both welfare provision and the labor market, caregiving issues will take on increasing significance. It will be vital to respond appropriately on the basis of sound research data.

☐ References

Ahmed, W., & Atkin, K. (1996). *"Race" and community care*. Milton Keynes, England: Open University Press.

Allen, I., & Perkins, S. (Eds.). (1995). *The future of family care for older people*. London: Her Majesty's Stationary Office.

Anderson, R. (forthcoming). The role of the European Union in stimulating actions to improve the situation of working carers. In G. Naegele & M. Reichert. (Eds.), Working and caring: The situation in Germany, Europe, and North America. Hanover, Germany: Vincentz, Verlag.

Arber, S., & Ginn, J. (1993). *Gender and later life*. London: Sage.

Askham, J., Grundy, E., & Tinker, A. (1992). *Caring: The importance of third age carers* (Research Paper No. 6.) Carnegie Inquiry into the Third Age. Dunfermline, Scotland: The Carnegie Trust.

Atkin, K. (1998). Ageing in a multi-racial Britain: Demography, policy and practice. In J. Phillips & M. Bernard (Eds.), *The social policy of old age: Moving into the 21st century.* (pp. 163–183). London: Center for Policy on Ageing.

Baldwin, S. (1995). Love and money: The financial consequences of caring for an older relative. In I. Allen & S. Perkins (Eds.), *The future of family care for older people* (pp. 119–141). London: Her Majesty's Stationary Office.

Berry-Lound, D. (forthcoming). Corporate programmes and policies in Great Britain. In G. Naegele and M. Reichert (Eds.), *Working and caring: The situation in Germany, Europe and North America*. Hanover, Germany: Vincentz, Verlag.

Carpenter, M. (1994). *Normality is hard work: Trade unions and the policies of community care*. London: Lawrence and Wishart.

Dalley, G. (1996). *Ideologies of caring*. London: Macmillan.

European Commission. (1997). *Social Europe: Progress report on the implementation of the medium term Social Action Programme 1995–7*. Luxembourg: Author.

Evandrou, M. (1992). Challenging the invisibility of carers: Mapping informal care nationally. In F. Lazcko & C. Victor (Eds.), *Social policy and elderly people* (pp. 1–30). Aldershot, England: Avebury.

Evandrou, M., & Winter, D. (1992). *Informal carers and the labour market in Britain* (Welfare State Discussion Paper No. 89). London: London School of Economics.

Gilhooly, M., & Redpath, C. (1997). Private sector policies for caregiving employees: A survey of Scottish companies. *Ageing and Society, 17*, 399–423.

Glendinning, C. (1988). Dependency and interdependency: The incomes of informal carers and the impact of social security. *Journal of Social Policy, 19*, 469–497.

Gooch, R. (1990). Skills shortages. *Local Government Employment, 34*(5), 5.

Graveling, M. (1989). *Combining work with care: A survey to assess the needs of carers at work*. Unpublished paper. Great Yarmouth, England: Anglia Harbours NHS Trust.

Help the Aged. (1994). *Seniorcare surveys*. London: Author.

Jones, D. (1992). Informal care and community care. In J. George & S. Ebrahim (Eds.), *Health care for older women* (pp. 16–27). Oxford: Oxford University Press.

Joshi, H. (1995). The labour market and unpaid caring: Conflict and compromise. In I. Allen & S. Perkins (Eds.), *The future of family care for older people* (pp. 93–119). London: Her Majesty's Stationary Office.

Lazcko, F., & Noden, S. (1992). Combining paid work with eldercare: The implications of social policy. *Health and Social Care in the Community, 1*, 81–89.

Lewis, J. (1996). What does contracting do to voluntary organisations? In D. Billis & M. Harris (Eds.), *Voluntary agencies: Challenges of organisation and management* (pp. 98–113). London: Macmillan.

Lewis, S., & Lewis, J. (Eds.). (1996). *The work-family challenge: Rethinking employment.* London: Sage.

Lewis, S., & Taylor, K. (1996). Evaluating the impact of family-friendly employer policies: A case study. In S. Lewis & J. Lewis (Eds.), *The work-family challenge: Rethinking employment* (pp. 112–128). London: Sage.

Mann, K. & Anstee, J. (1989). *Growing fringes: Hypotheses on the development of occupational welfare.* Leeds, England: Arnley.

Martin, J., & Roberts, C. (1984). *Women and employment. A lifetime perspective.* London: Department of Employment.

McLaughlin, E. (1994). Legacies of caring: The experiences and circumstances of ex-carers. *Health and Social Care, 2,* 241–253.

Means, R., & Smith, R. (1994). *Community care: Policy and practice.* London: Macmillan.

Metcalf, H. (1990). *Retaining women employees: Measures to counteract labour shortages* (Institute of Manpower Studies Report No. 190). London: Institute of Manpower Studies.

Morgan, P. (1994). Double income, no kids: The case for a family wage. In C. Quest (Ed.), *Liberating women from modern feminism* (pp. 2–12). London: Institute of Economic Affairs Health and Welfare Unit.

Moss, P. (1996). Reconciling employment and family responsibilities: A European perspective. In S. Lewis & J. Lewis (Eds.), *The work-family challenge: Rethinking employment* (pp. 20–34). London: Sage.

Office of Population, Census and Surveys. (1990). *General Household Survey.* London: Her Majesty's Stationary Office.

Parker, G. (1990). *With due care and attention: A review of research on informal care.* (Occasional Paper 2). London: Family Policy Studies Centre.

Parker, G., & Lawton, D. (1990). *Different types of care, different types of carer: Evidence from the General Household Survey.* London: Her Majesty's Stationary Office.

Phillips, J. (1991). *Working caregivers: Care review and productivity report.* Unpublished paper. Norwich, England: University of East Anglia.

Phillips, J. (1994). The employment consequences of caring for older people. *Health and Social Care in the Community, 2,* 143–152.

Phillips, J. (Ed.). (1995). *Working carers: International perspectives on working and caring for older people.* Aldershot, England: Avebury.

Phillips, J., & Penhale, B. (Eds.). (1996). *Reviewing care management.* London: Jessica Kingsley.

Phillips, J., & Waterson, J. (1997). *Older people: Hospital discharge and entry to private residential and nursing care.* Unpublished report prepared for South-Cheshire Health Trust and Cheshire County Council Social Services Department, England.

Pickard, J. (1992, December). Staff health gets a new checkout. *Personnel Management Plus,* pp. 16–17.

Princess Royal Trust for Carers. (1995). *Carers in employment.* London: Author.

Pringle, K. (1995). *Men, masculinities and social welfare.* London: University College London.

Ramsey, D. (1994) *Carers at work: A survey of informal care responsibilities among social work staff in Fife regional council.* Unpublished paper, Fife Social Work Department, Fife Regional Council, Scotland.

Reading, P. (1996). *Community care and the voluntary sector.* Birmingham, England: Venture Press.

Rossi, I. (1996). *An assessment of employer-sponsored initiatives for assisting employees who are caring for elderly dependants in the Netherlands and the UK.* Unpublished master's thesis, University of Bath, England.

Stevenson, O. (1994). Paid and unpaid work: Women who care for adult dependants. In J. Evetts (Ed.), *Women and career* (pp. 87–100). London: Longman.

Turner, M. (1995). *Older people with disabilities* (European Resource Centre Briefing Paper 7). London. Unpublished manuscript.

Twigg, J. (1989). Models of carers: How do social agencies conceptualise their relationship with informal carers. *Journal of Social Policy, 18,* 53–66.

Twigg, J. (Ed.). (1992). *Carers: Research and practice.* London: Her Majesty's Stationary Office.

Twigg, J., & Atkin, K. (1994). *Carers perceived. Policy and practice in informal care.* Milton Keynes, England: Open University Press.

Ward, C., Dale, A., & Joshi, H. (1996). Combining employment with childcare: An escape from dependence? *Journal of Social Policy, 25,* 223–249.

Whatmore, K. (1989). *National Carers Survey: Vol. 1. Care to work.* London: Opportunities for Women.

CHAPTER

Jenny Brodsky
Brenda Morginstin

Balance of Familial and State Responsibility for the Elderly and Their Caregivers in Israel

☐ Introduction

Patterns of care for the elderly have their origin in the exceptional mix of modern and traditional values that are Israel's foundation. On one hand, modern aspirations for a higher standard of living have propelled industry, education, and technology into the twenty-first century. On the other, traditional expectations of familial accountability and commitment have not vanished. The majority of elderly people are still cared for at home, and a number of interesting programs have been developed to help families cope with this situation. Reliance on informal caregivers assumes that women are available to fill caregiving responsibilities. However, the increasing numbers of women who are joining the labor force make it crucial to understand the implications of labor force participation for caregiving, and how the burden of care affects the caregiver's work responsibilities. Further, the service system is challenged by the need to adapt to the patterns of care and expectations specific to each of Israel's ethnic and cultural groups. Policy makers have begun to wonder how much longer the existing balance of familial and state responsibility for the elderly will hold.

The authors will describe the particular configuration of the aging process in Israel and the notable role of Israeli families who care for elderly relatives. Families are confronted with many responsibilities when meeting the needs of an elderly relative while continuing to fulfill obligations to their jobs and families. The authors will describe solutions that have been created to alleviate some of this burden. While innovative, these solutions are far from comprehensive, and raise questions about the direction that service development should take.

☐ Work-Family Issues

The Demography of Aging in Israel

The number of people age 65 and over had reached 537,500 by the end of 1995, representing 10% of Israel's total population. While Israel's general population is still significantly younger than that of other Western countries, its relatively high birth rate masks phenomenal growth in the absolute number of elderly. Since 1955, this population has increased sixfold, while the general population has increased threefold. The rate of increase of those age 75 and over is even greater—eightfold.

Broad changes in the age structure of the society are reflected in changing societal support ratios (Kinsella & Taeuber, 1993). These ratios indicate the number of youth or elderly persons per 100 persons age 20 to 64 years, principal ages for participation in the labor force. The "elderly support ratio" (persons age 65 and over per 100 population age 20 to 64) in Israel has increased from 10 in the early 1960s to nearly 19 in 1994. In contrast, the "youth support ratio" (persons under age 20 per 100 adults age 20 to 64) has declined. Consequently, the "total support ratio" (youth plus elderly in relation to the working-age population) has declined (Central Bureau of Statistics, 1962, 1973, 1984, 1995), and is expected to decline over the next decade (Beer, 1997). A decrease in the proportion of children, who are dependent and major users of social resources, does not necessarily balance the increased need for resources generated by the growing proportion of the elderly in the population. Not all elderly persons require support, however, and not all working-age people actually work or provide direct support to elderly family members. Workers do provide indirect support through taxes and social welfare programs. Thus, these statistics are rough indications of the overall support burden on working-age adults (Kinsella & Taeuber, 1993).

The main source of population aging in Israel, as in other countries, has been a decline in the fertility rate. The increase in life expectancy also has an effect on the age structure of the population, especially life expectancy at the age of 65. However, one crucial factor in Israel is immigration. In the past, the immigrant population tended to be relatively young; thereby, having the effect of slowing the rate of aging of the overall population (Brodsky & Bergman, 1993; Habib & Tamir, 1994). Of special note is the recent recurrence of large-scale immigration, primarily from the former Soviet Union. These immigrants are older than the general veteran population and, therefore, contribute significantly to the growth in the number of elderly (Beer, 1997).

The influx of elderly immigrants into Israel also has augmented the cultural heterogeneity of Israel's elderly population. Approximately 94% of the elderly population are Jews, while 6% are non-Jews (Moslems, Christians, and Druse). Among the Jews, only 6% actually were born in Israel, while 26% were born in Asia and Africa (e.g., in Morocco, Yemen, Iraq, India), and 68% in Western and Eastern Europe, and North and South America.

Compounding the increase in the elderly population is the proportionally greater increase in the number of elderly who are disabled (i.e., who need assistance in personal care activities such as washing, dressing, and eating). It is very interesting to note that the disability rates among the Arab and immigrant elderly populations are far higher than those of the veteran Jewish elderly population—22%, 14%, and 8%, respectively (Beer, 1996). Many factors may contribute to the explanation of these differences among the three groups, such as education, income, health behavior and habits, accessibility to health care services, health care utilization patterns, and genetics. The changes that have taken place in the age, gender, and ethnic composition of Israel's elderly population have contributed to the increase in the number and proportion of disabled elderly. In 1994, there were 68,000 disabled elderly in Israel, constituting about 13% of all elderly. By the year 2005, the number of disabled elderly people is expected to have increased by 48%, raising the proportion of disabled elderly to 16% of the elderly population. Thus, the increase of the disabled elderly population is expected to be twice that of the total elderly population (Beer, 1996).

Women and the Labor Force

It has been documented in Israel and elsewhere that mainly women bear primary responsibility for provision of care to the elderly. Little study has been made of how the burden of care affects the caregiver's work responsibilities, in spite of the fact that, in Israel as in other Western countries, the proportion of women in the labor force is continuously increasing. For example, 64% of the women age 25 to 44 were in the labor force in 1994, compared to 32% in 1970 (an increase of 98%); 63% of the women age 45 to 54 were in the labor force in 1994, compared to one third in 1970 (an increase of 86%); and 32% of the women age 55 to 64 were in the labor force in 1994, compared to 22% in 1970 (an increase of 47%). The majority of these women are working full time. Interestingly, the proportion in the labor force of men of the same ages has decreased by 9%, 6%, and 22%, respectively (Central Bureau of Statistics, 1971, 1995) Among the Arab population, the proportion of women in the labor force also has increased over time, even in the most traditional sectors. For example, the proportion of Moslem women in the labor force increased by 34% between 1980 and 1994 (Central Bureau of Statistics, 1981, 1995).

In contrast to the tendencies of some groups in the United States to encourage women to stay at home and care for children, in Israel, there is a strong emphasis on encouraging women to work. This is true for all sectors of the society, including the more traditional ones. It is interesting to point out that, contrary to expectations, even among the Orthodox religious communities in Israel, women play an important role in the workplace. In fact, because the highest value in Orthodox communities is on enabling the men in the family to devote their time to religious studies for as long as possible, women most often are the primary breadwinners. Furthermore, Israel's income tax credit system offers a strong economic incentive for both spouses to work, rather than only the husband or the wife. Moreover, the system of child day care in Israel is very well developed, with much political pressure to continue expanding affordable child care for all sectors of society, thus enabling the women to work. It is worthwhile to mention that, in recent years, there has been much discussion of raising the age for pension eligibility for women from 60 to 65. Already women are entitled to continue working until age 65, if they choose. Israel's government recently has appointed a special commission to make recommendations concerning a gradual increase of pension age, which stands today at 65 for men and 60 or 65 for women, as they choose.

Reliance on informal caregivers assumes that women are available to fill caregiving responsibilities. However, the increasing number of women from all sectors who are joining the labor force makes it crucial to understand the implications of labor force participation for caregiving, for the system of informal care, and, hence, for the economy. While many studies consider the cost of alternative types of service, few have factored in the cost of care provided by the family. Certainly, the implications of labor force participation for the family, for employers, and for the economy also should be considered.

Furthermore, the trend of the aging of the population, together with most primary caregivers being women, may have implications for the future of the informal support system. The "parent support ratio by females" (that is, the ratio of those age 80 and over to women age 50 to 64) provides a rough indication of the expected burden of care on women (Kinsella & Taeuber, 1993). The "parent support ratio" for Israeli women has increased from 11 in the early 1960s (that is, 11 elderly persons for every 100 women age 50 to 64), to nearly 40 (that is, 40 elderly persons for every 100 women age 50 to 64) (Central Bureau of Statistics, 1961, 1973, 1984, 1995). This means far fewer women will be available to care for the increasing population of elderly.

Informal Care of the Elderly in Israel: Characteristics of Primary Caregivers

As noted, family structure has remained fairly traditional in Israel. Thus, while Israel's socioeconomic structure moves ever closer to that of developed countries, its value system is still like that of some developing countries (Brodsky & Habib, 1997; Noam & Habib, 1992). Many families desire and expect to keep elderly relatives at home and care for them. At present, the vast majority of the elderly live at home. It is clear that such a situation would be impossible without a great degree of family involvement. Moreover, no society can offer viable cost-effective community care options for the elderly, unless it can rely on the commitment of families.

Elderly men enjoy greater access, at least potentially, to informal support than do elderly women. Approximately 60% of the elderly are married, and twice as many elderly men as women are married. Not surprisingly, the proportion of elderly women who live alone is more than three times higher than that of men. The total percentage of elderly people who live alone has increased (from 12% in 1961 to 24% in 1995), while the percentage of elderly people who live with a child has decreased (from nearly 50% in 1961 to 18% in 1997). However, Arab Israelis and recent immigrants from the former Soviet Union are more likely to live with family than are veteran Jewish Israelis (Azaiza & Brodsky, 1996; Naon, King, & Habib, 1993; Strosberg & Naon, 1997). It is worth noting that the percentage of Arab elderly who live with their children has decreased; thus, while it appears that the immigrants and Arabs have greater access to informal support—for entirely different reasons—the authors may expect that these populations increasingly will fit Western models, as does the veteran Jewish population.

These findings do not necessarily indicate a lessening of family willingness to provide help and support. Most of Israel's elderly have an informal support system. The majority of them have at least one child, and the overwhelming majority of them are in close contact with their children (Brodsky, Sobol, Naon, King, & Lifshitz, 1991; Noam & Habib, 1992). A study of caregivers of disabled elderly living in the community found that, although the extended family forms a network of informal care, one individual usually takes on primary responsibility for provision of care. Most (66%) primary caregivers are women (Brodsky et al. 1991). When possible, spouses assume the role of primary caregiver; about 40% of all primary caregivers are spouses. Children are next most likely to serve as primary caregivers and, in fact, comprise 50% of all primary caregivers; most of them are married with families of their own. When neither a spouse nor child is available, other relatives, friends, and neighbors may offer assistance (Brodsky et al., 1991).

The Burden of Care on Primary Caregivers

In addition to providing emotional support, research has shown that primary caregivers of disabled elderly invest between 20 and 45 hours a week in the actual provision of care, depending on the elderly person's level of disability (Brodsky & Naon, 1993a, 1993b[1]). This involves running errands, accompanying the elderly relative to physicians' appointments, assisting the relative with activities of daily living, doing household chores, and the like. It should be remembered that children who are primary caregivers also have obligations to their own families and to jobs. Physical care of, and constant worry about, an elderly relative thus can add a heavy burden to the caregiver's life. More than 85% of caregivers reported being constantly worried about their elderly relative's condition, and approximately 60% reported suffering physical and emotional strain due to the infringement on their lives and the need to perform unpleasant tasks. Overall, more than two thirds of primary caregivers reported that the burden of care was too great (Brodsky & Naon, 1993a, 1993b).

It seems that a major strain on caregivers is their feeling that they shoulder all or most of the responsibility for caring. About two thirds of primary caregivers reported that there was no one else who could replace them, even for a short time. It thus is not surprising that the vast majority (80%) of them were worried that they would not have sufficient assistance if the functional capacity of their elderly relative deteriorated.

Although copious studies have been conducted in Israel and elsewhere on the effect of caregiving on the caregiver's emotional well-being, little study has been made of how the burden of care affects the primary caregiver's work responsibilities. Do caregiving responsibilities necessitate absence from work and, if so, how often? Do primary caregivers decline the opportunity to work because of their caregiving responsibilities? The one prominent study conducted in Israel found that one third of all primary caregivers of disabled elderly were in the labor force, and that 50% of those who were not spouses were in the labor force (69% of the men and 40% of the women). Twenty-five percent of those who were working claimed that they had to reduce their work hours because of their caregiving responsibilities, and 20% claimed they had to miss work hours during the month before the interview because of their caregiving responsibilities (Brodsky et al., 1991). On average, primary caregivers missed 3 days of work a month.

The need to care for an elderly relative also can cause the caregiver to leave the labor force. Feuerbach and Erdwins (1994) indicated that the major issues influencing the decision to retire were income, personal health, and the need to care for a disabled spouse, parent, or other relative. They found that women, in particular, were apt to consider retirement not only because of their own health problems, but because of an obligation to care for a sick spouse or aging parents. The findings of the authors' study indicate a similar trend. Of those primary caregivers who were not working, 28% indicated that they had to stop working or that their responsibilities prevented them from seeking a job.

The formal system of care in Israel has been structured to complement the informal support system available to most elderly. During the past decade, a fair number of services—some of them quite innovative—have been created with the aim of balancing limited public resources with family resources. The authors will now describe current efforts to maintain a balance that will benefit both the elderly and their families, and discuss areas for further development in light of the existing supports

☐ Supports for Employed Caregivers and Elders

Table 5-1 lists the supports available in Israel for the elderly and for employees with elder care responsibilities.

Special Services for and Policies Concerning Family Caregivers

The wide range of services for the elderly in Israel was established with the intention of enabling the family caregiver to maintain a normal lifestyle, including participating in the labor force. However, few of the services are designed to meet the needs of families. Specifically, there is no statutory or established response to the family caregiver's need to balance work and caregiving responsibilities. The increasing number of women joining the labor force, coupled with the desire of the formal service system to maintain elderly people in the community, however, is inducing policy makers to address the needs of families.

Temporary Work Leave. One promising response to the needs of employed caregivers is a recent labor agreement that allows employees to take 6 sick days for the express purpose of caring for a disabled elderly parent, much as they would take sick days to care for an ill child. These sick days are taken off of the employee's total allotment of sick days; if more time is needed to care for an elderly relative, it must be taken from vacation days. This agreement represents an advance; however, it does not provide an appropriate and comprehensive response to the vast needs of women caregivers. In Israel, employers do not as yet offer formal elder care programs. Research needs to be conducted on how employers are coping with employees' need to care for elderly relatives.

Israel's Labor Union: Implications for Employed Caregivers

Israel is a country which finds itself in the flux of transition from a more traditional, socialist economy, with a heavy emphasis on the public sector and on the importance of protecting workers' rights through general labor agreements, to an economy which is moving in the direction of restructuring, privatization, and individual work contracts. As such, there has been a severe erosion in the role and power of Israel's major labor union, the General Federation of Labor (the Histadrut), which is struggling to redefine its position and readjust to the requirements of a newer, faster moving economy.

The Histadrut was founded in Palestine in 1920 by the representatives of fewer than 5,000 Jewish settlers. One of its main objectives being the provision of jobs for Jewish workers, it had a historic mission dedicated to building up an economic infrastructure for the future state of Israel. By the late 1980s, its membership had grown to 1.6 million, and it has been acknowledged as one of the most important organizations in the country. It not only is a trade union, but also an economic instrument and a provider of social services. Economic collectives affiliated to the Histadrut, and the business corporations which it owns together, accounted for a fifth or more of Israel's national product and employment in the early 1990s (Shalev, 1992). Its Sick Fund (health maintenance organization [HMO]) was the dominant health care provider until 1995, when

TABLE 5-1. Israel's supports for employees with elder care responsibilities

Government Initiatives	Nongovernmental Organization Initiatives	Union Initiatives	Workplace Initiatives
For employed caregivers Income tax reductions for caregivers of elderly persons in nursing homes Reduction in property tax for disabled elderly receiving home care under Long-term Care Insurance Law Medical leave to care for disabled elderly persons requiring assistance with basic activities of daily living Indirectly, for older persons Social Security National Health Insurance Community long-term care insurance Social- and health-related services provided by the Ministry of Health, the Ministry of Labor and Social Affairs, and local authorities	Involved in service development and providing direct care (home care, day care, nursing homes, sheltered housing) The Association for the Planning and Development of Services for the Elderly in Israel (ESHEL) Local associations for development and provision of services for the elderly Advocacy organizations for specific high-risk groups, such as the Israeli Alzheimer's Association Private (for-profit) organizations	National Union of Retired Persons (part of the General Federation of Labor) National lobbying by interest groups, especially for protection of pension rights and health care benefits	Policies: Work scheduling Parental sick leave, paid as option of part of personal sick days or vacation days Flextime work (voluntary) Workplace services Social welfare counseling

the National Health Insurance Bill was implemented in Israel, and concomitantly the Sick Fund was disassociated from the Histadrut.

The Histadrut still holds an extensive role in the area of pensions and supports a ramified network of services in education, sports, day care, and other public interest spheres. As a trade union, it claims the vast majority of all wage earners and represents most of the workers in negotiating collective agreements, which often are legally binding on the entire relevant labor force. Collective bargaining takes place both nationally and locally. Economy-wide "framework agreements" (typically concluded every 2 years for each sector) and the cost-of-living allowance, periodically renegotiated between the Histadrut and the association of private employers, constitute the highest level of the system. The government plays a major role at this level in steering the outcomes of negotiation, and as a negotiator, ultimately delineating tripartite "package deals" (Shalev, 1992).

The Histadrut is not a roof organization of federated trade unions, but a unitary direct membership organization. It assigns its members to national trade unions (generally industry-based unions or occupationally based organizations of professional workers), most of which it created. The internal structure of the Histadrut is centralized, hierarchical, and permeated by political parties. Histadrut institutions are governed by party nominees (Shalev, 1992). Up to 1977, Israel was governed by the Labor Party and, at the same time, the Labor Party dominated the Histadrut in its dual role as a trade union and as the owner of economic enterprises. Despite differences in emphasis resulting from the role of each of these entities, the leadership of all three represented the same social ideals and the same political stances (Kleiman, 1987). In 1977, there was a political turnover, bringing to an end a long period of hegemony of the Labor Party. During the decade and a half of right-wing or coalition governments, as well as the changes in the economy during the past several years, the Histadrut has been confronted with new challenges, both as an economical enterprise and as a trade union.

It is unclear today to what degree the labor union will find itself able to expand benefits for employed persons, since it is struggling to maintain some of the protections and rights which have been fought for over the past few decades. During this period, for example, future activities of labor unions most probably will emphasize protection and expansion of basic pension rights rather than obtaining family-focused services or benefits. The authors do not envision that, in the foreseeable future, there will be increased public pressure from the unions on the government to provide more assistance to employed caregivers. On the other hand, advocacy groups, such as women's organizations, which are an offshoot of the Histadrut, have taken on themselves the role of protecting and expanding support services for women in the workplace.

Formal Services

Responsibility for services for the elderly is shared by numerous government, public, and voluntary organizations, and, increasingly, the private sector has been providing services. Financing for services comes from a variety of sources (including general taxation, payroll taxes, local taxes, and out-of-pocket expenditures) and is provided by various government and public agencies (Brodsky, Kaplan, & Barnea, 1995). The main government agencies involved in care for the elderly are the Ministry of Health, the Ministry of Labor and Social Affairs, and the National Insurance Institute (Israel's Social Security Administration). The principal public and voluntary organizations responsible for the development of services for the aged are the four major health insurers (similar to HMOs): the Association for the Planning and Development of Services for the Aged in Israel (JDC-ESHEL) and the Division of Services of the Elderly of the Histadrut (MISHAN). In addition, many smaller voluntary organizations provide services throughout the country (e.g., local associations coordinate services at the local level).

The authors will now focus on the most important of the services developed for the frail elderly, and describe how they have affected the families of the elderly in all sectors of Israeli society.

Institutional Care

The responsibility for institutional services is shared by the Ministry of Labor and Social Affairs and the Ministry of Health (according to the level of disability of the elderly person). These ministries are not involved in the direct delivery of long-term care services, but rather refer elderly people to either private, for-profit or public, nonprofit institutions. The financing of institutional care is shared by the two ministries, and by the elderly and their families.

Interestingly enough, adult children are required (according to the Alimonies Law, which provides for filial responsibility) to contribute to the cost of nursing care, depending on their economic situation and that of their elderly parent. This is an expression of the responsibility posed on children toward their aging parents.

Even though Israel has an established system of institutional care, families and professionals always have preferred to enable the elderly to remain at home for as long as possible. In fact, Israel has maintained a relatively low institutionalization rate—4.5%. As noted above, the disability rates among the Arab and immigrant elderly populations are far higher than that among the veteran Jewish elderly population: however, the institutionalization rates of the former are significantly lower than that of the veteran Jewish population because of the relatively more intense involvement of family in caregiving. Institutionalization is particularly low in the Arab sector, although it is rising as family structure changes (Azaiza & Brodsky, 1996). Similarly, when immigrants first arrive in Israel, they have a notably low need for institutional services (Strosberg & Naon, 1997), although experience has shown that their need for institutionalization matches that of the veteran Jewish population with time.

Home Care Services

There are two major types of home care: professional home care and nonprofessional home care.

Professional Home Care.   Besides providing all acute care, the Sick Funds provide professional medical care to disabled people in their homes. This care includes visits by physicians, nurses, and physiotherapists, and hospice care. With the recent introduction of the National Health Insurance Law and the attendant concern with providing quality service within a predetermined, limited budget, the Sick Funds have begun considering the provision of additional types of medical care in the home. For example, home hospitalization is being examined as an alternative to costly hospital stays. However, they have yet to consider the additional burden that this will place on families. Data are being collected on the utilization, cost, and impact of home hospitalization programs (Bentur, King, & Brodsky, 1998).

Nonprofessional Home Care.   Concern about the growing number of people who will need long-term care, and awareness that existing programs are insufficient, induced the Knesset (Israel's Parliament) to enact the Community Long-Term Care Insurance (CLTCI) Law in 1980, to be administered by the National Insurance Institute (Morginstin, Baich-Moray, & Haron, 1989).

In 1980, an 0.2% Social Security payroll tax was levied to develop a reserve fund for implementation of the new law. Enactment was completed in April 1986, and full implementation in April 1988. This innovative law reflected the government's commitment to providing a basic level of home care to a vulnerable population (Morginstin, 1988). This commitment also was politically crucial, given the reduction in per capita spending on health and welfare at that time (Habib & Factor, 1993).

The primary aim of the CLTCI Law was to universally provide home care services to dependent elderly on the basis of personal entitlement and clearly defined eligibility criteria. This represents an important shift from budgeted programs to entitlement programs, and from largely selective benefits to universal ones. The basic entitlement is for in-kind services, carefully delineated as a "basket of services" closely related to the direct care functions normally provided by families, such as personal care and homemaking. Benefits also may be used to purchase day care services, laundry services, absorbent undergarments for the incontinent, and an alarm system (for medical and other urgent situations). The benefit entitlement, set at 25% of the average market wage, with severely disabled elderly receiving an additional 50% of this level, is translated into in-kind services (equivalent to 10 or 15 hours of care per week, respectively) (Morginstin, 1987).

The first effect of the law was to tremendously increase the resources earmarked for community care. This resulted in a more balanced allocation of public resources between institutional and community care. Prior to the law, 15% of public spending for long-term care went to community services; following the law's implementation, close to 50% of public funds were spent on community care.

Given the small amount of caregiving hours provided under the CLTCI Law, families continue to be the primary caregivers (Brodsky & Naon, 1993a, 1993b). However, the CLTCI Law is an implicit recognition of the economic value of caregiving: No longer is care by the family regarded as a free, unlimited resource. The government now shares at least some of the burden of caring for the elderly. The implementation of the CLTCI Law has increased the coverage of home care for the total elderly population, from 1.5% prior to the law to 10% today. Among the Arab elderly population, 11.8% receive services under the law. This high rate may be explained by the high rate of disability and low rate of institutionalization among this population (Weihl, 1991, 1995). It is worth noting that this level of utilization of services was made possible by the flexibility of the CLTCI Law, which allowed Arab family members to provide actual services that are provided in the Jewish sector by hired caregivers, as Arabs were reluctant to allow strangers to care for their elderly relatives. The successful implementation of the law in the Arab sector also spurred Arab families to take advantage of other community services, such as day care centers and senior clubs.

Policy makers were concerned that the increase in formal services might cause families to relinquish their caring responsibilities; however, experience has not substantiated this concern. In Israel as in other countries, no evidence has been found of a decrease in the amount of informal services because of the provision of formal services (Hanley, Wiener, & Harris, 1991; Moscovice, Davidson, & McCaffrey, 1998). It appears that community services supplement, rather than supplant, informal care and significantly reduce caregivers' sense of burden (Brodsky & Naon, 1993a; Morginstin & Baich-Moray, 1992). The presence of formal caregivers enables family members to choose what care they will provide. In addition, knowing that formal care is guaranteed by statute and, therefore, reliable, may give families emotional relief, enabling them to continue providing significant levels of care (Brodsky & Naon, 1993b).

It seems that a system in which eligibility is based on principles of entitlement has a major impact on demand (Factor et al. 1991). In fact, demand for services has exceeded what was forecast, and the CLTCI Law has become a deficit program. The authors' findings also indicate that, despite the improvement brought about by the expansion of formal services, elderly people still have many unmet needs, and caregivers still feel burdened (Brodsky & Naon, 1993; Morginstin & Baich-Moray, 1992). Given that this basic level is proving insufficient, the authors must ask whether the Israeli government should extend entitlements or allow the development of discretionary programs to supplement this basic level of care (Morginstin, Baich-Moray, & Zipkin, 1992).

Homemaking Services and Meals-on-Wheels

The Ministry of Labor and Social Affairs provides homemaking services for the less severely disabled elderly. This is a means-tested discretionary program, which benefits just over 2% of the elderly population. In addition, through local authorities and various voluntary organizations, the ministry provides frail elderly with two forms of meals: hot meals delivered daily and frozen meals delivered once a week. Elderly people who are unable to cook are eligible and are required to pay the full price of the products used in the meals (half of the total cost). The cost of preparation and delivery is subsidized by the Ministry of Labor and Social Affairs, according to income level.

Day Care Centers

Day care centers are a significant service which enables the elderly to remain in the community, improves the quality of their lives, and releases the family from caregiving duties during the day, freeing them to work and attend to other tasks (Habib & Factor, 1993; Korazim, 1994). A network of approximately 125 day care centers serves over 8,000 disabled elderly, or approximately 1.5% of the elderly (Beer, 1998). In the Arab sector, demand for day care services is growing. At present, there are more than 6 day care centers in Arab villages, serving about 1.8% of the Arab elderly. It is thought that day care centers are becoming a substitute for the traditional gathering place of elderly Arabs (diwan), which gradually is disappearing (Azaiza & Brodsky, 1996).

Day care centers usually operate 5 or 6 days a week and offer social and recreational activities, personal care, hot meals, transportation, counseling, and health promotion. In addition to freeing the family from some care responsibilities, the centers give the elderly opportunities for social contact and provide them with stimulation that helps maintain their functional and cognitive capacity. Day care centers in Israel differ from centers in many other countries, as they emphasize social rather than medical care, and thus are relatively lower in cost (Brodsky et al. 1995; Habib & Factor, 1993).

Another significant development within the day care network has been the establishment of special programs for the cognitively impaired, including elderly people with Alzheimer's disease and other dementias. This is a result of the forecast increase in the number of cognitively impaired and of the attendant need for a community-based service, which will benefit these elders and their families. Recently adopted standards for adult day care in Israel mandate that all new facilities set aside a special place for the cognitively impaired elderly.

Respite Care

Respite care is a relatively new service in Israel, which provides a temporary alternative residence for elderly people who usually live at home. It often is used as a transitional residence after discharge from the hospital following an acute event, prior to returning home. It also provides a place for an elderly person to stay if his or her other primary caregiver is absent, becomes ill, or needs a rest from the burden of care. The service is provided in two ways: in facilities designated for respite care and in institutional long-term care facilities. In both cases, the service is intended to be short term and institution based.

Data from a recent study showed that there are only four frameworks formally providing respite care at present, with a total of 170 beds. Another 150 beds are available for use in this capacity, but only if they are not being used by long-term care patients. In 1995, some 3,000 elderly people (approximately 0.5% of all elderly people) availed themselves of respite care beds. The average length of stay in a respite care bed was 24 days (Cahan, Brodsky & Berencik, 1998). This service is not sufficiently developed in Israel. Policy makers are considering expanding it, particularly for the benefit of families caring for disabled elderly and elderly with cognitive impairment (e.g., Alzheimer's disease, dementia).

Other Living Arrangements in the Community

Two other types of community service allow the elderly to "age in place," and enable their families to care for them within a supportive framework that relieves some of the burden of caregiving. The first of these is sheltered housing, which has developed in response to the increased demand of elderly people to live independently (King & Shtarkshall, 1997).

In most of these frameworks in Israel, the elderly person or couple lives in a normal apartment with kitchen facilities, in a building that provides an alarm system (for medical or other urgent situations) and offers meals in a dining hall and organized recreational activities. As of late 1995, there were 9,000 housing units for elderly people in Israel; that is, 18 housing units per 1,000 elderly people (Beer, 1996). Development of this service is shared evenly by the public, government, and private sectors, although the latter is becoming increasingly involved in constructing sheltered housing projects. Recently, the government has begun developing sheltered housing expressly to meet the needs of elderly immigrants.

The second, and most innovative, type of living arrangement is the supportive neighborhood for senior citizens. This encourages the elderly to remain in their neighborhoods by providing a variety of supportive services to meet their needs, including a crisis and referral system, an emergency beeper system, counseling and guidance, meals-on-wheels, medical care, and recreational activities. Many of these services are coordinated by a housemother or housefather and involve the participation of volunteers, some of whom are younger residents of the neighborhood. The elderly people pay a monthly fee, which covers approximately 70% of the program's costs (Brodsky, et al., 1995). To date, the program has been successfully implemented in 14 neighborhoods in cities in Israel, and plans are being made to expand it further.

☐ Future Trends: Issues and Problems

Background

The situation in Israel, as in other Western countries, is extremely complex. There are three related trends, which will influence how the formal system responds to care needs. First, the aging of the elderly population is causing astonishing growth in the number of disabled elderly. Second, concern that the increased number of disabled elderly will cost the formal care system more than it can afford to spend is causing policy makers to seek less expensive care solutions in the community. This, in turn, creates a third problem: Increasing pressure is being put on families to care for their elderly relatives, precisely when many women (the majority of primary caregivers) are joining the labor force and have less time to devote to care of elderly relatives. Some of the services developed during the past decade partially resolve this situation. Israel's innovative CLTCI Law, together with universal health care coverage, have created an infrastructure that provides at least a modicum of care to all elderly. However, more effective use can be made of existing resources and problems remain, the solutions of which will lie in policy decisions.

Expanding the Flexibility of the Existing System

Given a decade of experience in establishing a stable program that ensures a basic level of home care for the elderly, many professionals believe it is time to increase the program's flexibility. Services purport to meet the needs of families but, in fact, they are limited in scope and type. Families do not have enough choices in how to use the services to which they are entitled. For example, instead of receiving 3 hours of home care in one block of time, as is the current practice, a family could receive home care for brief intervals evenly spaced throughout the day, in direct response to their work or other obligations. Conversely, a family might prefer support services at night, freeing them to leave the house. No such services are currently available. One way of making services more flexible would be to establish neighborhood teams of home care workers who would share responsibility for a number of families; this also would be cost effective. At present, formal caregivers are not able to use their discretion in service provision, and informal caregivers are not able to choose among different alternatives in making use of services.

One service that was expected to provide a ready-made answer to the needs of the elderly was day care centers. Policy makers also expected this service to allow family caregivers more free time. Despite its rapid and extensive expansion, this service is not being used to full capacity or advantage. Those who do use the service seem to be very satisfied with it (Korazim, 1994), making it difficult to understand why it is not used more widely. Apparently, something deters families or the elderly from taking advantage of it. It also is possible that professionals are not making sufficient referrals to day care centers. Efforts are being made to investigate whether the problem is one of accessibility, cost, inappropriate hours of operation, and so forth.

One service that has been shown to be crucial to the well-being of family caregivers, but which has been insufficiently developed in Israel, is respite care. The success of existing inpatient respite care programs indicates that more such programs are needed, as are home-based respite care programs. Given the growing tendency to keep hospital stays brief, respite care can provide a patient the period of adjustment that he or she needs before returning home, while enabling the family to make arrangements for the elder's return.

Policy Regarding Entitlements and Spending

One indicator of the success of the CLTCI Law also is a reflection of its shortcomings: It is now running on a deficit. The enormous demand for services indicates that the need is even greater than was forecast 10 years ago. At the law's inception, a decision was made to provide a few services to all those in need; this commitment to universal care is what makes the law unique, but it has proven to be expensive. Moreover, the gap between needs and services has not been sufficiently bridged.

One way of bridging the gap would be to raise the payroll tax from which the law culls its funding and, thereby, maintain a basic level of coverage for all disabled elderly. Another would be to introduce more stringent eligibility criteria to reduce the target population to only the most severely disabled. Yet another way would be to increase the number of eligibility categories, providing fewer services to the less severely disabled and more services to the more severely disabled. Finally, it might be desirable for other organizations to begin supplementing the services provided under the CLTCI Law on a discretionary basis. In fact, Sick Funds have begun providing home hospitalization, augmented by nonprofessional home care services. The Ministry of Health also is considering providing nonprofessional home care services to the severely disabled as a way of reducing both expenditures and lengthy waiting lists for institutionalization.

Another of the system's shortcomings is its fragmentation. The elderly and their families may easily be confused about their rights and about who provides which service. An attempt was made to introduce case management and other coordination mechanisms into the system, with only moderate success (Brodsky & Sobol, 1992). Problems of coordination must be solved at both the level of policy and the level of service provision.

In light of forecast demographic changes, changes in family structure and labor force participation, ever-dwindling resources, and the desire to keep institutionalization low in Israel, there is a need for statutes that will help caregivers balance their familial and work obligations with that of caring for elderly relatives—particularly, if they are to continue to be the most important component of the system of care. Employers could make policies that would enable employees who care for an elderly relative to use their work time more flexibly. Research is needed in Israel that will examine the implications of caregiving for earnings and career advancement. Perhaps, this will enable Israel to calculate the true cost of caregiving and find more appropriate support that will reduce both the emotional and financial cost of care.

☐ Note

1. The study was based on a follow-up of 400 disabled elderly and their caregivers. Participants were identified from a representative sample of 1,780 elderly out of a total of 16,000 elderly living in communities in 10 different areas of Israel.

☐ **References**

Azaiza, F., & Brodsky, J. (1996). Changes in the Arab world and development of services for the Arab elderly in Israel during the last decade. *Journal of Gerontological Social Work 27*(1/2), 37–53.

Be'er, S. (1996). *Estimates of the needs for services for the elderly in Israel by geographic region, 1994–2005.* Jerusalem: JDC-Brookdale Institute of Gerontology and Human Development. (in Hebrew)

Be'er, S. (1997). *National information center reports.* Jerusalem: JDC-Brookdale Institute of Gerontology and Human Development. (in Hebrew)

Be'er, S. (1998). *Clients of day care centers for the elderly: Findings from a 1994 national census.* Jerusalem: JDC-Brookdale Institute of Gerontology and Human Development. (in Hebrew)

Bentur, N., King, Y., & Brodsky J. (1998). *Home hospitalization in Israel: An evaluation study.* Jerusalem: JDC-Brookdale Institute of Gerontology and Human Development. (in Hebrew)

Brodsky, J., & Bergman, S. (1993). The aged in Israel. In E. Palmore (Ed.), *Developments and research on aging: An international handbook* (pp. 165–186). Westport, CT: Greenwood Press.

Brodsky J., & Habib, J. (1996). Strategies for assisting frail elderly to maintain dignity and independence. *Ageing International 23*(2), 21–32.

Brodsky J., & Habib, J. (1997). New developments and issues in home care policies. In Home care: Developments and innovations in health provision [Special issue]. *Disability and Rehabilitation Journal 18*(4), 150–154.

Brodsky, J., Kaplan, E., & Barnea T. (1995). Experience counts: Innovative programs for the elderly in Israel that can benefit Americans. In M. C. Bard (Ed.), *The American-Israeli cooperative enterprise.* Maryland: AICE.

Brodsky, J., & Naon, D. (1993a). *Implications of the expansion of home care following the implementation of the Community Long-Term Care Insurance Law.* Jerusalem: JDC-Brookdale Institute of Gerontology and Human Development. (in Hebrew)

Brodsky, J., & Naon, D. (1993b). Home care services in Israel: Implications of the expansion of home care following implementation of the Community Long-Term Care Insurance Law. *Journal of Cross-Cultural Gerontology 8*, 375–390.

Brodsky, J., & Sobol, E. (1992, September). Coordinated care teams: Improving health and social care of older Israelis. *Ageing International*, 81–93.

Brodsky, J., Sobol, E., Naon, D., King, Y., & Lifshitz, C. (1991). *The functional, health, and social characteristics and needs of the elderly in the community.* Jerusalem: JDC-Brookdale Institute of Gerontology and Human Development. (in Hebrew)

Brody, E. M. (1988). The long haul: A family odyssey. In L. F. Jarvik & C. H. Winograd (Eds.), *Treatments for the Alzheimer patient* (pp. 107–122). New York: Springer.

Brody, E. M., Johnsen, P. T., Hoffman, C., & Schoonover, C. B. (1987). Work status and parent care: A comparison of four groups of women. *The Gerontologist, 27*, 201–208.

Cahan, P., Brodsky, J., & Berencik, B. (1998). *Mapping and evaluation of respite care in Israel.* Jerusalem: JDC-Brookdale Institute of Gerontology and Human Development. (in Hebrew)

Central Bureau of Statistics. *Annual Reports* (1961, 1962, 1971, 1973, 1981, 1984, 1995). Jerusalem: Central Bureau of Statistics.

Factor, H., Morginstin, B., & Naon, D. (1991). Home-care services in Israel. In A. Jamieson (Ed.), *Home care for older people in Europe* (pp. 157–187). Oxford: Oxford University Press.

Feuerbach, E. J., & Erdwins, C. J. (1994). Women's retirement: The influence of work history. *Journal of Women and Aging 6*(3), 69–85.

Habib, J., & Factor, H. (1993). Services for the elderly: Changing circumstances and strategies. In A. Kruger, D. Morley, and A. Shachar (Eds.), *Public services under stress: A Canadian-Israeli policy review.* Jerusalem: Magnes Press.

Habib, J., & Tamir Y. (1994). Jewish aged in Israel: Sociodemographic and socioeconomic status. In Z. Harel, D. Biegel, & D. Guttmann (Eds.), *Jewish aged in the United States and Israel: Diversity programs and services* (pp. 47–60). New York: Springer.

Hanley, P., Wiener, J. M., & Harris, K. M. (1991). Will paid home care erode informal support? *Journal of Health Politics, Policy and Law 16*, 507–521.

King, Y., & Shtarkshall, M. (1997). *Public-governmental sheltered housing projects: Residential characteristics and needs, and organizational and operational characteristics.* Jerusalem: JDC-Brookdale Institute of Gerontology and Human Development. (in Hebrew)

Kinsella, K., & Taeuber, C. M. (1993). *An aging world. II* (International Population Reports P95/92-3). Washington, D.C.: U.S. Department of Commerce Economics and Statistics Administration, U.S. Bureau of the Census.

Kleiman, E. (1987). The Histadrut economy of Israel: In search of criteria. *The Jerusalem Quarterly, 41*, 77–94.

Korazim, M. (1994). *Day care centers for the elderly in Israel: An evaluation study.* Jerusalem: JDC-Brookdale Institute of Gerontology and Human Development. (in Hebrew)

Liebig, P. S. (1993). Factors affecting the development of employer-sponsored eldercare programs: Implications for employed caregivers. *Journal of Women and Aging, 5*(1), 59–78.

Morginstin, B. (1988). Response of formal support systems to social changes and patterns of caregiving. *Journal of Welfare and Social Security Studies,* 103–126.

Morginstin, B. (1987). Long-term care insurance in Israel. *Ageing International 11*(2) 10–13.

Morginstin, B., & Baich-Moray, S. (1992). *The impact of long-term care insurance on informal caregivers of dependent elderly.* Jerusalem: National Insurance Institute.

Morginstin, B., Baich-Moray, S., & Haron T. (1989). *The implementation of long-term care insurance: Demonstration project.* Jerusalem: National Insurance Institute.

Morginstin, B., Baich-Moray, S., & Zipkin, A. (1992). Assessment of long-term care needs and the provision of services to the elderly in Israel: The impact of long-term care insurance. *Australian Journal on Ageing 11*(2), 16–24.

Moscovice, I., Davidson, G., & McCaffrey, D. (1988). Substitution of formal and informal care for the community-based elderly. *Medical Care 26*, 971–981.

Noam, G., & Habib, J. (1992). Family care of the elderly in Israel. In J. Kosberg (Ed.), *Family care of the elderly* (pp. 139–157). Newbury Park, CA: Sage.

Naon, D., King, Y., & Habib, J. (1993). Resettling elderly Soviet immigrants in Israel: Family ties and the housing dilemma. *Journal of Psychology and Aging 17*, 299–314.

Shalov, M. (1992). *Labour and the political economy in Israel.* Oxford, England: Oxford University Press.

Strosberg, N., & Naon, D. (1997). *Absorption of elderly immigrants from the former Soviet Union: Follow-up of the housing problem and its effect on various dimensions of absorption.* Jerusalem: JDC-Brookdale Institute of Gerontology and Human Development. (in Hebrew)

Weihl, H. (1991). *Welfare services for the elderly in the Arab sector in Israel, Report of surveys conducted by ESHEL.* Jerusalem: Association for the Planning and Development of Services for the Aged in Israel (ESHEL). (in Hebrew)

Weihl, H. (1995). *Implementation of the Community Care Law in the Arab sector.* Jerusalem: National Insurance Institute. (in Hebrew)

6

CHAPTER

Masako Ishii-Kuntz

Japan and Its Planning Toward Family Caregiving

☐ Introduction

The proportion of the elderly (65 years old or over) in Japan doubled from 7% in 1970 to 14% in 1994 (Ministry of Health and Welfare, 1995a). While the comparable increase in the elderly population took 115 years in France, 85 years in Sweden, 75 years in the United States, and 45 years in Great Britain, it took only 24 years in Japan. The elderly population in Japan continues to rise. In 1996, the population age 65 or over constituted 15% of Japan's population. According to the 1997 projection issued by the Institute of Population Problems, approximately 27% of Japan's population will be 65 years old or over in 2025. In addition, the rise in the elderly population will be particularly sharp among those who are above 75 years of age (Management and Coordination Agency, Statistical Bureau, 1997a).

These demographic changes have raised considerable concern among the Japanese public and government over the issue of caring for the elderly. Also, the Japanese mass media has been reporting a high level of stress and burden experienced by caregivers. For example, one talk show focused on death by fatigue *(karoshi)* of a middle-aged woman who had been caring for her bedridden mother-in-law for 3 years (Ishikawa, 1990). An unfortunate incident such as this has begun to change the public perception of *karoshi*, a term which previously had been used to describe death of workaholic, salaried men. In response to these growing concerns, the Ministry of Health and Welfare issued its Ten-Year Strategy for Promoting Health and Welfare Services for the Elderly (the so-called "Gold Plan") in 1989, which promoted home care for the frail elderly and assistance for home caregivers. Before this plan, nearly 90% of the budget for elderly welfare at the Ministry of Health and Welfare went to institutional care (Sodei, 1996). Although there have been improvements in the Gold

I wish to thank Takako Sodei and Katsuko Makino of Ochanomizu University in Tokyo, Japan, for their support.

Plan, as reflected in the 1994 New Gold Plan, one area that has received relatively little attention is the issue of elder care by employed persons.

Today nearly 90% of caregivers in Japan are female (Sodei, 1997). If frail elders are male, their wives are the primary caregivers; whereas, if frail elders are female, then middle-aged daughters-in-law or daughters are most likely to take on the role of caregiver. With their increased participation in the labor force, middle-aged, married women are now facing difficulties in pursuing both work and caregiving for elders. Additionally, with the rise in women's labor force participation and changes in women's attitudes toward familial roles, elder care is also becoming a central concern for many Japanese men. It thus is clear that the Japanese government and work organizations need to pay greater attention to reducing difficulties experienced by employed caregivers.

In brief, these two trends—the dramatic increases in the elderly population and in women's labor force participation in Japan—have raised public and governmental concerns over elder care. In this chapter, the author will first describe work and family concerns as they relate to the care of the elderly in Japan. Second, the types of support (e.g., policies, benefits, programs, and services) available for employed caregivers in Japan will be explained. Third, the demographic, sociocultural, historical, political, and economic factors that have contributed to Japan's configuration of policies and services for employed caregivers and for elders will be discussed. Finally, likely future trends in elder care among employed persons will be outlined.

☐ Work and Family Concerns

Results from several studies, including nationwide surveys, have revealed that the majority of frail elderly are cared for at home by family members rather than in institutions (Ministry of Health and Welfare, 1995b, 1997; Okamoto, 1996; Sodei, 1996, 1997). Overall, approximately 4.9% of the elderly age 65 and over are cared for at home, while 3.3% receive institutional care. Among the frail elderly who need care, 60% live at home, while the rest live in institutional care settings.

Employment and Caring for the Elderly

Several national surveys sponsored by the Japanese government have reported the extent of elder care among employed persons. The Demographic, Social and Economic Survey (Ministry of Health and Welfare, 1995a) was conducted to assess the extent of elder care among family members of deceased elderly. This survey reported that 67% of caregivers were family members living in the same household; 6% were other relatives; 16% were professional care providers; 6% were others, including friends; and the remaining 5% were unknown.

Sixty-four percent of male and 53% of female caregivers were employed at the beginning of the caregiving experience. Among them, 28% of males and 35% of females had to alter their employment by (1) quitting (14.4% of males and 21.5% of females), (2) taking extended leave from work (12.2% of males and 11.7% of females), (3) changing jobs (1.3% of males and 1.6% of females), or (4) making other nonspecified arrangements (4% of males and 3% of females). Interestingly, however, the majority of these caregivers (68% of males and 62% of females) continued to work, thereby maintaining the dual roles of caregiver and worker.

In general, the impact of caregiving on employment is much greater for female than for male caregivers. The Survey of Working Caregivers (Ministry of Labor, Women's Bureau, 1991), which was conducted at firms with more than 30 employees, showed that among 1,319 full-time employees who had been caring for elders at home for the previous 3 years, 44% were females and 56% were males. Although more males reported having elderly care recipients at home, their wives, daughters, or daughters-in-law generally gave the actual care. Only 7% of males were primary caregivers, whereas 43% of the females were primary caregivers. Among men who had care recipients at home, approximately 75% provided some assistance to the primary caregiver, and 25% did almost nothing. Gender differences also were found in employees' use of work leaves (mostly unpaid) to care for frail elders; 64% of females and 27% of males took such leaves, with the average length of the leave being 138 days. Clearly, Japanese working women are more strongly affected by caregiving than are their male counterparts. Stated another way, elder care among the employed in Japan is a highly female-dominated activity.

Changing Roles and Attitudes of Women

As is common in other countries, caring for the frail elderly is almost always the role of women in Japan. However, in contrast to most of the Western nations where wives and daughters usually are the primary caregivers, daughters-in-law also are primary caregivers in Japan (Sodei, 1997). In 1989, daughters-in-law cared for 39% of elderly males and 63% of elderly females (Ministry of Labor, 1989). Indeed, daughters-in-law have formed the core of caregivers; however, the number of Japanese who want to be cared for by their daughters-in-law in their old age is declining. According to the Survey on Life and Care in Old Age (Management and Coordination Agency, 1991), those who preferred their spouse as caregiver totaled 51%, daughters-in-law 16%, daughters 10%, sons 5%, and the remaining 18% preferred institutional care.

The heavy reliance on women (whether wife, daughter, or daughter-in-law) to care for the elderly at home has become a major problem with the increase in labor force participation among middle-aged, married women. The proportion of female employees to total male workers was 32% in 1955. Many were family workers who helped their self-employed fathers or husbands. However, the expansion of tertiary industries (such as sales, commerce, and services) has increased employment opportunities for women. Consequently, while there were only 5 female workers for every 10 male workers in 1970; by 1991, the ratio had increased to 7 female workers for every 10 male workers (Sodei, 1997).

In 1995, nearly 7 out of 10 women in their forties and fifties were employed. The increase in women's labor force participation is particularly evident among middle-aged and married women. Among female employees, the percentage who were married was only 30% in 1962, a little over 50% in 1975, and nearly 60% in 1990. Moreover, those women age 40 and over accounted for 19.5% of all female employees in 1970, but reached 49% in 1991 (Ministry of Labor, Women's Bureau, 1993). Many of these middle-aged women are part-time workers who work no more than 35 hours a week. The number of female part-time employees was 1.3 million (12% of total female employees) in 1970, 2.56 million (19%) in 1980, and 5.01 million (28%) in 1990 (Ministry of Labor, 1990). Of female part-time workers, 34% were age 35 to 44, 32% were age 45 to 54, 15% were age 55 or over, and 18% were under age 35 (Ministry of Labor, 1991). It is clear that the majority of part-time workers are middle-aged women.

In addition to women's increased participation in the labor force, there have been changes in women's attitudes toward caregiving. According to the survey conducted by one of Japan's nationally circulated newspapers, *Asahi Shimbun* (1994), less than 30% of Japanese women in their forties and fifties felt responsible for taking care of their elderly parents. The same survey also reported that less than 50% of men and women in any age group wanted to take care of their frail elderly parents.

Managing Work and Elder Care

Elder care responsibilities can influence various aspects of caregivers' daily lives. Research has documented that the number of hours spent caring for frail elders is similar for employed and nonemployed caregivers (Ministry of Labor, 1989); thus, the former group has to give up their free time or leisure hours in order to meet the demands of the frail elderly. Interestingly, however, the time demands placed on employed caregivers are not necessarily associated with an increased level of stress. Previous studies, for example, show that the amount of stress experienced by employed caregivers actually is less than that experienced by nonemployed caregivers (e.g., Sodei, 1997). According to the survey conducted by Women's Bureau (Ministry of Labor, Women's Bureau, 1986), 26% of nonemployed (and 27% of employed) wives reported frequent physical fatigue. However, 59% of nonemployed women compared to 47% of employed women reported psychological stress as a result of elder care. Stated another way, slightly more employed women caregivers experienced physical fatigue, but fewer experienced psychological stress than did their nonemployed counterparts. Sodei (1989) also confirmed this finding in her study of caregivers who utilized day care facilities. In her sample of 391 employed and nonemployed caregivers, she found that nonemployed caregivers reported twice as high a level of stress as did employed caregivers.

Several explanations may exist for this unexpected finding. First, nonemployed caregivers are likely to be older and have some illness that prevents them from working. Employed caregivers tend to be younger, healthier, and more likely to care for elders with less severe disabilities. Therefore, it may not be employment per se that affects the stress level. Second, the opportunity to leave home for work, and thus spend some hours a day away from the caregiving environment, can be seen as a stress reduction strategy. In fact, 5% of male and 7% of female caregivers in Sodei's sample cited their employment as a way to reduce the stress caused by caregiving activities (Sodei, 1989).

In addition to affecting caregivers, the combination of work and elder care has a significant impact on relationships between men and women. The low rate of Japanese men's participation in elder care is due, in part, to their typically long commutes and work hours. At the same time, caregiving for an elderly family member is frequently considered women's work; thus, men are reluctant to take it on. However, elder care involves more than direct physical care. In fact, many Japanese caregivers (i.e., women) rely on their spouses' (i.e., husbands') emotional support to continue caring for the elderly. Nonetheless, as more Japanese men take part in child care (Ishii-Kuntz, 1994, 1996), men's active participation in elder care also can be predicted to increase in the foreseeable future. This trend is evident by a currently best-selling book by Ochi (1998), entitled *Oya ga 65-sai o sugitara otoko ga yomu hon* (A Book to Be Read by Men Whose Parents Are Older than 65). The book emphasizes the importance of men's participation and responsibility in caring for frail elderly parents.

The increase in caregivers who also are employed has necessitated some changes in the workplace. A survey conducted by Japan Labor Institute showed that 53% of employed caregivers wanted to choose the hours they would work, 38% wanted parental care leave, and 9% wanted home-based work (Ohshima, 1996). Due to the increase in the elderly population and the demand for caregiving, the workplace has begun to consider ways to accommodate these needs.

☐ Supports for Employed Caregivers

Japan has a relatively long history of welfare services for the elderly; however, it was not until the 1990s that the topic of work and caregiving began receiving attention from the government, work organizations, and other organizations. Table 6-1 summarizes the major types of supports for employed caregivers offered by these bodies. It also lists supports for elders, such as home care, which make it easier for employed caregivers to manage their dual responsibilities. As described below and shown in Table 6-1, Japanese government policies and those of workplaces and other organizations are closely intertwined.

Government Initiatives

Long-Term Care Leave (Kaigo Kyugyouhou).   The government policy that is most relevant for employed caregivers is the Long-Term Care Leave Law (enacted in 1999). This law mandates businesses to grant temporary work leaves to employees caring for frail family members. Due to the increase in women's participation in the labor force, combined with the low birth rate and the rapid aging of the population, the Ministry of Labor has become greatly concerned with child care and elder care. As a result of cooperative efforts between the ministry and private businesses, the Child Care Leave was first inaugurated in 1992. This was an important development for Japanese parents with infants because, for the first time, the government allowed fathers or mothers to take parental leave (Ishii-Kuntz, 1996). However, it was far from an ideal supportive measure for employed parents because it did not guarantee pay, and it also reduced benefits.

The government's focus on employed caregivers of frail elders emerged after the 1989 Gold Plan, which shifted the government's emphasis from institutional to home care for the elderly. In February 1995, the proposal for the Long-Term Care Leave was submitted to Japan's Parliament (the Diet). This proposal was in direct response to the more than 80,000 workers who were forced to resign from their jobs in order to care for elderly family members. Subsequently, the proposal was incorporated in the Law for the Welfare of Employees Engaged in Infant Care or in the Care of Family Members, which was passed in June 1995.

The law will help employed caregivers continue their employment and caregiving duties, and, in doing so, employed caregivers will be able to maintain their contribution to the economy and to society. The major stipulations of the law are (1) employees are allowed to take 3 months of leave to care for a family member (spouse, parent, child, parent-in-law) who needs "constant attention" as defined by medical personnel; (2) approximately 25% of salary will be paid during the leave, and this compensation will come from the employee insurance program; (3) the leave can be taken one time only (however, once the leave is taken, employers must allow employees to work shortened days to care for an elderly family member); (4) employers cannot fire indi-

TABLE 6-1. Japanese supports for employees with elder care responsibilities

Government Initiatives	Nongovernmental Organization Initiatives	Union Initiatives	Workplace Initiatives
For employed caregivers Long-Term Care Insurance (2000) Long-Term Care Leave (1999) Financial assistance for caregivers Financial assistance for companies Implementation advising for companies Part-time work Telework, satellite office Home care support center Counseling for employed caregivers Fure Fure Telephone Service Dependent tax credits Housing assistance (loans) Research funding Seminars, job referrals New Gold Plan Indirectly, for older persons Health Insurance for the Aged National Health Insurance Provision for retirees Provision for the elderly National Pension (Kokumin Nenkin) Senior recreational centers Training for "manpower" (i.e., retraining) Life education Counseling for health maintenance	For Employed Caregivers Home help service Short stay service Day service Indirectly, for older persons Senior citizens clubs Sports clubs, culture centers, Life education fair Silver Service (identify services that meet acceptable standards) Counseling for senior citizens Barrier-free transportation system Silver Personnel Center (employment service)	Political and work organization influence Federal and prefectural lobbying Union and management negotiations Services Health insurance Pension, research	Policies: Work Scheduling Long-Term Care Leave Sick, vacation, personal leave Medical leave Counseling and support Part-time work, flextime Relocation policies Telework, satellite office Benefits: Income assistance Welfare Pension (Kousei Nenkin) Fure Social Health Insurance Dependent tax credits Corporate pensions, retirement benefits Services Educational materials, seminars Resource and referral, counseling

viduals solely because of the leave they took. Although taking the leave does not constitute legal grounds for firing employees, there are no penalties imposed on employers who do not comply with this provision.

The law's original implementation date was to be April 1996; however, this date was delayed until 1999 because of several unresolved issues. These issues include financial compensation during the leave, special leave to care for a dying family member, and an emergency leave. There is an on-going discussion concerning the provision of a maximum of 3 months of leave. On the one hand, 3 months is almost too short a leave, since elder care frequently is a long-term activity. At the same time, however, many businesses cannot afford to grant more than 3 months of leave to their employees. Unless these critical issues are solved, the Long-Term Care Leave Law will not be an effective law.

Despite these issues, the government has proposed several additional measures to promote the Long-Term Care Leave. These measures include increasing the employee salary replacement beyond 25%; providing financial support to those companies who incur extra costs, such as the hiring of another person to replace the employee on leave; and advising companies on how to implement the law.

Although the government delayed enactment of the law, several companies have already created long-term care provisions for their employees, as discussed below. However, because the government does not yet mandate the Long-Term Care Leave, the number of companies with such provisions is still low.

Other Policies, Programs, and Services.   Because part-time workers constitute a large proportion of employed caregivers, the government improved benefits for part-time workers in 1993 and 1994. Additionally, in 1996, the Ministry of Labor revised the law to improve the conditions and benefits of workers who substitute for those on Long-Term Care Leave. The main purpose of the latter revision was to increase the number of temporary workers who can fill the vacancies created by employed caregivers on leave.

Second, the Ministry of Labor has been working to promote teleworking or satellite working (working at home using various modes of communication, such as phone, Fax, and electronic mail) for employed caregivers. This alternative work style will reduce the long hours of commute that many Japanese workers experience, thereby allowing them to care for their homebound elderly family member.

Third, the government sponsors or partially funds various services to support employed caregivers and their families. Some examples of these services include counseling for employed caregivers, Fure Fure Telephone Service (telephone counseling and advising), seminars on work and elder care management, and job referrals. Finally, the government has subsidized some research projects concerning the care of the elderly. However, most of the research funds have been allocated to projects that focus on medical, technological, and telecommunication (e.g., cable television, e-mail) aspects of aging.

Public Insurance Scheme for Long-Term Care (*Kaigo Hoken*).   In April 1994, the National Welfare Tax Bill, which proposed to raise the consumer tax to 7%, failed to pass the Diet under Prime Minister Hosokawa. As a result, the Ministry of Health and Welfare had to formulate a new plan to raise money to care for the elderly. It was with this background that the concept of Long-Term Care Insurance was born. After several years of negotiation and debate, the Diet finally passed the bill proposing Public Insurance Scheme for Long-Term Care in 1997. This has set the stage for the April 2000 launch of the system, which is to be funded by premiums paid by everyone age 40 and older and funds from the government. This insurance system will provide services for the elderly who are bedridden or who suffer from senile dementia and other age-related difficulties. It also will pay for professional caregivers (at least on a part-time basis) and pay for day care centers, thereby increasing elders' use of such centers. This increase will also encourage more openings of day care centers. Therefore, the availability and easy access to day care centers will reduce the burden of caring among employed caregivers.

Financial Incentives.   Two programs that encourage home-based elder care are particularly relevant to employed caregivers: the tax deduction for elderly dependents and housing assistance, including low-interest loans. First, family members who earn taxable income can claim a tax deduction for elderly dependents regardless of the elder's health status. According to the 1997 Tax Guide, 380,000 yen ($2,900) can be deducted for each dependent. Also, if the dependent is age 70 or over, an additional 200,000 yen ($1,500) can be deducted.

Second, there are several types of housing assistance and programs for families with elderly dependents. For example, the "being filial to elderly parents" Oyakoko Loan allows adult children with elderly dependents to take out housing loans from the government at lower interest rates. In addition, low-interest housing loans are available for families who remodel their homes to create a "barrier-free" environment for the elderly, such as the installation of home elevators. Other housing-related policies include priority ranking for families caring for the elderly to obtain publicly funded apartments, and to be placed on the first floor in such apartment buildings.

Indirect Initiatives.   In addition to the above initiatives, there are initiatives that enhance the lives of frail elders which, in turn, benefit the lives of employed caregivers. These include Health Insurance for the Aged, National Health Insurance (Kokumin Hoken), National Pension, senior recreational centers, health counseling for seniors, geriatric training for health care workers, and lifelong education programs and workshops (Management and Coordination Agency, Statistical Bureau, 1997b).

Union Initiatives

Several trade labor unions in Japan have advocated for the needs of employed caregivers and have aggressively lobbied the government and employers on behalf of this group. Japanese Trade Union Confederation (Rengo) (1994), an organization to which more than 60% of labor unions belong, conducted research to identify the needs and problems of families with at least one household member who is older than 55. Using data collected from 9,800 households, they found that the average age of the caregiver was 52, 60% of the sample households cared for their frail elders at home, and the average length of caregiving was 6 years. In addition, the study identified that caregiving has been a psychological, physical, and social burden for many family members. Based on these findings, the federation submitted a proposal to the government detailing its suggestions for Long-Term Care Leave. The Shinshinto Party incorporated most of the suggestions in legislation that it proposed. Although heated debates took place between the Shinshinto Party and the Liberal Democratic Party, the latter party's proposal eventually was adopted and passed in June 1995. Although defeated in the end, the federation's proposal contributed to increasing awareness of the importance of a Long-Term Care Leave.

Workplace Initiatives

Long-Term Care Leave.   Several companies allow their employees (mostly females) to take leave for caregiving. The Female Employment Management Basic Survey found that 14% of female employees took leave to care for a frail elderly family member in 1989 (Ministry of Labor, 1990). The ministry conducted a second study in 1991 of employees in 1,105 randomly selected companies that employed more than 30 persons (Ministry of Labor, Women's Bureau, 1993). According to this survey, 21% of the companies provided a Long-Term Care Leave provision. Interestingly, only 30% of these companies specified the allowable length for such a leave; the rest did not impose any limitation. Additionally, 91% of these companies approved of an extension of the Long-Term Care Leave. Women took almost all of the leaves (93%). Of large companies with more than 5,000 employees, 56% provided no monetary compensation during the leave. This was the case even more for medium-sized companies (70%) and small-sized companies with 30–99 employees (80%). These figures indicate that, although employees in some companies are allowed to take Long-Term Care Leave, they risk a major financial setback. The government's Long-Term Care Leave policy guarantees that the company will pay at least 25% of its employee's salary during the leave; thus, employed caregivers will benefit greatly when it is implemented.

Other Leave Policies and Work Scheduling.   Employees can take other types of leave to care for frail elderly. These include sick, vacation, personal, and medical leave. Flextime also can be used to accommodate the needs of employed caregivers. Relocation decisions, likewise, can be made with consideration to elder care. Several private businesses, in cooperation with the government, have begun investigating the feasibility of telework or satellite offices as an alternative workplace options for their employees caring for frail elders. Finally, some employers offer flexible work hours and extended leave with a job guarantee to part-time workers caring for elderly parents or parents-in-law (Ministry of Labor, Women's Bureau, 1993).

Benefits.   Most of the benefits available through employment are directed toward elderly retired workers rather than their caregivers. For example, Employees' Pension Insurance, Social Health Insurance (Shakai Hoken), corporate pensions, and retirement benefits are given to retirees regardless of their health status. The tax deduction for dependents, as described earlier, is the only financial benefit currently available for employed caregivers.

Services.   In preparation for implementing the Long-Term Care Leave, some businesses have begun developing educational materials concerning the leave. These efforts include creating pamphlets and hosting seminars on care leave. In addition, some companies offer counseling to their employees with elder care duties or elder care referral services.

Initiatives by Nonprofit and For-Profit Organizations

Since the 1980s, many nonprofit and for-profit organizations have offered various kinds of services for seniors. They include home help service, day service, short stay service, senior citizens clubs, culture centers, sport clubs, life education, barrier-free transportation system, and counseling. In addition, the Silver Personnel Center offers opportunities for the elderly to work, including the provision of daytime home care for frail elders (Management and Coordination Agency, Statistical Bureau, 1997b). Nonprofit organizations that serve elders include the Community-Based Citizen's Group, the Regional Women's Association, the Cooperative Association, and the Agricultural Cooperative Association. An example of a for-profit organization is the Foundation for Promotion of Silver Services, established in 1987, which provides high quality services to the elderly, including consumer advocacy activities. The provision of services from profit-making and nonprofit organizations is likely to increase in the near future (Okamoto, 1996).

Overview of Initiatives for the Elderly: The New Gold Plan

Japan's first long-term care project to set numerical goals for services and institutions for the elderly was prescribed in the 1989 Gold Plan. This project was enacted under the agreement of three ministries; the Ministry of Health and Welfare, the Ministry of Finance, and the Ministry of Home Affairs. According to the plan, the goals to be attained by 1999 include 100,000 home helpers, 50,000 beds for short-term stays in institutions, 10,000 day care service centers, and 240,000 beds in nursing homes. Although the Gold Plan was considered to be an innovative long-term plan, the proposed services were expected to meet only half of the needs of the elderly population (Sakamoto, 1996).

In February 1990, revisions to the eight laws on welfare services were made, including revisions to both the Welfare Law for the Aged and the Health Law for the Aged. In conjunction with these amendments, all municipalities and prefectures in Japan were obliged to develop 10-year long-term plans for the health service and welfare for the elderly. In March 1994, it became clear that more services were needed to achieve the goals set in the Gold Plan. Therefore, in December 1994, the Gold Plan was amended and became the New Gold Plan. In this revised plan, new measures for the care of senile elderly were stipulated. The revised plan also reinforces the notion of home-based care for frail elderly by expanding the variety of services targeted for homebound elderly. It is expected that the achievement of these goals and the enactment of both the Long-Term Care Leave Law and the Public Insurance Scheme for Long-Term Care will significantly improve care of the elderly in Japan.

Strengths and Weaknesses of Supports

Post–1989 government plans, such as the Gold Plan and the New Gold Plan, have included various measures that will assist employed caregivers. Both the Long-Term Care Leave and the Public Insurance Scheme for Long-Term Care are also expected to greatly benefit employed caregivers. Several strengths surrounding these newer policies include long-range goal setting, greater emphasis on home-based care, and cooperation among government, work organizations, and other organizations.

At the same time, however, several weaknesses are noted with these policies and programs. First, although Long-Term Care Leave is likely to benefit employed caregivers, it is uncertain how many companies will comply with such requests from their employees. This is likely to be especially problematic, since no penalty system is expected to be attached to the law. Second, the government's goal of increasing the number of elderly cared for at home will be difficult to achieve unless other support systems are established. For example, the government has yet to achieve the goal of increasing the availability of home helpers. Since it may be difficult to rely solely on family caregivers, it is important that the caregivers be given the option to hire home helpers. Stated another way, although the Japanese government is extremely organized in making plans, it takes a long time to implement these policies. This was also seen in the delay in enacting the Long-Term Care Leave Law. Third, many policies and programs in Japan are targeted toward improving the lives of the elderly rather than caregivers. The Long-Term Care Leave is an exception, because it directly assists employed caregivers. However, problems remain concerning the financial compensation for workers on leave. For example, the 25% of salary compensation is quite problematic for low-income workers; thus, it likely will discourage them from taking leave.

Although Japan appears to be ethnically homogenous, there are a significant number of minorities. Traditionally, this minority population consists mainly of Koreans and their descendants who were forcefully brought to Japan for cheap labor. The Japanese minority population has been diversified somewhat with the increase of foreign laborers who have come from other parts of Asia and South America. However, because these recent labor immigrants are young people, it is the Korean ethnic elderly in Japan who are largely affected by the government initiatives for elderly care. In general, the Japanese government's policies for elder care apply only to the citizens of Japan. However, many Korean ethnic elderly, who were never granted Japanese citizenship despite their long residence in the country, are excluded from such policies.

The limited access for government-sponsored health care also has become a problem when the Japanese National and Social Health Insurance Schemes were introduced. However, with the revisions to the law, foreign residents who obtain an alien registration card are now eligible to purchase National and Social Health Insurance. In order to alleviate the problem of limited access to Long-Term Care Leave and Public Insurance Scheme for Long-Term Care that the Korean ethnic elderly may experience, the Ministry of Health most likely will inaugurate these laws in a similar fashion as the health insurance schemes.

☐ Factors Contributing to Supports for Employed Caregivers and Elders

The initiatives outlined in the previous section were developed in response to demographic, sociocultural, historical, political, and economic factors which increased the needs for a systematic approach to caregiving in Japan. How and why these factors influenced policies, programs, and services for employed caregivers are discussed in this section.

Demographic Factors

As a consequence of women's increased participation in the labor force, the care of dependent family members and housework can no longer be considered solely as women's work. Although Japanese men are slowly, but steadily, beginning to realize child care responsibilities (Ishii-Kuntz, 1996), elder care remains mostly the responsibility of women. The gap between the demands for elder care, caused partly by the greater proportion of women in the labor force and the shortage of reliable professional assistance, inspired the government as well as other organizations to consider long-term plans, such as the New Gold Plan. The rapid aging of the population also pressured the government to develop various initiatives, including the 2000 Public Insurance Scheme for Long-Term Care. In addition, the Japanese government has been greatly concerned with the recent rapid decline in birth rates. One such concern is the lack of eventual family support for the elderly. Therefore, the government initiatives for the Long-Term Care Leave and the Public Insurance Scheme can be seen as preventive measures for the lack of family support resources to care for the elderly in the near future.

Sociocultural Factors

In addition to institutional changes after World War II and the influence of American democracy, industrialization and urbanization have been changing Japanese people's attitudes from an extended family orientation to that of a nuclear family. Although shared living arrangements have been decreasing, the number of elderly living close to their children is increasing. Today, Japanese elderly and younger generations seem to prefer "intimacy at a distance."

This contemporary "intimacy at a distance" arrangement seems to work as long as the elderly parents are healthy. However, when the elders become frail, to the extent that they need constant caregiving, then daughters or daughters-in-law are more or less expected to step in. This trend also is reflected by the increase in Japanese elderly parents who either live or want to live with their daughters rather than sons.

The feminization of caregiving is deeply rooted in Japanese society, as is the case in many other societies. Sodei (1997) argued that this is due to the patriarchal social structure, feudalistic ideology, expectations from others, and women's identification with the caregiving role. First, under the patriarchal ideology, gender roles are clearly segregated, with men as the economic providers and women as the homemakers. Because of this segregation, men frequently are excused from caregiving, which is considered to be the role of women. Second, under feudalism, women are expected to obey their husbands. This feudalistic decision making is seen frequently among Japanese couples, in which husbands make important decisions on caregiving and wives simply are expected to follow their husband's directions. Third, Japanese society (including the workplace, relatives, and friends) expects women to be care providers and men to be financial supporters for such activities. This is true regardless of women's employment status. One could argue that the reason why mainly women end up quitting their jobs to care for elderly parents is because of their lower pay and inferior job situations, compared to those of their husbands. However, even when both the husband and the wife occupy management level positions, it usually is the wife who ends up seeing to most of the caregiving needs at home. Fourth, because of feudalism and related expectations for women, many wives find caregiving activities to be affirming of their feminine identity (Sodei, 1997).

Due to the lifelong employment system (guaranteed job for life), Japanese companies and their employees have paternalistic relationships where employers and employees are loyal to each other. Under this system, employees' commitment to work is expected to be high, and promotion is based largely on seniority. Therefore, if employees need to take care of the elderly by sacrificing work hours, it may be seen as a sign of less commitment. However, since the bursting of the "bubble economy" (sustained economic growth), many Japanese companies have become more achievement-oriented (as opposed to seniority-oriented), and now do not always guarantee lifelong employment (Ishii-Kuntz, 1996). Workers' views also are changing; they no longer assume that long work hours always lead to greater productivity and promotional opportunities. Consequently, Japanese men have become much more concerned with their families than were the fathers in previous generations (Ishii-Kuntz, 1994, 1996). When asked about the importance of work and family, approximately 46% of employed men indicated that their family was much more important than their work (*Asahi Shimbun,* 1989). This is a remarkable increase from the 1978 survey, which showed the comparable figure of 23% (*Asahi Shimbun,* 1989). Because of these changes in the workplace and workers' attitudes toward families and work, there is room for introducing the idea of home-based care. Although major improvements still are needed with respect to financial compensation, today's workers may welcome the idea of Long-Term Care Leave more readily than did workers in previous decades.

Additionally, the Japanese government gives economic assistance to companies far more frequently than in the United States (Lodge & Vogel, 1987). This close relationship also is seen in the case of the Long-Term Care Leave to be implemented in 1999 (Ohshima, 1996). The government already has begun advising companies on how to implement such a leave and is outlining financial assistance for companies that actively pursue their employees' needs for Long-Term Care Leave.

Historical Factors

The period of 1961 to 1975 was characterized by high economic growth, with an average annual gross national product (GNP) growth of nearly 10%. As a result, both national and local governments were able to improve benefits and start new programs. For example, the Welfare Law for the Aged, enacted in 1963, aimed at providing health care services, home help services, and institutional care for the elderly. This prosperous period, however, ended with the oil crisis of 1973. The impact of the oil crisis on the economy became apparent after 1974, and the government became more cautious about expanding social welfare programs.

In addition to financial difficulties, the rapidly aging population required a reexamination of the entire Japanese Social Security System. The welfare program that the government proposed in the 1960s came under attack because too much governmental support might make people dependent. Self-help, the traditional Japanese family, and the traditional Japanese community were suddenly reevaluated. These traditional values initially had been targeted for eradication due to their feudalistic nature. However, the government warned that the sheer imitation of a Western welfare system was not constructive because the problems faced in Western societies were not the same as those faced in Japan. The government report thus emphasized the reevaluation of the patriarchal stem family system *(ie)* and praised the virtues of family care of the elderly.

Political Factors

Since the Meiji Restoration, Japan has been a nation with a strong centralized government. The 1989 Gold Plan asked local governments (city, town, and village) to take responsibility for health care and welfare services for the elderly. In 1989, the Ministry of Health and Welfare issued the Gold Plan. As previously discussed, this plan shifted more emphasis to home care rather than institutional care because, on the one hand, home care costs less than institutional care and, on the other hand, aging at home is more effective for promoting a better quality of life for the elderly. The elderly, themselves, also wanted to stay at home (Sodei, 1997).

Because of changes in household structure from the extended to the nuclear family and to the single-person household, the increase in employed women, and the recession following the collapse of the so-called "bubble economy," Japan's Social Security System is now undergoing a major change. The government faces difficulties in reforming the entire system with limited financial resources. The major concern is establishing an equitable balance between the supports and the supported (or the contributors and the beneficiaries) to alleviate the burden on the younger generation. It is under these guidelines that Long-Term Care Insurance and Nursing Leave were passed.

Prior to the enactment of the Gold Plan, the government had passed many laws concerning elder care, but they were mostly for short-range objectives. Also, the content of the plans on which the laws were based varied from one administration to another. Given the short terms of Japanese prime ministers in the late 1980s and early 1990s, there was a need to establish clear guidelines and policies concerning elder care. The Gold Plan was the first long-range planning (10 years) to occur concerning care of the elderly. The New Gold Plan of 1994 is another example of long-range planning. As demonstrated by this plan, the Japanese government has been engaging in more comprehensive and long-range planning concerning the care of the elderly. This trend is likely to continue in the foreseeable future.

The Japanese government also has long dictated social policy to work organizations. With long-range planning for elder care, the government has been working closely with private businesses to implement the new policies. Although companies attempt to work cooperatively with the government, the delay in implementation on the side of the government also caused a major delay for workplaces. For example, the Long-Term Care Leave was delayed 3 years, as stated earlier, because of several unresolved issues. In reality, however, the delay in the implementation also was politically motivated. That is, the initial date of the implementation (April 1996) was proposed by labor unions through minority political parties who also made other demands, such as 1-year rather than a 3-month leave and several leaves rather than one-time-only leave. Because, in part, the government needed some time to persuade labor unions and minority political parties to agree with the proposed plans, it decided to delay the implementation of the Long-Term Care Leave. In response to the bureaucratic barriers and ongoing political power struggles, which have prevented the plans from being carried out, some companies independently established their own policies concerning employed caregivers. For example, some companies began implementing their own Long-Term Care Leave policies in response to internal pressures. Although strong ties exist between the government and companies concerning workplace policies and their enforcement, it also is important for the government to grant more autonomy for firms, such as establishing a firm's own guidelines for the welfare of its employees.

Economic Factors

Japan's economic development allowed the government to begin to focus on providing comprehensive welfare for the elderly. However, economic downturns, first in the early 1970s and more recently in the early 1990s, and the rapid aging of the population, have meant that the country no longer can afford to provide 100% financial assistance for the care of the elderly.

An additional economic factor that has influenced policy makers has been the accumulation of wealth by the elderly. The elderly as a group have become an attractive target for the market economy (Okamoto, 1996), referred to as the "silver market." Along with the increased aging of the population and the development of the public pension system, the elderly have become powerful consumers. The pension income of some elderly who receive Employee's Pensions and Mutual Aid Pensions exceeds the income of average workers. Further, more than 80% of Japanese elderly own their homes. This affluence of the elderly is one of the determining factors for the government to propose the Public Insurance Scheme for Long-Term Care, which requires the elderly to contribute to the insurance. The notion of the elderly paying into the insurance is a rather significant departure from the past policy of social welfare for the elderly.

It is, however, important to note that not all Japanese elders are affluent. Some elderly live on only a small income from the National Pension. In 1992, the average monthly payments were 37,000 yen ($250) for the National Pension, 156,000 yen ($1,040) for the Employee's Pension, and 203,000 yen ($1,360) for the Mutual Aid Pensions Fund. The percentage of the elderly age 60 and over receiving public assistance in 1994 was 43%. While, in general, the proportion of the Japanese population that receives public assistance is decreasing, the proportion of elders who receive public assistance is growing. Because of this reality, a lower cost option for caregiving, namely home care, must be considered. Therefore, employed caregivers are seen as important resources for the caregiving of elderly family members.

☐ Future Trends

There are several possible future trends that will have an impact on employed caregivers. These include privatization in elder care, household-based to individual-based caregiving, and an increase in men's participation in caregiving.

First, privatization in elder care inevitably will exclude bureaucratic intervention and, as a result, may lower the cost of caregiving. Today, the so-called "silver service market," which aims at selling goods and services to elders (such as wheelchairs, lifts, special beds for nursing care, home care services, and retirement homes) is expanding rapidly. Some local governments entrust the private sector with home care because these services are more effective and cheaper than services provided by public sector employees. Although most services are expensive and not many people can afford them, the cost to individuals will decline if a new social insurance can be used to buy such services (Sodei, 1996). Such cost reductions will reduce the financial burden currently experienced by some employed caregivers and elders.

Second, when the government considers elder care issues, the unit of service provision usually is the household rather than the individual. Therefore, eligibility for receipt of services or payments for services is based on household income. In households where elders live with their adult children, the children's income is counted. *The New Eldercare System,* which was published in 1995 by the Council of Health and Welfare for the Aged, is based on the New Gold Plan. This report clearly mentions that everyone will receive needed services, regardless of income or living arrangement. In order to achieve this ideal, though, the service unit should change from household to individual. If this change takes place, elders and double-income families will benefit because financial assistance for caregiving will not be based on household income but rather on the needs of frail elderly family members.

Finally, as more women enter the labor force, it is necessary for men to realize that they, too, need to participate in caregiving. However, given the pay inequity between men and women and the limited financial compensation during leave, men are less likely to take a Long-Term Care Leave. Unless the leave were to guarantee higher financial compensation, it is not likely that men will actively participate in caregiving. Although men's attitudes toward caregiving seem to be undergoing a transition, a change in attitudes alone will not bring about equal participation in caregiving between men and women.

☐ References

Asahi Shimbun. (1989, June 22). Opinion about fathers, p. 8.

Asahi Shimbun. (1994, November 13). Public survey, p. 7.

Council of Health and Welfare for the Aged. (1995). Atarashii Kaigo Shisutemu [The New Eldercare System]. Tokyo: Author.

Institute of Population Problems. (1997). *Nihon no shourai suikei jinko* [Projected population of Japan]. Tokyo: Management and Coordination Statistics Bureau.

Ishikawa, K. (1990). *Isha no me ni namida* [Tears from doctor's eyes]. Tokyo: Shufu to seikatsusha.

Ishii-Kuntz, M. (1994). The Japanese father: Work demands and family roles. In J. C. Hood (Ed.), *Men, work and family* (pp. 45–67). Newbury Park, CA: Sage.

Ishii-Kuntz, M. (1996). A perspective on changes in men's work and fatherhood in Japan. *Asian Cultural Studies, 22,* 91–107.

Japanese Trade Union Confederation (Rengo). (1994). *Youkaigosha o kakaeru kazoku ni tsuite no jittai chousa* [Survey on families with care recipients]. Tokyo: Author.

Lodge, G. C., & Vogel, E. F. (Eds.). (1987). Ideology and national competitiveness. Boston: Harvard Business School.

Management and Coordination Agency. (1991). *Rougo no seikatsu to kaigo ni tuiteno chousa* [Survey on life and care in old age]. Tokyo: Author.

Management and Coordination Agency, Statistical Bureau. (1997a). *Nihon no toukei* [Statistics of Japan]. Tokyo: Author.

Management and Coordination Agency, Statistical Bureau. (1997b). *Kourei shakai hakusho* [White report on aging society]. Tokyo: Author.

Ministry of Health and Welfare. (1995a). *Annual report on health and welfare.* Tokyo: Author.

Ministry of Health and Welfare. (1995b). *Demographic, social and economic survey.* Tokyo: Author.

Ministry of Health and Welfare. (1997). *Annual report on health and welfare.* Tokyo: Author.

Ministry of Labor. (1989). *Roujin kaigo to kateinai roudou ni tsuite no chousa* [Survey of elder care and family work]. Tokyo: Author.

Ministry of Labor. (1990). *Roudouryoku chousa* [Labor force survey]. Tokyo: Author.

Ministry of Labor. (1991). *Kyuuryou kouzou ni kansuru kihon chousa* [Basic survey on wage structure]. Tokyo: Author.

Ministry of Labor, Women's Bureau. (1986). *Roujin kaigo ni kansuru chousa* [Survey on elder caregiving]. Tokyo: Author.

Ministry of Labor, Women's Bureau. (1991). *Roujin kaigo o suru roudousha ni tsuite no chousa* [Survey on working caregivers]. Tokyo: Author.

Ministry of Labor, Women's Bureau. (1993). *Kaigo o okonau roudousha ni kansuru sochi ni tsuiteno jittai chousa* [Survey on treatment for working caregivers]. Tokyo: Author.

Ochi, T. (1998). *Oya ga 65-sai o sugitara otoko ga yomu hon* [A book to be read by men whose parents are older than 65]. Tokyo: Benesse.

Okamoto, T. (1996). Welfare for the elderly in Japan. In T. Sodei (Ed.), *Decline of fertility and population aging in East Asia* (pp. 46–57). Tokyo: International Longevity Center.

Okamura, K. (1996). Tomokasegi to kaji roudou no henka [Dual-earners and change in household labor]. In T. Sodei, K. Okamura, M. Nagatsu, & K. Miyoshi (Eds.), *Tomokasegi kazoku* [Dual-earner families] (pp. 47–86). Tokyo: Kasei Kyouikusha.

Ohshima, C. (1996). Kaigokyugyo housei no seiritsu katei [Process of development of nursing care leave]. In S. Sakamoto & T. Yamawaki (Eds.), *Koureisha kaigo no seisaku kadai* [Policy goals for elder care] (pp. 225–239). Tokyo: Keiso Shobo.

Sakamoto, S. (1996). Koureisha kaigo to hoken, iryo, fukushi seisaku no tenkai katei [Development process of health, medical, and welfare policies for elder care]. In S. Sakamoto & T. Yamawaki (Eds.), *Koureisha kaigo no seisaku kadai* [Policy goals for elder care] (pp.9–29). Tokyo: Keiso Shobo.

Sodei, T. (1989). Josei to roujin kaigo [Women and elder care]. In M. Ozawa, S. Kimura, & H. Ibe (Eds.). *Josei no life cycle* [Women's life cycle], (pp. 127–149). Tokyo: University of Tokyo Press.

Sodei, T. (1996). Tomokasegi to roushin kaigo [Elder care among dual-earner Couples]. In T. Sodei, K. Okamura, M. Nagatsu, & K. Miyoshi (Eds.), *Tomokasegi kazoku* [Dual-earner families] (pp. 165–188). Tokyo: Kasei Kyouikusha. Sodei, T. (1997). Care of the elderly in twenty-first century in Japan. *Ochanomizu University Human Science Journal, 50,* 311–330.

CHAPTER

Lars Andersson

Sweden and the Futile Struggle to Avoid Institutions

☐ Introduction

Sweden has proportionately more elders and more working women than almost any other country in the world. In Sweden, caring for the elderly is a responsibility divided between the family and society. In 1956, the legal right for elderly parents to demand care for their children was abolished; moreover, the Swedish Social Services Act, effective since January 1, 1982, emphasizes the legal right of the individual to assistance from society (Svensk författning-Ssamling [SFS], 1980). Society, here, principally means the municipalities. The municipal governments are responsible for social welfare services as well as for medical services and care for the elderly.

The role of the public sector in Sweden (as well as in all the Nordic countries) differs from that in the rest of Europe. The public sector not only has an indirect role, functioning through legislation and financing (in common with the rest of Europe), but also a direct role as a major provider of services. Although private contractors have been providing an increasing share of the care needed in the past few years, in 1997, this share still represented only about 6% of the total volume of care provided to elders.

In sum, this means that care is an area that is dealt with by the individual and his or her family, together with the public sector. Other actors, such as companies (e.g., where a relative is employed) or voluntary organizations, are not expected to be involved in social or health care when continuity and professional work are necessary. Through taxation, each individual contributes to society and, in turn, is supported by public social welfare activities.

This chapter will examine the experiences of employed caregivers and evaluate the type and level of supports available to these caregivers and to elders. Possible reasons for Sweden's particular configuration of policies, benefits, and services for employed caregivers and for elders are explored. The chapter ends with a look into future trends in the type and level of supports.

☐ Work-Family Issues

In 1995, 80% of women age 40 to 65 and 85% of men in this age range were in the workforce (International Labor Office [ILO], 1996). Although there are almost as many women as there are men in the workforce, 39% of women work part time (less than 35 hours per week), compared to only 9% of men (Statistics Sweden, 1997).

Sweden was ranked third oldest among 100 developed and developing nations in 1996 in a report compiled by the United States Department of Commerce (U.S. Bureau of the Census, Department of Commerce, 1996). In 1995, the percentage of people age 65 and older was 17.5% (1,543,000) (Statistics Sweden, 1997). In the near future, projections (main alternative) show that the percentage of seniors will decrease from 17.5% to 17.4% between 1995 and 2000 (Statistics Sweden, 1998). At the same time, those age 80 and above will continue to increase, from 414,000 (4.7%) in 1995 to 499,000 in 2010 (5.5%). Since the increases will take place among the oldest old, who also are the major recipients of care, a strain on public resources, as well as on family caregivers, will remain.

Prevalence of Employed Caregivers

The number of persons who work and also care for elders is unknown. There are several possible reasons for the lack of data. Managing work and caregiving may not be perceived as a social problem because of Sweden's emphasis on public service support. Unlike other advanced capitalist countries, where prevalence surveys are useful for influencing the development of government and workplace policies, such surveys may be considered less critical in Sweden. Another possibility is that employed caregivers primarily are part-time working women, who have not had a voice in the matter. Still another possible reason is that the media does not find them particularly interesting because they primarily are lower-middle-class or working-class women.

Managing Work and Elder Care

Only a few studies touch on the experiences and consequences of maintaining the dual roles of work and elder care in Sweden (Furåker & Mossberg, 1994, 1997). One study of family caregivers (of all age groups) found that, among those who had a job, one third had made no changes in their work life, while 28% had stopped working, 18% had changed their work hours, 9% had made other changes (e.g., leave of absence), and 7% had changed occupation. Reasons for changes in previous work included "didn't work out with the hours" (spouses 19%, children 16%), "help round the clock" (spouses 37%, children 29%), and "didn't manage" (spouses 41%, children 43%) (Furåker & Mossberg, 1994).

Other than the above study, family caregiving has been researched in Sweden either in relation to formal caregiving or, to some extent, as a problem of strain put on informal caregivers to demented elderly. In the former line of research, studies have often dwelled on the proportions of formal to informal care (Andersson, 1986; Andersson & Johansson, 1996; Herlitz, 1997; Johansson, 1991; Statistics Sweden, 1993; Sundström, 1994; Szebehely, 1993). Families, the informal caregivers, have been credited with providing two thirds of the care. Although the basis for this figure is uncertain, this statistic has become accepted.

The division of labor between spouses varies for particular household tasks and particular types of physical care. Generally, wives are considered to provide more care for their husbands than the opposite. However, some Swedish data have shown a more equivocal picture of this issue. At least one study reported as many male caregivers as female caregivers (Sundström & Thorslund, 1994). In the county of Stockholm, the representative Health Attitudes and Health Behavior in a Longitudinal Study of Aging (HALSA) study even found more married women (age 69 to 78) reporting help from their husbands (21%) than the converse (10%) (unpublished data). But, there are also representative studies that indicate what is commonly assumed: that is, that proportionately more women than men care for their spouses (c.f., Andersson & Sundström, 1996).

In research about caregiver strain, Grafström (1994), for example, found that relatives of demented elderly reported higher physical and psychological burden and greater social and affective limitations than relatives of nondemented elderly. Relatives of demented elderly in institutions reported feelings of burden similar to those experienced by relatives providing home care, but they used less psychotropic drugs. On the other hand, they used more somatic drugs and medical facilities. Daughters were most burdened, whether parents were demented or not. The heaviest burden was reported when the elderly person was mildly demented. Behavior problems and moderately decreased activities of daily living (ADL) functions were strongly associated with burden.

☐ Supports for Employed Caregivers: Description and Evaluation

In the mid-1980s, Parliament declared that municipalities and other authorities responsible for providing health care should play a more active role in informal care. This included educating municipal care personnel about the needs of informal caregivers. It also covered carrying out active outreach programs to inform informal caregivers about support available from the municipalities and country councils. And, third, it included paying more informal caregivers to provide assistance to their elders. The contributions of relatives, friends, and neighbors, however, were to be viewed as supplementary to the primary responsibility borne by the public sector. Thus, in addition to playing a major role in the formal provision of elder care, the municipalities also were expected to attend to the burdens of informal caregivers.

Today, there are basically two forms of economic help available to individuals who work and who provide informal elder care: the paid caregiver program and paid temporary work leaves.

Paid Caregiver Program

If an elderly person is deemed in need of care because of chronic illness or disease, the municipality can employ a family member. The family member is then recognized as a paid caregiver. This program has been available since the 1960s. Salary is determined by the elder's care needs and is paid in proportion to the number of hours needed to perform the necessary care. Choosing this option requires the caregiver to give up some or all of his or her regular work. The salary given to the paid caregiver can be viewed as compensation due to loss of income from regular work. Payment is at a level (per hour) equal to that of a typical home helper employed by the municipality. While not the lowest paying work, home helpers are definitely on the lower rungs of the income ladder. The payment is considered income, and is taxed as such. The paid caregiver receives all the benefits of social insurance plus pension credits that he or she normally would have accrued in his or her regular employment.

Data from several studies have indicated that the vast majority of paid caregivers are women (about 85%), and that the average caregiver is between 50 and 65 years of age. Half of the caregivers care for a spouse, and approximately two thirds of paid caregivers live with the person they care for. Finally, about half of the paid caregivers combine care work with other types of work in order to round out the equivalent of full-time employment (Furåker & Mossberg, 1994; Sundström, 1984).

Despite the fact that the national government and Parliament have encouraged economic support for informal care, the number of paid caregivers in the home help system has continuously decreased during recent decades. In 1970, 18,500 were employed as caregivers. In 1980, the number was 10,600. Five years later, it was down to 6,000 and, in 1995, the number had decreased to 4,000. Reasons for these changes are discussed below.

Municipalities run paid caregiver programs. Compared to most other countries, Swedish municipalities (and county councils) enjoy an unusually autonomous position vis-à-vis the state. The social service and health care laws allow the municipalities (and the county councils) great freedom to plan and organize services as well as to impose taxes in order to finance them. Why, then, have the municipalities not supported the programs?

One likely reason is that these programs, which support informal care, have only a marginal position compared to public care. Johansson and Sundström (1994) offered further explanations: (a) informal care costs are negligible and affect only a minority; (b) there is a lack of pressure groups fighting for the programs; and, most importantly, (c) there is no general strategy. However, the last two points are soon to change. The strategic role of informal care has been strengthened with the new Social Services Act (effective January 1998), which recommends that the municipalities pay more informal care providers to provide assistance to their elders. Also, in February 1996, the Council of Relatives in Sweden (Anhörigrådet i Sverige [AHR]) was formed. Its purpose is to lobby, provide information, and support informal caregivers. Since the council is quite new, exact membership figures are not available. Pensioner membership, however, can be estimated to be at least 70%.

Even before the decrease in paid caregivers, the numbers of paid caregivers were fairly low. Why do families not claim the support that they properly are entitled to? One reason is a lack of knowledge pertaining to the availability of support. Another is that eligibility criteria vary in different parts of the country; some municipalities do not offer the support at all (Johansson & Sundström, 1994). The most likely explanation, however, is budget restrictions. Faced with the options of retaining their own regular staff or paying more informal caregivers, municipalities most often have supported the former. In addition, the restrictions on public care actually may have made relatives more reluctant to take up paid informal care—fearful that they might be trapped with informal care "for good" if the public support were to decrease. There also may be a sense of getting a "fair share" of public support. Or, it may be a cohort question: As pensions increase for the better, the newer cohorts of working age may be less interested in or less able to carry out paid informal care, given the relatively low salaries paid.

Paid Leaves of Absence

The most recent of the initiatives to support informal caregiving is the incorporation of a care leave policy into the Swedish social insurance system. In effect since 1989, the initiative entitles employed individuals to paid time off from work for the purpose of caring for an acutely, often terminally ill, family member. The level of compensation during the short period of the leave's existence has been changed several times, from 100% to 65% to 75% of one's salary. The allowance is taxable and corresponds to the individual's sick allowance reimbursement.

The informal acute care leave is limited to a total of 60 days in the lifetime of the individual receiving the care. It can be taken in many forms: full days, half days, or hours per day. It is not intended to be used for ongoing care. A doctor's statement of care needs, along with a written application, is necessary to procure a care leave reimbursement. Finally, the elderly person must give his or her consent.

One difference between the care leave and the paid caregiver program is that care leave reimbursement is dependent on actual income, which makes it an incentive in all societal segments; whereas, the paid caregiver program has a socioeconomic bias that attracts mainly working class women. Persons in higher income brackets lose economically in the paid caregiver program.

The care leave program has shown a modest increase. During 1990, care leave was taken by 2,574 persons. For each of the ensuing years 1991 through 1995, the figures were 1,972; 2,769; 4,094; 5,450; and 6,427, respectively (personal communication, National Social Insurance Board, Statistical Division, 1996). Plausible reasons for the increase are the following. Beginning in 1992, care leave not only was payable when the sick person was at home, but when the sick person was in a hospital or nursing home. Also, effective in 1994, Parliament extended care leave from the original 30 days to cover a period of 60 days of leave.

Together, the paid caregiver program and the paid care leave underscore a development in which the family, in most cases, is responsible for care in acute situations, while public care is present for more extensive chronic situations (Andersson, 1986, 1993).

Other Supports for Employed Caregivers

On the basis of its guidelines for care of the elderly in the 1990s, the government solicited the National Board of Health and Welfare to update and expand the support system for informal caregivers. The government made available special project funds to the board for this purpose. Municipalities and voluntary organizations designed local projects and applied for funding.

The purpose of the projects was to try to get a picture of the situation of informal caregivers and unveil what the public sector might do to help them take better care of the elderly and the sick. Project work was completed during 1992.

One purpose of the projects was to devise suitable respite mechanisms for both caregivers and recipients. For example, in the municipality of Nacka near Stockholm, the caregiver and care recipient could stay in a respite center for up to 2 or 3 weeks for a low daily cost. The caregiver received relief, as well as the opportunity to meet other caregivers and thus break the isolation so common to informal caregiving. Both long and short respites for informal caregivers were found to be appreciated. Also appreciated was a contact person who could provide psychosocial support. Organized meetings for informal care providers also were considered important. To many elderly persons, placement in an institution was not an acceptable alternative. Therefore, in some of the projects, day centers in residential areas were started. Elderly persons could attend a few hours a day, several days a week. In certain cases, overnight facilities also were created.

Taken together, the results from the projects showed that:

(1) Informal care situations should be immediately known to the municipalities so they can provide assistance to the caregivers.
(2) Relatives, friends, and neighbors who provide informal care do not spontaneously seek help from the public sector.
(3) Informal care providers feel a deep sense of responsibility for their task and are not eager to hand it over to someone else.
(4) Public sector back-up programs encounter difficulties in reaching informal care providers with information.
(5) Psychosocial support is important to informal care providers: knowledge that help is available and that there is someone to talk to is often sufficient.
(6) For many informal care providers the best back-up is targeted assistance in the form of good health care, nursing, rehabilitation programs, etc. (Hedin, 1993, p. 97).

Discussion of Supports for Employed Caregivers

Legal responsibility for care of the elderly lies solely with the municipality and, in heavy care situations, a vast majority of children and parents expect and desire public care. Most scholars have argued that informal help has increased during the past decade, even though convincing evidence has not been provided so far (Andersson & Johansson, 1996). If, however, adult children and their parents choose informal care, not many options are available. The chances of becoming a paid family caregiver are on the decrease, and the opportunity for receiving a tax reduction for care work is nonexistent. The adult child can attempt to negotiate a reduction in work time with his or her employer, but the drawback, besides loss of salary, is that the adult child's future pension is undercut unless the adult child enrolls in the paid caregiver program. Because proportionately more women than men are caregivers, these arrangements put women at a disadvantage in the market economy. Thus, gender inequalities continue to exist, in spite of Sweden's system of paid leaves and payments to those who assume elder care duties (Persson, 1990).

Workplace-Based Supports

The right to flexible work arrangements, such as part-time work and flextime, are ensured by either the law or through collective agreements. For example, the Working Hours Act (Arbetstidslag) states that exceptions to the law may be made, where a collective agreement has been reached. However, certain paragraphs, such as paragraph 5, which states that the regular working hours for employees (with exception for certain positions) is not to exceed 40 hours per week, cannot be altered by a collective agreement. The same general rule applies, for example, in the Parental Leave of Absence Act (Föräldraledighetslag) and the Educational Leave of Absence Act (Lag om arbetstagares rätt till ledighet för utbildning). However, no law covers leave of absence for employed caregivers. Individually adjusted work schedules can be negotiated with one's employer. The extent to which this is done is not known. No conclusive data on voluntary initiated flexible work schedules exist.

Impact of Caregiver Benefits on Employers

In Sweden, in any given week, the absenteeism rate at work for men and women can be as high as 15% because of the paid leave policies for child care, vacation, and sick time (Arbetskraftsundersoknigen [AKU], 1996). Employers are critical of their limited control over the workforce, arguing that, although state-paid absences can be advantageous during slack periods, they are problematic during peak work periods. For this reason, employers are pressuring the state and unions to give them more authority over work hours and other work conditions (Pierson, 1996).

In the case of paid family caregivers, the municipality faces a dilemma as both employer and protector. Under conditions of high unemployment, which have been a problem, the employer (i.e., the municipality) may be disinclined to pay family members as caregivers. Paying family members to care for elders could reduce the number of public employees needed to provide public home care services.

☐ Supports for Older Persons: Description and Evaluation

Sweden's social insurance program provides comprehensive and universal health care services and pension plans. These programs enable most seniors to live a fairly comfortable life. The state, employers, and employees contribute to the pension plan. Medical services are supplied to elderly people on the same terms as the rest of the population. The major part of the cost for health care is covered by a progressive tax levied by the county councils. Smaller amounts come from state grants and patient fees.

Home Care

A fairly high percentage of elderly persons receive assistance through the municipal home help services. It is the duty of each municipal social welfare committee to keep itself fully informed of local home help and other service needs. Every Swedish municipality provides home help service, a collective concept encompassing various forms of activities such as home help, meals-on-wheels, and security alarms.

Of those age 65 or older, about 12% used home help service in 1995, and of those age 80 or older, about 27% used the service (Socialstyrelsen, 1996a). The percentage of use of privately paid help is 7%, and regular help from voluntary organizations is practically nonexistent. Proportionally more of Sweden's elderly receive municipal formal home care than do their counterparts in the European Union, who receive private help as well as help from cohabiting children. In addition, more elderly in the European Union receive help from distant family members and from neighbors than do elderly Swedes (Andersson, 1993, 1994; Walker, 1993).

Institutional Care

In 1995, about 8.4% of people age 65 and older, and 23.2% of people age 80 and over, lived in some type of institution, including "service houses" which originally were considered ordinary living (*Socialstyrelsen*, 1996b). Service houses are a form of sheltered housing that consists of service-enriched forms of independent living, usually in an apartment complex of about 40 to 150 apartments. They correspond to the American congregate care model. Originally, the service houses were thought to be an intermediate form of living, where elderly people could move in and get along with minimal practical help (e.g., with cleaning and washing), and, when the resident became more frail, the home help could contribute more. It soon became clear, however, that the new residents were very old, frail, and dependent. The image of independent living was no longer possible to maintain. So, service houses, together with old age homes, group dwellings, and nursing homes, are regarded today as institutions under the common name of special housing (*särskilda boendeformer*).

Discussion of Supports for Elders

Today, major investments in public care have been effected, but what do the elderly themselves prefer? To what extent do the elderly receive the care that they want? In what direction do unfulfilled needs point: family care, public care, or other alternatives? Findings from the Swedish Eurobarometer indicate strong support for the supply of additional future care from local and regional governments: 86% said that the municipalities and counties should do more, whereas a mere 8% mentioned the family. Support for voluntary organizations and private care is scarce at best (Andersson, 1994).

The proportion of elderly during the past century has been on a steady rise. The increase has been particularly dramatic in the past 30 years. The National Board of Health and Welfare has estimated that, during the 10-year span from 1984 to 1994, the costs of Swedish elder care increased from 24.3 billion kronor to 56.5 billion kronor. With 1984 as the base year, this amounts to a fixed price increase to 33.3 billion kronor in 1994 (Socialstyrelsen, 1996b). In spite of the cost increase, also expressed in an increase in the number of employees in the public sector, public care for the elderly has covered the needs of a decreasing proportion of elderly in the past 20 years. Public care has concentrated its resources on heavier care cases, while elders predominantly in need of service have been omitted to an increasing extent. The proportion of people age 65 and over who received public home help decreased from about 17% in the 1970s and early 1980s to 12% in 1995 (Socialstyrelsen, 1996c). It has become apparent that the resources allocated for public care are insufficient if public care is supposed to manage both service needs and heavier care. Hence, there has been an interest in supporting informal care in various ways. Table 7-1 lists the supports available to employed caregivers and elders.

☐ Contributing Factors

A variety of factors (e.g., historical, cultural, political, economic) have helped shape Sweden's social welfare system. This section discusses these factors and then examines those that have contributed to Sweden's policies, benefits, and services that specifically concern Sweden's employed caregivers and older persons.

The Social Welfare System

Researchers have called attention to several factors that have been characteristic of the development of the social welfare system in Sweden (Antman, 1996; Elmér, 1975;

TABLE 7-1. Swedish supports for employees with elder care responsibilities

Government Initiatives	Nongovernmental Organization Initiatives	Union Initiatives	Workplace Initiatives
State initiatives	For employed caregivers	Political and work organization influence	Policies, work scheduling
Social Services Act	Study circles, support groups	State, county, municipal lobbying	Flextime, compressed work week[b]
Health and Medical Services Act	Indirectly, for older persons[a]	Cooperation with the Social Democratic Party	Part-time work, job sharing[b]
Earmarked subsidies to municipal projects	Friendly visiting	Union and management negotiations	Flexplace[b]
Care leave (Social Security)			Relocation policies[b]
County Initiatives			
Indirectly, for older persons			
Geriatric care			
Rehabilitation			
Municipal initiatives			
For employed caregivers[a]			
Back-up care, information			
Outreach activities, support groups			
Study circles, auxiliary staff			
Cash payments, salary for caregivers			
Indirectly, for older persons			
Home help services, home nursing			
Day care, sheltered housing			
Old age homes, nursing homes			

[a]Varying occurrence.
[b]Voluntary.

Esping-Andersen, 1985; Hedborg & Meidner, 1984; Korpi, 1978; Marklund, 1982; Odén, 1997). Some influential elements can be traced back hundreds of years; others have their origin in the 1930s.

One factor behind the fairly uniform solutions to various societal problems was Sweden's ethnic and religious homogeneity. This resulted in fewer alternatives, and it facilitated national support for movements, such as labor union development and the temperance movement.

In line with what is described by Putnam (1992) in his analysis of the Italian situation, a civic engagement at the community level thrived during the nineteenth century. Contributory factors were, among other things, the relatively independent position of the farmers, the widespread ability to read brought about by parish catechetical meetings in the homes of the residents (which created a solid ground for the introduction of the compulsory comprehensive school in 1842), and the strong impact of egalitarianism as a cultural value (Listhaug, 1990). Consistent with this value is the interest in improving the situation of those most in need of help. Income redistribution policies, such as progressive taxes, transfer payments, and social services, are a few examples.

One manifestation of a sense of community, where citizens feel empowered to engage in collective matters, is evidenced in the growth of labor unions. In 1996, 83% of all employees belonged to a union (Statistics Sweden, 1997). The strength and structure of the unions must be taken into consideration when the development of Swedish policies is analyzed (Esping-Andersen, 1985; Korpi, 1978). The unions and the Social Democratic Party have a long history of cooperation (Esping-Andersen, 1985; Hedborg & Meidner, 1984; Korpi, 1978). And, the labor movement has been the dominant political force, often in alliance with the center on the political scale (Marklund, 1982). Part of the explanation for the Swedish model is the balance of power between the labor movement and employers and other groups who automatically receive power in a capitalistic system (Hedborg & Meidner, 1984).

Social Welfare Goals Related to Employed Caregivers

Several of Sweden's social welfare goals benefit employed caregivers: (a) full employment, (b) state and family responsibility for elders, and (c) gender equity. They are discussed below.

Full Employment.   The goal of full employment is to employ every person who wishes to work. Incentives are given to encourage work. First, wages are such that employment provides a decent standard of living, making employment worthwhile. The early blue collar trade unions were very influential in establishing the policy of wage solidarity (Esping-Andersen, 1985). This policy has helped to ensure that the difference between the lowest and highest paid worker is moderate. Such arrangements lift wages at the lower end.

A second program that supports full employment is state-supported retraining for laid-off workers and others in need of skill enhancement. A third has been the absorption of nonattached workers into the public sector, which employs approximately 38% of the total work force (AKU, 1996). However, the number of public employees peaked in 1990. During the economic recession from 1991 to 1996, many public employees lost their jobs. When women began entering the work force in increasing numbers, starting in the early 1960s, many of them obtained jobs in the public sector.

Today, about 70% of public employees are women, as compared to about 50% in the total workforce (AKU, 1996).

Policies that support the joint roles of work and caregiving are an integral part of the full employment goal. Paid care leaves, part-time employment with minimal loss of benefits, and extensive home care services for elders provide caregivers with incentives to remain in the labor force.

When most adults work, the state is protected from the high cost of supporting non-working, dependent persons. Plus, employed adults generate tax revenues for the state. These contributions are necessary to support the comprehensive and universal social welfare activities in Sweden. Thus, in Sweden, both women and men are encouraged to work.

The state was able to implement these full employment policies and programs because of the strong alliance between the unions, the Social Democratic Party, and Sweden's balance of power model. In the past decade, however, small national economies with large international trade have become more dependent on the global market. The global market does not always support the suggestions put forward by a Social Democratic government and, through the global economy, the markets have access to currency speculation. In order to avoid currency speculation in Sweden, costs in the national budget are better reflected as unemployment benefits, not as costs for public employees. Hence, the possibility of realizing a policy of full employment is more restricted, today.

There are advantages and disadvantages for employers sharing power with the state and unions. Sweden's still rather centralized form of decision making helps to ensure a fairly high level of labor peace and wage and price stability, along with a moderate level of employer flexibility (Logue, 1983). Employers benefit from the wage restraint policy, which often is activated during economic downturns. These policies, though, are not always viewed favorably by employers.

State and Family Responsibility for Elders.   As noted above, the care of dependent persons is a shared responsibility. The state cannot afford to absorb all the dependent care costs. Programs such as paid care leaves and payments for caregiving enable persons to be employed (albeit for fewer hours) and to tend to the care of dependent elders. Thus, the supports for employed caregivers support the dual goals of full employment and shared responsibility for the care of elders. Possible contradictions do exist, though, between encouraging family members to care for elders and encouraging employment.

Gender Equality.   Another important goal is gender equality. In 1962, the Advisory Council to the Prime Minister on Equality Between Men and Women was established. The council submitted reports declaring that women and men should have the same rights to and responsibilities for work, family care, leisure, and participation in other social events (Liljeström, 1978). Paid leaves, payments for caregiving, and part-time employment are programs available to both men and women. Women more often than men, however, opt for these programs, as gender roles change slowly. Since many of the jobs in the public sector are care-related jobs, they are similar to what women traditionally have done on an unpaid basis. Also, wages in these jobs are in the lowest brackets. As a result, few men are attracted to these jobs (Persson, 1990).

Historical Developments: Elder Care

In medieval times, elderly persons without property were taken care of by the Catholic Church, which owned about one fifth of the land (the farmers owned about half the land, the nobility one fifth, and the state 6%). In 1527, King Gustav Vasa convinced the Parliament that the property of the Catholic Church should be confiscated (the Reformation). The Catholic Church's land was taken over by the state and to some extent by the nobility. From that point, the state-controlled Lutheran Church and its parishes assumed the main responsibility for support, or relief, of the poor. But, through the Poor Relief Ordinance of 1847, this responsibility was taken over by the municipalities. The church never developed as a real alternative care provider, making public authorities the main providers of care.

Among the early developments leading to the situation today, two periods in time are notable: the years 1912–1913 and 1947–1949, respectively. Each time span was characterized by paradigmatic shifts with respect to elder care. On the first occasion (1912–1913), poor relief and old age homes became targets of criticism in that they represented an old-fashioned and degrading mode of dealing with the negative effects of old age. The alternative put forward was the introduction of a new pension scheme. On the second occasion (1947–1949), old age homes again were targeted. This time, the solution lay in home care. Two key words describe the prevailing atmosphere in each period: Elderly persons were being humiliated and stigmatized.

1912–1913: Poor Relief and Old Age Homes Versus Pensions.   At the beginning of the twentieth century, two chief sociopolitical ideologies were at work in Sweden. One claimed that a humanized poor relief system would play a meaningful role in social politics and that modern social insurance would rest on a strictly actuarial ground (Edebalk, 1996). The other sociopolitical ideology was represented by supporters of a pension system proclaiming a newer principle of justice.

Advocates for Poor Relief Reform.   A small group of socially active persons formed at the beginning of the twentieth century. Referred to as "poor relief people," they were in favor of modernizing and humanizing poor relief (Edebalk, 1996).

The poor relief reformers were members of Stockholm's leading economic and social class. Their sociopolitical view was liberal and paternalistic. Like other bourgeois reformers of the time, they often spoke in terms of "upbringing and training" and believed that poverty could be abolished through education. A number of arguments lay behind this ideology. It was feared that supplemental pensions would result in a diminished will to work (when receiving compensation, one did not need to work) and a reduced desire to save money. Children's sense of responsibility to support their aged parents would be abolished, and moral dissolution would result. Poor relief supporters also expressed outrage against "unworthy" individuals receiving a pension (e.g., those reluctant to work, neglectful heads of family, and other "asocial" individuals) (Edebalk, 1996).

Poor relief could be characterized as differentiating and individualized; services would be available only to those who could demonstrate need and meet eligibility requirements. The forms of poor relief, thus, ought to be clearly spelled out and included in the law. Permissible forms for the elderly were home support and institutionalization (where old age homes can be seen as a logical consequence of the differentiation). However, no national organization for reforming and modernizing poor relief existed. This vacuum was soon to be filled by leading, vocal persons within the Central Organization for Social Work (CSA) and the Swedish Poor Relief Alliance (SFF) (Edebalk, 1996; Elmér, 1975).

Advocates for a Pension System.   According to the second ideology, poor relief should be more or less eliminated. The great errors in poor relief, it was argued, were that it made its entrance too late, after the damage had been done (i.e., after the individual had lost most of his or her belongings and could qualify as poor), and that it humiliated its recipients. Since social insurance intervened earlier, before the individual's economic and perhaps family situation reached bottom, it served a preventive function (Edebalk, 1996).

A national social insurance could relieve the burden on the economies of the municipalities and could provide each individual with a dignified form of compensation. Poor relief stigmatized, and, more, recipients lost their right to vote. Another motive for supporting a pension insurance was that grown children would be relieved of some of the burden of supporting elderly parents—something of particular relevance for poor workers. The hoped-for effects were that tensions in society would abate and that emigration would diminish (Edebalk, 1996).

Several pension models were proposed in Sweden around the turn of the century. Two of these were said to be impossible; one, a state-financed voluntary insurance and, the other, a universal tax–financed, fixed-value pension. Experience with the first model had demonstrated that a voluntary insurance plan would receive limited interest and participation and that those most in need would not participate. Thus, pension insurance would have to be compulsory. From the second model, it was clear that no financial means existed to offer adequate benefits, since compensation would have to be placed below the lowest wage in the job market (Edebalk, 1996).

Thus, the insurance would need to be universal and obligatory. The universal feature motivated the lost income principle,[1] since high-wage earners in other cases would not have benefited from any larger gains through the insurance program. Compensation would be financed by new surcharges paid by employers, employees, or by state taxes. Greater parity in municipal taxes could be achieved in this way (Edebalk, 1996).

The Confrontation.   In 1907, the Conservative government appointed a poor relief legislation committee. At the end of the same year, the government appointed another commission: the Old Age Insurance Committee (Ålderdomsförsäkringskommittén) (Edebalk, 1996; Odén, 1988).

The confrontation between the spokespersons for poor relief and the representatives of a more modern sociopolitical ideology took place during a few months beginning in November 1912, when the Old Age Insurance Committee presented its motion. On the basis of the committee's basically unanimous recommendations, an all-inclusive Old Age Pension Scheme was overwhelmingly approved by the Parliament in March 1913 (Edebalk, 1996; Elmér, 1960). This scheme was the first of its kind in the world to encompass, in principle, an entire population. It was constructed with two parts. The first was a surcharge, with roots in the obligatory German pension system, built on actuarial principles. Pension insurance would be paid in cases of invalidity and old age (67 years). In addition, to attain a quick sociopolitical effect, a tax-financed, income-related supplemental pension was addended. This enabled the pension to take immediate effect (Edebalk, 1996; Elmér, 1960; Odén, 1988).

Near unanimity was evident in the 1913 parliamentary decision; therefore, the political preconditions for reform were good. Right-wing political arguments for social insurance were usually based on socially pacifistic motives and calls for "national unity." The liberals deemed that the increased individual responsibility upheld their notion of self-help, and the Social Democrats had been striving for security in old age for urban and rural workers (Edebalk, 1996; Odén, 1988).

Even though pension insurance had its limitations and the amount provided was relatively low, the course was now charted. For advocates of the pension system, the reform signified a solid overtaking of the poor relief peoples' territory: It was estimated that the reform would liberate more than 80,000 elderly from poor relief (Edebalk, 1996).

In order to understand the outcome of the pension–poor relief battle, the strong position of the farmers, given the country's agrarian structure, is necessary to consider. Compared to continental Europe, the feudal system had had very little impact on Sweden. Instead, a long tradition of free farmers prevailed and, after 1866, they dominated the Parliament. In addition, the Swedish population overall was too small to have given rise to an influential upper middle class. The farmers were determined to fight against poor relief, which increased municipal taxes. They also were determined to have a decisive influence on the type of pension system to be implemented. For example, a pure employee insurance (with partial financing by employers) would be difficult to enact since farmers and small businessmen, who often did not have a higher material standard than their employees, would have to contribute without receiving any pension themselves (Edebalk, 1996; Elmér, 1975).

Odén (1988) noted that the most important effect of the reform was that the state now took responsibility for administering resources between rich and poor municipalities and for intervening in an area that, until then, had been the duty of the family and, in the last resort, the municipality. She wrote, "The parliamentary decision of 1913 must be regarded as a remarkable breakthrough—the beginning of a transition from familial to societal responsibility for the aging individual" (p. 44).

1947–1949: Old Age Homes Versus Home Care.   In 1946, an almost unanimous Parliament ratified a new National Basic Pension Law and, in 1947, it unanimously decided on a major reform of the municipal old age homes (Elmér, 1975).

The decision in 1947 concentrated on the expansion of old age homes—to build new units and to improve existing ones. The estimated cost of the investment was 450 million kronor over a 10-year period, an enormous sum at that time. That large sum may have had an opposite-than-anticipated psychological effect. Critics saw a threat in that the old age homes had a stigma attached to them, were still within the jurisdiction of poor relief authorities, and often exhibited a variety of poor conditions (Gaunt, 1995).

The aim of the decision was to house 10% of the elderly in modernized old age homes, with an additional 5% in nursing homes. Another ambition was that the old age homes would look more like the "retirement homes" (*pensionärshem*) which, with Danish inspiration, had been constructed in the preceding two decades (Gaunt, 1995). The retirement homes became very popular; above all, because they were modern and were not stigmatized. The drawback was that no care or supervision was available. Consequently, in order to allow elderly to remain in the retirement homes, a home help organization would be necessary.

At the same time, the old age homes were expected to house elderly with a "normal" level of difficulty, which meant that about half their residents would have to be moved to special institutions, such as hospitals, psychiatric hospitals, and homes for mentally retarded (Elmér, 1975). Here was ample reason for the municipalities to support the proposition: Severely ill and needy could be transferred to institutions run by the counties or the state and, at the same time, the municipalities could receive subsidies to build and repair old age homes. In addition, in many old age homes, the elderly barely composed half of the inmates, as these institutions still housed orphans, the disabled, mentally ill, destitutes, and so forth (Gaunt, 1995).

After the ratification of the proposition, Parliament did very little. The waiting period for financing was shortly accompanied by a sense of resentment. One of the new pensioners' organizations argued solely for home help, even at the expense of retirement homes, as they did not want to segregate the elderly from society. And, at the end of 1948, a media debate ensued. A laypersons' campaign led by a popular novelist and backed up by representatives of the pensioners' organizations defeated the state, as represented by high officials from the National Board of Health and Welfare. The battleground had been newspapers, magazines, and, above all, radio, where the only (public service) station had a tremendous impact. Within a year, the idea of a gigantic investment in old age homes had failed (Gaunt, 1995).

But, the number of old age homes did not decrease significantly after this turning point. In 1950, there were 1,385 old age homes in the country. In 1960, there were still 1,350, and the number of inhabitants had increased from 32,600 to 39,600. The number of inhabitants of old age homes reached its peak in 1974 with 58,100. And, although only 879 homes had survived the 1980s, they still housed approximately 39,000 elderly.

Obviously, it was easier to abolish old age homes in theory; in reality, the need for intermediate care in one form or another is ever present. However, the main effect of the battle was on the attitudes toward the anticipated increase in care need. From this point onward, the emphasis on the development of a home help service was irreversible.

☐ Future Trends

Care Options for Elderly Persons

At the time of this writing, there are no immediate plans for major changes in care of the elderly. In the longer perspective, several possibilities are open. Johansson (1997) suggested three scenarios. First, the situation could remain about the same, with public care providing more than 90% of the elderly care. Private care would remain a predominantly urban phenomenon. This scenario is most likely with the Social Democrats remaining in power (at the national level). The second scenario suggests a quite opposite development. If less money is allocated to elder care (and to public spending in general), and if major cutbacks are made, a situation could arise where more affluent people could "buy" the care they want (e.g., via insurance). This would open up a large private sector of elder care services, and an increased inequality in the population. For this scenario to materialize, it would be necessary for the Conservative Party to talk the center parties into this change. In the third scenario, there would be increased competition among care providers, with an increased share of private (although publicly financed) care providers. Johansson's optimistic prospect is that, in the future, the major competitive advantage in this case would be the quality of care. Perhaps, the most probable development is a mix between the first and the third scenarios. Due to the autonomous position of the municipalities, some (predominantly bourgeois) would emphasize the third way, while others (predominantly Social Democratic) would emphasize the first way. In any case, the result would be a greater discrepancy in the organization of elder care between municipalities.

With respect to the latter, Eliasson Lappalainen and Nilsson Motevasel (1997) have criticized the care of the elderly for becoming commodified in many municipalities, as a result of influences from private enterprise. The services are divided into segments and are termed as care products.

Other authors have identified developments, such as a decentralization of the decision-making process; a redefinition of lines of responsibility; and an increase in inequality concerning accessibility, cost, and quality of services, as well as a general lack of public discussion (Thorslund, Bergmark, & Parker, 1997).

Daatland (1997), taking a broader perspective, also anticipates changes in the future. He argued that changes in themselves are not critical. Rather, a lack of change in a changing society would indicate rigidity. He also argued that recent changes in Scandinavian welfare policies on aging, including a decline in access to most services, are minor adaptations to protect and sustain the Scandinavian model. The major result of the economically harsh period between 1991 and 1996 in Sweden has been a greater division of wealth and income (due, e.g., to lower compensation levels), while the structure of the welfare model has remained strikingly intact. However, Daatland also asked whether the changes represent a shift in balance from universality to need allocation.

He also speculated whether the Scandinavian trends indicate a change in direction to both the conservative insurance model of continental Europe and the liberal residual model of the United States. One contributing factor may be a more pluralistic and heterogeneous population. Daatland suggested that the image of a benevolent "state" may be dependent on an image of a homogeneous population. When the population becomes more segmented into heterogeneous groups, solidarity may perish and support for collective solutions may weaken. Thus, an emerging welfare pluralism may become a plurality of segmented groups in which inequality is growing.

Supports for Employed Caregivers

Changes in state initiatives for elders may affect employed caregivers. The new Social Services Act recommends that municipalities pay more attention to supporting the efforts of informal caregivers. Although these initiatives are not specifically directed to employed caregivers, they could benefit from them.

Changes in employer practices also may affect employed caregivers. For example, some Swedish employers have made headway in negotiating wages at the company level (Martin, 1995). Although this arrangement can increase an individual employer's competitiveness, wages determined at the local level, rather than the national or industry level, can be disadvantageous for employed caregivers, along with other employees. Job security, equitable wages, and leaves of absences could be threatened by enhanced employer autonomy. Although challenges to Sweden's full employment and wage solidarity policies are taking place, Martin (1995) believed the challenges will transform, rather than replace, the Swedish universalistic welfare state. So far, because Sweden is highly unionized, unions have blocked the majority of employer attempts to eliminate national- and industry-level bargaining.

☐ Note

1. The lost income principle (sometimes called the income replacement system) means that the individual is compensated for loss of income in proportion to his or her salary. If it is decided that, for example, 80% of the salary up to a certain income level will be paid in case of sickness, then wage earners receive 80% of their salary when on sick leave. Thus, those who earn more receive more. The lost income principle is considered important in order to give legitimacy to a universal system among the middle classes.

☐ References

AKU. (1996). *Arbetskraftsundersökningen. Årsmedeltal 1995. Grundtabeller* [Manpower investigation. Annual 1995. Basic tables]. Stockholm: Statistics Sweden.

Andersson, L. (1986). Önskemål om informell och formell hjälp och vård [Wishes for informal and formal help and care). *Socialmedicinsk Tidskrift, 63*, 225–233.

Andersson, L. (1993). *Äldre i Sverige och Europa* [Elderly in Sweden and Europe]. Stockholm: Socialstyrelsen.

Andersson, L. (1994). *Äldre och äldreomsorg i Norden och Europa.* [Elderly and elderly care in Scandinavia and Europe]. Stockholm: Socialstyrelsen.

Andersson, L., & Johansson, L. (1996). Äldres behov av och inställning till hjälp och vård. [Elderly individuals' need of and attribute to help and care]. In *Äldres hälsa, behov och bruk av service och vård.* [Elderly individuals' health, needs, and use of service and care]. (Ädelutvärderingen 96:6, pp. 89–103). Stockholm: Socialstyrelsen.

Andersson, L., & Sundström, G. (1996). Social networks of elderly people in Sweden. In H. Litwin (Ed.), *The social networks of older people: A cross-national analysis* (pp. 15–29). Westport, CT: Praeger.

Antman, P. (1996). *Barn och äldreomsorg i Tyskland och Sverige. Sverigedelen* [Child and elderly care in Germany and Sweden. The Swedish part] (Välfärdsprojektet, skriftserien No. 5). Stockholm: Norstedts.

Daatland, S. O. (1997). Welfare policies for older people in transition? Emerging trends and comparative perspectives. *Scandinavian Journal of Social Welfare, 6*, 153–161.

Edebalk, P. G. (1996). *Välfärdsstaten träder fram. Svensk socialförsäkring 1884–1955.* [The emergence of the welfare state: Social insurance in Sweden 1884–1955] *Lund studies in social welfare XII.* Lund, Sweden: Arkiv förlag.

Eliasson Lappalainen, R., & Nilsson Motevasel, I. (1997). Ethics of care and social policy. *Scandinavian Journal of Social Welfare, 6*, 189–196.

Elmér, Å. (1960). *Folkpensioneringen i Sverige med särskild hänsyn till ålderspensioneringen.* [Pensions in Sweden with special emphasis on old age pension]. Doctoral dissertation, Lund, Sweden, Gleerup.

Elmér, Å. (1975). *Från Fattigsverige till välfärdsstaten. Sociala förhållanden och socialpolitik i Sverige under nittonhundratalet* [From poverty to the welfare state in Sweden: Social conditions and social policy in Sweden during the twentieth century]. Lund, Sweden: Bokförlaget Aldus/Bonniers.

Esping-Andersen, G. (1985). *Politics against markets.* Princeton, NJ: Princeton University Press.

Furåker, B., & Mossberg, A.-B. (1994). *De anhöriganställdas vardag.* [The everyday life of employed caregivers] (Ädel-utvärderingen 94:1). Stockholm: Socialstyrelsen.

Furåker, B., & Mossberg, A.-B. (1997). *Vårdansvar och bundenhet. Om anställda anhörigvårdare i Sverige* [Responsibility for care and lack of freedom. On employed caregivers in Sweden]. *Socialvetenskaplig tidskrift, 4*(1), 3–20.

Gaunt, D. (1995). *Ivar Lo, de radikala pensionärerna och striden mot ålderdomshemmen 1949* [Ivar Lo, the radical pensioners, and the fight against the old age homes 1949]. *Socialvetenskaplig tidskrift, 2*(4), 370–389.

118   Most Developed Countries

Grafström, M. (1994). *The experience of burden in the care of elderly persons with dementia.* Doctoral dissertation, Karolinska Institute, Stockholm.

Hedborg, A., & Meidner, R. (1984). *Folkhemsmodellen* [The people's home model]. Borås, Sweden: Rabén and Sjögren.

Hedin, B. (1993). *Growing old in Sweden.* Göteborg, Sweden: The Swedish Institute and the National Board of Health and Welfare.

Herlitz, C. (1997). Distribution of informal and formal home help for elderly people in Sweden. *The Gerontologist, 37,* 117–124.

International Labour Office. (1996). *Yearbook of labour statistics* (55th issue). Geneva, Switzerland: International Labour Office.

Johansson, L. (1991). *Caring for the next of kin. On informal care of the elderly in Sweden.* Uppsala, Sweden: Uppsala University.

Johansson, L. (1997). Konkurrensutsättning av äldreomsorgen—några svenska erfarenheter [Competition in elderly care—Some Swedish experiences]. *Aldring & Eldre, 14,* 26–31.

Johansson, L., & Sundström, G. (1994). Payments for care: The case of Sweden. In A. Evers, M. Pijl, & C. Ungerson (Eds.), *Payments for care—The European and the North American experience* (pp. 87–100). Aldershot, England: Avebury.

Korpi, W. (1978). *Arbetarklassen i välfärdskapitalismen* [The working class in welfare capitalism]. Kristianstad, Sweden: Prisma.

Liljeström, R. (1978). Sweden. In S. Kamerman & A. Kahn (Eds.), *Family policy: Government and families in fourteen countries,* (pp. 19–48). New York: Columbia University Press.

Listhaug, O. (1990). Macrovalues: The Nordic countries compared. *Acta Sociologica, 33,* 219–234.

Logue, J. (1983). Social welfare, equality, and the labor movement in Denmark and Sweden. In R. Tomasson (Ed.), *Comparative social research* (Vol. 6). London: JAI Press.

Marklund, S. (1982). *Klass, stat och socialpolitik.* Lund, Sweden: Arkiv.

Martin, A. (1995). The Swedish model: Demise or reconfiguration? In R. Locke, T. Kochan, & M. Piore (Eds.), *Employment relations in a changing world economy.* Cambridge: Massachusetts Institute of Technology.

Odén, B. (1988). The role of the family and state in old age support: The Swedish experience up to 1913. *Comprehensive Gerontology, C 2,* 42–46.

Odén, B. (1997). Kunskap och handling i äldrepolitiken [Knowledge and action in elder policy]. In K. Jennbert & R. Lagercrantz (Eds.), *Äldrepolitik i förändring?* (Välfärdsprojektet, Skriftserien No. 9, pp. 17–31). Stockholm: Norstedts.

Persson, I. (1990). The third dimension—Equal status between Swedish women and men. In I. Persson (Ed.), *Generating equality in the welfare state: The Swedish experience,* (pp. 223–244). Oslo, Norway: Norwegian University Press.

Pierson, P. (1996, January). The new politics of the welfare state. *World Politics, 48,* 143–179.

Putnam, R. (with Leonardi, R. & Nanetti, R.) (1992). *Making democracy work: Civic traditions in modern Italy.* Princeton, NJ: Princeton University Press.

SFS (Svenskförfattningssamling). (1980). Socialtjänstlag. [Social Services Act]. SFS 1980:620. Stockholm.

Socialstyrelsen. (1996b). *Social service, vård och omsorg i Sverige 1996* [Social service and care in Sweden, 1996]. Stockholm: Author.

Socialstyrelsen. (1996c). *Vård och omsorg om äldre personer och personer med funktionshinder 1995.* [Care of elderly and handicapped 1995]. (Statistik, Socialtjänst 1996:7.) Stockholm: Author.

Statistics Sweden. (1998). *Statistical yearbook of Sweden.* Stockholm: Author.

Statistics Sweden. (1993). *Pensionärer 1980–1989* [Pensions 1980–1989] (Levnadsförhållanden, Rapport No. 81). Stockholm: Author.

Statistics Sweden. (1997). *Statistiska meddelanden* [Statistics reports]. (Am12SM9701). Stockholm: Author.

Sundström, G. (1984). *De gamla, deras anhöriga och hemtjänsten.* [The old, their relatives, and the home help service]. (Rapport i Socialt Arbete 22). Stockholm: Socialhögskolan/Stockholms Universitet.

Sundström, G. (1994). Care by families: An overview of trends. In *Caring for frail elderly people. Social Policy Studies 14.* Paris: Organization for Economic Cooperation and Development.

Sundström, G., & Thorslund, M. (1994). Caring for the frail elderly in Sweden. In L. Katz Olson (Ed.), *The graying of the world* (pp. 59–85). Binghamton, NY: Haworth Press.

Szebehely, M. (1993). *Hemtjänst eller anhörigvård? Förändringar under 1980-talet* [Home help service or family care? Changes during the 1980s]. Stockholm: Socialstyrelsen.

Thorslund, M., Bergmark, Å., & Parker, M. G. (1997). Difficult decisions on care and services for elderly people: The dilemma of setting priorities in the welfare state. *Scandinavian Journal of Social Welfare, 6,* 197–206.

U.S. Bureau of Census, Department of Commerce. (1996). *Global aging into the 21st* century. Washington, DC: U.S. Government Printing Office.

Walker, A. (1993). *Age and attitudes. Main results from a Eurobarometer survey.* Commission of the European Communities.

8

CHAPTER

Viola M. Lechner
Margaret B. Neal

The Mix of Public and Private Programs in the United States: Implications for Employed Caregivers

☐ Introduction

This chapter summarizes work and family issues in the United States. It then describes policies, benefits, and services available to assist employed caregivers and analyzes those factors that have contributed to the United States public and private configuration of supports. The chapter ends with a discussion of possible future trends.

☐ Managing Work and Care of Older Persons

In the United States, the number of persons who both work and care for frail elders has been increasing for a number of years and is expected to double in the near future (Moen, Robison, & Fields, 1994). This is due to the aging of the population and the continuous commitment of women to the labor force (Moen et al., 1994). According to two nationally representative studies of informal caregivers, the proportion of caregivers who are employed has increased from 55% in 1989 to 64% in 1997 (American Association of Retired Persons [AARP], 1989; National Alliance for Caregiving [NAC]/AARP, 1997). In terms of the United States workforce overall, based on their meta-analysis of 17 studies of employees, Gorey, Rice, and Brice (1992) estimated that from 7.4% to 11.8% were engaged in elder care duties in 1992. A nationally representative study of workers conducted by the Families and Work Institute (Galinsky, Bond, & Friedman, 1993) found that approximately 18% of employees expected to be providing care for an aging relative in the next 5 years. These increases in family and work responsibilities are unprecedented.

In spite of their employment commitments, families provide 80% of the help needed by elders (Select Committee on Aging, 1987). Their duties range from weekly shopping to 24-hour personal care (e.g., bathing, feeding). As reviewed by Gorey et al. in 1992, studies of employed caregivers reveal that employed caregivers' average age is 47, they primarily are women (62%), and most are married. Wagner and Neal (1994) cited studies indicating that the average length of time spent in caregiving is 5.5 to 6.5 years and that from 6 to 10 hours are spent weekly, on average, in caregiving.

The multiple family and employment responsibilities of men and women impact families, workplaces, community services, and government. Several studies have found that employed caregivers experience strain as a result of managing their twin roles (Lechner & Gupta, 1996; Neal, Chapman, Ingersoll-Dayton, & Emlen, 1993). Stress reactions can contribute to unwanted physical and mental conditions (Vitaliano, Scanlan, Krenz, Schwartz, & Marcovina, 1996; Wagner & Neal, 1994). Those reactions, in turn, can lead to higher health care costs for the treatment of those conditions.

Some caregivers have quit their jobs in order to care for their loved ones, while others have reduced their work hours or have forgone overtime, promotion, and training opportunities (NAC/AARP, 1997; Scharlach, 1994; Wagner & Neal, 1994). A nationally representative study of caregivers found that 28% of employed caregivers either quit their jobs (10%), took a leave of absence (11%), or reduced their work hours (7%) as a result of caregiving (NAC/AARP, 1997). Regarding the leave of absence, Hispanics (18%) and Asians (22%) were more likely than Whites (10%) to take a work leave. The same study reported that, of those with heavy caregiving responsibilities, 30% had had to give up work entirely. Reduced employment hours depress family incomes and can decrease future Social Security benefits.

Women are more vulnerable to these economic disadvantages, because they are generally the ones who reduce their employment hours (Abel, 1991). Minorities and gays and lesbians also are more vulnerable to income losses due to their less flexible work environments. For example, Lechner (1993) found that Black caregivers reported less support from supervisors and less flexible policies regarding family concerns than White caregivers. Very few gays and lesbians are entitled to use family-focused workplace benefits, such as family leaves, for the care of their partners (Lechner & Creedon, 1994).

Not all caregivers find the dual roles of work and elder care taxing. For some, outside employment gives them a break from their caregiving roles; for others, the dual roles are not perceived as burdensome (Petty & Friss, 1987; Scharlach, 1994). Many factors have been identified as predictors of whether the outcomes of caregiving are positive or negative. These include the number of hours spent in each role; race or ethnicity; the perceived level of burden of each role; personal coping strategies; and the level of and satisfaction with support from family, friends, religious affiliations, public and private agencies, and workplace programs (NAC/AARP, 1997; Lechner & Creedon, 1994; Neal et al., 1993; Scharlach, 1994).

Work organizations can be adversely affected by employees' elder care duties. A cost analysis performed by the Metropolitan Life Insurance Company revealed that elder care–related costs (e.g., employee absences, distractions while at work, health care costs) were $3,142 per year per employee (Coberly & Hunt, 1995). This conservative estimate was based on a select group who provided personal care (25% of all employed caregivers), such as bathing and feeding. Had caregivers who provide a greater range of services to elders been included, the costs would have been even higher. Lowered company profits reverberate throughout the economy. For example, government revenues derived from corporate profit taxes are lessened, stockholder dividends are reduced, and employee wages and benefits are negatively affected.

It is important to note that findings reported in this section have several limitations which reduce their generalizability. These limitations include the absence of longitudinal studies, a lack of consistency in definitions, the preponderance of middle-income White earners in studies, and a tendency among researchers to emphasize negative outcomes over positive outcomes. Nonetheless, research has shown that the number of employed caregivers in the United States is increasing, and families, work-places, communities, and government are affected by these changes.

☐ Supports for Employed Caregivers: Description and Evaluation

This section describes the various efforts by government, work organizations, unions, and human service agencies in the United States to assist employees with elder care responsibilities. The initiatives are listed in Table 8-1.

Government Initiatives

Supports for Employed Caregivers.   The United States government has legislated two tax policies and one family leave bill which are particularly helpful to employed caregivers. The federal dependent care tax credit, first initiated in 1976, enables employed persons who qualify to deduct some of their employment-related dependent care expenses from the taxes they paid in the previous year (Costello, 1996). Almost half of the states also have state dependent care tax credits, most of which are tied to the federal tax credit (Dunken & Alt, 1992).

The second tax policy is the federal Dependent Care Assistance Plan (DCAP), first initiated in 1981. DCAPs allow qualified employees to exclude from their taxable income up to $5,000 of their elder care expenses. DCAPs are available only to employees whose employers have set up such a plan. Employers who administer these plans pay no Social Security taxes or unemployment taxes on employee DCAP contributions. Although the DCAP and the dependent care tax credit can be used simultaneously, the same expenditures cannot be claimed twice. Low-income earners generally save more with the dependent care credit; higher earners gain more from DCAPs (Costello, 1996).

Although these tax policies could save employed caregivers a modest amount of money, government restrictions limit their use. For example, both tax plans require employees to spend 8 hours a day (essentially live with) their elders, yet only 15% of nonspousal caregivers fit this category (U.S. Bureau of the Census, U.S. Department of Commerce, 1995). DCAPs require employees to be paying at least 51% of the elder's care-related expenses, which excludes many caregivers (Costello, 1996).

The Family and Medical Leave Act of 1993 requires employers to grant employees an unpaid leave for up to 12 weeks to care for a frail relative or sick child. Benefits are continued during this period, and job reinstatement is guaranteed (Family and Medical Leave Act of 1993). Although many caregivers can now take time-limited leaves without fear of losing their jobs, those who work for employers with fewer than 50 employees typically do not have this option. This is because employers with less than 50 employees are not mandated to provide this temporary leave of absence. Even among the employees who do have access to this leave, many cannot afford to take advantage of it because it is unpaid. Employers also have created barriers to utilization of the leave. For example, a study of 980 California firms found that 40% were out of compliance with at least one of the required provisions, such as posting notices, preparing leave request forms, and training supervisors (Scharlach, Sansom, &

TABLE 8-1. U.S. supports for employees with elder care responsibilities

Government Initiatives	Nongovernmental Organization Initiatives	Union Initiatives	Workplace Initiatives
For employed caregivers Federal and state dependent tax credits Dependent Care Assistance Plan (DCAP) Family and Medical Leave Act Indirectly, for older persons Social Security, Medicare, Medicaid Area Agencies on Aging (AAAs) and other community services	For employed caregivers Care management, work-family vendors Indirectly, for older persons Home care, day care, nursing home	Political and work organization influence Federal and state lobbying Union and management negotiations Services Member assistance program Sensitivity training for union negotiators and other staff	Policies: Work scheduling Parental and family leave (usually unpaid)[a,b] Flextime, compressed work week[a] Part-time work, job sharing[a] Flexplace, relocation policies[a] Policies: Corporate culture Top-level management support[a] Management sensitivity training[a] Work and family task forces[a] Community resource development[a] Benefits: Income assistance DCAP (administration of)[c] Subsidized dependent care assistance plan[a] Long-term care insurance (administration)[a] Subsidized care and vouchers,[a] discounts for care[a] Services Educational materials, counseling and support[a] Resource and referral[a] Case management services[a] On-site care center and other direct services[a] Employee assistance program (EAP)[a]

[a]Voluntary.
[b]Government mandated.
[c]Government encouraged.

123

Stanger, 1995). A number of states (34) also have enacted time-limited leave legislation. In some cases, federal and state requirements are contradictory (Commission on Family and Medical Leave & U.S. Women's Bureau, 1996).

Some countries (e.g., Sweden) provide compensation to family caregivers who provide care to elders. In the United States, there is no federal provision for such compensation; however, in 69% of the states and jurisdictions, some form of financial payment of relatives is at least possible (Linsk, Keigher, Simon-Rusinowitz, & England, 1992). Such payments typically are restricted to family caregivers for elders who are at high risk of institutionalization and who qualify for federal Medicaid funds (which are administered by the states) or for other income means-tested forms of assistance. Many states exclude certain kin, for example, spouses, adult children, adult siblings, or grandchildren, from receiving compensation. Several states will permit payments only if the caregiver and the client do not coreside. One quarter of the jurisdictions that allow payments to family caregivers require these caregivers to give up outside employment if they are receiving caregiver compensation (Linsk et al., 1992).

In addition to, or instead of, cash grants to family caregivers, several states provide services intended to prevent exhaustion among family members by allowing caregivers time off, such as respite care and day care services. In 1990, respite care was offered in 47 states and territories. Of jurisdictions not providing respite care in 1990, two allowed some type of family payment, while three did not. Forty-six jurisdictions provided day care in 1990; 32 of these also allowed for some type of family payment (Linsk et al., 1992).

Supports for Older Persons.   Several government programs indirectly assist employed caregivers by providing income continuation, health insurance, and social services for older persons. If these programs were not in place, family members would have considerably more financial and health care responsibilities for seniors.

The Social Security Act of 1935 established the nation's first federal pension plan for seniors. Social Security (Old Age, Survivors, and Disability Insurance [OASDI]) is a federally administered program which provides income protection to approximately 90% of Americans who are 65 years old and older (Social Security Administration, 1995). Presently, the Social Security Fund is solvent, but the 1994 Trustee's Report predicts that the fund's reserves will begin to decline after the year 2010, when members of the post–World War II baby boom generation begin to retire (Myers, 1995). A couple of approaches have been considered to build up the reserves: increase the tax rates and increase the normal retirement age to a higher age (Myers, 1995). Privatizing Social Security also has been discussed as a possible solution (Williamson, 1997). Such changes could decrease pension benefits, especially for middle- and high-income earners. If these changes occur, employed caregivers' financial costs for their elders may increase.

Amendments in 1965 to the Social Security Act established two health insurance programs: Medicare (for persons age 65 and older and for disabled persons under the age of 65) and Medicaid (for poor persons) (Friedland, 1995). Medicare is a federal program that covers the majority of persons age 65 and older. Medicaid is a joint federal and state program for impoverished persons who meet income eligibility requirements which vary from state to state. Both health insurance programs cover hospital care and physician and allied health professional services. Medicare, however, does not pay for prescription drugs and pays for only a limited amount of home care and nursing home care; Medicaid pays for all three (Friedland, 1995).

Health care costs in the United States are very high, and there is much concern about the nation's ability to pay for the health care costs of older persons in the future, especially as the baby boomers age. Many changes have been implemented to limit these costs, including raising Medicare deductibles and copayments, limiting the number of covered medical procedures, and curbing physician and hospital reimbursements (Friedland, 1995). Efforts are under way to enroll the majority of Medicare and Medicaid recipients in managed care programs, such as health maintenance organizations (HMOs) (Friedland, 1995). Managed care programs limit hospital stays; for many elders, this results in extensive posthospital medical assistance from family members and other nonhospital personnel. Thus, these changes in Medicare and Medicaid are likely to require increasing financial and medical assistance from relatives.

One of the biggest weaknesses in government health programs for older citizens is the lack of support for affordable home care and nursing home services. Many frail seniors, unable to pay for their health care privately but also not able to meet Medicaid eligibility requirements, must rely totally on their relatives or be left unattended (Abel, 1991). Questions also arise about the quality of care that seniors receive, particularly in light of the cost-saving strategies employed by managed care companies. Income, race, and ethnicity also affect the type of care received. According to a large federal study of Medicare recipients, Blacks and lower income people of all races get less preventive care and less optimal management of chronic diseases than do Whites and upper-income people in general, due to racism and culturally insensitive provider practices as well as attitudes of recipients (Gornick et al., 1996).

A final government initiative for older persons is the Older Americans Act of 1965. This legislation was designed primarily to coordinate services for elders at the state and local levels and, secondarily, to appropriate funds for services to persons age 60 and older, regardless of income. Such services include advocacy services, multipurpose centers, access services (resource and referral, transportation, and outreach services), nutrition programs, and home-delivered meals (Gelfand, 1995). This act established State Units on Aging and local Area Agencies on Aging (AAAs). Recently, the National Association of AAAs established the Eldercare Locator, a toll-free telephone service that connects callers to health and social resources for elders in their locality.

Workplace Initiatives

Work organizations have developed a range of benefits for their employees; most are useful to all employees, although a few are limited to employees with dependent care responsibilities. A list of benefits relevant to employed caregivers appears in Table 8-1, column 2. These benefits are grouped into four types of support: work scheduling arrangements, income assistance, services, and strategies that promote family-friendly corporate cultures. Although most employee benefits are voluntary, some are government mandated (e.g., family leaves), and a few are government encouraged through tax incentives (e.g., DCAPs), as noted above. Benefits (e.g., health care, pension, family) constitute a substantial amount of employer costs: approximately 40% of an individual's total compensation (Rosenbloom, 1996).

Work Scheduling Arrangements.   Employed caregivers consistently report that time to take care of their elders' health, financial, social, and personal needs is a crucial need (Creedon, 1995). Opportunities to choose the number of hours worked, when, and where address this need. Options that have been implemented by employers include: (1) granting temporary leaves to care for frail elders, (2) initiating flexible work schedules (e.g., varied workday start and end times), (3) reducing the number of hours worked (e.g., part-time schedules), and (4) changing where work is done (e.g., working at home) (Lechner & Creedon, 1994; Neal et al., 1993).

Income Assistance.   Employers are required by law to provide several employee benefits that protect employees against income loss due to retirement (Social Security), job loss (unemployment insurance), and disability (workers' compensation and Social Security disability). These benefits are useful because they provide income replacements, which can help employees continue in their caregiver role. In addition to DCAPs, described above, a few employers help employees pay for elder care services by providing subsidies, vouchers, or discounts for particular services, such as adult day care and respite programs, or by making available long-term care insurance (Lechner & Creedon, 1994; Neal et al., 1993).

Services.   Some employers have provided educational information on work and elder care issues through newsletters, lunchtime seminars, and caregiver fairs (local providers of service set up tables or booths at a work site). A few large employers have sponsored resource and referral and case management services, which enable employees to locate health care and social services for their elders and to determine appropriate courses of action the family can take for immediate and long-term care arrangements. Case management involves performance of a detailed needs assessment, development of a care plan, and provision of regular follow-up (Ingersoll-Dayton, Chapman, & Neal, 1990; Lechner & Creedon, 1994). Counseling and resource and referral services also are offered by some employers. Less frequently, employers sponsor on-site or near-site adult day care facilities and respite programs (Wilson, Nippes, Simson, & Mahovich, 1993).

Some employers have determined that the best way to help their employees is to contribute funds to expand the supply and improve the quality of local elder care services. Contributions may be made solely or in partnership with other companies. For example, the American Business Collaboration for Quality Dependent Care is a consortium of 137 companies, with 11 corporate giants (including IBM and AT&T) serving in leadership and coordination roles (Lechner & Creedon, 1994). Consortia of small businesses also have been formed to provide some economies of scale in offering elder care benefits and services to employees (Lechner & Creedon, 1994).

Promotion of a Family-Friendly Work Environment.   Some employers have conducted training sessions for managers to sensitize them to the needs of employed caregivers. Supervisors have been found to play a key role in employee awareness and utilization of employee benefits (Galinsky, Friedman, & Hernandez, 1991; Wagner & Hunt, 1994). Because employees' needs are ever changing, the development of family-focused benefits must be a continuous and dynamic problem-solving process. Given this, some employers have established work and family task forces (Lechner & Creedon, 1994). Companies with task forces and manager training sessions are more likely to incorporate their work-family agenda into their mission statements and to institutionalize their work-family benefits (Galinsky et al., 1991).

Evaluation of Workplace Initiatives.   As shown in Table 8-2, most work organizations in the United States offer at least one family-focused benefit. The most fre-

TABLE 8-2. Percent of full-time employees with select elder care benefits in 1994 (By size and type of work organization)

	Unpaid Family Leave	Dependent Care Assistance Plan	Flextime	Employee Assistance Program	Resource and Referral	Cash Subsidies	Supervisor Training
Small companies[a] (under 100 employees)	47%	19%	6% (BLS) NA (GAO)	15%	NA	NA	NA
Large companies[b] (over 100 employees)	99%	52%	6% (BLS) 28% (GAO)	62%	7%	1%	3%
Government[c] (local, state, and federal employees)	93%	64%	11% (BLS) 69% (GAO)	68%	25%	4%	8%

Note. From General Accounting Office (GAO; 1994a, 1994b); U.S. Department of Labor, Bureau of Labor Statistics (BLS; 1994, 1996a, 1996b).

[a]49 million full-time employees.
[b]34 million full-time employees.
[c]18 million full-time employees.

quently offered supports are those that the government mandates, (e.g., unpaid family leave) or encourages through tax incentives (e.g., DCAPs). The next most frequently offered supports are those available regardless of whether or not an employee has family responsibilities, such as flextime and employee assistance programs (EAPs). Disparities in findings for flextime are most likely related to differences in definition of flextime. Least frequently provided are voluntary services and programs targeted specifically to employees with family responsibilities, such as elder care resource and referral services.

Also, as shown in Table 8-2, employees in government and larger work organizations have access to more family-focused benefits than those in smaller companies (under 100 employees). Employees in alternative work arrangements (independent contractors, on-call workers, temporary workers, and contract workers), currently 10% of the labor force, and part-time workers, currently 18% of the labor force, typically have even fewer benefits than those in small companies (U.S. Department of Labor, Bureau of Labor Statistics, 1997).

Even when supports are available, government, employer, and employee barriers exist that reduce utilization of workplace benefits. As mentioned above, government requirements limit the number of employees who can use the tax relief plans or afford to take leave. Many employers do not adequately publicize workplace supports. Also, insensitive supervisors have overtly or covertly discouraged employees from using workplace benefits, and workplace cultures have limited management's interest in implementing, and employees' willingness to use, family supports (Galinsky et al., 1991; Wagner & Hunt, 1994).

Labor Union Initiatives

American unions, as shown in Table 8-1, have responded in a variety of ways to the needs of their members. Some have established member assistance programs which, like EAPs, provide counseling, education, and resource and referral services (Lechner & Creedon, 1994). They also have recognized the need for sensitivity training on work-family issues for union negotiators and other staff. For example, the New York City Labor Council introduced a module on elder care issues in its ongoing Peer Counseling Training Program (Lechner & Creedon, 1994).

In addition to these efforts, most of the larger unions have negotiated specific work-family provisions in their contracts with American companies (Bureau of Labor Management Relations, 1992). Overall, unionized employees have more generous family-focused benefits than nonunion employees (U.S. Bureau of the Census, U.S. Department of Commerce, 1997). Senior union leaders have made strong statements of support for a union-based family agenda (Lechner & Creedon, 1994). These statements outline the basis for legislative action and collective bargaining on dependent care issues. The Coalition of Labor Union Women and the American Federation of Labor and Congress of Industrial Organizations (AFL-CIO) have published important guides for negotiation of family benefits (Lechner & Creedon, 1994), and unions actively lobbied Congress to pass the Family and Medical Leave Act of 1993 ("Family and Medical Leave Policy," 1988).

Several unions have done a great deal to advance the cause of employees with elder care duties, and unions seem a natural resource for such support. However, according to the Bureau of Labor Management Relation's (1992) review of 452 labor-management agreements, only half of the contracts contained work-family provisions. Unions have multiple agendas, such as job security, membership recruitment, and political organizing. These issues can dwarf work-family issues, especially if union leadership is not strongly committed to family concerns.

Public, For-Profit, and Not-for-Profit Human Service Agencies

Supports for Older Persons.   Human service agencies for the elderly offer a range of services, such as home care, adult day care, and nursing home care. Seventy-one percent of nursing homes are proprietary (for-profit) agencies; the government owns only 5%. Of home health care agencies, 44% are privately owned, and 19% are government owned (U.S. Bureau of the Census, U.S. Department of Commerce, 1995). Overall, long-term care services are expensive, inadequately regulated, and unevenly distributed. Some religious-based and other not-for-profit agencies are more affordable, but they are few in number (U. S. Bureau of the Census, U.S. Department of Commerce, 1995). Many long-term care services are not publicly financed: Approximately 37% of long-term care services are paid for by individuals out of their own pockets (Friedland, 1995). Moreover, issues of quality abound. In one study, reviewers of patient records from 47 home care agencies found quality of care deficiencies (e.g., failed to provide prescribed nursing services) in 43.8%; 14.4% of these records had deficiencies with potential or actual adverse effects for the patient (Jette, Smith, & McDermott, 1996). Abel (1991) suggested that the lack of public funds and the discriminatory practices of proprietary agencies create formidable problems for low-income and racial and ethnic minority elders seeking long-term care services. Elders unable to obtain long-term care services must rely on their relatives to meet their needs. Abel also noted that minority elders remain in the community with higher levels of functional impairments than do Whites.

Supports for Employed Caregivers.   The number of human service agencies serving employed caregivers is much smaller than the number serving the elderly. One service available to caregivers is geriatric case management. This service will assess, recommend, provide for, and supervise the care needs of frail relatives (Lechner & Creedon, 1994). This can be an especially useful service for caregivers who live at some distance from their frail relatives.

Several private and public agencies specializing in dependent care services have contracted with employers to provide to their employees a number of elder care services, such as resource and referral services, case management, education, and counseling. These vendors have a major influence on what employers offer to their employees; they also act as advocates for services and workplace policies which may become the centerpieces of work and family programs in the future (Lechner & Creedon, 1994). Like long-term care services, services for employed caregivers are expensive, unevenly distributed, and poorly regulated.

Partnership Arrangements

In an effort to provide cost-effective services to employed caregivers, partnership relationships have emerged among public, private, and not-for-profit agencies. The American Business Collaboration for Quality Dependent Care mentioned above is one example of a private and not-for-profit partnership. Public agencies also have entered into collaborative relationships. For example, the New York City Office on the Aging (an agency which receives funds through the Older Americans Act) has contracted with more than 35 companies to provide education, counseling, and information and referral services to employees in these companies (Garrison & Jelin, 1990).

In conclusion, the support programs for employed caregivers and their elders in the United States represent a strong public and private mix of initiatives that are varied and innovative. At the same time, these supports are limited in scope and unevenly distributed, which is the end result when the federal government does not play a primary role in setting the basic minimum of benefits and services for employed caregivers and their elders (Kamerman & Kahn, 1987). As Davis and Krouze (1994) noted, "The United States consistently falls behind other industrialized countries in its treatment of family-related issues" (p. 20). Many supports found in other industrialized countries are missing in the United States, such as paid family leaves, comprehensive health insurance coverage, and universal liveable wages.

☐ Factors Contributing to Supports for Employed Caregivers

This section examines several interrelated factors (demographic, historical, political, economic, and sociocultural) that have contributed to the particular public and private mix of supports for employed caregivers and elders in the United States.

Demographic and Social Pressures

Several demographic and social trends have influenced the development of elder care supports for employed caregivers in the United States. First, gains in longevity have occurred, and the segment of the oldest old, those who are those most likely to need assistance, has grown the fastest (Select Committee on Aging, 1987). With increasing numbers of frail elders, the demand for informal care has increased. The fertility rate also has declined, which means there are fewer adult children to care for a growing number of elders. Also, due to increasing rates of divorce and remarriage, adult children have a greater number of aging parents to care for, including stepparents and parents-in-law. At the same time, high divorce rates among adult children have resulted in more single-parent households and fewer spouses to rely on for help in parent care (Neal et al., 1993). Contributing to the increased demand for informal care and to the decreased availability of family caregivers have been changes in the reimbursement and financing of health care. These changes have resulted in earlier hospital discharges and more complex home care regimens, increasing the need for informal caregivers for persons who are frail or who have disabilities (Neal et al., 1993).

At the same time, since the 1930s, the number of women (the primary caregivers of elders) who have entered the workforce has been steadily increasing, to the point where women now comprise 46% of the entire labor force (U.S. Bureau of the Census, U.S. Department of Commerce, 1997). Among women age 40 to 60, 73% were employed in 1995 (International Labour Office [ILO], 1997). These employment commitments can make it more difficult for women to provide "hands-on" care, although women's involvement in other aspects of caregiving is not necessarily decreased (Linsk et al., 1992; Neal et al., 1993).

Since family problems become work issues, employers have been forced to address these issues. In order to attract and keep desired workers, and to maintain productivity levels, employers began implementing workplace supports for employees with elder care duties in the mid-1980s (Lechner & Creedon, 1994). Once one company started, others in the same industry followed in order to remain competitive.

Government and union officials, likewise, have been influenced by women's strong commitment to the labor force. With heightened media attention and pressure from various interest groups, they too became involved in legislating or negotiating family-friendly workplace benefits, although overall results have been somewhat weak.

Cultural and Ideological Factors

Characterizing any country's belief system is difficult, because of internal diversity among its people and regions, and because of evolutionary changes over time. Global comparisons have been made, however, between a country's commitment to individualism (concern for individual freedom) versus communitarianism (concern for the group or community needs) (Lodge & Vogel, 1987). Much has been written about the American preference for individual freedom and for limited government involvement in family life and in the economy (Brinkley, 1995; Gans, 1988; Lodge & Vogel, 1987). Personal, social, economic, and political independence is highly valued. With these freedoms come the expectations of responsibility to use self-initiative and to care for one's self and one's family members. Clark (1993) noted that individualism is the American quality that, more than any other characteristic, defines who Americans are and how they organize their relationships and their lives.

Government's limited response to the work–elder care dilemma can, in part, be explained by this ideological belief. The government does not want to usurp the role of the family in caring for its elders. The fear is that comprehensive programs would increase the family's dependency on the state. Also, to fund these programs, increases in personal income taxes would be needed, and increases in taxes are seen as decreases in personal freedom.

The public supports for employed caregivers and for elders offer good examples of the value placed by Americans on individualism. The Family and Medical Leave Act guarantees only job reinstatement, not a paid leave. Families are expected to finance their own time off, even though most are unable to do so. The shared household requirement of the DCAP stipulates a fairly high level of family involvement in the day-to-day demands of elder care. Medicare coverage is such that older individuals are required to pay privately for most of their long-term care services or obtain these services from family members.

Workplace responses are consistent with the American pursuit of individual freedom in economic affairs. Employers can withdraw their voluntary work-family benefits at any time. Withdrawals can occur during economic downturns, during increases in the pool of desirable workers, or when supports are no longer needed to enhance company image (Stevens, 1984). Although workplace supports in the United States are social in nature, they actually are designed to meet economic goals. Under these conditions, employers are inclined to establish as few supports as possible and to establish supports that easily can be dismantled. Such employer flexibility fits well with the American form of capitalism and ideology of individualism.

It is important to note that workplace and public policies that stem from the cultural ideology of individualism place a disproportionate burden on women. This is because family care of elders typically means female care of elders (Hooyman & Gonyea, 1995), although among the employed population, this gender disparity has been found to be less pronounced (e.g., Neal et al., 1993 found that 63% of employed caregivers were female, compared to 72% as found by Stone et al., 1987 in their national study of both employed and not employed caregivers). The limited nature of workplace and government supports diminishes caregivers' personal freedoms in terms of life choices and financial security.

Historical Precedence

Although employer responses have been modest, what is surprising is that they have occurred at all. This section explores the historical legacies that have contributed to the role played by employers and labor unions.

Employers' Role.   Employers have a long history of providing corporate social welfare programs. The earliest employer benefit dates back to the eighteenth century, when Galatan Glassworks offered a profit-sharing plan to its employees in 1797 (Employee Benefit Research Institute, 1990). Corporate social welfare programs peaked during the Industrial Revolution, with the emergence of company towns in the 1880s (Brandes, 1976; Heald, 1970). Railroad, mining, and other manufacturing companies offered—over a 40-year period of time—a wide array of benefits, including education, housing, health care, and social services. A dependent care service was even offered: Employees with sick wives received housekeeper services (Brandes, 1976).

The comprehensive benefits of the early twentieth century faded away due to economic downturns and emergence of public social welfare programs. In spite of these changes, however, several work organizations continued to provide a moderately high level of corporate social welfare programs, such as child care centers during World War II and pensions and health insurance since the 1920s (Kamerman, 1983; Lechner & Creedon, 1994; Neal, 1998; Stevens, 1988). About 25% of all social welfare benefits in the United States are provided by work organizations (Stevens, 1988).

Historical legacies, then, have facilitated employer responses to their employees' elder care–related needs. Employers were accustomed to implementing and maintaining employee benefits, and had the necessary organizational structure (e.g., human resource departments), skills, and ideological commitment to initiate family benefits.

Labor Unions' Role.   Although labor unions could be considered a natural advocate for family-focused workplace supports, their responses have been slow and limited. Two factors may explain this: (a) the predominance of males in unions and (b) unions' organizational structures.

Unions have a long history of organizing White men more than women or minorities (Crain, 1994; Foner, 1978; Moody, 1988). The early unions were against including women as members, fearing women's lower wages would depress their own (Foner, 1978). Even today, membership discrepancies exist. Heavily unionized industries are those where males predominate, such as manufacturing and construction, even though the greatest job growth has been in the service economy, where women predominate (U.S. Bureau of Census, U.S. Department of Commerce, 1997). In 1996, 17% of male workers compared to 12% of females were members of unions, even though studies suggest that women are more interested in unionization than men (Crain, 1994). Moreover, few women are in union leadership positions (Moody, 1988).

The primary concern of male members is economic. Women members, too, are concerned about wages and job security, but they also are concerned about social issues, such as elder care and sex segregation. Historical male dominance has caused union organizers and contract negotiators to push for "bread-and-butter" economic issues and to shy away from social issues (Crain, 1994; Moody, 1988).

In addition to gender issues, the organizational structure of labor unions presents barriers to negotiating for more comprehensive social and economic benefits. Early unions in America organized by industry (e.g., steel, textiles), instead of nationally. This decentralized structure continues today. Western (1994, 1995) noted that, because unions in the United States lack a strong central union confederation, they have less influence over macroeconomic policy making. That is, they are less equipped to pursue the goals of full employment, livable wages, and paid family leave policies for all workers. They win employee benefits (generally, better wages and job security) on an industry-by-industry basis rather than on a national basis, which would affect *all* workers. Contributing to the decentralized structure of unions in America has been federal legislation. The Taft Hartley Act of 1947 made it almost impossible for unions to organize a general strike that would include the majority of workers in America. This act also banned union control over welfare funds (employee benefits) that were financed by employers (Stevens, 1988).

Thus, the unions' great emphasis on economic issues and their decentralized structure have made it difficult for them to focus on social issues and on benefits for employed caregivers with elder care duties.

Political and Economic Aspects

The only institution in the United States that can implement policies and programs which would ensure uniform benefits for employed caregivers is the federal government. Work organizations are concerned with their employees only, and labor unions, for the most part, only with their members. Government has the responsibility to serve all members of society. Scholars have analyzed possible political and economic reasons for the reluctant role taken by government. Three areas related to political and economic factors are discussed below: government decision-making processes, the relationship between government and the business community, and the political strength of unions.

Government Decision-Making Processes.   The Constitution of the United States ensures the division of power among all levels of government, business, labor, and political parties (Weir, Orloff, & Skocpol, 1988). Liebig (1993) noted that this was intentional, so that no one group would be in control. For example, political elections are not a winner-take-all political process. Instead, the president often has had to deal with a Congress that is not representative of his or her party. Under conditions of shared power, decisions are more likely to be the result of coalition building (Skocpol, 1995). The interest group(s) with the most power are most likely to get their way. Although family caregiving is a societal issue, it has been perceived as a women's issue (Abel, 1991). Women, subordinate racial or ethnic groups, and those in the lower classes tend to have less political power; thus, government decisions in their favor are limited (Abel, 1991).

Also, as Skocpol (1995) stated, since the United States lacks strong administrative bureaucracies that can reach directly into localities or the economy (the business community), national-level politicians tend to enact programs that rely on a combination of financial incentives and laws to get things done. For example, the federal government uses tax incentives (such as DCAPs) to "bribe" employers and legislative mandates (such as the Family and Medical Leave Act) to "boss" employers around. Since many compromises must be made to win the approval of those sharing power, policies that are approved can be uneven, very complex, and, in some cases, expensive to implement. Exemplifying this are the baffling eligibility restrictions for DCAPs and the dependent care tax credit plan, the unpaid nature of the mandated family leaves, and the exclusion in the Family and Medical Leave Act of small businesses from the requirement to offer leaves (paid or unpaid). All resulted from government compromises with the business community. Interestingly, a report prepared for small businesses indicated that a guaranteed unpaid family leave would not adversely hurt small firms (Bureau of National Affairs, 1991). In this case, the wishes of the employers won out over the needs of employed caregivers.

Thus, to answer, in part, the question of why the government has not implemented policies that would offer more support to employed caregivers, legislative decision-making processes need to be taken into account. Decentralized power and reliance on coalition building make it very difficult for the government, even if it wanted to, to develop coherent and comprehensive family policies that would ensure long-term care services for all, paid family leaves, guaranteed livable wages, and other family-focused benefits.

Employer-Government Relationships. Employers always have resisted union and government efforts to impose employee benefits and work conditions (Skocpol, 1995; Stevens, 1988). A 1994 General Accounting Office report revealed that 80% of private employers with 100 or more employees did not want the federal government to pass laws or develop regulations which would govern company provision of elder care benefits (General Accounting Office, 1994b). Employers prefer voluntary, nonmandated benefits because they can change them at will.

Stevens (1988) argued that the extensiveness of corporate welfare benefits (25% of all social welfare programs) gives employers considerable power in negotiations with unions and the government regarding the social welfare needs of employees. For example, when employers provide work conditions, benefits, and wages competitive with union collective bargaining agreements, they reduce employee demand for unions (Western, 1995). Likewise, employers can and have persuasively argued against government-mandated benefits when these employee benefits already are in place. The business community lobbied heavily against the Family and Medical Leave Act, saying employers did not need government mandates because many companies already voluntarily offered this benefit ("Family and Medical Leave Policy," 1988). Employers' efforts won them several favorable concessions, such as exclusion of paid leaves and the exclusion of small businesses from the unpaid leave requirements of the act. Business also successfully lobbied against President Bill Clinton's 1993 health care reform proposal, which would have required *all* employers to offer a standard health care insurance plan.

In addition to weakening union and government power over business, corporate welfare programs foster employee loyalty (Stevens, 1988). Employees are less likely to change jobs when benefits are not portable. Employees also may join employers in their fight against government mandates. For example, many citizens opposed President Clinton's health care plan, because they already had adequate health coverage and could not see the benefit of government intervention (Skocpol, 1995).

Another way employers gain power is through the establishment of complex networks of providers. For example, employers have turned over elder care programs (e.g., resource and referral services, educational seminars) to for-profit vendors to establish and operate (Lechner & Creedon, 1994). These vendors, in turn, subcontract with local providers (often public and not-for-profit agencies) for these services (Lechner & Creedon, 1994). In the health care arena, many employers contract with management consulting companies, which assist them in contracting with private and not-for-profit health insurance providers. These providers, in turn, subcontract with hospitals and utilization review agencies. These provider networks, emerging from corporate social welfare programs, become extensive and institutionalized. Once corporate social welfare programs are established, it is difficult for citizens, interest groups, and the government to add on to them, change them, or unravel them (Stevens, 1988).

In summary, the business community became involved in the provision of elder care benefits because there was an unmet need. Filling this need helped business meet its economic goals and also meant that the government and unions would be less likely to impose mandatory regulations or agreements. Because of the difficulty of changing established corporate social welfare programs, new government- and union-initiated programs will meet resistance.

Unions.   Several barriers exist which limit unions' influence over national goals. In some countries, unions are political parties; because of this, electoral wins considerably enhance the unions' power in the social policy arena. Although unions in America are closely aligned to the Democratic Party, they do not actually comprise a political party. So, unions, just like any other interest group, must find ways to influence political decisions. Recently, American unions have become more aggressive in influencing electoral wins, particularly for the Democrats, and they have begun speaking out for national concerns, such as raising the minimum wage (Toner, 1996).

The power of the unions also is influenced by the size of their membership: More members mean more power. However, union membership has declined, from 20% of the workforce in 1983 to 14.5% of the workforce in 1996 (U.S. Bureau of Census, U.S. Department of Commerce, 1997). Western (1995) found that, worldwide, decentralized union structures (such as that in the United States) are related to membership declines. Decentralized unions, unable to organize national strikes and to collectively influence macroeconomic policies, are more vulnerable to membership declines during periods of layoffs, stagnant wages, and rising employer power and clout, all of which have been occurring in many economic sectors in the United States. The decline in unions' strength, as measured by declines in membership and by concessions to employers, further increases unions' hesitancy to push for family issues (Moody, 1988). This hesitancy may change with the realization that membership opportunities exist in the service industries and among women in those industries.

Summary.   Support programs in the United States for employed caregivers are based on a strong public and private mix. Employers have played a primary role in the shaping of these benefits. Historical and continued weakness of unions has prevented the emergence of a powerful interest group, which would push for more adequate work conditions, wages, and benefits overall and work-family benefits in particular for *all* working people in the United States (Stevens, 1988).

☐ Future Trends

As noted above, a variety of factors have influenced the development of existing supports for employed caregivers of elders in the United States. These, as well as current situational factors, likely will shape the direction that such supports will take in the future.

Several demographic, social, and labor force trends point to the likelihood of increased support being provided to employed caregivers based on the need for such support. These trends indicate that there will be an increasing demand for informal care, and a decreased availability of informal caregivers (Linsk et al., 1992; Neal et al., 1993). In addition, women—the primary caregivers of elders—are increasingly part of the labor force. Thus, in concert with population changes due to the decreasing fertility rates and the increasing proportion of elderly, the composition of the workforce is changing. The declining number of White males in the labor force will lead to an increasing dependence on women, as well as minority males and immigrants, as sources of labor (Johnston & Packer, 1987). There are, then, clear and growing demographic, social, and economic imperatives for response to the needs of employed caregivers. It seems most likely that this response will come from employers, particularly medium-sized and large employers. Competition for workers, at least in some economic sectors, should result in greater attention on the part of employers to offer family-friendly benefits as recruitment and retention tools. Most likely candidates include the relatively low-cost options, such as resource and referral services, employee assistance (counseling) programs, facilitation of use of federal and state tax credits, and increased flexibility in work schedule and place of work. Some employers are broadening the scope of eligibility for "family" benefits to include domestic partners as well as spouses, but it is unclear how widely this development will spread. A few employers have made available to employees the option to purchase, at group rates, long-term care insurance for themselves and their parents—another example of the broadening definition of family to include members beyond marital or nuclear family relationships.

It is doubtful, however, that many employers will offer paid leaves of absence without a government mandate to do so and, given the difficulty encountered in passing the federal legislation that mandated unpaid leave, such a mandate is not foreseen. Moreover, the reluctance of Americans to pay increased taxes in order to fund additional government-sponsored programs seems intractable. Recent changes in public welfare which limit the amount of time that benefits can be received and require recipients to find work illustrate the continued dominance of the value placed on individualism—the view that people should take care of themselves.

At the same time, there is a burgeoning number of private-sector services aimed at helping families manage their work and family responsibilities. There are agencies that provide resource and referral services, case management services, and convenience services (e.g., preparation and delivery of home-cooked meals, housekeeping services, errand services). New forms of supportive housing for elders, such as assisted living facilities, allow elders to live in their own apartments but with the benefit of meal services, housekeeping, medication management, and home care services. Such arrangements can help to ease some of the burden on employed caregivers. Unfortunately, these various types of private sector services typically are available only to those who can pay privately for them. Thus, employed caregivers with low-paying jobs are unlikely to be able to take advantage of them.

With regard to the future role to be played by labor unions, a variety of factors combine to make it unlikely that leadership in the arena of work-family benefits will be forthcoming from this source. These factors include the decline in membership, unions' decentralized structure, and their primary interest in "bread-and-butter" economic issues rather than social issues.

In sum, demographic, social, and economic trends in the United States point to the need for support for employees with elder care responsibilities. Ideological and political traditions, however, are likely to counterbalance these trends, resulting in essentially the same public and private mix of policies, benefits, and services for the foreseeable future, except for families of considerable economic means, and except for a few additional low-cost options implemented by employers.

☐ References

Abel, E. (1991). *Who cares for the elderly? Public policy and the experiences of adult daughters.* Philadelphia: Temple University Press.

American Association of Retired Persons. (1997). *Family caregiving in the U.S.: Findings from a national survey.* Washington, DC: Author.

Brandes, S. (1976). *American welfare capitalism: 1880–1940.* Chicago: University of Chicago Press.

Brinkley, A. (1995). *New Deal liberalism in recession and war.* New York: Knoff.

Bureau of Labor Management Relations. (1992). *Work and family provisions in major collective bargaining agreements* (Report No. 144). Washington, DC: Author.

Bureau of National Affairs. (1991). *Small business leave policies: Excerpts from a Small Business Administration report* (Report No. 40). Washington, DC: Author.

Clark, P. (1993). Public policy in the United States and Canada: Individualism, familial obligation and collective responsibility in the care of the elderly. In J. Hendricks & C. Rosenthal (Eds.), *The remainder of their days: Domestic policy and older families in the United States and Canada* (pp. 13–49). New York: Garland.

Coberly, S., & Hunt, G. (1995). *The MetLife study of employer costs for working caregivers.* Washington, DC: Washington Business Group on Health.

Commission on Family and Medical Leave & U.S. Women's Bureau. (1996). *A workable balance: A report on family and medical leave policies.* Washington, DC: Commission on leave, Women's Bureau, U.S. Department of Labor.

Costello, A. (1996). Dependent care programs. In J. S. Rosenbloom (Ed.), *The handbook of employee benefits: Design, funding and administration* (4th ed.) (pp. 401–411). Chicago: Irwin.

Crain, M. (1994). Gender and union organizing. *Industrial and Labor Relations Review, 47,* 227–248.

Creedon, M. (1995). Eldercare and work research in the United States. In J. Phillips (Ed.), *Working carers* (pp. 93–115). London: Avebury.

Davis, E., & Krouze, M. (1994). A maturing benefit: Eldercare after a decade. *Employee Benefits Journal, 19*(3), 16–20.

Dunken, H., & Alt, R. (1992). *Impact of federal tax changes on state tax system.* Washington, DC: Federation of Tax Administrators.

Employee Benefit Research Institute. (1990). *Fundamentals of employee benefit programs* (4th ed.). Washington, DC: Author.

Family and medical leave policy. (1988, May). *Congressional Digest. 67*(4), 129–157. Washington DC: Author.

Family and Medical Leave Act of 1993. Pub. L. No. 103-3, 107 Stat. 6–29. (1993).

Foner, P. (1978). *From colonial times to the founding of the American Federation of Labor, Vol. 1.* New York: International Publishers.

Friedland, R. (1995). Medicaid, Medicare. In G. Maddox (Ed.), *The Encyclopedia of aging* (2nd ed., pp. 605–610). New York: Springer.

Galinsky, E., Bond, J., & Friedman, D. (1993). *Highlights: The national study of the changing workforce.* New York: Families and Work Institute.

Galinsky, E., Friedman, D., & Hernandez, C. (with Axel, H.) (1991). *Corporate reference guide to work-family programs.* New York: Families and Work Institute.

Gans, H. (1988). *Middle American individualism.* New York: Oxford University Press.

Garrison, A., & Jelin, M. (1990, October). *The Partnership for Eldercare research study*. New York: New York City Department for the Aging.

Gelfand, D. (1995). Older Americans Act. In G. Maddox (Ed.), *The Encyclopedia of aging* (2nd ed., pp. 706–709). New York: Springer.

General Accounting Office. (1994a). *Support for elder care could benefit the government workplace and the elderly* (GAO/HEHS-94-64). Washington, DC: Author.

General Accounting Office. (1994b). *Private sector elder care could yield multiple benefits* (GAO/HEHS-94-60). Washington, DC: Author.

Gorey, K., Rice, R., & Brice, G. (1992). The prevalence of elder care responsibilities among the workforce population. *Research on Aging, 14*, 399–418.

Gornick, M., Eggers, P., Reilly, T., Mentnech, R., Fitterman, L., Kucken, L., & Vladeck, B. (1996). Effects of race and income on mortality and use of services among Medicare beneficiaries. *New England Journal of Medicine, 335*, 791–799.

Heald, M. (1970). *The social responsibilities of business: Companies and community, 1900–1960*. Cleveland, OH: Case Western Reserve University Press.

Hooyman, N., & Gonyea, J. (1995). *Feminist perspectives on family care: Policies for gender justice*. Thousand Oaks, CA: Sage.

Ingersoll-Dayton, B., Chapman, N., & Neal, M. B. (1990). A program for caregivers in the workplace. *The Gerontologist, 30*, 126–130.

International Labour Office. (1997). *Working papers: Economically active population 1950–2010: Vol. IV. North America*. Geneva: Author.

Jette, A., Smith, K., & McDermott, S. (1996). Quality of Medicare-reimbursed home health care. *The Gerontologist, 36*, 492–501.

Johnston, W. B., & Packer, A. L. (1987). *Workforce 2000: Work and workers for the twenty-first century*. Indianapolis: Hudson Institute.

Kamerman, S. (1983). *Work in America Institute studies in productivity: Vol. 33: Meeting family needs: The corporate response*. New York: Pergamon.

Kamerman, S., & Kahn, A. (1987). *The responsive workplace: Employers and a changing labor force*. New York: Columbia University Press.

Lechner, V. (1993). Racial group responses to work and parent care. *Families in Society: Journal of Contemporary Human Services, 74*, 93–103.

Lechner, V., & Creedon, M. (1994). *Managing work and family life*. New York: Springer.

Lechner, V., & Gupta, C. (1996). Employed caregivers: A four-year follow-up. *Journal of Applied Gerontology, 15*, 102–115.

Liebig, P. (1993). The effects of federalism on policies for care of the aged in Canada and the United States. In S. A. Bass & R. Morris (Eds.), *International perspectives on state and family support for the elderly*. New York: Haworth.

Linsk, N., Keigher, S. , Simon-Rusinowitz, L., & England, S. (1992). *Wages for caring: Compensating family care of the elderly*. New York: Praeger.

Lodge G., & Vogel, E. (Eds). (1987). *Ideology and national competitiveness: An analysis of nine countries*. Boston: Harvard Business School.

Moen, P., Robison, J., & Fields, V. (1994). Women's work and caregiving roles: A life course approach. *Journal of Gerontology: Social Science, 49*, S176–S186.

Moody, K. (1988). An injury to all: The decline of American unionism. London: Verso.

Myers, R. (1995). Social Security. In G. Maddox (Ed.), *The Encyclopedia of aging* (2nd ed., pp. 876–884). New York: Springer.

National Alliance for Caregivers/American Association of Retired Persons. (1989). *Working caregivers report*. Washington, DC: Author.

Neal, M. (1998). Employers' elder care activities in the United States: History and Evolution. In G. Naegele and M. Reichert (Eds.), *Working and Caring: The Situation in Germany, Europe and North America*. Dortmund, Germany: Forschungsgesellschaft für Gerontologic C. V. Institut für Gerontologic.

Neal, M., Chapman, N., Ingersoll-Dayton, B., & Emlen, A. (1993). *Balancing work and caregiving for children, adults, and elders*. Newbury Park, CA: Sage.

Petty, D., and Friss, L. (1987). A balancing act of work and caregiving. *Business and Health, 4*(12), 22–26.

Rosenbloom, J. (1996). The environment of employee benefit plans. In J. S. Rosenbloom (Ed.), *The handbook of employee benefits: Design, funding and administration* (4th ed.) (pp. 3–5). Chicago: Irwin.

Scharlach, A. (1994). Caregiving and employment. *The Gerontologist, 34,* 378–385.

Scharlach, A., Sansom, S., & Stanger, J. (1995). The Family and Medical Leave Act of 1993: How fully is business complying? *California Management Review, 37*(2), 66–79.

Select Committee on Aging, Subcommittee on Human Services. (1987). *Exploding the myths: Caregiving in America* (Committee Publication No. 99–611). Washington, DC: U.S. Government Printing Office.

Skocpol, T. (1995). *Social policy in the United States: Future possibilities in historical perspective.* Princeton, NJ: Princeton University Press.

Social Security Administration. (1995). *Basic facts about Social Security* (SSA Publication No. 05–10080). Washington, DC: Author.

Stevens, B. (1988). Blurring the boundaries: How the federal government has influenced welfare benefits in the private sector. In M. Weir, A. Orloff, & T. Skocpol (Eds.), *The politics of social policy in the United States* (pp. 123–148). Princeton, NJ: Princeton University Press.

Toner, R. (1996, July 17). Battered by labor's ads: Republicans strike back. *The New York Times,* p. A1.

U.S. Bureau of the Census, U.S. Department of Commerce. (1995). *Statistical abstract of the United States: 1995* (115th ed.). Washington, DC: U.S. Government Printing Office.

U.S. Bureau of the Census, U.S. Department of Commerce. (1997). *Statistical abstract of the United States: 1997* (117th ed.). Washington, DC: U.S. Government Printing Office.

U.S. Department of Labor, Bureau of Labor Statistics. (1994). *Employee benefits in medium and large private establishments, 1993* (Bulletin 2456). Washington, DC: Author.

U.S. Department of Labor, Bureau of Labor Statistics. (1996a). *Employee benefits in small private establishments, 1994* (Bulletin 2475). Washington, DC: Author.

U.S. Department of Labor, Bureau of Labor Statistics. (1996b). *Employee benefits in state and local governments, 1994* (Bulletin 2477). Washington, DC: Author.

U.S. Department of Labor, Bureau of Labor Statistics. (1997, December). *Contingent and alternative employment arrangements.* (USDL97–422). Washington, DC: Author.

Vitaliano, P., Scanlan, J., Krenz, C., Schwartz, R., & Marcovina, S. (1996). Psychological distress, caregiving, and metabolic variables. *Journal of Gerontology: Psychological Sciences 51B,* P290–P299.

Wagner, D. L., & Hunt, G. G. (1994). The use of workplace eldercare programs by employed caregivers. *Research on Aging, 16,* 69–84.

Wagner, D. L., & Neal, M. B. (1994). Caregiving and work: Consequences, correlates, and workplace responses. *Educational Gerontology, 20,* 645–663.

Weir, M., Orloff, A., & Skocpol, T. (1988). *The politics of social policy in the United States.* Princeton, NJ: Princeton University Press.

Western, B. (1994). Unionization and labor market institutions in advanced capitalism, 1950–1985. *American Journal of Sociology, 99,* 1314–1341.

Western, B. (1995). A comparative study of working-class disorganization: Union decline in eighteen advanced capitalist countries. *American Sociological Review, 60,* 179–201.

Williamson, J. (1997). A critique of the case for privatizing Social Security. *The Gerontologist, 37,* 561–571.

Wilson, L., Nippes, J., Simson, S., & Mahovich, P. (1993, March). The status of employee caregiver benefits. *Employee Benefits Journal, 18*(1), 10–12.

MORE DEVELOPED COUNTRIES

Ursula Karsch
Corina Karsch

CHAPTER **9**

Migration and Urbanization in Brazil: Implications for Work and Elder Care

☐ Introduction

Brazil is the fifth largest country in the world. It occupies about half of the landmass of South America (Instituto Brasileiro De Georgrafia e Estatística [IBGE], 1993). The country has vast natural resources, including fertile agricultural lands, natural gas, and minerals. The Portuguese colonized Brazil from 1500 to 1822; to this day, the official language is Portuguese. The population is multicultural, consisting primarily of Portuguese and Africans plus millions of persons from southern and eastern Europe, the Middle East, and Japan (Alexander, 1981). A few hundred thousand American Indians still live in the Amazon Valley area.

Brazil's total population is 150 million inhabitants, and it is still growing at a rate of 2% a year (Berquó, 1996). The population is dispersed throughout five main regions: North (7% of total population), Northeast (29%), Southeast (43%), South (15%) and Central West (6%). Most people (75.5%) live in the urban areas, especially the large cities, such as SΔo Paulo, Rio de Janeiro, and Belo Horizonte in the Southeast region (IBGE, 1991).

Brazil's older population is rapidly growing, and women are increasing their commitment to the labor force. Yet, the country has not focused on issues concerning managing work and care of frail elders, nor has it given much attention to issues concerning the aging of its population. Much of Brazil's efforts and resources are dedicated to strengthening its economic base. After World War II, the country experienced many political and economic crises, resulting in spiraling inflation and rising foreign debt. Brazil is a country with a long history of flexibility and openness to outside ideas. Now, it is once again reinventing itself to solve its economic and social problems. Characteristics of a developing nation, however, make these changes more difficult. A large proportion of the population is illiterate, malnourished, and impoverished. It is within this context that the situation of employed persons with caregiving responsibilities for frail elders is analyzed.

This chapter examines the following questions: What is the extent of work-family problems in Brazil? What supports, if any, have work organizations and governmental and nongovernmental organizations put in place to help employed caregivers better manage their dual roles? What factors (e.g., demographic, cultural, historical, political, and economic) have contributed to Brazil's present configuration of supports for employed caregivers and frail elders? What changes in supports are likely to occur in the future?

☐ Work-Family Problems

This section examines data on employment and aging trends, followed by a review of two studies of family caregivers of older persons in Brazil.

Employment and Income Trends of Men and Women

In 1995, 61% of the population 10 years of age and older were economically active; of these, 60.4% were men and 39.6% were women (IBGE, 1995). The labor force participation rate of women age 40 to 60 (a likely age for caregivers to elders) more than doubled from 1980 to 1995; it went from 20.5% to 43% (International Labour Office [ILO], 1997). Present increases in female employment rates are, in part, related to the opening up of the current market economy to female workers (*Revista Veja*, 1994). More women in urban areas are employed than in rural areas. For example, in 1990, 51% of urban women compared to 44.5% of rural women age 40 to 49 were economically active (IBGE, 1993). Unfortunately, data differentiating part-time from full-time workers are not available.

Income.   The income of many workers may not be sufficient to take care of basic necessities, such as food and shelter. In 1990, 78.5% of persons 10 years of age and older earned less than U.S.$260 a month (IBGE, 1993). In this same year, 43% of all households were poor, having incomes amounting to less than twice the cost of a basic basket of food (United Nations Economics Commission for Latin America and the Caribbean, 1996). Inadequate incomes can make it harder for employed caregivers to financially assist family members in need of aid. More adjustments in the physical and social environment, such as improvements in basic sanitation services, greater access to primary health care services, adequate incomes, and more equitable educational and employment opportunities would help employed caregivers better manage their twin roles (IBGE, 1993).

Gender and Rural and Urban Differences in Income.   Men earn more money than women, and persons in urban areas earn more money than those in rural areas. In 1990, 26% of economically active men (10 years of age and older) earned more than U.S.$260 a month, whereas only 14.5% of women earned this amount. In this same year, almost 24% of all urban workers earned less than U.S.$52, whereas, 48% of rural workers earned less than this amount (IBGE, 1990).

Data on incomes since 1991 are not available; however, government interventions in the mid-1990s to stabilize inflation (Plano Real) increased the buying power of the lower classes. The poor now have more money to spend on products and services (*Revista Veja*, 1996). Women still earn less than men do but, hopefully, the gender differences have decreased, along with urban and rural differences.

Regarding Elders

Growth in Number of Elders.   Until the1970s, Brazil had been characterized as a country primarily of young people. Nowadays, the number of younger persons is decreasing, while the number of older persons is increasing. Declines in fertility rates and increases in longevity rates have contributed to this changing picture. In a 30-year period, from 1960 to 1991, the fertility rate dropped 60%, falling from 6.2 to 2.5 (Berquó, 1996). Life expectancy advanced from 38.5 years of age in 1940 to 55.9 years in 1960 (Veras, 1994) and 67 years in 1995 (World Bank, 1997).

Decline in mortality and sizeable reductions in fertility tend to be more marked in urban than in rural areas (Karsch, 1998). The overall life expectancy of elders in the rural areas is less than elders in urban areas; however, great differences in life expectancy are present among rural elders. This difference is related to migration experiences (Karsch, 1998). In the 1960s and 1970s, a considerable number of young persons from rural areas in the North region migrated to the South, where opportunities for higher incomes from employment existed. The youths traveled to metropolitan areas in the Southeast region of Brazil and to the country's capital, Brasília, which was then being built. The generation that migrated to the South region returned to their original hometowns 30 years later. The returnees, now in their fifties, are healthier than their peers who stayed in the rural areas in the North region. The returnees have a longer life span, receive monthly pensions, and practice healthy lifestyles (e.g., exercise, good nutrition) which they developed when they lived in the cities. For those who did not migrate to the cities in their formative years, their life expectancy at birth is about 45 years of age, much less than the national average of 67 years, noted above (Karsch, 1998). The migration movement has highly influenced family structures in some regions of Brazil, particularly the Northeast region.

The number of persons age 60 and older is expected to grow from a projected 14 million in 2000 to 34 million in 2025 (Veras, 1994). Those 80 years of age and older also will increase, during this same time period, from 1.5 million to 3.7 million (Veras, 1994). The number of the aged in both age groups will increase about 145% from 2000 to 2025, profoundly affecting Brazil for years to come. With the decline in the younger population, it is not surprising that the proportion of retired persons to workers will increase. In 1990, the ratio between persons age 65 and older to those 20 to 64 years (working age) was 8 elders to every 100 working age persons. This ratio is projected to be 11:100 in 2010 and 16:100 in 2025 (Kinsella & Taeuber, 1993).

The aging of the population is increasing more rapidly in the urban areas than in the rural areas. This makes aging in Brazil an urban phenomenon, as it is in most developing countries in Latin America. If this trend persists, the projections for the year 2000 assume that 82% of all Brazilian elders will live in the cities (55% of women and 45% of men) (Berquó, 1996).

Increases in Elders Living with Chronic Disabilities.   Changes in the past two decades in the causes of death and morbidity contribute to the rapid increases in life expectancy. Epidemiological transitions have resulted in changes in the leading causes of death from infectious and acute diseases to chronic and degenerative diseases. According to Kalache and Aboderin (1995), "the observed declining trend in case-fatality suggests that one must expect an increase in the prevalence of stroke related disability in the coming decades" (p. 9). Heart and pulmonary diseases and cancer also are on the rise. These chronic conditions contribute to increased fragility, reduced functions, disabilities, impairments, and loss of independence in later years. Older persons today are living longer with chronic conditions, which oftentimes require assistance from others.

Data reveal that, in 1981, 3% of Brazilian men and women age 50 to 59 and 7% of those age 60 and older considered themselves disabled (United Nations, 1993). Information on specific types and severity of disabilities is not available due to the lack of systematic and reliable data reporting and collecting procedures in Brazil. For the same reason, up-to-date disability data are lacking.

Living Arrangements.   The proportion of elderly living alone is increasing, especially for women. The percentage of older women living alone grew from to 9.4% in 1970 to 14.5% in 1989 and, for older men, it increased from 6% to 8% (Berquó, 1996). The decline in the number of elderly living with their children or other relatives explains the increase in the number of elderly living alone (Berquó, 1996). A 1989 study of 1,602 elders (age 60 and over) in the city of São Paulo revealed that 90% of the elders lived with at least one other person: 31% lived with persons of the same generation (mainly spouses); 34% with their children; and 25% lived together with children and grandchildren (Ramos, Santos, Rosa, & Manzochi, 1991). Of the 10% surveyed who lived alone, 8% were women and 2% were men (Ramos et al., 1991).

Two Brazilian studies report on the experiences of persons caring for frail elders. Medeiros (1998) examined the quality of life of 62 caregivers of persons suffering from rheumatoid arthritis. The patients' average age was young, at age 46. Rheumatoid arthritis is a disease that can occur at early ages (including childhood). The average age of the caregivers was 40 years of age; almost all caregivers were women (82%), and the majority worked or studied (61%). The families' average monthly income was U.S.$425. Forty-five percent of the caregivers received informal support from others (e.g., family members, friends, neighbors); only 5% paid someone to take care of the patient. No information was given on the impact of caregiving on caregivers, on managing work and caregiving duties, or on government or workplace supports for the caregivers.

Karsch and Kalache surveyed 102 caregivers of first episode stroke patients, from 1992 to 1995 (Karsch, 1998). The patients and caregivers were followed for 1 year. They received three home visits during the study period. The sample included 14 employed caregivers. The majority of caregivers (87%) were women; 72% of the total sample were 40 years of age and older, although 22% were over age 64. Most of the caregivers were spouses (44%), followed by daughters (31%), daughters-in-law (6%), sons or sons-in-law (6%), other relatives (11%), and friends or neighbors (2%). Female caregivers were most likely to perform personal care tasks (e.g., feeding), whereas male caregivers were most likely to perform instrumental care tasks (e.g., financial assistance).

Almost all of the caregivers lived with the stroke patient; however, two patients lived in a Brazilian slum *(favela)*. Family incomes were low; 63% of the families earned less than U.S.$500 a month and 10% earned less than U.S.$100. In spite of the families' financial situations, they still managed to care for the patients. Assistance from other family members, friends, and neighbors helped make this possible. Most of the patients had regular contact with family members, including siblings, adult children, and grandchildren.

The following vignette highlights the lengths to which an employed caregiver, with limited resources, adapted his life and surroundings to accommodate the disabled relative.

A separated 63-year-old alcoholic stopped drinking and went back home to take care of his 52-year-old wife. He took a job as a bricklayer, earning U.S.$250 a month. Without proper equipment or knowledge of patient care duties, he created his own coping strategies. At first, he bathed his wife in bed and carried her in his arms to the bathroom as needed. Afterward, he began transporting her by putting her feet onto his feet, like they were dancing; he walked backwards with her, taking his wife to the toilet or to any place where she could get some sun.

Impact of Caregiving.   Findings from the study revealed that many (30%) of the caregivers felt emotionally stressed and physically unwell. They complained a lot about the physical efforts needed to perform their roles. In spite of the strains, the caregivers expressed a strong desire to care for their relatives. They also expressed an interest in sharing their experiences with other caregivers and learning new coping strategies from professionals.

The caregivers expressed several reactions to combining work and elder care. Many (42%) of the caregivers who did not work indicated that they would like to work outside the home; however, 24% reported this would not be possible because they needed to look after the patient. The 14 caregivers who were employed complained about difficulties in managing their twin roles; they experienced time and schedule conflicts and increased travel demands to take care of elders. Eight of the 14 caregivers either left their jobs or changed their work schedule in order to have more time to care for their dependent relatives.

Summary and Discussion

Demographic data suggest that an increasing number of Brazilian elders will need assistance in the coming years. Families may be less available, however, to care for frail elders because of their employment commitments. Although, in Brazil, families are responsible for the care of frail elders, little is known about caregivers' experiences. The caregiver studies discussed in this section reveal that many family caregivers would like to work, but their caregiving duties prevent this. Those who manage the twin roles of work and caregiving reported that the severity of time and schedule conflicts necessitated either quitting their jobs or making other work adjustments. Here is an emerging societal problem. How can families meet both their employment and family caregiving responsibilities? Successful accomplishment of these tasks not only is important to families, but to the Brazilian society. Economic productivity and cost-effective elder care are important aspects of Brazil's economic and social development efforts.

☐ Supports for Employed Caregivers and Elders

In this section, government, workplace, and nongovernmental supports for employed caregivers and for elders are discussed. Supports for elders are reviewed because such supports indirectly assist employed caregivers. For example, elders receiving pension benefits will need less financial help from their families. Table 9-1 lists the supports for employed caregivers and their elders.

Employed Caregivers

Little information exists about trade union and workplace initiatives to assist employed caregivers. Some industries or companies might provide assistance, such as

TABLE 9-1. Brazilian supports for employees with elder care responsibilities

Government Initiatives	Nongovernmental Organization Initiatives	Union Initiatives	Workplace Initiatives
For employed caregivers	For employed caregivers	None	Policies: Work scheduling
Sistema Único de Saúde (SUS)	Churches		Flextime, compressed work hours
Social Security system	Indirectly, for older persons		Benefits: Income assistance
Indirectly, for older persons: Local and	Home care programs		Social Security
state initiatives	Nursing homes		Medical care
Medical care	Travel programs		Services
Social assistance			Counseling and support
Home care programs			Educational seminars
Day care programs			Case management services
Community centers			Employee assistance programs (EAPs)
Monthly benefits for the very poor			
Nursing homes			
Activity projects for personal fulfillment			

employee assistance programs, flexible work schedules, and reduced work hours. Nothing is official, however, or government mandated; employee benefits are determined by the internal policy of each work organization. Trade unions have limited their activities to protecting workers affected by technological advancements and structural changes at the workplace, such as downsizing and the hiring of temporary workers. The unions' main concern is job security rather than enhanced benefits, policies, and services for workers with family responsibilities.

Similarly, no formal public policies exist to assist employed caregivers. Although the government is very interested in keeping the elderly in the community with their families, the recent 1996 National Politics of the Elderly legislation does not focus on support strategies to assist caregivers, employed or not. This legislation focuses primarily on providing home care programs for elders (Ministério da Previdência e Assistência Social, Secretaria da Assistência Social [MAPS, SAS], 1996). Community services provided to elders by health care professionals exclude the caregivers. Primary care networks have not developed information and education programs on coping strategies for family caregivers.

Possible reasons for the lack of support to employed caregivers are as follows. First, population aging in Brazil is a recent demographic issue. Government, media, and other influential groups have focused on this issue only in the past 2 to 3 years.

Second, the Brazilian people receive daily information about poverty, abandoned children, malnutrition, violence, and Brazil's inadequate heath care and education system. These concerns have been and still are Brazil's main priorities. Assistance to employed caregivers has not become a central concern.

Third, the Brazilian society perceives the family as the unit responsible for the care of frail elders, regardless of other responsibilities. In this sense, elder care is "hidden" from the public; it is not considered the state's concern because of cultural reasons.

Older Persons

The Brazilian government provides pension coverage to retired workers and health care to all citizens through its Social Security program. Nongovernmental organizations also provide some assistance to elders. These programs are described below.

Old-Age Pension.   In 1975, the National Security and Assistance System was created for the whole country. This system is the main service organization for workers, their dependents, and retired persons. The system collects 18.5% of each worker's monthly salary; employers contribute 10% and employees contribute 8.5% (IBGE, 1993). In rural areas, contributions mainly come from a 2.5% levy on sales of rural products (Maddison and Associates, 1992).

Eligible persons can receive pension benefits in several ways: (a) once they reach a certain age (65 years old for men and 60 years old for women), (b) once a required number of years of employment are completed (35 years for men and 30 years for women), and (c) when a disability prevents an individual from working. In 1992, slightly over 13 million monthly benefits were distributed to persons in the five main regions of Brazil: North, 3.3%; Northeast, 28%; Southeast, 49%; South, 16.5%; and Central West, 5% (IBGE, 1993). In 1992, about 1.7 million (24.8%) of almost 7 million retired workers (urban and rural) received monthly benefits for having worked until the age of 65 (men) and 60 (women) (IBGE, 1993). In 1995, the Social Security program covered 43% of the labor force (IBGE, 1995). The remaining workers were not covered.

Pension benefits vary according to previous earning history, with a minimum of 70 reais (100% of minimum wage in 1994) to a maximum of 583 reais (U.S. Social Security Administration, 1995).

Health Care Services.   The state's duty to guarantee health care to all citizens is stipulated in Articles 197 and 199.1 of the Brazilian Constitution. Health services in Brazil are divided into public and private; both sectors receive financial aid from the government via the Unique Health System (Sistema Único de Saúde [SUS]). SUS, established by the 1988 Constitution, Article 196, helps ensure universal and equal access to health promotion, protection, and rehabilitation services. SUS also performs fiscal and regulatory functions for the health care system, which is decentralized and hierarchic for federal funds that are distributed to the local health authorities in the cities according to need. Health needs are differentiated by age group and by gender. Appropriate interventions for each group are defined and assigned to various health care facilities, from health care centers to hospitals. SUS constitutes the public services network in partnership with private services because federal funds go to both public and private institutions (Ministério da Saúde, 1994).

In Brazil, there are almost 12,000 private hospitals and almost 24,000 public health services that include mainly hospitals (IBGE, 1993). Health services are concentrated in the large urban areas; 36% are located in three major metropolitan areas in the Southeast region: São Paulo, Rio de Janeiro, and Belo Horizonte. The frail elderly are cared for in these urban centers more than anywhere else.

Hospitals are the most expensive and most used health services in the country. In 1992, 33% of hospital stays, paid with public funds, were for terminal and chronic illnesses, such as those frequently found among older persons. The average length of stay was 21 days, including internment for mental disorders (IBGE, 1993).

No data exist on the number of people who have access to nursing homes or other long-term care services. Systematic record keeping and report mechanisms have not been established. Very recently, in order to avoid rehospitalization of persons 60 years of age and older, a few public and private health agencies organized medical, nursing, and physical therapy home assistance services for this age group. The primary reasons were to decrease the length of in-patient stays and to decrease the number of readmissions. In some impoverished zones of Brazilian cities, informal visits to impaired elders are carried out by religious and voluntary organizations.

Recent Legislation

The goals of two recent laws, the 1994 and the 1996 National Politics of the Elderly, are to: (1) improve the coordination of elder care services among all branches of government, (2) strengthen regulations of health care providers, (3) decentralize elder care services to the state and local levels, (4) improve long-term care services, and (5) increase awareness of aging as a societal issue. To address these goals, the Health Ministry's Plan to Integrate Government Actions established the following subgoals: (a) create health prevention and promotion programs; (b) regulate norms of operation at the institutions; (c) include geriatrics as a clinic specialty; (d) regulate current geriatric services; (e) train professionals; (f) increase research on aging; (g) implement policies based on data resulting from the research; and (h) offer alternative services, like home care services.

The ministry's plan consists of creating a system of medical assistance involving long-term hospital care and follow-up by the primary care network. The plan will give discharged elderly patients the right to ambulatory care, local health services, and assistance from home care agencies. Criteria are being established to regulate and decide the placement of elders in day hospitals, day centers, and home care services. The plan has not been in existence long enough for an evaluation of outcomes. It is still being studied and reformulated. The government has increased funding for various elder care services; however, the Health Ministry could cut funds if elder care issues drop in priority.

Local and Small Community Initiatives

Traditionally, a substantial part of social assistance to elders has been provided by nongovernmental organizations. These organizations include churches of all denominations, pensioners' associations, and various advocacy groups concerned with elder care issues. No surveys exist on the number of these organizations, their services, or their effectiveness. Information on local community initiatives for elders has been loosely disseminated through research and conferences.

☐ Strengths and Weaknesses of Supports

There is a growing awareness of aging as a societal issue and the need for the government to become involved in strengthening the coordination and regulation of elder care services. In spite of this strength, several weaknesses exist.

First, no known supports (other than health care) exist for employed persons with elder care duties and, more importantly, the specific situations of employed caregivers are unknown.

Second, the pension and health care services have been criticized because they provide inadequate levels of benefits. In 1991, health care expenditures constituted only 2.9% of the gross domestic product (GDP) (United Nations Economics Commission for Latin America and the Caribbean, 1994). The medical assistance system has been plagued by shortages of hospital beds, material, equipment, and personnel. The media has uncovered many cases of fraud and abuse among the privately contracted services.

Third, low-income workers and elders have fewer supports than higher income persons. A great many low-income insured persons face long waiting lines and very poor service at the government system for health care (Maddison and Associates, 1992). Those who are better off are able to afford private hospital services, physicians, and clinics. They are able to purchase very expensive professional home care support services for their frail or handicapped relatives. Higher income persons probably will continue to obtain elder care services from the private sphere (Maddison and Associates, 1992).

Fourth, data collection methods are inadequate and research on aging is very limited. Such limitations make the development of informed policy decisions less likely. The following are examples of the data-related problems that exist. The demographic census, which is supposed to systematically be done every 10 years, did not occur in 1990 as it should have, but instead in 1991. The official system of death notification is seriously flawed. Frequently, death certificates list only the acute symptoms that led to the death and, commonly, these are denoted as "symptoms not well defined." Chronic diseases are rarely identified. The small amount of available data have not been sufficiently analyzed and interpreted yet. Furthermore, data on the SUS have not been adequately analyzed. Important information is missing, such as expenditures by elders on hospital stays, causes of death in the hospital, diagnosis, and reasons for hospitalization. In 1994, the Health Ministry proposed guidelines for an information policy concerning health indicators for the SUS (Ministério da Saúde, 1994).

Recently, a few scholarly publications on epidemiological transitions and demographic aspects of aging have appeared. Scientific productivity on aging issues, however, still occupies a very "slim" place on the country's research and social planning agenda.

Gerontology, the discipline responsible for the production of knowledge about the aging process and its implications, has not been recognized by the Brazilian national system of science and technology or by the postgraduate programs. Interdisciplinary research on aging as a multifaceted phenomenon is only now emerging.

Research on aging in Brazil is very difficult to conduct because of theoretical deficiencies, difficulties in finding specific data about population needs and services, and inadequate bibliographic references. Data problems weaken the ability of social planners and government officials to evaluate and interpret available data. Information is necessary for the development of social policy programs, such as Social Security and health care. The paucity of health care and aging data impedes thoughtful planning and implementation of elder care services and further increases inequalities in the provision of services to elders and their caregivers (Maia, 1996).

☐ Factors Contributing to Limited Supports for Employed Caregivers and Elders

This section reviews several factors (political, economic, demographic, cultural, historical) that may have contributed to Brazil's limited number of services, policies, and benefits for employed caregivers and for elders.

Political and Economic Factors

Economic and Social Problems.   Brazil has had, and is still dealing with, fairly serious social and economic problems. In 1990, 43% of all households were poor. This number is higher than the 39% average of poor persons for all Latin American countries (United Nations Economics Commission for Latin America and the Caribbean, 1996). In this same year, 19% of the population 15 years of age and older were illiterate, which is higher than that in Argentina at 5% or Chile at 6% (United Nations Economics Commission for Latin America and the Caribbean, 1996). Brazil ranks among the most inequitable societies in the world. In 1995, the wealthiest 10% of the population collected 51.3% of the income, while the poorest 10% received only 0.7%. In the United States, the richest 10% earned 25% of the income (World Bank, 1997).

Severe economic problems have made it very difficult for the country to deal with its numerous social problems. Between 1990 to 1994 the consumer price index increased an average of 1,664% per year, a much higher inflation rate than that of almost all other Latin American countries (United Nations Economics Commission for Latin America and the Caribbean, 1996). Many regions and municipalities have been near bankruptcy, and the federal government is only slightly better (Maddison and Associates, 1992). The state of São Paulo has accumulated a debt of U.S.$36 million

(Maddison and Associates, 1992). The GDP was at −4.4% in 1990 and nearly −1% in 1992, both much lower rates than the averages for all Latin American countries. Fortunately, the GDP has increased since 1993 and, in 1994, was 4%, which was above the Latin American average of 2.8% (United Nations, 1996).

The government has made major revisions to the Constitution in an effort to strengthen the economy; decrease poverty; increase educational levels; and address the social, economic, and health needs of the country's large number of dependent persons. The federal government's current economic and social goals are to: (a) privatize state-owned enterprises (e.g., banks, oil, telecommunications); (b) increase foreign investments; (c) increase state and municipal accountability and responsibility; (d) distribute the tax burden in a more equitable way; and (e) redirect the efforts of government to address social welfare, education, and health issues (Brazilian-American Chamber of Commerce, 1996).

Problems of Brazil's Youth.   Children and adolescents have constantly required the state's attention, with respect to education, medical assistance, and child protection issues (e.g., child abandonment, drugs, and criminal involvement). Despite many efforts by the government and by nongovernmental groups, the social scenery has worsened because the legal and judiciary systems as well as other instruments of social control have made only minor progress in resolving these problems. Although the proportion of the population that comprises persons 15 years of age and younger is declining, the actual number of youths is increasing. From 1980 to 2000, the number of youths is projected to increase 25%, from 45.5 million to 57 million. In order to compete in the global market, Brazil needs a well-educated and healthy workforce with a strong work ethic. Thus, it is likely that the problems of the young will be given a higher priority than the problems of older persons and their employed caregivers.

Costs for Social Security Programs.   Politicians and Social Security administrators are creating a new model of social protection for seniors. Brazil wants to strengthen its economy so that it can attract foreign investments and export products and services at competitive prices. One way to strengthen the economy is to keep government costs as low as possible. State-administered pensions for older persons can be expensive, especially as the number of persons eligible for pensions rapidly increase, as in Brazil. Therefore, the Brazilian government is proposing legislation that will decrease the number of persons eligible for early retirement benefits. Under the new plan, the minimum age for retirement will be raised to age 60 years from age 50 for men who have contributed to the system for 35 years and to age 55 for women who have contributed for 30 years (Project of the Social Assistance and Security Ministry, 1998). Thus, it will take longer for workers to start receiving pensions, and the state will spend less on retirement benefits. As such, one can suppose that, after this change, workers (including employed caregivers) will depend on their salaries for a longer period of time.

Media and Other Interest Group Influence

The media has played an important role in raising the awareness of issues related to elders. In May 1996, the Brazilian press publicized the death of 98 elders in a long-term care institution in the city of Rio de Janeiro. This private institution received U.S.$17 a day/per capita from the Health Ministry. Follow-up investigations conducted by health authorities determined that diarrhea and dehydration from infected food and water caused the deaths. Also, the elders with chronic illnesses were put together with persons with mental disorders and with abandoned children. In June 1996, the Health Ministry closed this facility. It then created a technical commission comprised of doctors, nurses, social workers, and nutritionists. The commission's task is to routinely inspect all long-term care institutions. Meanwhile, the World Health Organization's (WHO) Aging and Health Program in Geneva, together with staff from the ministries, universities, and advocacy groups, organized an international seminar on population aging in Brasília. The purpose of this seminar was to discuss possible intervention programs for the elderly population and to explore the fit between these programs and Brazil's overall social and economic goals. A specific goal of this seminar was to pressure the federal government to support the 1996 National Politics of the Elderly. This goal was reached when the president signed this legislation on July 3, 1996. The authors believe that the well-publicized tragic deaths of the 98 elders, together with the seminar event in the nation's capital, performed an important role and greatly influenced the president's decision to sign the new legislation.

In addition to the efforts of the media and concerned advocacy groups, elders are starting a social movement of their own. For example, the various associations of retired persons are growing and gaining strength. Also, some local politicians have promoted public debates on the problems of the elderly, proposing laws that would benefit elders.

It is important to keep in mind, however, that the aging of the Brazilian population has been compressed into a few decades and has occurred simultaneously with profound social, economic, and cultural changes that do not favor the provision of services, social policies, or other forms of care and support to the elderly or to their informal caregivers.

Trade Unions

Trade unions emerged in Brazil at the beginning of the industrialization process and gained strength from 1930 to 1950. In the 1960s and through the early 1980s, they suffered a retraction because of the military dictatorships (1963–1985). During the dictatorship years, companies gained more control over workers' wages and hiring and firing decisions. As a result, the trade unions lost members because they were unable to effectively bargain for job security and better wages. A recent defeat of the oil workers' strike has furthered weakened the public reputation of unions and particularly the Central Única de Trabalhadores (CUT) (Keller, 1995; Martinez-Lara, 1996).

In addition to the military dictatorships, other external influences have limited the goals of unions (Keller, 1995). During the years of high inflation, the trade unions worked only on balancing the value of wages with currency devaluation. Also, structural changes in production and changes in the labor market, such as the expansion of unemployment and of informal labor relations, have led to a fragmentation of class interests (Keller, 1995). These changes have weakened the capacity of the trade unions to represent the collective interests of the workers. The consequence of the trade unions' loss of force was the development of a bureaucratic syndicalism dependent on the state. The bureaucratic syndicalism is a structure that intermediates workers' and employers' interests according to the federal law (Keller, 1995). Thus, the external pressures described here have prevented unions from negotiating family-friendly benefits for employed caregivers, higher wages for employed persons, and better working conditions for all workers.

Demographic Factors

The growth of the elderly population in Brazil is occurring in all five main regions of the country, but the increases are greatest in the major cities of the Southeast region. For example, 47.6% of all elders (43.7% of men and 56.3% of women) live in the Southeast region alone. This critical mass of elders has raised awareness of the present and future social and financial costs of aging. Thus, politicians and other government officials are beginning to respond to the aging of the population.

The situation of employed caregivers is less pressing. In 1995, 55.8% of women age 15 and older were not attached to the workforce (ILO, 1997). Women not engaged in employment outside of the home are most likely to be available to care for frail elders. Thus, a critical mass of employed persons who also are caregivers probably has not yet been reached. With the declining birth rate, demographers anticipate that the women's employment rate will continue to increase as it has done in other industrialized countries (Maddison and Associates, 1992). As Brazil positions itself to become stronger economically, more women may be needed to increase productivity output rates. Of course, another scenario is that technological advances and corporate downsizing will limit employment opportunities and increase unemployment. However, it is expected that, with the relatively low urban unemployment rate of 5.6% in 1993, women workers will be in demand in the cities (United Nations Economics Commission for Latin America and the Caribbean, 1994). Already, it is in the urban areas where a high number of economically active women reside. Their labor force participation rate increased 9% from 1970 to 1980 (IBGE, 1993). Because elders also have gravitated to the cities, these employed persons will be geographically close enough to provide family care to frail elders.

The authors believe that those families with increased employment responsibilities will need assistance as they combine work and elder care duties. This is particularly true of persons born in the 1940s and 1950s. They have been steadily increasing their employment commitment at the same time that elders have been living longer, many with increased frailties. Eventually, younger cohorts also will face this situation.

Cultural and Historical Factors

Another factor affecting private and public sector responses to employed caregivers, and the elders they care for, concerns the role of women in the Brazilian society. Industrialization in the 1880s brought about a number of changes; however, changes in women's roles effectively began only in the past two decades. Up until the 1970s, when influenced by the women's liberation movements abroad, women were socially designated to the roles of mother and housewife, and very rarely worked outside of their homes. Moreover, only a few women had the opportunity to go to school because of the limited number of educational institutions. They also were exposed to social pressures to remain in the home. They were brought up to submit to their parents, husbands, and children, and to take care of the house. In fact, they were not given the right to vote until 1932. Thus, it is not surprising that the rate of education of women age 65 and older was only 35% in 1960. It reached 41% in 1980, and 53% in 1993 (Berquó, 1996). Consequently, many elders, particularly women, are exposed to difficulties related to their lack of education, such as lack of awareness of their rights.

As stated above, women are the main caregivers in Brazil. Neri (1993), the first author to investigate the roles of caregivers in Brazil, noted that providing aid to frail elders is considered a normative family role that is part of the family life cycle.

Caregiving is especially expected of married woman, daughters, eldest daughters-in-law, and single and widowed daughters. Undoubtedly, the societal expectation that females care for dependent family members retards the seeking of solutions to assist busy caregivers. The study by Karsch and Kalache (1995) found that only 13 of the 102 caregivers studied were men (5 husbands, 5 sons, and 3 brothers or brothers-in-law). It still primarily is the responsibility of women to deal with the difficulties of combining paid work and care for elders.

☐ Future Trends

In the near future, it is unlikely that employed caregiver issues will emerge as important workplace or government policy concerns. Brazil's numerous social and economic problems will have the greatest priority. Elder care issues are gaining some attention and support, however, so it is possible that employed caregivers will benefit indirectly from enhanced services for elders, such as the provision of affordable home care assistance. On the other hand, reductions in pension payouts and increases in costs for health care and social services most likely will expand employed caregivers' financial responsibilities to their frail relatives.

The authors hope and expect that the Brazilian society will become more and more aware of the aging process, its implications, and its consequences. Aging is the country's only problem that is not specific to a particular social class, ethnic group, or other cultural group. Data show that both the rich and the poor are getting older in Brazil and becoming dependent on others. They require special attention for their health care and autonomy needs.

Some evidence exists that allows the authors to think that a gradual movement toward awareness of aging concerns is happening among citizens, advocacy groups, scholars, researchers, and government officials. Although the evidence is weak and recent, examples include:

- the emergence of aging research and theory building in universities and other survey centers, along with the addition of new courses in gerontology and geriatric services;
- the appearance of different forms of advocacy instigated by international organizations like WHO and the Pan-American Health Organization of Washington, DC;
- the development of educational programs and political support at the local level for the development of human services and other resources to assist elders;
- the rebuilding of the Social Security system and the creation of programs that help elders prepare for retirement;
- an increase in national and international nongovernmental organizations that promote cultural attention and social assistance to aging issues; and
- a new image of elders in the media, which shows them actively engaged in their social environment. The media message also encourages families to keep elders occupied for longer periods of time.

It is important to underscore that the government cautiously will increase benefits and services for seniors. This is due, in part, to economic, but also cultural, reasons. The government still will emit the "subsidiarity" principle in which interventions at the highest level (federal government interventions) are of secondary importance to the obligations of smaller units (e.g., family and community). The subsidiarity of state principle is based on the view of society in which responsibilities are conditioned by the closeness of people's relationships. Interventions at higher levels of society have to be seen as subsidiary to the smaller social units (Spicker, 1991).

The concentration of elders in the cities suggests that most interventions, such as social policies and programs on behalf of elders, will occur in the cities rather than in the rural areas. Also contributing to this is the fact that medical care is more advanced in the cities than in the rural areas. Furthermore, the per capita income is higher, work conditions are better, and the infrastructure (e.g., transportation, communication, public services, water supply, electricity) are more developed in the cities than in the rural areas. Overall, the cities allow for better living conditions for impaired elders.

What will happen to rural elders and their caregivers is less clear. Will their needs be recognized? Historically, the less well off have received smaller shares of limited resources. Also geographic distances between towns may make it harder to provide support services. On the other hand, there may be a trickle-down effect. That is, rural elders may benefit, at least, from the increased awareness of aging issues brought about by urban elders.

Considering the higher life expectancy for women than for men, the fact that elderly women in Brazil are more likely than men to live in urban centers appears to be related to the reality that women at advanced ages are more likely to have chronic illnesses. Urban homes may give older women, (especially, widows) proximity to their children and to specialized health and social services, like in many developed and developing countries (Kinsella & Taeuber, 1993).

Aging well in Brazil does not depend solely on the individual, but on the solidarity coming from the family and others in society. The authors believe that the media has a special responsibility to construct a picture of the elderly as ordinary citizens, not as poor souls. Aging as a process represents new demands for the Brazilian society, which require that the state develop aid and support through benefits and services for the solidarity of the society. The beginning of the twenty-first century will find Brazil with 8.7 million people age 65 and older, which means 1 in every 20 Brazilians will be elderly, a proportion that will increase gradually over the years, reaching 1 elder for every 13 Brazilians in 2015 (Berquó, 1996). This perspective illustrates the challenge that faces the country.

Frail elders are typically cared for by Brazilian women. Future caregivers probably will be women in their fifties and sixties who will be working outside the home. Support policies and services need to be implemented to help employed caregivers manage their dual responsibilities. In the absence of workplace and government supports, employed caregivers with the heaviest demands may need either to quit their jobs or to place their elders in nursing homes. Workplace and government supports could help avoid unnecessary job cessation and other unwanted outcomes among the caregivers. Supports also would help avoid unnecessary nursing home placements.

☐ References

Alexander, R. (1981). Brazil. In A. Blum (Ed.), *International handbook of industrial relations: Contemporary developments and research* (pp. 49–70). Westport, CT: Greenwood Press.

Berquó, E. (1996). Algumas considerações demográficas sobre o envelhecimento da população no Brasil [Some demographic considerations about the Brazilian population aging process]. In *Anais do I Seminário Internacional do Envelhecimento Populacional: Uma agenda para o final do século* (pp. 16–34). Brasília: MPAS, SAS.

Brazilian-American Chamber of Commerce. (1996). *Business review directory*. New York: Author.

Instituto Brasileiro De Geografia e Estatística. (1990). *Anuário estatístico do Brasil* [Brazilian statistic yearbook]. Rio de Janeiro: Author.
Instituto Brasileiro De Geografia e Estatística. (1991). *Anuário estatístico do Brasil* [Brazilian statistic yearbook]. Rio de Janeiro: Author.
Instituto Brasileiro De Geografia e Estatística. (1993). *Anuário estatístico do Brasil* [Brazilian statistic yearbook]. Rio de Janeiro: Author.
Instituto Brasileiro De Geografia e Estatística. (1995). *Anuário estatístico do Brasil* [Brazilian Statistic yearbook]. Rio de Janeiro: Author.
International Labour Office. (1997). *Economically active population: 1959–2012: Vol. III.* Latin America (3rd ed.). Geneva, Switzerland: Author.
Kalache, A., & Aboderin, I. (1995). Stroke: The global burden. *Health Policy and Planning, 10*(1), 1–21.
Karsch, U. (1998). *Envelhecimento com dependencia: Revelando cuidadores* [Aging in dependence: Revealing homecarers]. Catholic University of São Paulo: EDUC/Novartis.
Keller, W. (1995). Neocorporativismo e trabalho: A experiência Brasileira recente [Neocorporativism and work: The recent Brazilian experience]. *São Paulo em Perspectiva, 9*(4), 73–83.
Kinsella, K., & Taeuber, C. (1993, February). *An aging world. II.* (International Population Reports P95/92-3, (p. 43). U.S. Bureau of the Census, U.S. Department of Commerce. Washington, DC: U.S. Government Printing Office.
Maddison, A. and Associates. (1992). *The political economy of poverty, equity, and growth: Brazil and Mexico, A World Bank comparative study.* Oxford: Oxford University Press.
Maia, R. (1996). *O processo de envelhecimento como campo de investigação* [The aging process as a field of investigation]. In *Anais do I Seminário Internacional Envelhecimento Populacional: uma agenda para o final do século,* (pp. 71–76). Brasilia, D.F., Brazil: MPAS, SAS.
Martinez-Lara, J. (1996). *Building democracy in Brazil: The politics of constitutional change, 1985–95.* New York: St. Martin's Press.
Medeiros, M. (1998). *Impacto da doença e qualidade de vida dos cuidadores primários de pacientes com artrite reumatóide: adaptação cultural e validação do caregiver burden scale.* [Impact of disease and life quality of primary caregivers of patients with rheumatoid arthritis: Cultural adaptations and validation of the caregiver burden scale]. Unpublished doctoral dissertation, Escola Paulista de Medicina, São Paulo.
Ministério da Previdência e Assistência Social, Secretaria da Assistência Social. (1996, July). Política nacional do idoso: Perspectiva governamental. [National politics of the elderly: Government perspective]. In *Seminário internacional, Envelhecimento Populacional: Uma Agenda para o Final do Século.* Brasilia, D.F., Brazil: Author.
Ministério da Saúde. (1994). *Uso e disseminação de informações em saúde; Subsídios para a elaboração de uma política de informações para o SUS.* Relatório final [Use and dissemination of health information; Subsidies to the elaboration of an information politics for SUS. Final report]. Rio de Janeiro: ABRASCO.
Neri, A. (1993). *Qualidade de vida e idade madura* [Quality of life and mature age]. Campinas, São Paulo: Papirus.
Project of the Social Assistance and Security Ministry. (1998). Voted on by the National Congress in March 1998. Folha de São Paulo, January 15, 1998.
Ramos, L., Santos, C.A., Rosa, T., & Manzochi, L. (1991). Perfil dos idosos residentes na comunidade no município de São Paulo, segundo o tipo de domicílio: O papel dos domicílios multigeracionais [Profile of elder residents of São Paulo's urban community according to type of domicile: The role of multigeneration homes]. In *A população idosa e o apoio familiar. Informe demográfico no. 24* (pp. 11–86). São Paulo: SEADE.
Revista Veja. (1994, August–September). [Special issue on women]. p. 12.
Revista Veja. (1996, December 18). Year 29, No. 51, p. 50.
Spicker, P. (1991). The principle of subsidiarity and the social policy of the European Community. *Journal of European Social Policy, 1*(1), 2–14.
United Nations. (1993). *The demographic yearbook—Special issue: Population/ageing and the situation of elderly persons* (p. 460). New York: Author.

United Nations Economics Commission for Latin America and the Caribbean. (1994). *Statistical yearbook for Latin America and the Caribbean, 1993.* New York: Author.

United Nations Economics Commission for Latin America and the Caribbean. (1996). *Statistical yearbook for Latin America and the Caribbean, 1995.* New York: Author.

U.S. Social Security Administration. (1995). *Social security programs around the world.* Washington, DC: U.S. Government Printing Office.

Veras, R. (1994). *País jovem de cabelos brancos: A saúde do idoso no Brasil* [A young country with white hair: The health of the elderly in Brazil]. Rio de Janeiro: Relume Dumará.

World Bank. (1997). *World Bank development report 1997: The state in a changing world.* New York: Oxford University Press.

CHAPTER

Raquel Bialik

Urbanization in Mexico Affects Traditional Family Caregiving of the Elderly

☐ Introduction

Mexico, a country of over 90 million inhabitants, has one of the fastest growing aged populations in the world (U.S. Bureau of the Census, U.S. Department of Commerce, 1991). It also is experiencing a growth in the number of women entering the paid workforce. With these changes, families may be less available to care for the growing number of elderly. This chapter examines, for the first time, issues related to managing work and the care of frail elders. Government, workplace, and community supports for elders as well as for employed persons are investigated to gain some knowledge of the current level of support, outside of family, that is available to employed caregivers. These supports are then evaluated. In an effort to understand Mexico's particular configuration of supports, various contributing factors are examined, such as social and economic factors. Having summarized the level of current supports and explored possible reasons for them, the chapter ends with a projection of future trends.

☐ Work-Family Problems

No known studies exist on the impact of managing employment and the care of frail relatives on employed persons, elders, work organizations, or society as a whole in Mexico. This topic has received no academic, media, or political attention. One possible reason is simply a lack of awareness of these issues. Another possibility is that other social and economic problems overshadow those of employed caregivers. The third possible reason is cultural; basically, caring for elders, regardless of employment status, is seen as the duty of the family. Findings from caregiver studies suggest that there is no specific policy to favor caregivers of the old, because this is done inherently as a task within each family (Montes de Oca, 1995).

Although data are lacking on employed caregivers, several related topics are discussed in the hope of shedding light on issues related to managing work and family duties. First, employment and aging patterns are reviewed, and then the relationship between job conditions and caregiving is explored.

Employment Patterns of Men and Women

Although fewer Mexican women work outside the home than women in many other nations, the National Work-Force Surveys (1988, 1991, 1993, 1995) have demonstrated a steady increase of women in economic activities (21% in 1979, 31% in 1989, and 33% in 1993). In 1995, 37% of women 40 to 60 years old were employed (International Labour Office [ILO], 1996). This is the group who would most likely be caregivers, at least as determined by data from more developed countries. Employment figures for males indicate that 93% of men 40 to 60 years old were employed in 1995 (ILO, 1996).

A large percentage of working women (62%) are involved in "dual work," while only 18% of working men are involved in domestic chores (National Work-Force Survey, 1993).

According to the 1996 National Work-Force Survey (1996), 50% of all employed women work full time (40 hours per week or more) and the others work part time: 18% work 24 to 39 hours a week; 20% work between 15 and 23 hours a week, and 12% labor less than 15 hours per week. This survey also reports that 60% of the almost 11.5 million employed women are employed in the informal sector, where they receive no benefits at all (e.g., Social Security, paid vacations, health insurance, and health care services).

Elderly Population

The population age 65 and older, at present, is a little over 6 million, with women outnumbering men, 55% and 45%, respectively. Seventy percent of all elders live in urban areas; however, men are more likely than women to live in rural areas. In 1995, persons 60 to 64 years old comprised 2.5% of the population, those age 65 to 74 comprised 2.7%, and those age 75 and older comprised 2% (National Work-Force Survey, 1995).

The elderly population is projected to grow to 7 million by the year 2000 and to 17 million by 2030 (Sepúlveda, 1994). By 2030, the aged will comprise 12.3% of the total Mexican population (Ham, 1993).

The number of younger persons available to help care for the elderly is diminishing, as in most other nations. The birthrate has declined to 30 births per 1,000. Whereas youngsters (15 years of age or younger) represented 39% of the population in 1990, they are expected to become less than 30% in 2010 (Bialik, 1992).

Health Status.   Although the health status of Mexicans has improved throughout the years, Mexico still presents a dichotomized health profile. On the one hand, it has the characteristics of underdeveloped countries: 40% of its infant population has some degree of malnutrition (2% of which is severe). Epidemics in the past 20 years (e.g., measles, malaria, equine encephalitis, typhoid fever, dengue melindre) have resulted from an unhealthy environment and inadequate public health services (drinking water, drainage, and very poor health education). On the other hand, like developed countries, Mexico has seen an increase in chronic degenerative diseases (62% of the total deaths), accidents, and neoplasias.

The main cause of old age disability for Mexicans is some type of chronic degenerative disease, which increases with age: among those 60 to 69 years old, 38% had some type of chronic condition; among those 70 to 79, 45%; and for those age 80 and older, 46.5% (Sepúlveda, 1994). These diseases result in limiting the elder's daily activities. Partial as well as total limitations of daily activities increase with age and affect 12.5% of males and 8% of females. The overall distribution of limitations due to disability is: 20% for those age 80 and older (10.4% with total limitation), 11.5% for persons age 70 to 79 (5% total limitation), and 7% for those age 60 to 69 years of age (2.5% total limitation). The other two main causes of old age disability are accidents (mainly, falls) and violence (Sepúlveda, 1994). Sixty percent of all falls occur among the elderly, with a 7:2 ratio between women and men. Falls limit mobility and cause loss of independence (Sepúlveda, 1994).

Living Arrangements.   In a study of 770 elderly women, Bialik (1989) found that 34% of the women in urban areas lived with their daughters or sons (compared to 40% among the rural aged population), 23% of those in urban areas lived in institutions (compared to 7% of the rural elders), while 13% of both groups lived alone. According to Montes de Oca (1995), 86% of males who are 65 years of age and older are household heads, compared to 35.8% of females. It is interesting to note that 34% of women age 65 and older live in extended households of a relative, while only 12% of males have such arrangements.

It is a fact that the elderly are dependent on their families, but it also is true that they (particularly, elderly women) take care of their grandchildren and perform household chores for their working children (especially, their daughters) (Garcia, 1988).

Managing Work and Elder Care

Although most men and many women work, their incomes and benefits, for many, are insufficient to adequately support themselves and their family members. The minimum actual average wage was U.S.$93 monthly in 1997. Thirty percent of those in the workforce actually are underemployed and in very precarious conditions, especially women, the very young, and the working elderly (Parker & Pacheco, 1995). Inadequate incomes may make it harder for family members to provide financial, emotional, and concrete (e.g., personal care, shopping) assistance to elders. For this reason, it is necessary to understand the relationship between employment, income, and benefits.

The Mexican workforce consists of the formal and the informal sectors (Jusidman, 1993). The term *informal sector* was first mentioned in 1971 by anthropologist Keith Hart of the Institute of Development Studies at Sussex University (Jusidman, 1993). In his study of occupations in Ghana, he identified the formal labor sector with paid work and benefits and the informal sector with several other characteristics. Workplaces in the informal sector usually are small, unregulated, family-owned facilities that depend on local resources and simplified technology. Jobs in this sector are easy to access because working abilities are acquired by experience outside the formal educational system. Hours of employment will depend on the needs of the employer and thus can be flexible and unpredictable. The informal sector is a cheap and useful alternative for the consumer. It also guarantees the survival of the family group, because the informal sector can absorb the surplus manpower in an urban setting that cannot be absorbed otherwise. Work in this sector is a subsistence strategy (not cumulative), because it does not provide for future needs, and consumption is for immediate coping. Benefits (e.g., medical care, paid vacations, retirement pensions, loans) are not provided in this sector, whereas they are in the formal sector. Wages are low (less than half of wages in the formal sector). More women than men and those with very low schooling, particularly the young and the old, work in the informal sector (Garcia, Muñoz, & de Oliveira, 1982).

The informal sector is growing more and more, now representing 38% of the working population. It contributed nearly 11% of the gross internal product in the 1990s. Ninety-five percent of informal businesses have two or fewer workers, and 50% operate in private places (their own or their clients'). Prices are set according to what others charge for similar services (Jusidman, 1993). If income distribution remains unaltered, Mexico will need to increase its economic development to 9% during the next two decades; only in this way will it be able to satisfy the basic needs of its lower strata. A typical household will need an average income of two to three times the minimum wage (which, at present is U.S.$3 a day), in order to provide for the needs of its members (Jusidman & Eternod, 1994).

While the informal sector has benefits to the overall Mexican economy, the low wages and the lack of benefits for employees in this sector strain families' abilities to care for themselves financially. Families struggling to survive may find it more difficult to help their elders with their everyday needs.

Men and women tend to be segregated into different occupations; women are more likely to be in manufacturing jobs, such as textiles and the *maquiladora* (in bond) industries, while men are in commerce and service (Garcia, Blanco, & Pacheco, in press). Male-dominated jobs pay higher wages than female jobs, and jobs in the formal sector, overall, pay men twice as much as women.

☐ Supports for Employed Caregivers and Elders

Employed Caregivers

Mexican work organizations and the government have not developed any policies, benefits, or services targeted to employees who care for frail elders. Some programs, however, have been developed to assist employees with infants, such as the establishment of nurseries and the provision of medical assistance (Montes de Oca, 1995). Employers pay 1% of payroll, up to a ceiling of 25 times the minimum wage, for the child day care program (U.S. Social Security Administration, 1995).

The author interviewed 12 program staff and decision makers of the Mexican Institute of Social Security (IMSS) and the Employment Ministry, and 12 top researchers from El Colegio de Mexico and the National University. After extensive research, only three government programs were identified that assist unemployed persons with dependent care responsibilities. These programs were not developed for persons with elder care duties, but they can be used by them. Since 1984, unemployed workers (age 18 to 55) who have dependents under their care have job placement priority over other unemployed persons. Also, they can enter into a "scholarship program" where they receive the minimum wage (at present, U.S.$90 monthly). Finally, they can receive free transportation and 3 to 6 months training in trades that are in demand in the marketplace. About 500,000 scholarships are provided yearly.

Supports for Elders

Besides the family, which traditionally has been responsible for the care of its elderly, there coexist in Mexico several types of government, workplace, and community supports for people 60 years of age and older. These include pensions, pre- and postretirement programs, health care, long-term care, social services, and advocacy services.

Pension System.   The two main government institutions that provide pensions to retired workers are IMSS, which covers most workers, and the Institute of Social Security and Services for Civil Servants (ISSSTE), which serves state employees. Together, the IMSS and the ISSSTE provide coverage to 60% of the economically active population (*Presidential Annual Report,* 1995). The term "economically active" does not include those looking for work, those who are partially employed, or those in nonformal work. When those persons are included, coverage amounts to only 12% of the total urban population and 3% of the rural population (*Presidential Annual Report,* 1995).

The government pension system is financed through mandatory employer and employee contributions. A chronological review of the amount of this pension shows how it has increased throughout the decades, but also demonstrates the insufficiency of this pension for economic independence. In 1940, the pension amounted to 33% of the minimum general salary (mgs); from 1944 to 1988, it varied between 27% and 33% mgs; in 1989, 70% mgs; in 1991, 80% mgs; in 1993, 90% mgs; in 1994, 95% mgs; and, in 1995 to 1996, 100% of the mgs, which, as mentioned above, amounts to U.S.$90 a month (Mexican Institute of Social Security [IMSS], 1995). Throughout the 90s, to date, there have been a million and a half pensioners (in 1994, 318,161 pensioned widows). If a worker dies before reaching retirement age, the ascendants (parents, grandparents) may inherit 20% of the pension if the deceased worker has no widow, concubine, or orphans (General Law of the Social Security, Article 137, 1994).

In addition to the government system, there is a complementary system of pensions, the Mexican savings system for retirement (Seguro de Ahorra para el Retiro [SAR] and Ahorro para el Fondo del Retiro [AFORES]). These programs are administered for each individual by private banks. The complementary system is mandatory; monthly deductions are taken from the worker's paycheck. Thus, the worker has two pension plans; one through the government and the other through the private sector.

Pre- and Postretirement Programs Offered by Work Organizations.
One year prior to retirement, workplaces in the formal sector offer preretirement programs for the worker and his or her family to help prepare the worker for a more integral retirement. Legal, psychological, social, and biological aspects of aging are discussed. And, after retirement, there is a network of places (day care centers) and productive activities and cooperatives (of 10 or more people) where the retired elder can socialize and feel useful.

IMSS commenced, in the workplace, a program called Decalogue, designed to enhance older persons' self-esteem (IMSS, 1994). Through bulletins and other forms of mass media communications, the following messages are relayed: (1) pay attention to your daily appearance, (2) keep alive your love toward life, (3) cherish physical exercise, (4) accept yourself with dignity, (5) talk about your age with pride and respect, (6) cultivate optimism above anything else, (7) be useful to yourself, (8) work with your hands and your mind, (9) keep alive and cordial human relationships, and (10) live the moment. . . . the present is yours too.

Medical Care.   Private and public health care services are available in Mexico. The public medical program is financed by employee, employer, and government contributions. The government not only administers the public program, it operates its own hospitals, clinics, pharmacies, and other medical facilities (U.S. Social Security Administration, 1995). According to the latest National Health Survey, 40.5% of people age 60 and older make use of private medical facilities, 31% use the public social security facilities, and 10% use the services of the public government sector. Overall, more older women than men use health services: 59% to 41% (Sepúlveda, 1994). Government expenditures per capita on health care, by client group, are very uneven: In 1983, U.S.$3,000 was spent on state employees, U.S.$1,829 on nonstate insured workers, and U.S.$169 on uninsured workers (Maddison and Associates, 1992).

Geriatrics and gerontology are still young disciplines and are neither well developed nor popular. There were only 87 certified geriatricians in 1992. Geriatric services are found only in Mexico City, in six general hospitals. (Thirty percent of hospital beds are occupied by people age 60 and older, with a median hospital stay of 21 days.) Only two to three geriatricians attend 1,000 elderly a year. Twenty percent of all outpatient consultations are for persons 60 years of age and older.

Long-Term Care Services and Social Services.   Numerous government programs provide assistance to older persons. One program consists of public institutions for the "open population" (e.g., those without Social Security benefits). Another program is the National System of Integral Development of the Family (DIF). This program includes 37 nursing homes that provide assisted living; food; integral medical, rehabilitation, and psychological assistance; occupational, cultural, and recreational therapies; and a specialized service for terminally ill patients. A third program is the National Institute for the Aged (Instituto Nacional de la Senectud [INSEN]), which has over 1 million affiliates. This program provides economic assistance programs, such as discounts for transportation, medical services, pharmaceuticals, basic need articles, and laundry. INSEN also provides day care centers and seven nursing homes. The fourth program, the department that governs Mexico City (Departmento del Distrito Federal [DDF]) provides four nursing homes and assistance centers. A fifth program, the National Institute for Adult Education (Instituto Nacional de Educación para Adultos [INEA]), assisted 166,598 elderly in 1995 in three educational programs, teaching them to read and write, providing elementary education, and providing informal training for jobs. Last, the Program for Retired Teachers provided 6,000 retired teachers with economic assistance for their help and involvement in cultural and community activities.

In addition to the numerous public programs, several community or private institutions offer assistance. A representative sample includes: (1) the Junta de Asistencia Privada (JAP) which groups 66% of all the associations that assist the elderly (e.g., foundations, 30 nursing homes), (2) philanthropic organizations (like the Lions and Rotary Clubs), (3) nongovernmental organizations, (4) self-support groups, and (5) other voluntary associations (vide infra).

As to specific institutions, there are private nursing homes for the elderly that are financed by wills and foundation funds (like the Dr. Ignacio Medina Lima and the Antonio Haghenbeck for elderly persons with sight problems). Religious orders, like the San Vincent Foundation and the Mexican Association of Malta, promote family participation and intergenerational communication.

Universities, especially private ones (like the Panamerican University, the Universidad Iberoamericana, and the Tecnológico de Monterrey) have implemented extension programs where students assist elderly nursing homes residents. Students are guided in organizing and participating in activities that make the elderly feel cared for and wanted.

Advocacy Services.   More and more nongovernmental organizations, like Project Light, have become active in the media, not only nationally, but internationally. This organization sponsored May 28 as the "day of the old old" (defined as persons age 80 and older). The goal was to promote elders' personal development within their families and the community, without isolating them. At present, August is the month of the elderly, where activities are concentrated to remind society of elders' civil rights and care needs.

Recently, other initiatives have been developed, such as LOCATEL. This program, in operation since 1996, provides an emergency telephone number to report and help locate lost elderly. Local committees, called the Third Age, have organized in the 16 precincts of Mexico City to act as an official channel for conveying needs and solutions related to elders. And, the program, Adopt a Granny, was initiated to promote the civil society to visit and help take care of the elderly in public nursing homes.

Summary.   As shown in Table 10-1, the work environment, government, and private sector responses described in this section indirectly help employed caregivers through their assistance to elders. Elders with sufficient incomes, medical care, and social services will be less dependent on their younger relatives to assist them. In one way or another, these policies, services, and benefits help take care of the biological, psychological, social, cultural, and recreational needs of the old. They also extend programs to family members and to society in general (educational, integrative, sensitizing, and elevating the self-esteem of this segment). The responsibilities of the family are never usurped, however. In Mexico, government policies toward elder care have emphasized family responsibility to keep the elderly in their homes, in the midst of the family, and their own milieu.

☐   Strengths and Weaknesses of Supports

Essentially no programs exist to directly help employed persons with caregiving duties. Along with this, many employed caregivers are underemployed or receive very low wages. Mexico's economy will need to grow substantially in the coming years in order to increase current wages and to create enough jobs for those willing and able to work.

Elders and caregivers of the indigenous population (the Indians of Mexico) receive fewer governmental and workplace services than the rest of the Mexican population. For this reason, elders, within the indigenous population, rely almost totally on their extended families for assistance.

Among elders with various benefits and services, an uneven distribution is present. Many retirees, particularly those who were in the informal sector, have no Social Security benefits. Even among those who are covered, inequalities exist. For example, state employees have much better health coverage and higher paying pension plans (through the ISSSTE) than employees in other jobs that provide Social Security insurance. (i.e., through the IMSS)

TABLE 10-1. Mexico's supports for employees with elder care responsibilities

Government Initiatives	Nongovernmental Organization Initiatives	Union Initiatives	Workplace Initiatives
For employed caregivers Unemployed workers' job placement, scholarship, and training programs Indirectly, for older persons Social Security pension, medical care, and long-term care programs	For employed caregivers None Indirectly for older persons Private pension plan Economic assistance Counseling and support groups Nursing homes Advocacy	For employed caregivers None specific to caregivers Indirectly, for older persons Negotiations for better retirement benefits	For employed caregivers None Indirectly for employed caregivers Pre- and postretirement programs that include family members

A total of just U.S.$64 per capita is spent yearly for health, representing 2 to 5% of the national gross product. Only 15% of total health care costs goes for prevention. Since the beginning of the 1980s, there has been a reduction in health expenditures in Mexico (Sepúlveda, 1994). Such reductions probably have adverse effects on access to and the quality of health care that employed persons and elders alike receive.

On a positive note, Mexico's combined public sector and mandatory private sector retirement savings plans may help reduce the costs to government of retirement benefits. Savings from these programs could be used for economic and social programs of benefit to elders and their employed caregivers. Mexico's public and private mix is a model that several advanced nations, concerned with rising retirement costs, are only now exploring.

Although employed caregivers have no workplace benefits, a mechanism exists which could be adopted for this group. Presently, the government has mandated employers to contribute 1% of payroll to help fund child care services. This mechanism could be used to help finance elder care programs if such services become a priority in Mexico.

☐ Factors Contributing to Strengths and Weaknesses of Supports

Although Mexico has had a strong ideological commitment to government support for the income, health care, and social needs of all of its citizens, the support for elders is less than sufficient, and supports for employed caregivers is essentially nonexistent. This section examines the many interacting forces that have shaped Mexico's current configuration of supports.

Historical Factors and Economic Conditions

In 1943, Mexico enacted legislation that was to provide a basic level of income protection, health care, and social services for the entire population under the IMSS (Tracy, 1991). Had this legislation accomplished its goals, employed caregivers and their elders would be in better financial shape today. This early legislation was based on the ideological notion of "social solidarity," reflecting a strong commitment of the wealthiest and most able to share with the poorest and least able. Because program expansion was linked to the economic strength of the society, the social welfare goals of the 1940s never were reached due, in part, to a series of economic downturns.

For some time, Mexico has struggled with developing a stable economy. Such stability is an essential condition for gaining the financial strength necessary to meet public policy commitments concerning citizens. Past and present economic conditions have presented, and continue to present, barriers to adequate income and health care supports for elders as well as for employed caregivers.

The modern Mexican economy can be divided into four different periods: (a) growth with inflation and devaluation (1940–1958); (b) growth with price stability (1958–1970); (c) economic crisis and recession (1970–1990), with a few years of recuperation; and (d) after 1995, again a recession. In the 1970s, there was a period of stagnation, with a sharp decrease in private investments, especially in industry. These economic changes precipitated massive rural-urban migrations to three or four of the developing urban centers as well as emigration to the border with the United States. As a result of the serious decline in private investments, the government adopted neoliberal strategies. These strategies consisted of abandoning the previous industrial imports model and, instead, increasing internal productivity and favoring exports. Taxes on imports were increased, while those on exports and national investments were decreased. Bureaucratic barriers to internal production also were reduced. Although these policies have helped increase Mexico's economic strength, fairly serious economic and social problems continue to exist.

Public deficit, as a proportion of the gross internal product (which had a median annual rate growth of 6.7% in the decade 1970–1980) increased from 1.6% to 15% from 1970 to 1980. Inflation, which reached 22.05%, caused a disastrous effect on the prices of goods and services and a severe devaluation of the Mexican currency. High inflation rates continue today; in the 1990s, it is 26.7%. Unemployment has risen from 4.9% in 1987 to nearly 8% (Instituto Nacional de Estadistica Geografía e Informatica [INEGI], 1995).

The number of persons age 14 to 64, in which the economic activity rests, will increase considerably at the close of the century, to 66.5 million people. Such changes represent an unrealistic challenge for the creation of new jobs that will meet this population's growth (estimated at 3% annually).

Salaries have dropped as much as 50%. In the mid-1990s, however, the economy started a slow growth due to the North American Free Trade Agreement (NAFTA). According to Watkins (as cited in United Nations Development Program, 1997, p. 88), NAFTA has resulted in winners and losers. Winners include those who have obtained jobs or enhanced business profits due to increased exports to the United States and Canada, and through increased investments from the United States to Mexico. Some of the losers will be approximately 750,000 agricultural workers whose livelihoods will be lost as the price of maize (the country's staple food) drops as a result of competition from cheaper imports. A related struggle is that the economy is still very much technologically dependent; Mexico exports natural resources and buys finished goods for its consumption due to this slower technological development, especially in electronics (Gonzalez & Aguilar, 1990).

Mexico's high unemployment, inflation, and external debt has limited the availability of financial resources for social programs for all of its citizens, including the elderly and their employed caregivers. NAFTA has not benefited those who care for older persons and, furthermore, it has raised overall costs due to inflation, globalization, and the entrance of expensive medical equipment and medicines.

Cultural Factors

Since pre-Hispanic times, family links have been strong. The family always has been the basic social, economic, and legal institution in Mexico, with rights, responsibilities, and expectations of cooperation among its members. It is a socially recognized responsibility of the family to take care of all its members, including its elderly, sick, and poor. This includes all members of the extended family.

Politically, socially, and psychologically, family members are prepared to assume the responsibility to take care of their elderly relatives, but priorities have changed. Young adults first meet their necessities and those of their children; only after that, are the needs of the elders considered. Although the elderly do receive care, it may not be sufficient. In addition, elders may want their grown children to assist them more than they presently do. A study by Bialik (1989) of 770 elderly women (both urban and rural) found that elderly women expected their daughters to provide love and care (e.g., assistance with everyday activities) and their sons to provide economic help and sustenance. These expectations were greater among the rural elderly than among the urban dwellers. Rural and urban differences may be related to the more extensive network of support among urban elders; they had formed social networks that included neighbors and the church. Twenty-three percent of the sample said their lives at present were good, while 4% said life was not good for them, due mainly to loneliness; more than half had a fatalistic attitude about their future.

Cultural expectations affect not only the family's attitude about responsibility for the care of older persons, but that of politicians and employers. When families are seen as the primary care providers, there is less incentive to create workplace and public policies that would assist employed persons with their elder care duties.

Political Factors

Political System.   Mexico has had an authoritarian and highly centralized political system (Maddison and Associates, 1992) but, since 1995, it has opened up to a more democratic process with citizenship participation. The outcome is still too premature to evaluate. One political party, the Partido Revolucionario Institucional (PRI), until recently, had been in power since 1946. The major unions are affiliated with the PRI and have tended to support government policies (Maddison and Associates, 1992). This centralized structure could, in theory, facilitate national goals related to comprehensive public and workplace policies that would benefit the masses. This has not occurred, however, as evidenced by the fairly high level of income inequality in Mexico. For example, in 1992, the one fifth of the population ranked highest by personal income received 55.3% of total income, while the one fifth of the population ranked lowest by personal income received only 1.6% of total income (World Bank, 1997). Also, wages and benefits of public sector employees and union members generally are higher than those of other workers (Maddison and Associates, 1992). The recent election in Mexico has signaled a desire to use the centralized decision-making process in a more equitable manner. There is a renewed commitment to reduce favoritism and fraud.

Unions.   Unions in Mexico were created for the first time in 1918, with a huge national Central Union. They have a long history of struggles defending workers' rights against the owners and bosses. Their main focus has been on salaries and working conditions. Since 1971, democratic groups were created within the main unions (like the Confederacion Regional Obrera Mexicana, [CROM]). The democratic unions are fighting to become independent from the state and the official unions. Only recently have elder care issues been put on the unions' agenda. The goal has been mainly, if not solely, to increase retirement payouts (*Presidential Annual Report*, 1995).

General Public.   Mexico only recently has shown political pressure from the civil society to move elder care issues to the nation's agenda and, hopefully, to raise awareness about employed caregiver issues. Pickets and protest marches by retired persons are occuring and are quite a new experience for the Mexican people. About 3,000 pensioners marched to Congress to protest the very low pensions they receive and to demand a raise to two minimum salaries (instead of one). They also spoke out for free public transportation and free taxation. The pensioners stopped vehicle circulation for over 8 hours in very dense traffic avenues in Mexico City.

Demographic Pressures

The growth of women in the workforce and the increases in the number of elderly are becoming more acknowledged. Self-help groups of elderly and several nongovernmental organizations are becoming more and more visible politically. Newspaper editorials are appearing throughout the country highlighting the problems of the elderly, as shown in this recent quote.

> Mr. President: the problem of the Mexican elderly is still unsolved, getting worse and worse every day. The system of social assistance—addressed for only a few—is totally surpassed. The nongovernmental organizations (NGOs) do not solve the elderly overall problem. They are only palliatives sustained by a "culture of donations." The sectors of pensioners and retired persons endure deprivations, and there is an uneasiness due to this situation. The critical condition of the Mexican families makes them see their elders as a burden. (*Excelsior*, 1996, p. 4).

The civil associations consider it urgent to change the paternalistic political system to one that is more participatory, where the aged are given the opportunity to be productive once again. One mechanism is the establishment of training centers in multiple technologies, which are managed by the elderly themselves. The government recently funded some of these workshops.

☐ Future Trends

It is very unlikely that the Mexican government, work organizations, and unions will, in the next few years, develop policies, services, and benefits targeted to employed caregivers of frail elders. Not one group (e.g., media, family, religious bodies) has focused on employed caregiver issues, except for those related to employees with young children. Government and work-related institutions are unaware of the situation of employed caregivers of elders. Even if concerns were raised, it is doubtful, given Mexico's many other economic concerns, that employed caregivers would become a priority.

Demographic and cultural factors also help explain the anticipated lack of response to employed caregiver issues. Employed women with elder care duties may be too small a minority to have the power to influence government, work organization, and union policies and agendas. Although the employment rates of women are increasing, they are low in comparison to countries that have given this issue attention. And, half of the employed women work part time which, in some cases, could make it easier to balance work and elder care duties. Cultural expectations among the women themselves also may limit the likelihood that they even would want to raise this issue.

The situation of older persons presents a more promising picture. The old of today and the coming generation of elderly are pressing for adequate and equitable benefits, policies, and services for elders. Having many children once ensured, in some ways, the certainty of having someone who would care and provide for one's old age. Now, under the present difficult economic and social times, this no longer is the case. Moreover, the elderly have had to contribute, even in their old age, economic assistance for their families with unemployed household heads by caring for their grandchildren and doing household chores. Thus, having their mature daughters seek work outside the traditional domestic roles has had a "boomerang effect."

In Mexico, the elderly have started to organize themselves and, as a group, have publicly begun to be noticed. This strategy to exert pressure on the government is working; senior issues are becoming a bilateral family-government responsibility. The author foresees a growing empowerment of the the elderly segment, because the decision makers of today are on the brink of becoming the old of tomorrow. The media and other groups will continue to raise awareness of how vulnerable are the social and economic conditions of the old.

Economic pressures, however, may make it difficult for Mexico to respond favorably to the older generation. Budget deficits, high inflation, and trade imbalances may need to be altered before the Mexican government is in a stronger economic position. At the very least, jobs with reasonable wages and benefits would help family members to better care for their dependents as well as themselves.

Public speech and policies in Mexico are directed at encouraging the family to take more responsibility for caring for the aging population. In order to strengthen informal care of elders, family caregivers will need realistic and practical deeds. Such deeds include decent wages and government and workplace benefits for employed caregivers who assist their elders. Such supports are essential in order to have a society where the family and state, together, take care of its old.

☐ References

Bialik, R. (1989). Profile of the Mexican elderly woman: A comparative study. In *Midlife & older women in Latin America & the Caribbean*. Washington, DC: PAHO-AARP.

Bialik, R. (1992). Family care of the elderly in Mexico. In J. I. Kosberg (Ed.), *Family care of the elderly: Social & cultural changes* (pp. 31–46). London: Sage.

Excelsior. (1996). Editorial, "Letters to the Editor." p. 4, la. secc. Mexico City.

García, B. (1988). *Desarrollo económico y absorción de fuerza de trabajo en México 1950–1980* [Economic development and workforce absorption in Mexico 1950–1980]. Mexico City: El Colegio de México.

García, B., Blanco, M., & Pacheco, E. (in press). Género y trabajo extradoméstico en México [Gender and extradomestic work in Mexico]. In El Colegio de México (Ed.), *Mujer, género y población en Mexico* [Woman, gender and population in Mexico]. Mexico City: El Colegio de México.

García, B. , Muñoz, H., & de Oliveira, O. (1982). *Hogares y trabajadores en la ciudad de México* [Homes and workers in Mexico City]. Mexico City: El Colegio de México/UNAM.

Gonzalez, C. P., & Aguilar, C. H. (Coordinators). (1990). *Mexico ante la crisis* [Mexico in the presence of crisis]. Mexico City, Mexico: Siglo XXI Editores.

Ham, C. R. (1993). México: País en proceso de envejecimiento [Mexico: A country in the process of aging]. *Comercio Exterior, 43*, 688–696.

International Labour Office. (1996). *Yearbook of labour statistics,* (55th issue). Geneva, Switzerland: Author.

Jusidman, C. (1993). *El sector informal en México* [The informal sector in Mexico]. Mexico City: Secretaría de Trabajo y Previsión Social.

Jusidman, C., & Eternod, M. (1994). Serie monografías censales: *La participación de la población en la actividad económica en México* [Participation of the population in the economic activity in Mexico]. Mexico City: INEGI, IISUNAM.

Maddison, A. and Associates. (1992). *The political economy of poverty, equity, and growth: Brazil and Mexico, A World Bank comparative study.* New York: Oxford University Press.

Mexican Institute of Social Security. (1994). *Centros de día para pensionados y jubilados* [Day care centers for pensioners and retired persons]. Marco Normativo para la organización y funcionamiento. Mexico City: Author.

Mexican Institute of Social Security. (1995). *Bases gerontológicas para la organización de actividades en centros de día para Pensionados y Jubilados* [Gerontological bases for the organization of activities in day care centers for pensioners and retired persons]. Dirección de Prestaciones Económicas y Sociales. Mexico City: Author.

Montes de Oca, Z. V. (1995). Evejecimiento en México. Condición social partipación económica de la población cón 65 años y más en la ciudad de Mexico [Aging in Mexico. Social condition and economic participation of the population aged 65 and over in Mexico City]. Master's thesis, El Colegio de México, Mexico City.

National Work-Force Survey. (1991, 1993, 1995, 1996). Mexico City: National Institute of Statistics, Geography and Computer Science, Ministry of Work.

Parker, S., & Pacheco, E. (1995). *Labor market entries, exits & unemployment: Longitudinal evidence from urban Mexico*. Paper presented at the International Seminar, El Colegio de México, Mexico City.

Presidential Annual Report. (1995). Mexico City: The Mexican Presidency.

Sepúlveda, J. (Coordinator). (1994). *La salud de la población de edad avanzada* [The health of the elderly population]. Mexico City: Cuadernos de Salud, Secretaría de Salud.

Tracy, M. B. (1991). Mexico: Government commitment to social policies for the elderly. In M. B. Tracy (Ed.), *Social policies for the elderly in the third world*. New York: Greenwood Press.

United Nations Development Program. (1997). *Human development report 1997*. New York: Oxford University Press.

U.S. Bureau of the Census, U.S. Department of Commerce. (1991, September). *Global aging: Comparative indicators and future trends*. Washington, DC: Author. (Wallchart is available from the National Institute on Aging, Washington, DC).

U.S. Social Security Administration (1995, July). *Social security programs throughout the world—1995* (Research Report No. 64, SSA Publication No. 13–11805). Washington, DC: U.S. Government Printing Office.

World Bank. (1997). *World development report, 1997: The state in a changing world*. Oxford: Oxford University Press.

LESS DEVELOPED
COUNTRIES

CHAPTER

Iris Chi

China and the Family Unit: Implications for Employed Caregivers

☐ Introduction

The world's elderly population (age 60 and older) in 1991 was nearly half a billion persons. China alone is home to more than 20% of the global total. China has had a relatively "young" population; only 9.8% of the total population was age 60 and older in 1995 (*China Statistical Yearbook*, 1995). Given its rapidly declining fertility due to the one-child policy, China is expected to have a substantially older population in the middle of the twenty-first century. According to a number of projections, the proportion of the Chinese population age 60 and older is projected to be 24% by the year 2020, and 31% by the year 2040 (*China Statistical Yearbook*, 1995). At the same time, the age 75 and older population is projected to increase from 1.9% of the total population in 1991 to 4.1% by 2020 (U. S. Department of Commerce, 1996). As a result of population aging, the demand for elder care in China is expected to increase substantially.

Traditionally, the Chinese family, and its extended set of blood-related kin, was a self-sufficient little society on which one had to depend for job, education, support, and assistance in times of difficulties (Leung, 1992). For the Chinese elderly, family is the predominant mode of support. In fact, the Marriage Law still stipulates that children have the duty to provide support for their aged parents, and violators are subject to criminal penalties (Leung, 1995). Policies for elder care always assume that the family will play a primary role, whereas nonfamily-based welfare providers play a somewhat secondary role. A number of surveys carried out in cities in the 1980s all confirm that the family is the basic unit of support to the elderly. The 1984 survey in Tianjin shows that 96.4% of the elderly were taken care of by their family members during recuperation. Findings of another health care survey in Beijing in 1984 also indicate that 87.4% of elderly patients were taken care of by immediate family members, 8.3% by relatives (such as siblings and nephews), and 1.2% by neighbors (Yuan, 1989).

In a national survey of caregivers for the elderly, less than 5% of the care was provided by a nonfamily member in the city; in the village, it was only 2% of the care

(Wang & Xia, 1994). This survey also showed that women, especially wives, are the primary caregivers (Wang & Xia, 1994). A study of the distribution of responsibilities in housework in urban families (Sha, 1994) found that one third of the families took care of elderly persons. Wives caring for husbands or daughters-in-law caring for elderly parents were the primary caregivers in 54% of these families, whereas husbands or sons were primary caregivers in only 21% of these families. All family caregivers, regardless of sex, on average spent more than an hour a day providing elder care.

Rapid social changes associated with modernization and industrialization have led to repercussions in Chinese families. The capacity of the Chinese family as a primary source of help and support is being challenged and undermined. In fact, the family already has emerged as a focus of social problems, which include disputes over the care of the elderly. Among various factors that diminish family care capabilities, the most profound probably are high female employment and economic reforms. China's female employment rate is very high; among the labor force in 1990, 45% were women. The rate of women's participation in the labor force reached almost 90% for those between the ages of 20 and 44, and were only slightly lower than men (Cheng, 1995). Accordingly, family-work conflict, especially among women, may be widespread in China. Increasingly, when elders need care, people have to resort to means beyond families. Nevertheless, there are very few studies on family caregiving, and virtually no study exists on the impact of managing work and caregiving. One possible reason for the lack of studies is an insufficient awareness of the problem.

In China, social welfare benefits and services for persons in rural areas are very limited. Rural China has not yet established an aged care system. Rural elders rely on their families to provide for food and shelter. Some rural areas adopt a collective approach to pool resources together to care for the young, the old, and the disabled. However, no regulations or consistent way of handling elder care issues or the needs of employed caregivers exist in rural China. This chapter focuses on the provision of supports for urban elders and employed caregivers.

Benefits and services for older persons and for workers in urban areas are provided through China's employment-based welfare system. As a socialist country, China has a very different employee benefits system than most of the Western industrialized countries. Chinese economic enterprises take the form of work units, which are either directly or indirectly state owned. Enterprises refer to various economic units, such as industries, institutions, government administrative organizations at various levels, and social organizations (*China Statistical Yearbook*, 1995).

This chapter will focus on the problems of the employment-based welfare system and the responses to these problems by the state. Since China is still undergoing major economic reform, very few explicit records could be located. Data are lacking on the range of national responses, including policies, benefits, and services initiated by the government and the workplace that directly or indirectly help employed caregivers manage their dual work and family caregiving roles. In order to fill this gap, the author conducted a study of enterprises (businesses) and workers in Guangzhou to explore the kinds of support available to employed caregivers and to determine how these supports help the workers and their frail elderly relatives. Major findings from this study, which used a case study and focus group discussion method, are summarized in this chapter. Although the study is not representative of employed caregivers in China, it nonetheless is a first of its kind.

This chapter also will describe family caregiving values and their changes. Finally, this chapter will discuss the strengths and weaknesses of China's particular configuration package on work and family and outline future trends.

☐ The Components of the Welfare System in Urban China

As a socialist country, welfare is perceived by the government and the people as a government responsibility and every citizen's right. Welfare implies holistic well-being of a person from birth to death rather than service provision based on individual needs. All along, the Chinese government has advocated a decentralized and informal welfare system with a high emphasis on self-protection, self-help, and mutual help. The spirit of Communism, which is based on the values of "altruism," "to serve the people," and "mass line" (mass line implies everyone and a grassroots approach) encourages the participation of the people as natural helpers to solve their own problems rather than to rely on governmental and professional services (Leung, 1992). As a society based on "collectivism," the practice of mutual help and self-help presumably is widespread.

☐ Employment-Based Welfare

The Chinese Communist Party created an employment-based welfare system in 1949. Regulations were enacted to centralize control over the recruitment and allocation of employees. All work units were prevented from recruiting or dismissing workers, and graduates from schools and colleges were not allowed to choose their jobs. Work assignments came under the labor and personnel Departments of local governments, which allocated workers to jobs on a permanent and lifelong basis.

Not only were workers from state-owned enterprises guaranteed lifelong employment, they also enjoyed generous benefits and services. Therefore, the importance of the work unit in China is not simply a place where one works, it also is a place where one acquires various forms of services such as housing, medical care, education, and Social Security (Laaksonen, 1988; Lam, 1988; Walder, 1986). Thus, in addition to basic protection, state-owned enterprise workers enjoy a host of benefits, subsidies, and personal services. Functioning as a "small society" or "mini-welfare state," the work units exhibit some basic characteristics of the traditional pattern of an extended family. They bear the total responsibility of taking care of all of the social and economic needs of their members (Leung, 1992).

The large majority of all organized social services in China is found in enterprises or work units. For example, the majority of the hospitals and primary schools (some 225,000 hospitals and 3 million primary schools) are operated nationally by state-owned enterprises. Only a very insignificant number of these social services are run by nonstate enterprises. In 1992, the total fringe benefits expenditure in enterprises amounted to 131 billion yuan, representing almost one third of the total wage. (Yuan is the official currency in China. In 1992, the official exchange rate was: U.S.$1 = 8.50 yuan). Typical benefits and services within a state-owned enterprises can be divided into four major areas (Leung, 1992):

(1) Labor insurance: This is a scheme which provides benefits to cover retirement, sickness, injury, medical care, disability and death, funeral expenses, survivorship, maternity and sick leave.
(2) Allowances: China does not distinguish the difference between fringe benefits and welfare. Various benefits in cash include subsidies on food, meals, housing, bathing, haircuts, and transportation, and the one-child allowance (In order to encourage one-child per family, an allowance is given to the family that only has one child).

(3) Collective welfare: Most enterprises operate a number of services, which include clinics, primary schools, day care centers, nurseries, bathhouses, kindergartens, sport facilities, canteens, recreational centers, libraries, and theatres.

(4) Individual welfare: The enterprises, especially the state-owned ones, have the responsibility to take care of workers who have personal and family difficulties. These personal services, provided mainly by union staffs at the grass-roots level, include job placement for the physically disabled, mediation of family, individual and industrial disputes, promotion of family planning and family education, assistance to low-income households, and care for the frail elderly.

Financial Problems Facing the Employment-Based Welfare System

The employment-based welfare system serves the employees of the state-owned enterprises and the various government departments, providing comprehensive and generous benefits and services to these employees. By 1992, these workers accounted for 74% of the employee population in the urban area. The major weakness in this system probably is the heavy burden of the welfare expenditures, which is especially serious as the population ages. For instance, the insurance and welfare fund soared from 7.81 billion yuan in 1978 (14% of the total payroll) to 131 billion yuan in 1992 (33% of the total payroll) (Leung, 1992, p. 25). The growth in welfare expenditure correlated with increasing numbers of people retiring from work. The number of retirees rose dramatically from 1978 to 1992, from 3 million to over 26 million, and the ratio of employees to retirees decreased from 30:1 to only 5.7:1 during that same period of time. (It should be noted that this ratio is an average, the range was 90:1 in some young enterprises to a mere 2:1 in some older enterprises.) Consequently, expenditures on retirees rose from 1.7 billion yuan in 1978 to 79.5 billion yuan in 1992. Far worse, demographic projections put the number of retirees by the year 2000 at 40 million, representing 17% of the employee population, with retirement expenditures expected to amount to 150 billion yuan (Leung, 1992). In addition to expenditures on pensions, the enterprises also have to pay for other welfare expenses of the retirees, such as housing and medical care. Estimates indicate that the pension itself accounts for only one half of the total expenditure on retirees.

Economic and Labor Reforms Since 1978

In response to its financial problems, China began instituting economic and labor reforms in 1978. The Chinese government is attempting to move the centrally planned economy toward a market orientation. One major change is to issue new enterprise laws and regulations, such as the profit retention scheme and the taxation system. In addition, the Enterprise Law in 1988 prescribes the separation of ownership and management. Enterprises are supposed to have more autonomy to decide their policy on labor welfare (wages, bonuses, benefits), personnel, production, marketing, and investment. But, along with greater autonomy, the enterprises must now also take up a larger share of the welfare responsibility. Thus, the issue of how welfare policy affects the efficiency and productivity of the enterprises becomes salient (Leung, 1992).

Another major change is to develop new categories of enterprise to replace state-owned enterprise. With the economic diversification that occurred in the 1980s, many new enterprises have been recognized. The enterprises can be classified into four main types: the state-owned enterprise; the collectively owned enterprise; the individually owned or private enterprise; and other types of enterprises, such as joint ventures with foreign partners. Except for the state-owned enterprises, the enterprises are not bound by the state to provide comprehensive employment-based welfare. Despite massive protection for the state-owned enterprises, industrial growth in recent years has been attained largely by nonstate-owned enterprises. It was reported that at least 40% of the state-owned enterprises were suffering losses in 1994 (*China Statistical Yearbook,* 1995). In the early decades of the People's Republic of China, employment-based welfare was depicted as a social and political asset but, today, it is held responsible for depressing economic growth. As a result, the proportion of new types of enterprises is increasing steadily every year, while the number of state-owned enterprises is decreasing. Some state-owned enterprises have been sold to collectives or foreign companies and more may be sold in the coming years.

China is making plans to overhaul its current pension system for urban workers. As mentioned above, most of the peasants in rural China do not have a pension system in place. Driving this push for reform are low coverage rates due to a declining ratio of workers to pensioners, and a huge growth in the number of persons reaching the age of eligibility for collecting benefits. In urban areas, both funding methods and benefits packages are slated for major changes. Under the previous urban pension system, the enterprise typically was responsible for administering retiree benefits, which also were funded out of current operating funds. Under the still-evolving reform, pension pools are being established at the municipal level, where Social Security offices are being set up for administrative purposes. The intent is for young enterprises to share the welfare burden of the older enterprises. At the end of 1992, about 58% of the employee population were included in the scheme. Fifty-nine percent of pension expenditures are paid through these funding pools. Participation in the funding pools is voluntary. The average contribution rate by enterprises to these funds is 15% of the total payroll, which is rather high, particularly for those money-losing state-owned enterprises. In cases of deficits in the funds, the local government would intervene to cover the losses. Currently, the employees are contributing 1% to 3% of their salary. The employees' proportion will grow by 1% every 2 years, while the employers' proportion will decline until the total premium costs are shared equally between the two. The contribution rate for the new system should generate a 10% surplus annually (U.S. Bureau of the Census, U.S. Department of Commerce, 1996).

Other than pensions, medical care is the second largest item of expenditure in employment-based welfare. Medical expenses for employees increased dramatically from 3.18 billion yuan in 1978 to 22 billion yuan in 1992, more than a fivefold increase. (The inflation rates in China before 1990 were extremely low.) Increased expenditure is attributed to wastage, problems in management, and the rising cost of medical care. The system of free medical treatment for employees is under criticism, and the consensus is that the system must be abandoned. The Chinese Communist Party leadership desires to diminish the responsibility of the enterprises in providing collective welfare to their employees (Leung, 1992).

To facilitate economic reforms, the state promulgated regulations in 1986 on dismissal, recruitment, bankruptcy, and the introduction of a contract worker system. In effect, the government has endorsed the following as new operating principles: economic enterprises that are not profit making should declare bankruptcy, employees with undesirable performance should be dismissed, and new recruits should be employed on contract rather than on a permanent basis. In contrast to permanent employees, contract employees and their employing work units are required to make monthly contributions to a trust fund. At the present time, the labor system tolerates the coexistence of several types of labor; namely, permanent employees, contract employees, and temporary employees. Since 1995, the Ministry of Education announced that all college graduates were allowed to look for employment by themselves. In short, the Chinese government has partially abandoned its commitment to full employment and the strategy of job creation through administrative procedures.

In addition, more experiments are being tried to lessen the financial pressure on the state-owned enterprises. For instance, some of the existing welfare facilities (such as canteens, kindergartens, nurseries, hospitals, and bathhouses) have been opened to nonemployees on a fee-for-service basis. Enterprises are beginning to sell some of the housing quarters to their employees at a relatively low price. In this way, the welfare responsibility of the enterprises can be reduced and, in return, they can obtain additional income for benefits and services.

The bottom line in the issue over employment-based welfare would seem to be an ideological one. How much of the welfare costs should be borne by the individual, by the enterprises, and by the state? In the debate over this issue, one argument put forth is that economic enterprises should put their emphasis on improving production rather than on noneconomic pursuits. Concomitant to this argument is that existing welfare functions, as far as possible, should be transferred to society, notably to local urban neighborhoods.

☐ Responses to Managing Work and Informal Care of Frail Elders

A case study method was adopted in 1994 to collect information on the employment-based welfare system from various types of enterprises in Guangzhou, the capital city of Guangdong Province in southern China. Guangzhou is one of the most rapidly developed cities in China. Compared with other cities in China, it is a pioneer in economic and social development and a model for many other cities considering economic reform. The numbers of individually owned and joint venture enterprises in Guangzhou have grown quickly in the past 10 years.

The data collection steps used in this study included reviewing the relevant literature and documents and interviewing responsible staff from the enterprises. A relatively structured schedule was used for the interviews and document review to avoid subjective interpretations and data omissions. The fieldwork started in June 1994 and ended in September 1994.

Through the assistance of the Municipal Labour Bureau, one enterprise for each type was identified as representative from the total listing of enterprises in 1993. Types included the state owned, collective owned, and individually owned and other enterprises, including joint venture enterprises, shareholding enterprises, and foreign-owned enterprises. In the beginning, the individually owned and the other enterprises refused to participate in the study, because they believed they did not have any specific program or service to support their workers' elder care needs. As a result, study goals and the interview schedule were modified to include employment-based welfare, regardless of family care responsibility.

A focus group discussion was held with workers (including retired workers) from these enterprises. The purpose of this group was to encourage the participants to talk about their elder care needs and their expectations for programs and services. Therefore, a relatively unstructured group discussion was conducted to allow for more qualitative data.

TABLE 11-1. The distribution of enterprises in Guangzhou in 1992

	Number of Enterprises	Number of Workers
State-owned	770 (23%)	927,400 (64%)
Collective	2,116 (63%)	354,150 (25%)
Others[a]	475 (14%)	158,361 (11%)
Total	3,361 (100%)	1,439,911 (100%)

[a]Includes individually owned, joint ventures, and all other categories.

Findings: Employer Supports

In order to understand the development of the economic reforms in urban China, the distribution of enterprises in Guangzhou is examined. According to the Labour Bureau of the Guangzhou Municipal (1993), the distribution of different types of enterprises in 1992 is shown in Table 11-1.

Table 11-1 demonstrates that, in 1992, the majority of the enterprises were the collective type, followed by the state owned, and, last, by the other types of enterprises. In terms of the number of workers, however, state-owned enterprises had the highest number, followed by collective enterprises, and, last, the other enterprises. Roughly over 80% of the population between the ages of 15 and 60 in Guangzhou were workers. According to the law, these workers received employment-based welfare. Those who were not included in these figures either were covered by another welfare system, were dependents of the workers, or were simply not covered.

Table 11-2 describes the size of the four enterprises participating in this study and the number of workers who were covered by employment-based welfare. These four

TABLE 11-2. Characteristics of the case-study enterprises

	State-Owned[a]	Collective-Owned[b]	Individually-Owned[c]	Other[d]
Total employees	626	443	137	326
Number of employees by types				
Permanent	535	391	124	231
Contract	41	27	6	15
Temporary	50	25	7	80
Number of employees having welfare	626	408	103	246

[a]Zhu Jiang Shirt Factory.
[b]Guangzhou Lamp Factory.
[c]Hua Nan Stationary Factory.
[d]Dong Fang Hardware Manufacturing.

enterprises were asked to provide the total number of employees for the year 1993, types of their employees (that is, permanent, temporary, or contract workers), and the proportion and number of employees covered by employment-based welfare. The typical state-owned factories are larger in size, as compared with the collective and other factories. The proportions of permanent workers for these four enterprises ranged from 71% to 90%. The number of contract and temporary workers hired by these factories varied each year. Except for the state-owned case, no other factories covered temporary workers. The total numbers of workers covered also included employees' dependents and retired workers. However, the proportions of noncovered workers were quite different among these four factories, ranging from none to 25%. Therefore, some flexibility is allowed for determining the proportion of workers covered by employment-based welfare by individual factory.

Table 11-3 reports employer responses among these four enterprises to the needs of caregiving workers. Two basic types of responses were solicited in the study. These were leave and work arrangement policies and benefit provisions. In principle, only permanent and some contract workers are entitled to employment-based welfare. The employer responses, in terms of leave policies and benefits, are not caregiver specific.

The state-owned and collective-owned enterprises tended to have better leave policies. As a matter of fact, when we interviewed these enterprises, both the managerial staff and the workers indicated that they would not have a problem getting leaves from their work units. For instance, the state-owned enterprise would allow its employees to take a paid sick leave for up to 3 months, as long as a medical certificate was obtained from the employee's work unit medical practitioner and endorsed by his or her immediate superior. Benefit rates vary, however, by length of service, job nature (such as administrative or laborer), and length of sick leave. In addition, employees in state-owned enterprises could request a personal leave for up to 3 months. Paid personal leave, however, is seldom granted for the care of frail parents. Both state-owned and collective-owned enterprises had a flexible policy on unpaid leave. These enterprises would grant unpaid leaves on an individual basis, and such leaves usually would be granted to employees caring for sick parents. Unlike the state-owned and collective-owned enterprises, the other and individually owned enterprises had very strict leave policies. In general, none of their leave provisions would

TABLE 11-3.   Employer responses among participating enterprises

	State-Owned	Collective-Owned	Individually Owned	Other
Policies				
Sick leave	3 months	1 month	1 week	1 month
Personal leave	3 months	1 week	None	None
Unpaid leave	Flexible	Flexible	None	1 month
Flexible work	Yes	Yes	Maybe	Maybe
Benefits				
Labor insurance	Yes	Yes	Yes	Yes
Allowance	Yes	Yes	No	Yes
Collective welfare	Yes	Yes	No	No
Individual welfare	Yes	No	No	No

consider family care reasons. In terms of providing flexible work schedules, the state-owned and collective-owned enterprises said that they would accommodate their employees' requests as much as possible, while the other and individually owned enterprises were hesitant to give a definite answer.

All four enterprises claimed that they provided labor insurance to their workers. One reason could be that they were referred by the Municipal Labour Bureau, which required this insurance from all enterprises. Those elderly who are eligible for retirement assistance under the labor insurance program received a pension, giving them a degree of financial security. To qualify for a wage-related retirement pension, workers have to satisfy a number of eligibility criteria, including age and length of employment. In terms of allowance, all enterprises, except the individually owned enterprises, reported that they gave individual allowances to workers, such as nursery fees, allowance for traveling, and housing allowance. However, the amount of allowance and number of covered items varied enormously from enterprise to enterprise.

Findings: Union Policies, Benefits, and Services

In urban China, approximately 75% of the workers are unionized (*China Statistical Yearbook*, 1995). However, the unions are sponsored by the Communist Party. The labor union is viewed by the Chinese Communist Party as an important bridge to facilitate communication between the party and the masses. Therefore, unions are supported by the work units in China, and the provision of maintaining a union is usually included in the individual welfare plans. Unions are found in major industries and in various geographical areas. Union workers' salaries are paid by the work units. Their major task is to work for the rights and interests of workers and staff. Unions are supposed to be the key official channel where suggestions to the party on recruitment, wages, subsidies, welfare, industrial safety, and women's rights are made. In contrast with the West, however, independent unions are suppressed. The party-sponsored unions are not supposed to use boycotting as a bargaining action. According to the official view, the fundamental interests of labor unions and the government are identical (Leung & Nann, 1995).

To a certain extent, unions might suggest and try to influence enterprises' responses to employees' elder care responsibilities, as long as the issues raised by the unions match the government's employment-based welfare policy. Due to their limited autonomy and fundamental influence on employment policy, the unions' contributions and responses to employed caregivers are insignificant. According to a national survey in 1986, most of the workers were not satisfied with the work of the unions, which were perceived as being preoccupied with recreational and cultural activities (All-China Federation of Trade Unions, 1987).

Table 11-4 describes the labor union responses to the issues of caregiving workers. Two basic types of response were solicited in the study. These were supportive services for the caregivers and elder care benefits negotiation. In principle, all types of workers are entitled to the services provided by the union. The union responses have become more caregiver-specific in recent years due to increasing demands from the union members. Since the other and individually owned enterprises seldom have unions, their caregiving workers usually do not receive union services, which are directly run by the work units.

In the present study, only the state-owned and collective-owned enterprises indicated that they had trade unions, and that these unions provided some elder care services to their retired workers and caregiving workers. As shown in Table 11-3, the

TABLE 11-4. Union responses

	State-Owned	Collective-Owned	Individually Owned	Other
Elder Care Services				
Voluntary day care	Yes	No	No	No
Support group	Yes	Yes	No	No
Visit frail elders	Yes	Yes	No	No
Meals	Yes	No	No	No
Home help	Yes	No	No	No
Barber	Yes	No	No	No
Health care	Yes	Yes	No	No
Ad hoc arrangements	Yes	Yes	No	No
Elder Care Benefits	No	No	No	No

state-owned enterprise provides more services than the collective-owned enterprise. The types of services provided included voluntary day care, support groups, visits to frail elders, meal preparation and delivery, home help, haircutting, health care, and ad hoc arrangements. Visits to elders are viewed as a major union duty in China, with the union staff responsible for carrying out these services. However, the unions have mobilized neighbors, retired workers, and unemployed people as volunteers to help provide this service. Health care is provided to the frail elderly through the medical staff in the work units. This service is usually home based. Ad hoc arrangements include helping workers who are in acute financial needs. To help these workers overcome this difficulty, the union would donate money as a special allowance to them or launch a campaign to collect money from other workers.

Table 11-5 gives a summary of current Chinese supports for employees with elder care responsibilities. Readers are reminded that most of these supports are not specifically designed for elder care. Nevertheless, due to the aging population, many of these supports now are more relevant than before to employees with elder care responsibilities.

Findings: Supports for Elders

The focus group format was used to obtain data on supports for elders. This unstructured format allows participants to freely express their views. Only three questions were asked. These focused on: the workers' need for elder care, the types of programs and services which would support their elder care needs, and their reactions to the changes in the employment-based welfare system. Approximately two to three workers (including the retired workers) from each enterprise participated in the focus groups.

One theme that emerged from the focus group discussion was that the families with frail elders were part of a network of community-based supportive services, including home help and day care. The network not only lessened their burden of care, but it also inhibited the development of feelings of social isolation. Although the Chinese welfare system provides no income support specifically for caregiving families, work units and street offices (neighborhood government offices that provide social welfare

TABLE 11-5. Chinese supports for employees with elder care responsibilities

Government Initiatives	Nongovernmental Organization Initiatives	Union Initiatives	Workplace Initiatives
For employed caregivers None Indirectly, for older persons Social Security[a] Medical care[a] Nursing home for elders without family[a]	For employed caregivers None Indirectly, for older persons Nursing home[b] Home care[b]	Political and work organization influence (Insignificant) Services Voluntary day care[b] Support group[b] Visiting frail elders[b] Meals[b] Home care[b] Barber[b] Health care[b] Ad hoc arrangements (e.g., respite care)[b]	Policies Sick leave[a] Personal leave[b] Unpaid leave[b] Flexible work schedule[b] Benefits Labor insurance[a] Allowance (e.g., food) Collective welfare (e.g., child care) Individual welfare (e.g., training)[b] Services Similar to those provided by the unions

[a]Mandated.
[b]Optional.

187

services to local residents) provide limited financial assistance to qualified families. Such assistance is temporary and based on recognized need, as decided by the respective management committees.

In principle, the Chinese institutionalize only those elders who are without family support. Absence of family support is defined by nonexistence of immediate kin. These elders most likely never married and are childless. Responsibility for these institutions largely remains a municipal job under the auspices of the municipal civil affairs bureaus. Little is known about the nature of these institute actions, beyond that they are available free of charge and that they accommodate a broad spectrum of elderly people. No systematic report has been made on the number of elderly in institutions, the profile of the residents, and the types of care they receive. In recent years, some of these institutions and other nonprofit institutions have accepted elderly people with families experiencing considerable conflict. These elderly have to pay for their services but, usually, the labor insurance program covers their fees.

Although support was present for the caregiving families, most of it came from the community rather than the state or employers. Respondents felt stigmatized and neglected by the state. Respondents noted that the Chinese traditional idea of welfare is centered on the family; thus, seeking outside assistance was disgraceful. However, work units were perceived as the institution that should be responsible for the people's livelihood. And, in most of the participants' past experience, work units were regarded as the most reliable and helpful source of support.

Findings: Employees' Evaluation of Supports

Many retired workers felt that they were the most vulnerable group in the society due to the economic reform. They are forced to retire from government-run factories. Their monthly pension of 400 yuan (about U.S.$50) is enough to cover the basic necessities, but not much more. Respondents believe they are the victims of a painful revamping of the Chinese economy that has been particularly hard on older workers and retirees. Chinese companies are taking drastic measures, including layoffs and forced retirements, to cut their losses and stay in business. Older workers are getting nudged out the door, and retirees are facing cutbacks in medical benefits. Many are getting partial pensions or none at all as their former employers struggle to meet payrolls. According to the respondents, for the elderly, economic reform translates into a loss of many of the cradle-to-grave benefits that they thought they were owed. Most recent retirees grew up under socialism. They spent their lives toiling for the state and expected the state to care for them until they died. Now, not only does the "iron rice bowl" (i.e., the guaranteed employment and welfare) no longer exist, but the economic reforms are changing family life in ways that make the elderly more vulnerable.

Adult children who want to help their parents are facing many difficulties themselves. Financially, they are less secure than their parents due to the economic reforms. They might get less pay or no pay at all if the enterprise does not make a profit. In some cases, the elders have to support their adult children who are in serious financial difficulties. In order to survive in the modern economy, the adult children need to work longer hours and take fewer leaves from their work. Consequently, they have less time available for elder care responsibilities. Those who live in the same city as their parents already are facing time and money constraints in providing elder care. Those who live far away from their parents are in even more compelling situations.

As more and more young people travel to other cities or abroad to seek their fortunes—a mobility that has come only with reforms—many older persons find themselves without their children's support. In general, the adult children who work in another province can afford to visit their parents only once a year, usually during the Chinese New Year holidays. These children hardly can provide any care to their frail parents. Therefore, it is becoming more and more common to find retirees left on their own and adult children with moral dilemmas.

Nowadays, it seems that only when profits are made by the enterprise are benefits to workers guaranteed. The enterprise can honor its welfare coverage to the workers only if it maintains a profitable business. As a result, financially weak enterprises can offer only welfare benefits that are much lower than those promised on official documents. For instance, a worker whom the author interviewed from the money-losing state-owned enterprise said that the factory did not cut back any welfare programs on paper (i.e., they did not change any of their welfare provisions). Instead, they gave workers only a 10-yuan (U.S.$1.25) allowance per month, regardless of the number of years they had worked. In addition, the factory was unable to reimburse workers and retirees in a timely fashion for their medicine; many had to wait over a month. Obviously, this practice hurt frail retired workers the most. In another situation, the factory had a higher ratio of retirees than workers. The medical costs of these retirees usually were higher than those of the workers; thus, the funds available for the medical insurance for the entire factory easily were used up.

Summary

This section attempted to explore some important dimensions of the employment-based welfare system in China. Only case study and focus group discussion methods were used in getting firsthand empirical information. Inevitably, the sample in this survey is biased, and the degree to which findings can be generalized to the general working population is uncertain. The findings of this study, however, can serve to highlight and illustrate some important characteristics of the employment-based welfare system, and it also can stimulate insights for future studies.

There are lots of variations in providing employment-based welfare among the different types of enterprises. This is due to the fact that different types of enterprises have different philosophies in providing benefits and services to their workers. The result is inequity in the provision of benefits. Very often the range of difference is significant, even with the same item of welfare provision. Study findings reflect that the present monitoring mechanism on supervising the employment-based welfare system is not effective and inequity is becoming a major issue. The support provided by the employers, while it exists, can cover only a small number of retired workers with a limited scope of services. Consequently, the majority of caregiving responsibility actually has fallen back to the families. Therefore, the issues faced by employed caregivers of frail elders in China are becoming urgent.

Moreover, the long history of emphasis on employment-based welfare by the state seems to have had an impact on the people's ideas of welfare. People seem to have high expectations for their work units to provide for their needs, especially in the domains of pensions and health care. Obviously, the economic reform has not yet taken elder care into consideration, and retired workers are facing great difficulties in their daily lives.

☐ Family Caregiving Values

The most important Chinese value that is relevant to family caregiving is "filial piety." This value prescribes a moral obligation on junior members of the family to respect and to take care of their elderly parents. Parents are required to care for their children and, later, adult children are expected to reciprocate. It is a "feedback model" of family care as contrasted with a "relay model" in the West (Zhu & Xu, 1992). The structure of the Chinese family is shaped on Confucian ideologies and principles of a hierarchical social order in which family power is based on seniority. Relationships within the family are governed by Confucian ethical principles that apply to general human behaviors and relationships in society. Relationships within the family organization are governed by a set of norms that apply to different relationships between family members. Filial piety is the most important principle that governs parent-child relationships. Engaging in unfilial behaviors is considered an unforgivable disgrace.

Family caregivers usually include spouses, sons, daughters, and in-laws. Family care obligations are shared among these caregivers, who assume different caregiving roles, defined mainly by common practices. Older persons also have very different expectations of the various caregivers. Among them, spousal support usually is not regarded as family support, although spouses always are the first port of help. Sons and daughters-in-law assume distinctive responsibilities, which are carried out by providing formally fixed amounts and kinds of support. Parent care is a formal obligation to sons and daughters-in-law and basically they should provide as much support to their parents as they can. Support by other caregivers is carried out mainly on a voluntary or convenient basis, although their obligation also is customarily and distinctively set. The social expectation on other caregivers is distinctively set by their relationship with the older persons who require care from them.

As a general code of behavior, filial piety both confers on the father's power and control over children and prescribes how children should behave toward their parents as well as their ancestors. Basically, it requires children to obey and honor their parents, and devote themselves to their well-being. Concrete norms and customs apply differently to relationships between parents and sons, parents and daughters, and parents and daughters-in-law.

Changes in Caregiving Values

Family relations have undergone marked changes since modernization and urbanization. Although Chinese culture still dominates, Western practices have been prevalent among the young and the educated. This encounter of different values is most apparent among the elderly, as most of them have come from an agrarian social and economic background and are now the first generation to grow old in an industrialized society. The results of the changes include:

1. Older persons tend to live separately from their married children and, therefore, their relations with children tend to be less intense than before.
2. When older persons live with their married children in one household, the authority of the household is usually in the hands of the children. However, children may still respect their parents, if the latter do not interfere with family affairs.
3. The roles of daughters and daughters-in-law as family caregivers have changed in the opposite direction. More daughters are assuming family caregiver roles to take

care of their own elderly parents, while fewer daughters-in-law are willing to care for their parents-in-law.

4. The mother-in-law and daughter-in-law relationship also has changed in the opposite direction. Instead of a daughter-in-law obeying the mother-in-law, it often is the daughter-in-law who gives the orders in the household. The former usually is satisfied if the latter does not dislike her.

5. In essence, the authority of older persons in the family depends on their economic independence.

In general, the status of older persons in their families has dropped. Although the majority of children are both willing and able to provide for their parents and perform their duty as family caregivers, the problem is that they may refuse to perform their duty due to a variety of factors, such as lack of economic resources and long distance caregiving. Family support depends heavily on the conscience or morality of the children.

☐ Future Trends

The author anticipates that further erosion of welfare benefits will continue. This is mainly because the majority of the state-owned enterprises are losing money and the costs of the employee welfare programs are now targeted as the main reason. However, cutting back on welfare benefits enjoyed by the working class of enterprises carries enormous political risks. In order to keep a balance between the need to achieve economic reforms and to maintain political and social stability, China's current welfare benefits display some features. First, the state is withdrawing from welfare commitments. The role of the state primarily is to be that of a regulator and enabler, promulgating laws, guidelines, and regulations on welfare policy rather than to be a service provider and financier (Leung & Nann, 1995). Second, local governments are encouraged to develop innovative welfare programs. The disadvantage of this policy is that it inevitably leads to different standards in different provinces. For those economically successful provinces, the local governments can afford to develop more aged care programs to meet the needs of frail elders. Third, the important role of the family is stressed in all aged care–related legislation. The Chinese government still holds that family care is the major policy direction for elder care.

Given the changes in filial piety among the younger generation, Chinese government has recently passed a Law on Protection of the Rights and Interests of the Elderly (China National Commission on Ageing, 1996). This law states that the elderly shall be provided for mainly by their families, and their family members shall care for and look after them. Supporters of the elderly shall perform the duties of providing for the elderly, taking care of them and comforting them, and catering to their special needs. The supporters referred to here are the sons and daughters of the elderly and other people who are under the legal obligation to provide for the elderly (China National Commission on Ageing, 1996).

Because of China's one-child policy, it is estimated that in 2017 approximately 30% of persons aged 75 or older will have only one child (Gai, 1999). The Chinese government recognizes the pressure on the only child, and for this reason, the government's new family planning policy allows and encourages the current only child cohort to have two children. It is hoped that the new measure will result in the presence of more grandchildren to help in the caring of their grandparents. Another measure to help ease the burden on the only child is a health education program that promotes healthy behaviors (e.g., nutrition, exercise, smoking cessation, obtaining needed medical care). Such programs are expected to reduce dependency in old age. Finally, the Chinese government is also developing aged care services and organizing young–old volunteers who can help in caring for frail elders in the community.

The one-child policy should have a positive impact on increasing the awareness of the needs of employed caregivers. Most of the current group of older people have more than one child. The caregiving tasks are shared by adult children, and some of them might not be working full time. Therefore, burden and stress are less obvious. The future group of older people will have only one child to provide support to them. Furthermore, their only child most likely will engage in a full-time job. Consequently, every employed person will experience parent care responsibilities. However, as a developing country, China is facing a lot of demands, such as building infrastructures to ensure further economic development. Some policy makers are worried that the responses to employed caregivers might slow down economic development, because these responses tend to increase business expenses.

Therefore, in order to have further economic development, the societal responses to employed caregivers may not consider formal care options, such as initiatives from government, unions, or private companies. Instead, social networks and informal care will become important channels for protection and welfare benefits.

In recent years, retired workers have expressed many concerns about the welfare cutbacks for elderly persons. Several protests and rallies have taken place in different major cities. Most of these demonstrations happened when inflation and the cost of living were too high for the retirees to maintain decent lives. Although the government has managed to settle the discontent in the past, it is anticipated that similar problems will arise from time to time in different cities at different times. Of central importance is the economic development of the enterprises. More successful development will ensure better provision of care to the aged and other employment-related welfare. The new generation is aware that the government can no longer be the sole provider for welfare and care during later life. Therefore, young people's expectations of government and work organizations are different from those of the current older cohort. Also, because more young people are educated and moving into the middle class, private and nonprofit responses to the needs of employed caregivers have been growing rapidly in recent years (such as in well-off cities like Shanghai, Beijing, and Guangzhou) and some families can afford to hire maids or pay for in-home health care services.

☐ References

All-China Federation of Trade Unions. (1987). *The survey on the existing conditions of workers.* Beijing: Workers' Publishers.

Cheng, X.Y. (1995). *Women's population issue and development in China.* Beijing: Beijing University Press.

China National Commission on Ageing. (1996). Law of the People's Republic of China on Protection of the Rights and Interests of the Elderly. Beijing: HuaLing. Publishing House.

China statistical yearbook. (1995). Beijing: China Statistical Publishing House.

Gui, S. X. (1999). Elder care in single-child families in China: problems and countermeasures. In I. Chi, N. Chappell, S. X. Gui, & J. Lubben (Eds.), *Elderly Chinese in Pacific Rim Countries* (pp. 37–46). Hong Kong: Chinese Professional Management Center.

Laaksonsen, O. (1988). *Management in China during and after Mao in enterprises, government and party*. New York: Walter de Gruyter.

Lam, C. W. (1988). *An appraisal of the system of occupational welfare in China*. Unpublished M.S.W. Dissertation, University of Hong Kong.

Leung, J. C. B. (1995). *Family support for the elderly in China: Continuity and change*. Hong Kong: University of Hong Kong, Department of Social Work and Social Administration.

Leung, J. C. B., & Nann, R. C. (1995). *Authority and benevolence: Social welfare in China*. Hong Kong: The Chinese University Press.

Leung, J. C. B. (1992). *Social welfare in China: Vol. 3. The transformation of occupational welfare in the PRC: From a political asset to an economic burden*. Hong Kong: University of Hong Kong, Department of Social Work and Social Administration.

Labour Bureau of the Guangzhou Municipal. (1993). *Report on the 1992 labour distributions in Guangzhou*. Guangzhou, China: Author. (in Chinese).

Sha, J. C. (1994). *The research on the population problem in the midst of reform and opening to the outside world*. Beijing: Beijing University Press.

U.S. Bureau of the Census, U.S. Department of Commerce. (1996). *International brief: Old age security reform in China*. Washington, DC: U.S. Government Printing Office.

Walder, A. (1986). *Communist Neo-traditionalism, work and authority in China's industry*. Berkeley: University of California Press.

Wang, M., & Xia, C. L. (1994). An analysis on the caring responsibilities of the elderly in Chinese families. *China Demographic Science, 4*, 37–43.

Yuan, F. (1989). The status and role of the elderly in Chinese families and society. *Chinese Sociology and Anthropology*, Fall/Winter, 58–86.

Zhu, C. Y., & Xu, Q. (1992). Family care of the elderly in China: Changes and problems. In J. Kosberg (Ed.), *Family care of the elderly: Social and cultural changes* (pp. 67–81). Newbury Park, CA: Sage.

CHAPTER

Caroline Njuki

Poverty and Economic Development: Implications for Work and Elder Care in Uganda

☐ Introduction

Uganda, with a land surface of 241,139 square miles, is a landlocked country. It is 800 miles from the Indian Ocean, the major route of transporting goods into the country. To the south, it is bordered by Tanzania and Rwanda; to the west, Zaire; to the north, Sudan; and to the east, Kenya. There are several physical features that make this country popular. Two are Lake Victoria, one of the largest freshwater lakes in the world, and the Nile River, one of the longest rivers in the world, which starts from Lake Victoria. In addition, the Rwenzori Mountains, also known as "the Mountains of the Moon," are located in the western part of the country. The highest peak reaches 5, 680 feet and is capped by snow. Toward the eastern part of the country is another range of volcanic mountains, the highest being Mount Elgon, with a peak of 4,800 feet. The area is rich with volcanic soil and is a major farming area. Uganda has plentiful rain, which is well distributed, except for the northeastern part of the country. The mean temperatures range between 50°F in the southwest, to 78°F in the northwest; however, in the northwest, temperatures can reach 94°F the whole year round. Because of the equatorial climate, there is plenty of sunshine moderated by the prevailing winds from Lake Victoria and the altitude of the country, most of which is relatively high. As a result of the abundant rainfall, good temperature, and rich soils in most of the regions, the country is extensively involved in agriculture. In the northern part of the country, which is less fertile, the population is basically pastoral (*Uganda: A Country Study*, 1994).

Uganda is a young country; it gained independence from the British only in 1962 (Rake, 1997). In the early 1970s, Uganda was highly visible internationally because of the infamous President Idi Amin. He contributed to the economic ruin and social disruption of a very promising country. The widespread AIDS epidemic, which began in the 1970s, further strained this country's economic and social development (World

Health Organization, 1994). Since 1986, the country has had a relatively stable government under the leadership of President Museveni (*African Farmer,* 1995). Yet, the problems of a very low-income country persist. Uganda is one of the poorest countries in the world. People are so poor that they cannot afford the basic necessities of life, such as salt, sugar, cooking oil, and soap. According to the World Bank (1997), 50% of the population live on less than U.S.$1 a day.

Almost all of the population live in rural areas (88%) and engage in agricultural activities (86%) (United Nations Development Program [UNDP], 1995). Living conditions are difficult; for example, 58% of the population had no access to clean water in 1995 (World Bank, 1997). From 1988 to 1991, there was only one doctor for 25,000 persons. This doctor to patient ratio is worse than the average for all sub-Saharan African countries (1 for 18,500), and considerably worse than the average for high-income countries (e.g., United States, Canada), which ranges from 300 to 600 persons per physician (UNDP, 1995).Considering these impoverished conditions, it is not surprising that the average life expectancy in Uganda is low, at 45 years of age (UNDP, 1995). Nevertheless, it has increased since 1960, when it was age 43 (UNDP, 1995).

Not only must Uganda deal with the problems of a developing country, hit hard by political and health crises, it also faces new challenges brought on by changes in the family and in types of employment. Ugandans have always worked (young and old, men and women), but the types of employment are beginning to change, from agricultural jobs in rural areas to service and industry jobs in urban areas. Also, the number of persons living into their senior years is steadily increasing. Thus, families, workplaces, and the government are facing new challenges. This is under conditions of mass migration to the urban areas and abject poverty.

Unfortunately, data on employed caregivers are nonexistent, and data concerning elders are very limited. So, in order to specifically explore issues related to work and caregiving, the author interviewed 150 Ugandans in 1996 from May to September. Those interviewed represent a cross section of Ugandans: 30 family caregivers from rural and urban areas, 21 elderly persons from rural and urban areas, 12 community leaders, 18 health care workers, 5 government officials, 16 food vendors, 28 rural farmers, and 20 teachers.

The following questions were asked:
(1) Do you have elderly relatives?
(2) Can the elders look after themselves? If not, who looks after them?
(3) Is the caregiver involved in any formal/informal type of work? If so, what type?
(4) Who relieves the caregiver when he/she has to perform work duties?
(5) Where is/are the elderly located? Urban or rural area?
(6) Does the government provide assistance to the elderly? If so, what type of assistance?
(7) Have you noticed any changes in traditional family relationships or in peoples' perceptions of the elderly? Please identify them
(8) What is the rural to urban migration trend today, and has it affected traditional structures (family, community) or affected the distribution in the division of labor?
(9) What are the similarities/differences between parents and children today as compared to a generation ago?
(10) How many eldercare facilities do you know of in this country?

Data gleaned from the interviews, along with the scant printed material on elders and on social and economic conditions in Uganda, are incorporated into this chapter. The following topics are discussed: (1) work and family issues, (2) supports for employed caregivers and for elders, (3) strengths and weaknesses of these supports, (4) factors contributing to the limited services for employed caregivers and elders, and (5) future trends.

☐ Work and Family Issues

Many issues are explored in this section, including statistical data on population, employment, and aging trends and descriptive data about the day-to-day experiences of workers and elders.

General Population Trends

Two population trends are significant to the care of elders. First, 50% of Uganda's population is under 15 years of age (International Labour Office [ILO], 1997). The large number of young dependents in need of care diminishes the resources available for elders and their caregivers. Second, the majority of AIDS cases have occurred among working age people (aged 16 to 40) (*Uganda: A Country Study,* 1994). In 1994, it was estimated that Uganda's population, which currently is 20 million people, would double by the year 2012; this estimate is now questionable due to the large number of premature deaths (*Uganda: A Country Study,* 1994). The cohort (age 16 to 40) may be burdened with extra responsibilities for the care of dependent children and for frail elders. Numerous premature deaths in this cohort will leave fewer persons of working age to take care of the large number of dependent persons.

Employment Conditions

The number of men and women who are economically active is quite high: 86% for persons 15 years of age and older. Among persons age 40 to 59 (the likely age of caregivers in Western societies), 97% of males and 90% of females worked in 1995 (ILO, 1997). As previously stated, Uganda is primarily an agricultural economy: 86% of the labor force work in agriculture, while only 4% work in industry and 10% in services (UNDP, 1995). Most jobs are in the informal sector (e.g., family farms, small businesses) where wages are very low and benefits are nonexistent. Some workers may be employed part time, as the employment figures do not separate part-time from full-time workers. It also is important to note that 45% of youth age 9 to 14 were in the labor force in 1995 (ILO, 1997). Employment earnings are most likely extremely low for the majority of workers, considering that 50% of the population earn less than U.S.$1 a day.

A study recently conducted in Kenya, a neighboring country, found that overall, including housework and paid economic activities, women work longer hours than men and receive considerably less income for their efforts (UNDP, 1995). The gender difference in hours worked per week is greatest in cash cropping and self-employment activities. In households that farm cash crops, women average 62 hours a week, while men average 42 hours per week. Self-employed urban women average 75 hours per week, and men average 61 hours (UNDP, 1995). Women's economic contributions often are underestimated. According to Food and Agricultural Organization of the United Nations and a number of other studies that have been carried out by various nongovernmental organizations, women produce 60% to 80% of all food in Africa (Food and Agriculture Organization of the United Nations [FAO], 1996). They also contribute significantly to the economy through their unpaid caregiving activities.

The Aging of the Population

In 1996, the number of persons age 60 and older in Uganda was 748,000, or 3.7% of the population. This number is projected to grow to 1,024,000 by the year 2025, an increase of 37% (U.S. Bureau of Census, U.S. Department of Commerce, 1996). This increase would be even higher had the AIDS epidemic not occurred (*African Farmer*, 1995). The premature deaths of young adults decrease overall the number of persons who would have lived into their senior years. Although the number of elderly is increasing, the percentage of the entire population age 60 and older actually will decline from 3.7% in 1996 to 3.1% in 2025. The likely reason for this decrease is the continuation of a high fertility rate, which was 6.7% in 1995 (World Bank, 1997).

Managing Work and Caregiving

Persons who work and care for elders in Uganda may face many problems. Caregivers have to give materially as well as emotionally to their aging relatives. Unfortunately, many times, employed caregivers are unable to tend to all of the needs of their frail elders. Problems which may be encountered by employed caregivers, such as financial concerns, generational conflicts, and harsh living conditions, are described below.

Financial Problems.   Government policies and organized, formal elder care services are lacking in Uganda. Families or others in the community always have assumed responsibility for the care of the elderly, just as they have assumed responsibility for the care of young people without families. Such arrangements have been the traditional way of caring for those who could not fend for themselves.

Most elders are financially dependent on their children because they have limited or no retirement funds. Most retired elders worked in the informal sector, where pension benefits were nonexistent and their wages were too low to save adequately for their retirement. Women, in particular, have been disadvantaged financially. Saving for retirement is hard for all but, especially, for women. Retired women who worked in the fields or in the marketplace spent most of their hard-earned money putting their children through school. For women who worked in the paid labor force, some or all of their money was taken by their husbands. Thus, most women were unable to save money. Those few who did save money did not know how to use the banking system. So, when old age arrived, they had nothing to fall back on, except their adult children (Mulira, 1994).

It is financially difficult for employed caregivers, most of whom have very low wages, to care for frail elders who often have no money of their own. Employed caregivers are not in a position to supplement elders' monthly incomes, purchase adaptive equipment for handicapped elders, or travel to the homes of relatives living some distance away. Most employed persons have difficulty in just supporting their immediate family.

Generational Conflicts.   In the Ugandan society, old people historically have been regarded with respect and as a blessing. Parents still look to the day when they can relax and be taken care of by their offspring or grandchildren. Since they gave sustenance and education to their children, they, in turn, expect to be supported by them when they need help (personal interviews with 10 male and 10 female elders, 1996). Ugandan society accepts that young people, since they owe the old, are responsible for honoring, respecting, and looking after the old. One of the unpardonable sins that children can commit is to show disrespect or ingratitude. The elderly in Uganda felt that their children were not as responsive to their needs and welfare as they had been to their parents' needs (personal interviews with 21 elderly Ugandans, 1996). The majority of these elders attributed their abject poverty to neglect by their children.

Many adult children and other young persons have moved to the cities to find employment and a better life. Geographic distances and exposure to life outside rural communities tend to change the younger generation's attitude about their responsibilities for frail elders (Archbishop Nkoyoyo, 1995). The changing meaning of the term old person *(Muzei)* described below offers one stark example of such an attitude shift.

In the rural areas, the word *Muzei* is used in connection with positive statements connoting "respect" but, in urban areas, many young persons use this same word in negative statements implying "old," as in stupid, useless, ugly, and unwanted. So, when young urbanites discuss old people and have a good laugh at them, they might say "how stupid the *Muzei* are to live in the city, or the *Muzei* have no self-respect; did you see how she was dressed?" (personal interviews with 20 food vendors at Nakasero Market, 1996).

The extent to which employed caregivers have negative attitudes toward their frail elders is unknown. It is likely, however, that they would be influenced by any widespread attitude shift. At the very least, important differences exist between the older and younger generation's expectations about elder care responsibilities.

Living Conditions and Caregiving.   The majority of homes in Uganda have no running water, indoor plumbing, or electricity. People must travel long distances and exert considerable physical energy to get water and firewood from the surrounding environment. Buying water is not an option for many because it is very expensive. Only 31% of the entire population and 28% of rural dwellers had access to safe water during the years 1988 to 1993 (UNDP, 1995).

In Uganda, the collection of water and firewood is the responsibility of the young and the adult women in the community. Frail older persons are unable to engage in these daily survival tasks. If a caregiver lives some distance from the elder, the elder's life is in jeopardy when others in the community are unable to help. Lack of firewood and water can result in a poor diet and missed meals, which can result in failing health (Mulira, 1995). Shelter also becomes problematic for the elderly, especially women, in Uganda. When a woman is widowed, she often is chased away by relatives of her deceased husband, who then take the land and the house that had belonged to the husband. The result is that many women are left destitute, some without a home, others in substandard housing with their adult children or another relative (Mulira, 1995). Many elderly Ugandan women are widows: In 1996, 53% of women 60 years of age and older were widowed, while only 11% of males were widowed at this age (U.S. Bureau of the Census, U.S. Department of Commerce, 1996).

Summary

In Uganda, out of necessity, many frail elders become totally dependent on their family members, not only for emotional support and for assistance with daily activities (e.g., cooking, personal grooming), but for all financial assistance and for basic survival needs of water, shelter, and food. Due to the elders' extraordinary dependency needs, adult children and other relatives, in some situations, have abandoned their caregiving role (personal interviews with 30 family caregivers, 12 community leaders, and 5 government officials, 1996). Geographic distances, low wages, and stressors related to living in poverty make caregiving very difficult for adult children and other relatives. Abandoning the caregiver role is problematic for all concerned, because caregiving is embedded in a long history of respect for the value and worth of older persons. The tensions between meeting the needs of Ugandan caregivers' immediate family and those of their elders likely will persist, however, as the care of the elderly continues to be viewed primarily as the responsibility of the family in Uganda.

☐ Supports for Employed Caregivers and for Elders

Table 12-1 summarizes the supports from the government, work organizations, and nongovernmental agencies that are available to employed caregivers and to elders.

Employed Caregivers

No documented workplace, government, or nongovernmental supports for employed caregivers could be identified. As previously mentioned, wages are very low, and benefits generally are nonexistent or meager. Free medical and maternity care is available to all citizens at government-run dispensaries and hospitals (U.S. Social Security Administration, 1995). However, the author's own experiences and information from the personal interviews suggest this generally is not the case. The majority of patients have to pay for health services. Evidence suggests that deficiencies exist in the availability and quality of Ugandan health care services. Only 42% of people in rural areas, where almost all of the population live, had access to health care services during 1985 to 1993 (UNDP, 1995). Although urban residents fared better (99% had access to health care services), they represent only 12% of the population. One international indicator used to assess quality of health care services is the maternal mortality rate, which in Uganda was 550 maternal deaths per 100,000 live births from 1980 to 1992. This rate is lower than the sub-Saharan African average of 608, but much higher than the average of 8 for high-income countries, such as the United States and Canada (UNDP, 1995).

Although systematic data are lacking, the author believes that a handful of employers provide some assistance to employed caregivers. These supports are listed in Table 12-1, under the heading, Workplace Initiatives. Some large international companies based in Uganda offer supports to employed caregivers, such as unpaid family leaves and flexible work schedules (e.g., flextime, part-time work) (personal interviews with 5 government officials, 1996). Such supports would be consistent with each company's worldwide employee benefits plans. Since few international companies exist in Uganda, these supports are available to only a handful of workers. Some small nongovernmental organizations offer paid bereavement leaves and paid leaves to care for sick elders (personal interviews with 5 government officials, 1996). In the Ugandan culture, participation in death rituals is very important to bereaved relatives, as is helping someone die. The small agencies recognize the importance of death and dying to the Ugandan culture; therefore, they are willing to grant temporary leaves. Some conflict exists, however, between employer and employee about the length of time for the leaves. Workers prefer leaves of many weeks so that they can adequately meet their cultural and family obligations, while agencies need their workers to be working and productive. Since the majority of workers in Uganda are family

TABLE 12-1. Supports for employees with elder care responsibilities in Uganda

Government Initiatives	Nongovernmental Organization Initiatives	Union Initiatives	Workplace Initiatives
For employed caregivers None Indirectly for older persons Pension plan (10% of population)	For employed caregivers Case management (very few provided by staff at residential facilities) Indirectly for older persons Home care (very few) Nursing home (only two are known of in the country)	None	Parental and family leave (usually unpaid)[a] Sick, vacation, personal leave (usually paid)[a,b] Flextime, compressed work week[a,b] Part-time work, job sharing[a] Flexplace[a]

[a]Voluntary.
[b]Government encouraged.

farmers or workers in small scale-businesses, very few workers receive the benefits discussed here.

Programs for the Elderly

Pension Plan.   The National Social Security Fund, legislated in 1967 and revised in 1985, provides limited pension coverage (U.S. Social Security Administration, 1995). Temporary employees and part-time employees are excluded. The fund includes a pension plan for government employees only. At age 55 or 50, the retired person receives a lump sum equal to total employee and employer contributions, plus accrued interest (U.S. Social Security Administration, 1995). Some retirement plans are offered by nongovernmental organizations, such as private companies. Only 10% of the employed population, however, is able to obtain pensions from their workplace or purchase them privately (personal interviews with 5 government officials and 20 community elders, 1996). Government employees are more likely to receive pension plans than other workers.

Long-Term Care.   Uganda's National Social Security Fund does not cover long-term care services, such as nursing homes and home care services for elders. The government depends on the extended family to provide this care to frail elders (Archbishop Nkoyoyo, 1995). The author was unable to locate studies that investigated elder care services in Uganda. The Church of Uganda provides several programs to elders, which are described below.

Residential Care.   The Church of Uganda is one of the first institutions to establish services for elders. One program, the Old Age Campaign Center, offers residential care to destitute elders who have no relatives who can care for them. At this facility, the elderly are given treatment, clothing, and all the necessary requirements for daily living. In the beginning, this facility was well equipped, with a staff of 25 people. Due to financial constraints, however, staff has been reduced to only one doctor, two nurses, and seven other health care personnel. The patient population has dropped from 60 to 13 (personal interviews with 30 elder care workers, 1996).

The health care personnel at the residential facility run by the Church of Uganda consists of three types: (1) the paid staff, (2) those who look after their relatives at the facility, and (3) volunteers. Residential care is new in Uganda, and it is unfortunate to note that most of the paid staff lack formal training in the care of the elderly. Instead, they are trained on the job. They are, however, very dedicated to their work. The low pay, lack of training, and widespread depression among the elderly make their jobs stressful, and many hold second jobs outside the facility (personal interviews with 30 elder care service providers, 1996).

Some relatives who cannot look after their elderly at home help take care of them at the facility, sometimes sharing responsibilities with other family members. There appears to be less stress in this group, since they do not have to spend too much time with a relative whose life is on the decline. Additionally, with this type of arrangement, the person receiving care does not feel isolated from relatives and family. Unfortunately, this type of arrangement is not always possible (personal interviews with 30 elder care service providers, 1996).

A third set of individuals who work at the facility is composed of people in the community who have volunteered to provide assistance to the elderly in the facility. The reasons that people volunteer are many. Some people are lonely and would like to spend time with others. Other volunteers are motivated by religion. Many are members of the church that started this project and feel a moral obligation to help those who cannot help themselves.

Volunteers contribute to the care of the elderly in a number of ways. For example, those who are well off contribute toward material needs in addition to donating their time. Others who are not as wealthy work with the elderly on various projects, such as exercise, crafts, off-site visits, counseling, washing clothes, and cooking. This group forms the majority of those actually providing care. It is important to keep in mind that, traditionally, caregiving always has been a voluntary service. Volunteers are the main service providers, whether in institutions or in the family. This will continue to be so for a long time (personal interviews with 150 people,1996).

Outreach Services.   In addition to residential care, the center also provides outreach services, such as home visits, counseling, referrals, and domestic help to 48 elders who live with their families in nearby communities (Archbishop Nkoyoyo, 1995). A second program run by the Church of Uganda, Young and Elderly in Society, helps destitute elders build homes where they can live permanently. This program also assists these elders in developing money-earning ventures, such as making baskets and raising chickens. The third program, Christian Outreach, provides several services, such as spiritual growth, home visits, counseling, and referrals to persons with disabilities, including elders, who live in the town of Mukono (Archbishop Nkoyoyo, 1995).

☐ Evaluation of Supports for Employed Caregivers and Elders

Employed Persons

As mentioned above, employed caregivers, at present, receive no assistance from the government or voluntary agencies and very limited forms of assistance from work organizations.

Elder Care

Long-term care is a new field in Uganda, and the facilities for the elderly are breaking new ground. The Church of Uganda has tried to provide services to the elderly, but it has faced many difficulties. Formally provided elder care is perceived as "un-Ugandan," necessary as it may be in today's changing world. It is seen as a radical departure from the care traditionally provided on an informal basis by the family. Few staff specialize in the field of geriatrics or receive formal training as nurses' aides. Most of the staff train on the job.

In 1996, the author conducted in-depth interviews with 18 health care workers and 30 elder care service providers. These interviews identified two problems in the provision of long-term care services. They are discussed below.

Financial.   The most pressing problem cited by the health care personnel is the financial aspect of caring for the elderly. Other than a few donations from the international community and from local churches, there is no other income for the programs for the elderly. The church finds it particularly difficult to obtain funds for such programs, because very few people are interested in the welfare of elders. Most donors prefer to give money to youth programs, because the young are seen as the hope for the future. The elderly who receive help from the church's programs are unable to contribute to their care due to frailty and lack of marketable skills.

Adjustment Problems.   Another problem identified by the health care personnel concerns elders' adjustment to living in a residential facility. These elders always have lived with their families or in their own homes, and they have managed their own lives. Communal living for the elderly, so far, has not been well accepted. The staff says that it is difficult to put old people together, because each resident has his or her own lifestyle. For example, some do not see the need for exercise, some feel demeaned when asked to play games for recreation, some are not willing to learn new skills such as making crafts, some have different dietary preferences, some have experienced a better standard of living than others and so their requirements and expectations are higher, some are educated and are not willing to share quarters with the less educated, and still others are too set in their ways to live communally.

In conclusion, not many organizations or donors are interested in the care of the elderly, because formal elder care is not yet culturally accepted and because of competition for support for programs for children and youth. Only a handful of voluntary agencies have organized programs to assist the elderly. The health care personnel who were interviewed were aware of only two other residential facilities in the entire country, but this has not been verified. Many people have yet to realize that the ability of the traditional source of care for elders—the family—is gradually eroding. At present, the family still is the main source of caregiving, and it will likely remain so for the foreseeable future.

☐ Factors Contributing to Lack of Services for Employed Caregivers and for Elders

This section explores possible reasons for the lack of programs for employed caregivers and the limited assistance provided to elders. It also examines factors that have contributed to the breakdown in the family's ability to care for its elders.

Political and Economic Factors

Civil wars of 1966, 1978–1979, and 1986, and wars with neighboring countries, have greatly destabilized the population and destroyed the infrastructure (e.g., roads, communication systems) (Rake, 1997). Since 1986, under President Museveni, the country has become more stable. Fewer wars have been fought, and more attention has been given to economic development (Rake, 1997).

Nonetheless, Uganda's weak economic base makes it very difficult, if not impossible, to provide adequate income, health care, and other social assistance to its citizens, including employed caregivers and their elders. Uganda's gross national product (GNP) per person was only U.S.$200 in 1994, making it one of the nine poorest countries in the world (Van Buren, 1997).

The cost of wars drains the resources available for social welfare programs (Rake, 1997). In 1986, the latest year in which data were available, 26.3% of total federal expenditures were for defense, while only 5.7% were spent on social services, including health care, social security, and other community services. The federal outlay for these social services was less than any other government program, including road construction (Van Buren, 1997). Building the country's infrastructure, attracting foreign trade, and investing in other economic services currently are taking priority over health care and Social Security programs.

The overall economy of the country is beginning to expand. The gross domestic product (GDP) in real terms grew by 4.5% in 1992, 6.4% in 1993, 9.4% in 1994, and an estimated 8.2% in 1996. The annual rate of inflation, which was at 200% in 1986, has declined to single digit rates, with the 1996 rate at 6% (Van Buren, 1997). Current economic growth, however, is not strong enough to adequately solve Uganda's economic, social, and national defense problems.

Not only are most people impoverished, many are illiterate and malnourished. Forty-four percent of the population 15 years of age and older are illiterate (32% of the men and 55% of the women) (United Nations Educational, Scientific, and Cultural Organization [UNESCO], 1996). Almost 1 million children under 5 years of age were malnourished in 1992 (UNDP, 1995). In a country with very limited financial resources, the competition among social welfare programs can be great. An educated workforce is essential for economic growth. Uganda's federal outlay for education in 1986 was 14.5% of the budget (Van Buren, 1997). Altogether, the needs of the elderly and family caregivers appear to be less essential at this time.

The Effect of Modernization on Family Caregiving and Social Welfare Programs

Industrialization, urbanization (rural to urban migration), and modernization (exposure to nontraditional values and beliefs) have redefined the relationships between family, work, and government. This section first reviews traditional family relationships, and then it explores the impact of urbanization and modernization on families, work organizations, and government.

Traditional Society.   A report by the Non-Governmental Organization Committee on Aging (1996) indicates that, in traditional society, old age was very respected. The elderly were an active and venerated force in the affairs of the community and the extended family. In traditional societies, elderly women, usually widows, were seen as offering continuity by passing on community history and culture from one generation to another. In the villages, where there was no electricity, the elderly were invaluable on those dark nights in passing on information and oral history to the younger generation. Parents and young people took these lessons very seriously, especially since words spoken by the elderly were believed to be words of wisdom. The elderly almost universally were seen as knowledgeable of most of the important elements that sustained the community, such as traditional ceremonies, folklore, herbs, medicinal herbs, plants, foods, and ways of cooking different foods (personal interviews with 150 people, 1996).

The elderly in rural African communities have been and still are perceived as possessing supernatural powers. Everyone believed that elders were equipped with worldly wisdom, because they had been around for such a long time. There always was a grown child, usually a daughter or daughter-in-law willing to take care of the aging parents (Brown, 1992). Such total and complete belief in the wisdom possessed by the elderly also caused the young to obey the old. Obedience to the older generation, therefore, did not have to be enforced. The community believed that the words of the elderly were prophetic. Indeed, if one were cursed by an old person, one could never succeed in life and one's life would be forever miserable. In this way, a place of respect for the elderly was guaranteed. When the elderly became infirm and inactive, their family took care of all their needs: financially, medically, socially, and emotionally. They remained an integral part of the family until they died (interviews with 150 people, 1996)

In Uganda, employment and caregiving were integrated into community life in the traditional society. Women, the traditional caregivers, took care of the frail while they engaged in agricultural work, such as household food production and small-scale cash cropping. Because their work was primarily agricultural, they could take the elderly with them to the fields. Unwell elders could stay at home with women engaged in homebound work tasks. Because women's work revolved around the home, it was easier for them to provide day-to-day care to frail relatives. Such care in the home also was beneficial to the elders, because they were assigned manageable tasks that made them feel useful (personal interviews with 18 health care workers and 30 elder care service providers, 1996).

When families and communities assume all caregiving functions, including financial supports, there is little pressure on the government to develop social welfare programs as we know them today (World Health Organization, 1997). Brown (1992) reported that, in Africa, the colonial British administration and the postindependence governments totally relied on the family's ability to take care of its elderly relatives. Uganda, having undergone the same colonial British system, subsequently has treated the issue of aging in exactly the same way.

Urbanization.   Young people migrated to urban areas to obtain employment and escape massacres in their villages during the wars of 1979 and 1986 (personal interviews with 150 persons, 1996). Between 1980 to 1995, the average annual urban growth rate was 5.2%; this rate is higher than the average urban growth rate of 4.0% for all low-income economies (World Bank, 1997). The new arrivals found few city jobs, however, because industries have become mechanized. Employers needed few people, and primarily wanted unskilled workers who would accept the lowest wages. The majority of people in urban areas, therefore, are poor. Women increasingly joined the paid labor force out of economic necessity (Mulira, 1995).

Rapid population growth in the cities led to the common problems of congestion, lack of basic services (e.g., schools, health care), a shortage of adequate housing, and declining infrastructure. The new arrivals found the crowded conditions in the cities unlike what they had been used to all their lives (Mulira, 1995).

Impact of Urbanization on Family Caregivers.   The rural-to-urban migration has resulted in the setting up of nuclear families that often live some distance from the elders in the family. As far as many young people are concerned, once they leave the rural areas, they do not want to be reminded of their responsibilities at home. Many others, even if they wanted to, would not be able to respond to the needs of those left behind, because they have more responsibilities than they can adequately handle in the cities (Mulira, 1995). The migration to the cities makes caregiving difficult, if not impossible. Furthermore, adult children and other relatives oftentimes are unable to take care of those elders who accompanied them in their move to the city. Many adult children in urban areas do not even have an income (personal interview with foster mother of 16 orphans, Mukono, Uganda, 1996). As a result, homelessness, which never used to be a problem in Uganda, is on the rise among the elderly as well as children (personal interviews with 150 persons, 1996).

Thus, the traditional supports for caring for elders have broken down. Urbanization requires government intervention in many areas, one of which is social welfare. Pension plans, access to health care, and help in finding employment are a few examples relevant to employed caregivers. Such an immediate and massive need for assistance likely would be overwhelming to any government in terms of cost, the expertise needed, and the commitment to following through. As discussed above, Uganda's economic base is weak. Thus, families are undergoing enormous change as they move from traditional to modern society, with very little support from the government.

Impact of Urbanization on Rural Communities and Rural Elders. Migration also has negatively affected rural communities. It has affected agricultural and livestock production, threatened the environment, undermined the rural economies, and eroded traditional values. Farming, the main source of employment in Uganda, has been neglected. There is less food being grown in the rural areas; therefore, food prices in the cities have become almost unaffordable for the average family. The urbanites do not revolt against the higher prices, because they realize that they are better off than the farmers who earn very little. The result has been a decrease in food production in rural areas (*African Farmer,* 1995).

Urban migration has especially affected the elderly in rural communities, as many have been left without the traditional support of family. Those left in rural communities either were the very young who needed to be looked after, the sick, or those dying of AIDS who could not move to urban areas and, instead, stayed in the rural areas to die (Mulira, 1995). The rural areas now predominantly are occupied by a relatively noneconomically productive population. To a certain extent, the elderly have become caregivers to children whose parents have died or are dying, (Ojulu, 1996) or who have migrated to the urban areas. Family members in rural areas who are committed to caring for their elders may find it difficult to care for them under these stressful conditions. Daily survival may be their most important consideration. Also, the added caregiving responsibilities for other relatives and dependent persons can easily tax the caregiver's available time, energy, and resources. Furthermore, in some cases, relatives previously available to help rural caregivers, have moved to the urban areas.

Impact of Education.   Modern education has resulted in the educated cutting ties that used to embrace the community. Research clearly shows that, as individuals become more educated in Africa, they tend to cut relationship or community ties (Apt & Crieco, 1994). The educated become more independent and physically far removed from communities where they grew up. They adopt new lifestyles in urban areas, where they are free from community ties. While in the past, young people spent time with the old, changes in society have resulted in a lack of communication between the young and the old. The young are no longer anxious to listen to stories or learn trades from the older generation (Apt & Crieco, 1994).

Summary.   Brown (1992) noted that urbanization works against old traditional beliefs. The breakdown of the extended family lessens the availability of family support to caregivers as well as to elders. Migration places new demands on the younger generation who moved to the cities. The result seems uniformly to be a disintegration of the family structure, which leaves employed persons with fewer resources to help them manage their employment and caregiving responsibilities.

Impact of AIDS on Family Caregivers

The U.S. government report, *Uganda: A Country Study* (1994) indicated that, in the 1980s, Uganda exhibited the highest incidence of AIDS of any country in the world, with an infection rate of 15 cases per 100,000 persons. This same report revealed that men and women were equally affected, and that the majority of AIDS cases occurred in people between the ages of 16 and 40 years. By the mid-1990s, approximately 1.3 million people in Uganda (primarily in Kampala, the capital) had HIV infections. This represents 14.5% of the population (United Nations Global Program on AIDS [UNAIDS], 1996). Uganda's successful AIDS education program has reduced significantly the number of newly infected persons (Uganda AIDS Commission, 1997).

The loss of so many young adults has reduced the number of available caregivers for older persons. In the traditional society, family members shared the caregiving duties. This is no longer possible when a family has lost a large number of its members. Surviving adults who care for frail older persons may feel particularly burdened, because of the limited number of family members to assist them and because of their own feelings of loss.

Women as Caregivers in Uganda

Prior to the twentieth century, polygamous marriages were common, and families were fairly large, with a number of wives and children. The various wives and their children collectively cared for the elderly and divided up the work equitably. Thus, no one individual wife felt overly burdened, because the caregiving duties were shared. By the turn of the century, polygamous marriages were no longer recognized and the traditional family structure that provided numerous support systems for women was lost. Today, in addition to the previously described problems that women face in caring for their elders, women now have fewer other women living in the same household who can assist them with their caregiving duties.

Prior to the 1920s, women could own land, cultivate crops for their own profit, and influence political decisions. Women occupied a special place in society. A number of men in Uganda still claim that this earlier society revered women. In fact, Ugandans believe that women, in earlier times, had traditional rights that exceeded those of women in the Western world (*Uganda: A Country Study,* 1994). For example, the senior wife always was given a superior role and sometimes could be given "male status" (personal interviews with a group of women at Namuwongo Market in Uganda, 1996). "Male status" gave the wife decision-making powers equal to those of men. Moreover, women were recognized as important religious leaders and sometimes led religious revolts that ended up toppling male-dominated regimes. Women also could own land, cultivate crops for their own profit, and influence political decisions.

With the introduction of high-earning cash crops in the 1920s, women's social and legal status declined. Growing cash crops became the domain of men because, in part, men were able to carry out the hard task of growing cash crops. Because they were viewed as the breadwinners, it was taken for granted that this was their domain. Essential information about ways to access local and international food markets was not shared with women. Thus, women were excluded from the cash crop business. Furthermore, women's lack of education and lack of political astuteness made it difficult for them to use the political system to their advantage. Poverty and the inability to raise funds to run for political office also kept women out of politics, leaving their voices unheard.

After the 1920s, women's legal status also changed. Once widowed or divorced, they could no longer own their own land, receive an inheritance, or obtain legal protection. Near the time of independence from Great Britain in 1962, the Uganda Council of Women ensured that a resolution was passed to ensure that women's concerns were addressed (whether in marriage, divorce, or widowhood) and to ensure that they received their rightful inheritance (*The Monitor,* 1998). The law today allows women to inherit or own land and property, and, when a women is widowed, the husband's property is divided up fairly between herself, the children, and the rest of the husband's family members. However, these laws are difficult to enforce, especially in remote rural areas, and, as discussed above, some women are chased off their land. Overall, however, women's lives are getting better. Uganda is one of few African states where women's issues are a priority to the government. In fact, it is the only African state with a female vice president. The new family structures and the new economic order, with its legacy of poverty, however, still place a lot of stress on female caregivers.

☐ Summary

This chapter has examined an emerging problem in Uganda: the family's lessening ability to care for a growing number of frail elders due to the processes of urbanization and modernization, conditions of severe poverty, and oftentimes unstable political regimes. Both the caregivers who move to the cities and those who remain in the rural areas have lost the support and assistance they previously had from extended family members. The demise of polygamous marriages has further reduced the number of helpers. Increased education, essential to economic growth, has contributed to the younger generation's lessened respect for and commitment to elders.

For employed caregivers in the cities, their low or nonexistent wages, along with cramped housing conditions, make it difficult for them to care for frail elders. Employed caregivers in the rural areas not only have dependent elders to care for, but also persons dying of AIDS and the survivors of AIDS victims.

Sadly, the government, which should offer assistance, is not in a position to help because of all the other needed services. Also, the government expects families to care for elders. Each individual family, therefore, has to fend for itself in the best way it can. There are no government programs set up to assist the destitute, such as Social Security or welfare, as found in the United States. It has been noted that over 90% of the employed population has no pensions or retirement benefits and, in the majority of cases, rely on support from their families. It also has been observed that there are no programs to train caregivers in the delivery of services to the elderly.

☐ Future Trends

It is unlikely that the government will improve the pension system or develop new policies, benefits, or services for the elderly or their caregivers, most of whom are employed. President Museveni's primary focus is on strengthening Uganda's economic base. He wants to attract foreign investors and improve the country's infrastructure (e.g., roads, communication system). Uganda will need a better educated and healthier workforce to attract foreign investors and to increase internal work productivity (President Museveni's interview on CNN which aired on January 17, 1998). To accomplish this, investments in social programs are likely to focus first on education and health care. Government spending on seniors most likely will be less important to the primary economic goals. President Museveni believes that, once the economy is strengthened, other social programs can be given attention. However, this could be many years away.

The decimation of so many youth and young adults by the AIDS pandemic is worrying leaders in Uganda. For the first time in the history of Uganda, orphanages are being accepted as an alternative type of family care for young children (Ojulu, 1996). Likewise, nursing facilities for frail elders, such as the one described above in Mukono, are becoming more visible. The author expects that Ugandans eventually will have to accept institutional care as an alternative to traditional family care for those who have lost their family members. Decisions will need to be made concerning who pays for these services, the role of government and private enterprises, and administrative procedures. The country, however, has not yet come to grips with these questions.

Strategies for the provision of care to elders, however, are particularly important, because families in Uganda are less able now than before to care for the growing number of elders. Studies from Western countries, presented in this book, have shown that work productivity is reduced when employed caregivers are overwhelmed with elder care duties. Also, family care of the elderly is far less expensive than formal care services. Thus, arguments can be set forth for the economic benefits of elder care strategies.

☐ References

African Farmer. (1995, May–Sept). pp. 19–21. A publication of The Hunger Project, New York).

Apt, N., & Crieco, M. (1994). Urbanisation, caring for elderly people and the changing African family: The challenges to social policy. *International Social Security Review, 47* (3/4), 111–122.

Archbishop Nkoyoyo. (1995, March). *Poverty and the elderly in Uganda: Cause and effect.* Comments to the Special Event Panel: Critical Emerging Issues for Older Persons, World Summit on Social Development, Copenhagen.

Brown, C. (1992). Family care of the elderly in Ghana. In J. I. Kosberg (Ed.), *Family care of the elderly: Social and cultural changes* (pp. 17–30). Newbury Park, CA: Sage.

Food and Agriculture Organization. (1996). Women and Population Division Sustainable Development Department. Rome, Italy: Food and Agriculture Organization of the United Nations.

International Labour Office. (1997). *Economically active population, 1950–2010: Vol. II. Africa* (4th ed.). Geneva, Switzerland: Author.

Mulira, R. (1995, September). *Problems of older women in Uganda.* Paper presented at the Fourth International Conference on Women, Beijing.

Non-Governmental Organization Committee on Aging. (1996). Washington, DC: American Association of Retired Persons.

Ojulu, E. (1996, September 14). Grappling with the orphans of Kakuutu. *The New Vision* (Uganda Press), p. 6.

Rake, A. (1997). Uganda: Recent history (based on an earlier version by Richard Walker). In *Africa: South of the Sahara, 1996.* (26th ed., pp. 1016–1021). London: Europa.

The Monitor (Uganda Press). (1998, January 7). p. 9.

U.S. Department of State. (1994). *Uganda: A country study.* Washington, DC: U.S. Government Printing Press.

Uganda AIDS Commission. (1997). The Ministry of Health, Entebbe, Uganda.

United Nations Development Program. (1995). *Human development report 1995*. New York: Oxford University Press.

United Nations Educational, Scientific, and Cultural Organization. (1997). *Statistical yearbook—1996*. Paris: Author.

United Nations Global Program on AIDS. (1996). *HIV/AIDS epidemic in Africa* (pp. 2–6). New York: Author.

U.S. Bureau of the Census, U.S. Department of Commerce. (1996). *Global aging into the 21st century*. Washington, DC: U.S. Government Printing Office.

U.S. Social Security Administration, Office of Research and Statistics. (1995, July). *Social security programs around the world—1995* (Research Report No. 64, SSA Publication No.13–11805). Washington, DC: U.S. Government Printing Office.

Van Buren, L. (1997). Uganda: Economy. In *Africa: South of the Sahara, 1996.* (26th ed. pp. 1021–1028). London: Europa.

World Bank. (1997). *World development report 1997: The state in a changing world*. Oxford: Oxford University Press.

World Health Organization. (1994). *Images of the epidemic* (WHO Library Cataloging in Publication Data, p. 36). Geneva, Switzerland: Author.

World Health Organization. (1997). *Ageing in Africa* (Prepared by Nana Apt, University of Ghana, Legon). Geneva, Switzerland: Author.

CHAPTER

Viola M. Lechner

Final Thoughts

This book has described how 11 economically, culturally, socially, politically, and geographically diverse countries have responded to the changing needs and demands of family members who care for frail elders. Altogether, the countries comprise a little over 2 billion people, or one third of the world's population.

This chapter synthesizes the contributing authors' findings with respect to: (1) their countries' work-family concerns; (2) the benefits, policies, and services available in each country to assist employed caregivers and their elders; and (3) the noted future trends. Several factors that have fostered the development of the most generous supports are then discussed. The chapter ends with recommendations for strengthening the availability of and access to supports for employed caregivers.

☐ Managing Work and Elder Care

Trends Regarding Employment and Aging

As revealed in all of the chapters and in Table 1-1 in chapter 1, women (traditionally the primary caregivers of elders) are increasingly committed to the labor force. Also, the number of persons age 60 years and older is projected to increase considerably. The greatest increases in overall proportion of elderly in the population will occur in developing countries; however, the most developed countries will experience the greatest growth in persons age 75 and older. (See Table 1-1 in chapter 1.)

In spite of their employment responsibilities, families in all 11 countries continue to be very committed to caring for frail elders. Most countries reported that about 80% of all the care needed by elders is provided by families; in Sweden, this projection is less (at 66%) and, in China, more (at 96%) according to the one available study.

Prevalence of Persons Managing Work and Elder Care

It is very difficult to accurately determine the number of employees with elder care duties. Differences in definitions of caregiving and data collection methods account for some of the differences in study findings. Most studies conducted in Great Britain and the United States have revealed that from 6% to 11.8% of employed persons in these countries are taking care of older persons. While the national work and family study conducted in Canada has identified a larger number of employed caregivers, 45% of the Canadian employees who were surveyed had some measure of involvement in assisting elderly relatives. Studies in Israel, Germany, Canada, and the United States have reported that from 33% to 64% of all informal caregivers to elders are employed. These prevalence rates suggest that combining work and caregiving is fairly common in developed countries. As the number of elders increases and as more women enter the workforce, the number of employed caregivers throughout the world can be expected to increase substantially in the coming years.

Characteristics of Caregivers

Gender.   The country-wide studies reported that most caregivers are women: for example, 70% in Great Britain, 66% in Israel, and 90% in Japan. Based on more limited studies, the authors from Uganda, Brazil, Mexico, and China believe that almost all caregivers in their countries are female. In Sweden one study reported as many male caregivers as female caregivers.

With respect to gender-related patterns in the type of care provided, a national study in Canada found that men are as likely as women are to perform instrumental tasks (e.g., help with transportation, shopping), but half as likely as women to provide personal care (e.g., assistance with eating, getting to the bathroom). This pattern was noted in other countries, too. Instrumental care is generally episodic, while personal care is daily and more labor intensive. Thus, women are more likely to assume heavier care responsibilities than men.

Hours of Care.   The number of hours that employed persons spend in caregiving activities varied considerably among the countries. For example, in Canada, 13% of employed women and 8% of men provide 5 or more hours of care per week; in Germany, 48% of employed caregivers are engaged in caregiving duties a couple of hours every day; and, in China, all family caregivers reportedly spend more than 1 hour per day. Differing methodological approaches account for some of these differences spent in caregiving hours. Nonetheless, data from all these studies suggest that employed persons spend a considerable amount of time helping their frail elders.

Diversity.   In all countries, research on caregiving and diversity is very limited. The authors describing Mexico and Canada stated that virtually nothing is known about the dynamics of elder care among their countries' indigenous peoples. In Germany, very little is known about the care situation of the "guest workers" from Turkey, Spain, Italy, Greece, and the former Yugoslavia. As a result of the formation of the European Union, ethnic diversity most likely will increase as workers move across country boundaries looking for work.

When diversity has been examined, various differences have been found in caregiving experiences based on racial or ethnic background, sexual orientation, and rural or urban location of the caregiver or care recipient. For example, in Canada, almost 30% of the older population do not speak English or French, presenting language and cultural barriers to accessing elder care services. In Israel, Arab elders and their family members are hesitant to use formal care services. Very few gays and lesbians in the United States are entitled to use family-focused benefits, such as family leaves. Discrimination was noted by the authors from Canada, Mexico, Great Britain, the United States, and Japan as one of the factors contributing to lessened access to and use of health care services and workplace benefits by minority groups and indigenous peoples.

In the chapters on China, Mexico, and Brazil, vast differences between rural and urban populations were noted in the availability of and access to public support for seniors. Basically, most rural elders do not have pension plans, and rural health care services are limited. Consequently, rural elders must rely totally on their families for financial and other types of support.

The data reported suggest that the experiences and needs of employed caregivers vary considerably within a given country by such factors as cultural background, geographical location, and sexual orientation; however, considerably more research in these areas will be needed if the needs of all employed caregivers are to be adequately addressed.

Impact of Managing Work and Elder Care

The studies reported in the preceding chapters identify both benefits and disadvantages related to combining work and caregiving for employees and employers alike.

Benefits of Combining Work and Elder Care.   Some employed caregivers experience no adverse effects of managing work and elder care and many experience benefits as well as challenges. As noted in several of the chapters, working has been found to be advantageous for many employed caregivers, because it gives them a break from caregiving. Another advantage is that the income earned from employment allows middle-class families, at least, in Brazil, Great Britain, and the United States to purchase services for their elders. This helps to reduce some of the employed caregivers' overall burden. Several chapter authors also noted that, as a result of the caregiving experience, employees bring to the workplace greater sensitivity to human needs and enhanced skills in managing difficult situations. Such attitudes and skills can improve communication and organizational abilities at work; thereby, contributing to increases in productivity at work.

Disadvantages to Combining Work and Elder Care.   A disadvantage to employees and employers alike is cutting back on the number of hours worked, or even the quitting of work entirely by employees in order to care for elders. These are the most frequently cited adjustments made by employed caregivers: In Canada, 9% had quit their jobs; in Germany, 16% had quit or reduced their work hours; in Great Britain, 40% had taken time off; in Israel, 25% had reduced their work hours and, on average, missed 3 days of work a month; in Japan, 28% of men and 35% of women had either quit, taken an extended leave, or changed jobs; in Sweden, 55% had either quit, reduced their work hours, or taken a leave of absence; in the United States, 28% had either quit, taken a leave of absence, or reduced their work hours.

For employers, reductions in work hours and job cessation have obvious adverse effects on workplaces through decreases in work productivity. The chapter on the United States revealed that one company estimated that a little over $3,000 dollars per employee per year are lost due to problems stemming from managing work and elder care. If losing valuable workers were included, the overall cost estimates would be much higher.

For employees in most countries a reduction in work hours results not only in lost wages but, ultimately, in reduced future pension benefits. In addition to these economic losses, caregivers no longer have their jobs to give them a break from caregiving nor do they have other benefits that jobs can provide, such as social contact and a feeling of competency. Employed caregivers also reported physical and emotional problems. In Germany, 58% of employed caregivers reported feeling strongly or very strongly burdened; in Great Britain, over 50% said that caregiving interferes with their work; in Japan, 27% reported physical fatigue and 47% reported psychological fatigue. The Canadian studies found that the greater the work-family conflict experienced by employed caregivers, the more likely they were to report reduced job satisfaction and increased absenteeism.

Special Problems in Developing Countries

Urbanization. Employed caregivers in countries undergoing urbanization, or movement from rural to urban areas, face particular problems in managing work and informal care of frail elders. The urban populations in China, Uganda, Mexico, and Brazil are steadily growing at 5.2%, 4.2%, 3.3%, and 3% per year, respectively (World Bank, 1997). Urban growth in the most developed countries is almost negligible, at about 1% per year (World Bank, 1997). In Uganda, young persons who move to the cities find it very difficult to care for their rural relatives, because of the substantial distances involved and the country's limited means of transportation. The new urbanites also are coping with economic and social disruptions of their own, given the limited jobs and crowded living conditions in the cities. Furthermore, the barriers to providing elder care create stress for persons whose cultural values dictate that they not only revere older persons, but that they provide any necessary care to them.

Low Wages and Unemployment. In countries such as Mexico, Brazil, and Uganda, many family members are employed in the informal sector, where wages are low, and benefits and job security are nonexistent. Helping older frail parents, many of whom have no retirement or health benefits, becomes difficult for employed caregivers struggling with their own economic insecurity. Unemployment is a growing problem in Mexico, China, Uganda, and Brazil. Although lack of a job may allow more time to help care for a frail elder, the resulting lack of economic security typically overrides this advantage for reasons previously noted.

Summary

In sum, throughout the world the combining of work with informal care to elders is a fairly common phenomenon that will become even more so in the future. For some employed caregivers, the dual roles have little negative impact for them or their employers. For others, this is not the case. In particular, caregiving is especially stressful for those employees who are assisting elders with heavy care needs, for those who assess their dual roles as conflictual, for those who lack adequate financial resources, and for those for whom programmatic supports are not available or accessible. Many workers have had to make considerable adjustments in their work schedules, resulting in lost wages and in reduced retirement benefits. Because women most often are the primary caregivers, they are the ones most vulnerable to economic losses and other stressors. Because of families' employment obligations, particularly those of women, the traditional reliance on families and especially on women to provide care to frail or disabled elders is becoming increasingly problematic.

☐ Supports for Employed Caregivers and Elders

Overall, awareness of and support for employed caregivers are limited in the countries described herein. In the countries in which supports are provided by the workplace or by some level of government, these programs typically are very recent. Oftentimes, such supports are not targeted to employed caregivers, but to all employees or to elderly persons themselves. This section summarizes the key government, labor union, work organization, and community policies, benefits, and services that the authors described as helpful to employed caregivers and their elders.

Supports for Employed Caregivers

Organizational or community interventions that prevent or limit the extent to which elder care involvement intrudes on work may substantially reduce the adverse workplace consequences experienced by caregivers.

Payment to Caregiver Programs.   As shown in Table 13-1, either local or federal governments in six countries (Sweden, Great Britain, Canada, Germany, Israel, and the United States) pay family members to care for their frail elders. Caregiving can be combined with employment in several countries, but work hours generally need to be reduced. In some countries, government contributions are made to caregivers' pension plans, in addition to payments to caregivers. Only three countries (Sweden, Germany, and Great Britain) offer the paid caregiver program to all caregivers who meet eligibility requirements. The programs in Canada and the United States are limited to a small number of people who live in those provinces or states that offer this benefit. Israel's program is available only to Arabs. Although the program in Great Britain is a universal program, few employed caregivers qualify, because the care allowance is targeted to those providing more than 35 hours of care. In all six countries, payment levels are generally low.

Work Leaves to Care for Elders.   As shown above in Table 13-1, many countries offer employees a temporary leave from work to care for frail relatives. In some countries, the leaves are mandated through legislation; in other countries, they are voluntarily initiated by work organizations; in still other countries, the leaves are both mandated and workplace initiated. Mandated leaves cannot be easily withdrawn, whereas workplace-initiated leaves can be discontinued at any time. Workplace leaves generally are available only to employees in large companies, especially those that have a high concentration of female workers. The length of the leave varies, as does whether or not financial compensation is provided. Although family care leaves do exist in Uganda and Brazil, only a handful of work organizations offer such leaves, and arrangements are entirely ad hoc. The most comprehensive and useful leave is that exemplified by Sweden—the leave is assured by the government, available to all, paid up to 80% of salary, and lasts for 60 days.

Work at Home Programs.   Many authors describing the most developed countries noted the increasing government and workplace interest in allowing employees

TABLE 13-1. Government, workplace, and union supports for employed caregivers

| | Government Initiatives | | | | | | Workplace Initiatives | | Union Initiatives | | | |
| | Pay Caregivers | | Mandated Work Leaves | | | | Work Leave | | Contract Negotiations | Lobby | Services | Educate Members |
Countries	Program Exists?	Universal	Program Exists?	Length	Paid	Universal	Program Exists?	Prevalence	Program Exists?	Program Exists?	Program Exists?	Program Exists?
Most developed												
Canada	Yes	No	No				Yes	Moderate	Yes	Yes	Yes	Yes
Germany	Yes	Yes	No				Yes	Few	Yes	Yes	No	No
Great Britain	Yes	Yes	No				Yes	Few	Yes	Yes	No	Yes
Israel	Yes[a]	No	Yes	6 days	100%	Yes	No	NA	Yes	Yes	No	No
Japan	No	NA	Yes[b]	3 months	25%	No	Yes	Few[c]	Yes	Yes	No	No
Sweden	Yes	Yes	Yes	60 days	80%	Yes	Yes	Unknown	Yes	Yes	No	No
United States	Yes	No	Yes	12 weeks	0%	No	Yes	Moderate	Yes	Yes	Yes	Yes
More developed												
Brazil	No	NA	No				Yes	Unknown	No	No	No	No
Mexico	No	NA	No				No	NA	No	No	No	No
Less developed												
China	No	NA	No				Yes[d]	Moderate	No	No	Yes	No
Uganda	No	NA	No				Yes	Rare	No	No	No	No

[a] Only pay Arabs to care for elders.
[b] Begins in 1999.
[c] Twenty-one percent of randomly selected companies with 30 or more employees offer work leave.
[d] Offered by state-owned enterprises.

to work from home or at a location close to home. For example, in Japan, several private businesses, in cooperation with the government, have begun investigating the feasibility of telework or satellite offices as alternative workplaces for their employees caring for frail elders. With on-going technological advances, more countries may consider this option.

Workplace-Initiated Supports Other than Work Leaves.   Work organizations in many countries have voluntarily initiated a variety of family-focused policies, benefits, and services. These include flexible work arrangements, subsidies to employees paying for elder care services, counseling, resource and referral services, and sensitivity training for supervisors. Generally, only large companies offer such programs. Small companies lack the financial resources to do so, unless they form a cooperative with other small companies and share resources and expenses.

Union-Initiated Supports.   As shown above in Table 13-1, some labor unions in the most developed countries have negotiated contracts with work organizations that include provision for family-friendly benefits. These unions also have pressured their respective national governments to pass legislation that is supportive of employed caregivers. In addition, unions in several of these countries have been active in educating and sensitizing their own members to work-family concerns. Finally, some unions have offered work-family services directly to their membership.

Community Agency Initiatives.   Very few private and not-for-profit agencies have evolved to assist employed caregivers. Such initiatives are most common in the United States, where private corporations contract with vendors to provide employees with work-family programs (such as referral to community services and educational seminars) to help them deal with their caregiving duties. Also, a few corporations offer elder care–case management services, primarily to employees whose relatives live some distance away.

Discussion of Supports for Employed Caregivers.   In none of the 11 countries does an explicit government policy exist that addresses the needs of employees who are informal caregivers to elders. Although 10 years ago, the Canadian Minister of Employment and Immigration recommended the development of a National Policy on Care for the Elderly, which would focus on the growing support needs of workers with elderly dependents, nothing seems to have come of this.

In those countries where family-focused supports are not universal, workers in the public sector and those employed by large corporations generally have more benefits than workers in other jobs. The uneven distribution of benefits typically hurts lower paid workers, who comprise mostly women and historically disadvantaged racial and ethnic groups. These latter groups often are the ones who need assistance the most, both because of their low wages and because they tend to have relatives who become frail at an earlier age due, in part, to the reduced access to health care by persons with low incomes. These employed caregivers have the fewest resources with the least assistance from the workplace.

It is important to point out that some employed caregivers do not use the supports that are available to them. The U.S., Canadian, British, and German authors suggested that some employed caregivers are reluctant to use workplace benefits because they fear such action would jeopardize their jobs. Employee reluctance also is related to having to negotiate for many of the benefits (e.g., flexible work schedules, place of work) with supervisors who may not be sympathetic. A third reason is lack of awareness of existing employee benefits and how to use them. A fourth is lack of identification of self as a caregiver. Finally, caregiving is sometimes seen as an expected role that is self-managed, rather than one where assistance can be expected from others.

Supports for Elders

Pensions and Acute Medical Care.   Almost all elders in the most developed countries receive public pension benefits and health insurance for acute care through their countries' public Social Security programs. In the developing countries, far fewer elders receive pension and health care benefits: Rural and low-income elders and those who did not work for the government receive the fewest benefits. In Brazil, only 43% of the labor force are covered through the country's Social Security pension program; in Mexico, 12% of the total urban population and 3% of the rural population have pension coverage; in China, almost all elders in rural areas are without pension benefits.

Access to health care is unevenly distributed in China, Mexico, and Brazil, with rural elders receiving the fewest services. In Brazil, the publicly financed health care services are of very poor quality. Uganda's health care system is the least developed; there is only one doctor for 25,000 persons, compared to one doctor for every 300 to 600 persons in the most developed countries.

In those countries without adequate pension plans, families provide 32% to 58% of financial assistance to elders, as shown in Table 13-2. Similarly, elders without adequate medical care must rely on their families for assistance.

Long-Term Care Services.   Long-term care (LTC) services include institutional care (such as nursing homes) and community care (such as home care, day care, respite care, and assistance with transportation). When elders become frail, they need LTC services far more frequently than acute medical care services. Countries vary considerably in their provision of these services, as shown in Table 13-2.

Most Developed Countries.   Sweden and Germany provide universal, publicly funded community and institutional care services. Japan and Israel provide publicly funded community-based programs. Canada's publicly funded LTC program emphasizes institutional care; community care services are neither comprehensively covered nor abundant. LTC services in Great Britain and the United States are not universal programs; they are means-tested programs, with eligibility determined by the elder's income. Private sector LTC services are most developed in the United States due to the absence of public sector support. In Great Britain, the federal government is the primary funder of LTC services, with services being provided by a mixture of private, not-for-profit, and public agencies competing with each other. It is important to note that, in all of the most developed countries except Sweden, the countries' governments are encouraging privatization of elder care services. Private sector elder care services could become more developed in Sweden, if the Conservative Party were to succeed in forming a government.

Countries with universal, publicly funded LTC programs generally have the most affordable LTC services. In all countries, however, the elderly still have unmet needs. There simply are not enough affordable LTC services to meet the present demand. The future portends even greater problems, with the projected growth in the number of elders over 75 years of age, especially in the most developed country.

TABLE 13-2. Long-term care and income supports for elders

Countries	Long-Term Care Services				Percentage of Seniors Receiving Income From		
	Public		Private	Other	Pension[c]	Family[c]	Work[c]
	Universal	Means-Tested					
Most developed							
Canada		X	X		97%	NA	19%
Germany	X		X		98%	NA	2%
Great Britain		X	X		100%	NA	13%
Israel	X		X		97%	NA	9%
Japan	X		X		97%	NA	9%
Sweden	X		X		100%	NA	0%
United States		X	X		94%	NA	20%
More developed							
Brazil		X	X		61%	32%	25%
Mexico		X	X		61%	32%	25%
Less developed							
China	NA		X	X[b]	13%	34%	45%
Uganda	NA		X[a]		13%	58%	47%

[a]Only a couple of voluntary organizations offer long-term care services.

[b]State-owned enterprises offer long-term care services.

[c]From *Averting the Old Age Crisis: Policies to Promote the Old and Promote Growth.* Copyright 1994 by the World Bank.

In all countries, the demand for LTC services has exceeded government budget forecasts. The overall trends are to reduce public sector costs and to encourage informal family care. Numerous approaches have been suggested to achieve these goals. One approach is to concentrate public care resources on heavier care cases. Another is to make home care services more cost effective; for example, by setting up neighborhood teams of home care workers who can serve numerous elders in a single day. Still another is to privatize community care services. Some approaches are designed to support the caregivers, such as the provision of respite care (someone else cares for the elder, either at home or elsewhere, while the caregiver takes a break).

Developing Countries. State-owned enterprises in China offer a few community-based LTC services to retired elders; nursing home care is available only to elders without family support. The scope and type of support varies from enterprise to enterprise, depending on the economic strength of the enterprise. In Mexico and Brazil, LTC services are poorly developed and are available primarily through the private sector. LTC services in Uganda are essentially nonexistent.

Discussion of Supports for Elders. Public supports for elders reduce some of employed caregivers' financial and other caregiving duties. Such supports make it easier for employed caregivers to balance work and elder care. The trend, however, is toward reduced government expenditures for the care of the elderly; thereby, increasing the burden on employed caregivers, particularly those with low incomes.

☐ Future Trends

Changes at the National Government Level

This section discusses three changes that are occurring among most countries' national governments: (1) privatization of public social welfare, (2) privatization of government-owned businesses, and (3) promotion of community and family-based care of the aged.

Privatization of Public Social Welfare Programs. Policy decision makers in all countries are carefully examining the appropriate role for government in the provision of social welfare benefits. The growing costs of public pension plans and health care services, especially for older persons, are raising concerns about existing and future government deficits. Deficits increase internal debt payments which, in turn, decrease monies available to strengthen countries' physical and social infrastructure, such as technological capacity, workforce quality (e.g., education and skill levels), and transportation systems. Deficits also can have an adverse effect on economic growth.

The preceding chapters described how national governments, in an effort to decrease government costs, have either partially privatized or are considering partially privatizing public pension benefits or LTC services. The authors noted that privatization of pension plans and other elder care services could benefit those with the financial resources and expertise to purchase them privately. On the other hand, reductions in government-funded pension plans and other services most likely would have an adverse effect on those employed caregivers and elders who have low to middle incomes or limited knowledge of the free market system. Thus, in the future, a substantial number of caregivers may need to financially supplement their relatives' lower pensions and provide elder care services no longer available from state-funded programs.

Privatization of Government-Owned Businesses.   The authors describing the developing countries noted that their national governments are selling state-owned businesses and enterprises to private individuals and companies. These governments want to shrink the size of government (e.g., personnel, responsibilities, expenditures) and, more importantly, they want to move toward a free market economy. The selling off of state-owned businesses in China, Brazil, and Mexico has left many people without jobs and without the more generous workplace benefits previously provided through government employment. Although those with the financial resources and know-how to successfully deal with the free market economy will benefit, many other workers will not.

Many influential economists, international organizations (e.g., the International Monetary Fund [IMF]), and state-level policy makers believe that smaller governments and privatization of social welfare programs and state-owned businesses are essential to economic growth (World Bank, 1997). For example, the IMF recently required Brazil to cut back on social programs in order to qualify for a $30 billion loan package (Schemo, 1998b).

Promotion of Community and Family-Based Care of the Aged.
Governments in 10 of the 11 countries are limiting expenditures on the more expensive institutional-based care of aged persons and, instead, are promoting the less expensive community- and family-based care of older persons. The exception is Uganda: Because Uganda has few institutional or community services for elders, families already provide the majority of care. Several innovative community care strategies were presented in the preceding chapters. Examples of programs that promote family care are paid informal caregiver programs, respite programs, and temporary work leaves to care for frail elders. Not all programs are supportive, though. Some governments are considering punitive measures to force families to assume care of frail elders. For example, in Canada, there is some concern that the 1921 law that declared children to be legally obligated to care for their parents will once again be enforced as a way to save the public purse.

Changes at the Work Organizational Level

As revealed in the preceding chapters, labor markets in all countries are in a state of transition; they are making significant changes in order to remain or become competitive in the global economy. In Japan, fewer companies guarantee lifelong employment; they have become achievement oriented as opposed to seniority oriented. Work organizations are restructuring, resulting in downsizing and increased reliance on temporary, part-time, and short-term contract workers. These workers generally receive fewer family-focused benefits, have limited job protection, and are paid lower wages. Corporate restructuring is expected to continue for some time.

Moreover, work organizations in all countries are pressing governments for more employer flexibility. Employers with the most flexibility can hire and fire at will and are the least restrained by government-mandated benefits and regulations. Increased employer flexibility can benefit those caregivers who prefer part-time or temporary jobs. But, for the majority of workers who want and need full-time employment, reductions in work hours and benefits will adversely affect them financially. In addition to financial losses, caregivers no longer will have the break from caregiving provided by employment that many have noted has been helpful in managing the care of elders.

Some of the work organizational changes, however, may benefit employed caregivers. Many countries have had flexible work scheduling in place for some time. Increasingly, work-at-home programs are becoming popular. Working from home may make it easier for workers to look after a frail elder while performing work tasks. In addition, the formation of common markets, such as the European Union, may allow for increased family-focused benefits for employees in countries with fewer present benefits. For example, as noted in the chapter on Great Britain, the European Union is considering new directives that, if implemented, will assist employed caregivers in all member states with respect to entitlement to leave, hours of work, and equal pay. One specific directive that is being considered is decreasing the average number of hours worked per week to help ensure employment for all who wish to work. This initiative would be helpful to employed caregivers, if benefits and wages were not reduced.

Changes Among Labor Unions

Several authors (Israel, Great Britain, United States, Brazil, and Mexico) reported that the power of labor unions in their country is eroding. One reason for this erosion is the unions' inability to effectively bargain for job security and better wages. Another reason is government legislation that weakens the strength of unions and increases the power of employers. Unions' failures have contributed to declines in union membership. Fewer members further decrease the strength of unions. Such changes weaken unions' abilities worldwide to bargain for family-focused benefits.

On a positive note, in an effort to increase union membership, labor unions are attempting to organize workers in the service industry, the fastest growing segment of the labor force. Because more women than men are employed in this industry, unions may be pressured into focusing on social issues that concern women, such as family-oriented benefits and discrimination. Such changes may bring favorable outcomes with respect to services for working families.

Families' Commitment to Care for Elders

Several authors noted that the processes of urbanization, migration, modernization, and economic globalization are affecting families' commitment and ability to care for elders. As discussed above, urbanization in the less developed countries and migration in the European countries among workers looking for employment are separating workers from their relatives and making it more difficult for them physically to care for elders. In the poorest countries, the new urbanites are experiencing personal, economic, and social problems that make caregiving more difficult. The processes of urbanization and migration are expected to continue for many years to come.

As noted in the chapters on Uganda, China, Japan, and Mexico, modernization (i.e., increased education or exposure to Western values) is resulting in changes in attitudes toward caregiving. Ugandan urbanites, once removed from their rural roots, are less committed to their traditional values, including those obligating the family to care for its elders. In China, exposure to Western values is weakening "filial piety" (the expectation that adult children will care for their parents). In Japan, less than 30% of Japanese women age 40 to 50 and less than 50% of men and women in any age group believed themselves to be responsible for taking care of their elderly parents. As noted in the chapter on Mexico, young people first meet their own necessities and those of their children; only after that are the needs of elders considered.

In each of the 11 countries discussed in this book, economic globalization or movement to a market economy have created a lack of jobs, contingency workforces, job layoffs, and underemployment. As a result, it is more difficult for families to financially assist their older relatives. This is particularly problematic for families in countries where elders have few health care and income security benefits.

Implications.   The changes occurring at the work organization, government, and trade union levels differentially affect elders and their employed caregivers. Many of these changes raise concerns about equity issues and decrease the likelihood that low-income workers and elders, especially those in developing countries, will get their basic needs met. Furthermore, these changes suggest a growing inequality between the better paid workers and those with low incomes from employment and from old age benefits. Women and historically disadvantaged minorities are the most at risk by any reductions in income and benefits from the state or the workplace. Inequalities are especially likely in the developing countries. Kuznets (1955) argued that when a low-income economy (e.g., Uganda, China, Mexico, and Brazil) moves toward a higher income economy, inequalities will increase. The emphasis will be on creating opportunities for economic expansion; thus, efforts will be made to reduce labor cost, by keeping wages low and limiting benefits. Under these conditions, a few people will make a lot of money, while the masses will not. State spending on social programs would be limited to developing the physical infrastructure (e.g., roads, telecommunications), which is necessary for promoting foreign investments and other capital investments. Table 13-3 overviews the distribution of income in all 11 countries. It clearly shows the disparity of income among the wealthiest and the poorest in all countries; the gaps are the greatest, however, in the developing countries. Kuznets also argued that, as low income countries become more affluent, the great differences in wealth will lessen because a sustained stronger economy will benefit the masses. This transition, however, will take years, leaving many people without decent incomes, housing or health care.

The next section examines those conditions that promote family supports. This information will be used to suggest recommendations for initiating supports for employed caregivers and their elders.

☐ Conditions That Foster the Development of Supports for Employed Caregivers and Elders

Drawing on data presented in the preceding chapters, here we suggest several factors that contribute to the development of supports for employed caregivers and for elders. The best supports are those that are comprehensive; that is, they are available to all, regardless of geographic location, workplace affiliation, or other limiting criteria. Exemplary programs are universal, affordable LTC services for elders and universal paid temporary work leaves for employed caregivers.

Three conditions are suggested that contribute to the development of supports: (1) external pressure, (2) ability, and (3) willingness. *External pressure* as it is used here, refers to presence of social needs (e.g., work and family conflicts) within a country that require its institutions (e.g., governments, work organizations, and trade unions) to respond. The response is necessary in order to ensure the institution's and, in some

TABLE 13-3. Distribution of income or consumption

Countries	Survey Year	Lowest 10%	Lowest 20%	Second Quintile	Third Quintile	Fourth Quintile	Highest 20%	Highest 10%
Most developed								
Canada	1987[e,f]		5.7	11.8	17.7	24.6	40.2	24.1
Germany	1988[e,f]		7.0	11.8	17.1	23.9	40.3	24.4
Great Britain	1988[e,f]		4.6	10.0	16.8	24.3	44.3	27.8
Israel	1979[e,f]		6.0	12.1	17.8	24.5	39.6	23.5
Japan	1979[e,f]		8.7	13.2	17.5	23.1	37.5	22.4
Sweden	1981[e,f]		8	13.2	17.4	24.5	36.9	20.8
United States	1985[e,f]		4.7	11.0	17.4	25.0	41.9	25.0
More developed								
Brazil	1989[c,d]	0.7	2.1	4.9	8.9	16.8	67.5	51.3
Mexico	1992[a,b]	1.6	4.1	7.8	12.5	20.2	55.3	39.2
Less developed								
China	1995[c,d]	2.2	5.5	9.8	14.9	22.3	47.5	30.9
Uganda	1992–1993[a,b]	3.0	6.8	10.3	14.4	20.4	48.1	33.4

Note. From *World Development Report 1997: The State in a Changing World.* Copyright 1997 by the World Bank.
[a]Refers to expenditure shares by percentiles of persons.
[b]Ranked by per capita expenditure.
[c]Refers to income shares by percentiles of persons.
[d]Ranked by per capita income.
[e]Refers to income shares by percentiles of households.
[f]Ranked by household income.

cases, the society's economic or social survival. *Ability* refers to economic and social infrastructure (e.g., capacity to administer a comprehensive pension program) within a country that enables its institutions to respond to the emerged social needs. *Willingness* refers to characteristics (e.g., strong unions) of a country that foster the development of comprehensive programs in response to the emerged needs. The three conditions (external pressure, ability, and willingness) are not mutually exclusive; they are interrelated and, moreover, in some cases, a combination of these conditions is essential for the development of comprehensive supports for elders and their caregivers.

External Pressures: Demographic and Social Changes

Institutional theory suggests that institutions (e.g., work organizations, trade unions, and governments) are most likely to respond to the needs of a particular group (e.g., employed caregivers) when they have become dependent on this group or have been coerced into responding (DiMaggio & Powell, 1991; Goodstein, 1994; Oliver, 1991). In many of the countries reviewed in this book, the proportion of women in the workforce is nearly equal to that of men. Work organizations have become as dependent on working women as they have been on working men. As previously noted in the chapters describing the most developed countries, one of the main reasons given for employers' initiation of voluntary workplace family benefits is to attract and keep female employees. Employers do this because they cannot afford to lose their valued female and male employees with caregiving responsibilities.

Work organizations also respond when they are coerced into doing so. In countries where unions have negotiated work-family benefits or governments have mandated family-supportive legislation, work organizations have acquiesced to the needs of employed caregivers. Noncompliance could result in an economic and, perhaps, a social loss for the work organization.

It is important to note that voluntary workplace responses, as well as union and government mandates, do not necessarily ensure that all workers have access to the same types and levels of support. Government mandates, however, are the most likely to cover the entire working population. Data from the preceding chapters suggest that family supportive programs, as well as higher wages, are more prevalent in large companies and government than in small- or mid-size companies. One reason for this is the higher visibility of large companies and governments as employers. This visibility makes these organizations more vulnerable to external pressures and, therefore, they are more likely to acquiesce. Large work organizations also have the economic means to initiate family support programs. Another consideration regarding uniformity of benefits and longevity of these benefits is that, during periods of high unemployment, some work organizations are more likely to withdraw their voluntarily initiated family support programs. Government mandates and union agreements, however, take longer to unravel and are more difficult to withdraw due to external pressures from employed caregivers. Thus, it appears that coercive strategies used by government and trade unions are the ones most likely to ensure supports that are equitable and long lasting.

According to institutional theory, governments and trade unions, as well as work organizations, are more likely to respond to the needs of employed caregivers if they become dependent on them or are coerced into responding. Evidence suggests that this is happening. The chapter on Sweden revealed that family policies were legislated in the 1960s to help ensure the participation of women in the workforce and the continuation of childbearing. Japan more recently legislated family supportive workplace policies, in part, to help slow down the country's declining fertility rate. In each country, the government became dependent on women and needed their cooperation in childbearing and employment; thus, accommodations were made to obtain a societal goal. Other countries have initiated benefits to make it easier for employed caregivers to continue to provide assistance to their dependent family members. Family assistance is far less expensive then public or private care services. Finally, worldwide attention is being given to the needs of the growing number of aged around the world. The year 1999 marks the United Nations Year of Older Persons. Events like this can pressure all countries to give greater attention and programmatic supports to older persons and their caregivers. In conclusion, work organizations, governments, and trade unions have initiated family supportive policies and benefits, in part, because of external pressures stemming from work and family conflicts. Such responses were initiated in order to ensure the institution's—and in some cases, the society's—economic or social survival.

Ability to Respond to Needs: Economic and Social Development and Infrastructure Capacity

Not all countries with high female employment rates or large numbers of elders in need of care have implemented family policies at the work organizational, government, and union levels. The situations in China and Uganda suggest that the needs of employed caregivers alone are not sufficient to foster the creation of family-friendly benefits. Both countries have very high female labor force participation rates, yet few, if any, employers have responded to the needs of employed caregivers. These inconsistencies suggest that, in addition to the presence of a social need, governments and work organizations must also have the *ability* to respond to external pressures.

A country's levels of economic and social development are good indicators of its ability to respond to emerging social needs. Basically, the most developed countries are able to respond to the needs of elders and employed caregivers because they have greater economic resources and fewer extreme social problems than are experienced in the other countries, as shown in Table 1-2 of chapter 1. This table shows that the gross national product (GNP) per capita in the less developed countries is very small compared to that in the most developed countries. Specifically, in 1995, Uganda's GNP was only $240, China's was $620, and Brazil's was $3,640, compared to Israel's GNP of $15, 000 and Japan's GNP of $40,000 in the same year. The less developed countries also have fairly serious social problems, as shown in the same table in chapter 1. Their poverty rates and infant mortality rates are high, as are rates of illiteracy. The authors from Uganda, Brazil, and Mexico suggest that the most basic social problems, such as inadequate health care, limited educational opportunities, poverty, and crime, are given the highest priority. Pension plans for elders are the only elder-specific social programs that are receiving some attention in these countries.

Although China has fewer extreme social problems and its gross domestic product (GDP) growth has been impressive (see Table 1-2 in chapter 1), the author from China noted that China's economic growth has not been sufficient to provide adequate public and employment-based social welfare support to the population of over 1 billion persons, especially the rapidly growing number of elders. Furthermore, average incomes are still very low. Here, the sheer numbers of low-income persons in need of services have overwhelmed China's economic growth factor.

In support of these observations, Wilensky (1975) and Kuznets (1955) argued that welfare states, such as those in the most developed countries, emerge once a country becomes affluent and can afford social programs, such as pensions, health care, and work-family benefits. Although there is a need for work-family programs in the less developed countries, the countries' weak economic bases and social problems make it more difficult for them to develop responsive programs.

A third condition that is necessary for the ability of a country to implement family-friendly supports is infrastructure capacity (e.g., efficient communication systems, administrative ability). In countries with a fairly rural population, such as in China and Uganda, pension plans are difficult to set up for a variety of reasons. Specifically, problems arise in setting affordable tax rates among the low-income farmers and traders whose profits can be destroyed by weather conditions. Also, collecting the taxes is difficult with poorly developed mail and banking systems. Furthermore, countries with weak administrative capacities (e.g., lack of knowledge of how to create and operate a sound pension system) will have a difficult time administering complex, comprehensive pension programs (Stiglitz, 1997). Finally, in countries where crime and corruption are high, the limited economic resources will be wasted and, thus, less available for social welfare programs. Thus, efforts to promote family-work benefits in Mexico, Brazil, China, and Uganda need to be balanced with the capacity of the government to engage in these activities.

Willingness to Provide Comprehensive Supports for Employed Caregivers and Elders

In the most developed countries, both "external pressure" and "ability" are present; yet, these countries vary in the degree to which country-specific supports are comprehensive. For example, Sweden's public social welfare programs provide fairly comprehensive LTC services to its elderly population and universal paid leaves and payments to informal caregivers. In contrast, public social welfare programs in the United States provide limited long-term care services to elders, offer no paid leaves to employed caregivers, and few payments to informal caregivers. Moreover, unlike all other most developed countries described in this book, the United States has no government-funded universal health care plan.

What accounts for the differences in type and level of supports among the most developed countries of Sweden, United States, Israel, Germany, Canada, Great Britain, and Japan? Wilensky (1975) suggested that a number of factors explain the differences in social welfare programs among "rich" countries. According to Wilensky, the welfare states with the most comprehensive and affordable supports tend to have (1) strong unions, (2) more centralized governments, (3) more developed public social welfare systems (i.e., universal health care), (4) less developed private sector initiatives, (5) more homogeneous populations, (6) meager self-employment experiences, (7) a middle mass that does not perceive its tax burden as grossly unfair to that of the rich and the upper middle class, and (8) citizens who do not feel a great social distance from the poor. Although all of these factors are important, the first four are considered here: unionization, centralized planning, public welfare programs, and private sector involvement. The other factors are not discussed, because data about those issues were not explicitly emphasized in this book.

Sweden has all of the four characteristics under discussion. Almost 90% of its labor force is unionized (U.S. Department of Labor, Bureau of Labor Statistics, 1997), which suggests a strong union presence. It engages in centralized planning. An example is where the national government, employers, and unions together negotiate employee wages and benefits, including family benefits. Swedish public social welfare programs are extensive and comprehensive, whereas the private sector is very small. Thus, it is not surprising that Sweden has comprehensive and affordable benefits for elders and paid caregiver leaves.

In contrast to Sweden, the United States has none of the four characteristics. Only 15% of employees in the United States workforce are unionized (U.S. Department of Labor, Bureau of Labor Statistics, 1997). The country's decentralization of political power among major institutions (e.g., government, business community, interest groups) and the country's reliance on coalition building make it very difficult for the government, even if it wanted to, to develop coherent economic and social policies that would lead to the initiation of LTC services for all, paid family leaves, and other family-focused benefits. Moreover, the private sector is much more developed in the United States than in the other developed countries, especially in the areas of LTC services and supports for employed caregivers.

The other five countries fall somewhere between Sweden and the United States on the four characteristics for willingness to provide comprehensive social programs (i.e., unionization, centralized planning, public and private sector initiatives). Israel's characteristics probably are closer to Sweden's. Its workforce is highly unionized, and labor decisions are made similarly to those found in Sweden. Israel's private sector is slightly more developed than Sweden's, but not as extensive as that in the United States. So, according to Wilensky, this is one of the reasons that Israel has fairly well developed public LTC services, a universal leave policy, and universal health care.

About one third of the workforces in Germany, Great Britain, and Canada are unionized (U.S. Department of Labor, Bureau of Labor Statistics, 1997). The preceding chapters suggest that private sector initiatives are somewhat developed in Germany, Great Britain, and Canada, but public support is still strongly present, especially in Germany. Germany's LTC services are universal and government initiated, whereas those in Great Britain and Canada are means tested and available only to select groups that meet income requirements.

As described in the chapter on Japan, its government has a long history of working closely with businesses, and the country engages in centralized planning, as exemplified in its series of 10-year plans. About one fourth of the workforce is unionized (U.S. Department of Labor, Bureau of Labor Statistics, 1997). Japan also has developed a universal LTC program, but its family leave program is available only to persons working for larger companies.

In conclusion, those countries with all four of the characteristics identified by Wilensky have the most generous supports for elders and employed caregivers. Those with the fewest characteristics have the least developed comprehensive supports, and those with some, but not all, of the four characteristics have a moderate level of comprehensive supports.

Wilensky's argument would suggest that the level and type of supports in the "more generous" countries would become more reflective of those found in the United States if their (1) private sectors were to become more developed, (2) levels of unionization were to drop, and (3) centralized planning were to become less prevalent. Given that these are the trends identified earlier in the Future Trends section (i.e., decline in union strength, shrinkage of the role of government, increases in private sector programs), it seems very possible that supports for employed caregivers and their elders will erode in the most developed countries and, furthermore, few (if any) supports will emerge in the developing countries. Despite the apparent bleakness of the situation, some steps can be taken to strengthen and enhance policies, benefits, and services for employed men and women who care for their frail elders.

☐ Recommendations

This book has established that, worldwide, the numbers of elders are growing, and many of these elders will need assistance from their family members when they reach their most senior years. The employment obligations of men and women make it more difficult for them to care for their dependent family members. As previously noted, because caregiving demands can adversely affect the economic and social goals of work organizations, trade unions, and governments, some of these institutions have acquiesced to the needs of employed caregivers and initiated family supportive policies and programs. It is important that, even within the context of the free market economy, work organizations, governments, and unions not lose sight of the benefits to them when they maintain or initiate family supportive policies and benefits. The needs of employed caregivers will only become greater as more assume the caregiving role.

The Role of the State

Only national governments can ensure equal distribution of resources and supports. Fishlow (1996) argued that government policies can do much to avert the tendency of social change and economic development to increase income inequalities. He suggested that government tax policies, regulations, mandates, and income transfers can help reduce income and social inequalities. For these reasons, we believe that national governments need to take the leadership role in establishing policies that will set a basic minimum of supports for all employed caregivers and elders. Basic minimums may vary somewhat from country to country. Possibilities include: (1) universal health care; (2) income security in old age; (3) paid temporary work leaves; (4) employment opportunities; (5) contributions to caregivers' pension plans during absences from the workplace due to elder care duties; (6) payments to informal family caregivers; and (7) various supportive services to employed caregivers, such as resource and referral services, case management, and education. The basic minimum either can be delivered by government, paid for by government, or mandated or encouraged by government. For example, some supports, such as a temporary family leave, can be mandated or encouraged (via tax incentives) through the workplace. Other supports can be directly administrated by national governments, such as pension plans. Other ways in which the government can be useful to employed caregivers is by raising awareness of issues related to balancing work and caring for older persons and by setting a good example of being family friendly by offering work-family benefits to its employees.

In countries with a strong capacity for centralized planning, the government is in the best position to take on a leadership role. But, national governments in all countries need to make work and family issues a priority. One way to do this is to set up an association consisting of representatives from all levels of government, business (including small and large employers), trade unions, for-profit and not-for-profit community agencies, and employed caregivers. This association would be charged with recommending cost-effective policies, benefits, and services for employed caregivers.

Partnership Arrangements

A model that fits well for future developments, and one that may help bridge the gap between a country's ability and willingness to help elders, emphasizes partnerships between unions, governments, work organizations, families, and community agencies. Some innovative partnerships have been described in previous chapters. One is a partnership between work organizations and for-profit and not-for-profit vendors to provide services to employed caregivers. Another partnership arrangement uses volunteers recruited from the community to work along with public home care workers to provide cost-effective assistance to elders. An example of a partnership between governments and families is the paid caregiver program. Tax incentives to work organizations are a form of partnership between public and private sectors. Governments have, in some cases, waived strict federal requirements in order to allow states, provinces, and so forth to develop more appropriate solutions to the work–elder care issue. Labor unions' efforts worldwide to reach out to women and address the social issues that affect them will strengthen a country's responsiveness to work and elder care issues.

Several programs described in this book offer affordable, universal assistance and are examples of programs that help reduce inequalities among employed caregivers. By assisting employed caregivers in better managing their dual roles, these government and workplaces both benefit. Family care is far less expensive than publicly funded formal care (e.g., nursing homes). Productive employees help work organizations increase corporate profits and maintain a competitive edge in a highly competitive global economy.

Developing Countries

As discussed above, developing countries have a limited capacity to respond to the needs of employed caregivers and to elders. As Stiglitz (1997) noted, governments in these countries may need to assume a greater role as providers of a social safety net than did the governments of the most developed countries when they were in similar stages of development. One reason is that, in developing economies, urbanization has resulted in less effective community-based safety nets. Urbanization has left elders with fewer support systems; they are more dependent than ever on employed caregivers who are less able to care for them. In transitional economies, state-owned enterprises are being sold, and the new private sector employers are cutting back pension and family-focused benefits in order to remain competitive.

We believe that program development efforts should balance the joint goals of economic growth and social development. Successful free market economies generate jobs and spawn the development of innovative, competitively priced private sector programs (Ohmae, 1995; World Bank, 1997). At the same time, social change and economic development, as discussed above, tend to increase income inequalities.

In developing countries, low-cost and efficient ways need to be identified to assist the informal caregiving system; to promote saving for retirement years, even among the very poor; and to encourage private sector and nongovernmental agency services for elders. The key word is *partnership* between families, the state, work organizations, and community agencies that service the elderly. One particular form of partnership that could be implemented concerns the pension system. Employers and employees would make contributions to a government-initiated pension system and, in addition, all persons of working age would be required to invest a portion of their earnings in the private sector, if banks and insurance companies are sufficiently stable and competent. Work organizations should be asked by the government to make accommodations to employed caregivers with heavy care demands. The government benefits by obtaining free family care. Only low-cost options, such as flexible work schedules and caregiving leave banks (all employees place a few ~~c~~   ~~··~~ vacation days in a central location so that, when the employee or another em~~p~~   ~~·~~tra leave days, they are available) can realistically be considered, how~~·~~   ~~·~~ould create more jobs via public works programs, utilizing lo~~·~~   ~~~~struc- tion and other infrastructure developments. The /   ~~~~nitiative in offering its family-focused benefits for employees ca~~ring~~

In developing countries with a partial pension system in place, u~~··~~ ~~··~~ is a need to standardize benefits across all work organizations and enterprises and to increase awareness of union officials and other groups, such as the street officers in China, of the need for standardized assistance to employed caregivers.

Employed Caregivers

Oftentimes, caregivers do not think of themselves as a group entitled to assistance from other institutions, yet, their voice is very important in pressuring institutions to acquiesce to their needs. Concerned human services workers, vested interest groups concerned with issues related to older persons, and groups that focus on employed caregivers can be effective in helping caregivers identify themselves and, further- more, recognize their rights to assistance from government, work organizations, unions, and other groups. Professionals who assist caregivers in organizing activities should give special attention to indigenous peoples and other minority groups that historically have received less support from major societal institutions. Along with a general recognition of caregiver needs, barriers to obtaining services and benefits (such as language, culture, religion, and disabilities) should be addressed.

Need for Research

Basic data on prevalence of employed caregivers, characteristics of these caregivers, and their experiences need to be more fully developed. Research is necessary to spe- cifically determine the types of supports that are most effective for employed care- givers and for elders. Future studies of employed caregivers should focus on groups that have been underrepresented in the research literature, including low-income workers, male caregivers, various racial and ethnic groups, and persons in gay and lesbian relationships. Causal relationships between caregiving and employment need to be established. Although a few rigorous studies of employed caregivers have been conducted, for the most part, country-specific studies need to be replicable, cross cul- tural, longitudinal, and evaluative. In addition, the methodologies used should be comparable, with similarities in definitions of, for example, "caregiver" and "level of care," and with similar methods of collecting data.

☐ Concluding Comments

In conclusion, with the increase in the numbers and proportion of elders worldwide, and elders of advanced age in the most developed countries, all countries will be un- able to ignore these elders and those who provide care for them. We believe that col- laborative efforts among each nation's major institutions can enable these countries to find cost-effective and humane ways to assist their citizens with dual work and elder care responsibilities. It is our hope that these countries will find the will to do so.

☐ **References**

Fishlow, A. (1996). Inequality, poverty, and growth: Where do we stand? In M. Bruno & B. Pleskovic (Eds.), *Annual World Bank Conference on Development Economics, 1995* (pp. 25–39). Washington, DC: World Bank.

Goodstein, J. (1994). Institutional pressures and strategic responsiveness: Employer involvement in work-family issues. *Academy of Management Journal, 37*(2), 350–382.

Kuznets, S. (1955). Economic growth and income inequality. *The American Economic Review, 14*(1), 1–28.

Ohmae, K. (1995). *The end of the nation state.* New York: Free Press.

Oliver, C. (1991). Strategic responses to institutional processes. *Academy of Management Review, 16*(1), 145–179.

Powell, W., & DiMaggio, P. (Eds.). (1991). *The new institutionalism in organizational analysis.* Chicago: The University of Chicago Press.

Schemo, D. J. (1998a, August 1). Brazil's economic half-steps. *The New York Times,* pp. D1-D2.

Schemo, D. J. (1998b, November 6). Brazil's austerity plan clears important hurdle on pension cost. *The New York Times,* pp. A11.

Stiglitz, J. (1997). Keynote address: The role of government in economic development. In M. Bruno & B. Pleskovic (Eds.), *Annual World Bank Conference on Development Economics, 1996* (pp. 11–23). Washington, DC: World Bank.

U.S. Department of Labor, Bureau of Labor Statistics. (1997). *Table 2: Union membership in twelve countries, adjusted data, 1985–1994.* (Unpublished data obtained from William McMichael, Division of Foreign Labor Statistics.) Washington, DC: U.S. Department of Labor.

Wilensky, H. (1975). *The welfare state and equality: Structural and ideological roots of public expenditures.* Berkeley: University of California Press.

World Bank. (1994). *Averting the old age crisis: Policies to promote the old and promote growth.* New York: Oxford University Press.

World Bank. (1997). *World development report 1997: The state in a changing world.* New York: Oxford University Press.

INDEX

2. Equality Law (Germany), 37

A Book to Be Read by Men (Ochi), 87
Abel, E., 121, 125, 129, 133
Aboderin, I., 145
Adopt a Granny (Mexico), 166
Advisory Council on Equality Between Men and Women (Sweden), 111
AFL-CIO (U.S.), 128
African Brazilians, 143
African Farmer, 195, 197, 206
African-Americans, 121, 125
Afro-Caribbean British, 60, 64
Age Concern (Great Britain), 59
Aging patterns, 3, 211
    Brazil, 145, 152, 154–155, 157
    Canada, 12, 21
    China, 180
    Germany, 39
    Great Britain, 54
    Israel, 73–74
    Japan, 94–95, 97–98
    Mexico, 161
    Sweden, 102, 108
    Uganda, 196–197
    United States, 120, 136
Agricultural Cooperative Association (Japan), 93
Aguilar, C. H., 169
Ahmed, W., 52, 60
AIDS, 3
    Uganda, 194–197, 206–209
AKU, 107, 110–111
Alberta, Canada, 11–12
Alexander, R., 143
Alimonies Law (Israel), 76
All-China Federation of Trade Unions, 185
Allen, I., 54
Alt, R., 122
Alzheimer's disease, 78–79
Amazon Valley, 143

American Association of Retired Persons (U.S.), 120–121
American Business Collaboration for Quality Dependent Care, 126, 129
Amin, I., 194
Andersson, L., 102–103, 105–108
Anstee, J., 56
Antman, P., 108
Apt, N., 206
Arab Israelis, 69–60, 71, 76–78, 212, 215–216
Arber, S., 13, 48
Area Agencies on Aging (U.S.), 123, 125
Asahi Shimbun, 87, 96
Asian Americans, 121
Asian British, 64
Askham, J., 48
Association for the Planning and Development of Services for the Elderly in Israel, 74, 76
AT&T (U.S.), 126
Atkin, K., 48, 52–53, 55, 60
Attendance allowance (Great Britain), 51
Averting the Old Age Crisis, 219
Avon Cosmetics Ltd. (Great Britain), 49
Azaiza, F., 71, 76, 78

Bäcker, G., 32, 34, 38, 43
Backes, G., 39
Baich-Moray, S., 77–78
Baldwin, S., 48
Barham, L., 21, 24
Barnea, T., 75
Bayer (Germany), 32
Beck, B., 29–31, 41
Beer, S., 69–70, 78–79
Beijing, China, 177, 192
Béland, F., 17, 21, 23, 24
Belo Horizonte, Brazil, 143, 150
Bengtson, V., 39
Bentur, N., 76

233

Berencik, B., 79
Bergman, S., 69
Bergmark, Å., 116
Berquó, E., 143, 145–146, 155, 157
Berry-Lound, D., 50, 53, 58
Better Government for Older People (Great
    Britain), 59
Bialik, R., 161–162, 169
Bispinck, R., 38
Blanco, M., 163
Blandford, A., 18
Bond, J., 120
Brandes, S., 132
Brasília, 154
Brazil, 143–159, 212–216, 218–224, 226–227
    aging trends, 3, 145, 152, 154–155, 157
    demographics, 143–144, 155
    future trends, 156–157
    per capita income, 3–5
    population size, 3–4
    social indicators, 4–5
    strengths and weaknesses, 151–152
    support factors, 152–156
    supports, 147–151
    women in the workforce, 1–3
    work/family concerns, 144–147
Brazilian Constitution, 150, 153
Brazilian-American Chamber of Commerce,
    153
Brice, G., 120
Brinkley, A., 131
British Household Panel Survey, 62
Brodsky, J., 69, 71–72, 75–81
Brody, E., 6
Brown, C., 204–206
Bureau of Labor Management Relations
    (U.S.), 128
Bureau of National Affairs (U.S.), 134
Business initiatives, 216, 221–222
    Brazil, 146–148
    Canada, 16, 19–21
    China, 179–185
    Germany, 32–34, 37, 42
    Great Britain, 50–52, 60
    Israel, 74
    Japan, 89, 92–93
    Mexico, 164, 167
    Sweden, 106–107
    Uganda, 199–200
    United States, 125–128, 132
Business-government relations (U.S.),
    133–134

Cahan, P., 79
Campbell, L. D., 12, 13, 14, 24

Canada Employment and Immigration
    Advisory Council, 19–20
Canada Health Act, 17
Canada, 11–28, 195, 199, 213–219, 221,
    224, 227–228
    aging trends, 3, 12, 21
    costs of caring, 13–14
    demographics, 11–12
    employee wants and needs, 19–21
    future developments, 21–24
    per capita income, 3–5
    population size, 3–4
    public policy, 15–18
    social indicators, 4–5
    women in the workforce, 1–3
Canada/Quebec Pension Plan, 16, 18
Canadian Aging Research Network, 11–13,
    19, 21–24
Canadian Minister of Employment and
    Immigration, 217
Canadian Ministry of Science and
    Technology, 11
Canadian Press, 23
Canadian Study of Health and Aging, 15
Caregiver characteristics, 212–213
Caregiver stress, 213–214
    Brazil, 146–147
    Canada, 13–14
    China, 188–189
    Germany, 30–31
    Great Britain, 48–49, 56
    Israel, 72–73
    Japan, 84, 86–87
    Sweden, 103
    Uganda, 207
    United States, 121
Caregivers Association of British Columbia,
    12
Carers (Recognition and Services) Act (Great
    Britain), 53
Carers Charter (Great Britain), 51–52, 58
Carers in Employment Survey (Great
    Britain), 56, 61
Carers National Association (Great Britain),
    59
Carey, E., 23
Carpenter, M., 52
Catholic Church (Sweden), 112
Central Änica de Trabalhadores (Brazil), 154
Central Bureau of Statistics (Israel), 69–71
Central Organization for Social Work
    (Sweden), 113
Central Union (Mexico), 170
Centre on Aging (Canada), 12
Chapman, N., 5, 121, 126

Chappell, N. L., 17–18
Chen, M.Y.T., 20
Cheng, X. Y., 178
Child Care Leave Law (Japan), 88
China National Commission on Aging, 191
China Statistical Yearbook, 177–178, 181, 185
China, 177–193, 211–214, 216, 218–224,
    226–227
  aging trends, 3, 180
  demographics, 177, 180
  employment-based welfare system,
    179–182
  family/work concerns, 177–178
  future trends, 191–192
  per capita income, 3–5
  population size, 3–4
  social indicators, 4–5
  supports, 183–189
  values, 190–191
  women in the workforce, 1–3
Chinese Communist Party, 179, 181, 185
Christian Outreach (Uganda), 202
Church of Uganda, 201–203
Churches
  Brazil, 148, 151
  Great Britain, 53
  Mexico, 165
  Sweden, 112
  Uganda, 201–203
Clark, P., 131
Clinton, B., 134
Coalition of Labor Union Women (U.S.), 128
Coberly, S., 121
Commission on Family and Medical Leave
    (U.S.), 124
Community Care Act (Great Britain), 52, 58
Community Long-Term Care Insurance Law
    (Israel), 74, 77–78, 80–81
Community-Based Citizen's Group (Japan),
    93
Community-based programs, 217–218, 221
  Brazil, 148–149, 151
  Canada, 17–18
  China, 179, 220
  Germany, 31–32, 35, 43
  Great Britain, 51, 53–54, 59
  Israel, 74
  Japan, 89, 92–93
  Mexico, 165–167
  Uganda, 200–202
  United States, 123, 129, 136
Confederacion Regional Obrera Mexicana,
    170
Confucianism, 190
Connidis, I., 24

Conservative Party (Sweden), 113, 115, 218
Contractual work, 221
  China, 181–184
  Great Britain, 55
Cooperative Association (Japan), 93
Costello, A., 122
Costs of caregiving, 29–32, 213–214
  Brazil, 146–147, 153
  Canada, 13–14, 17–21
  China, 180–182
  Great Britain, 47–49, 56
  Israel, 72–73
  Japan, 84–86
  Mexico, 168
  Sweden, 104, 107–108
  United States, 121–122, 125
Council of Health and Welfare for the Aged
    (Japan), 98
Council of Relatives in Sweden, 105
Coutts, J., 17–18
Crain, M., 132
Creedon, M., 5, 121, 125–126, 128–129,
    131–132, 134
Crieco, M., 206
Crossroads (Great Britain), 59
Cultural issues
  Brazil, 155–156
  China, 190–191
  Great Britain, 54–55
  Japan, 95–96
  Mexico, 169–170
  Uganda, 199–201, 204–206
  United States, 131

Daatland, S. O., 116
Dale, A., 55
Dalley, G., 55
Dallinger, U., 29
Davidson, G., 77
Davis, E., 130
Day care
  Brazil, 148
  Canada, 16, 20
  China, 180, 186–187
  Germany, 35–37
  Great Britain, 48, 50–51, 53
  Israel, 74, 78–79
  Japan, 87, 89, 92–93
  Mexico, 164–165
  Sweden, 106, 109
  United States, 123–124, 126, 129
Decalogue (Mexico), 164
Declining workforce, 180–181
  Canada, 21
  Germany, 40

Declining workforce (*continued*)
  Mexico, 161, 169
Democratic Party (U.S.), 135
Demographic, Social and Economic Survey
    (Japan), 85
Demographics, 225–226
  Brazil, 143–144, 155
  Canada, 11–12
  China, 177, 180
  Germany, 29–30, 38–39
  Great Britain, 47–49, 54
  Israel, 69–73
  Japan, 84–85, 94–95
  Mexico, 171
  Sweden, 102, 108
  Uganda, 196
  United States, 130–131
DeMont, J., 18
Dependent Care Assistance Plan (U.S.),
    122–123, 125–128, 131, 133
Deutscher Bundestag (Germany), 39–40
Diet (Japan), 88, 90
DiMaggio, P., 225
Disability insurance (U.S.), 126
Disabled persons
  Brazil, 145–146, 154
  Canada, 21–22
  China, 180
  Germany, 30, 39
  Great Britain, 54
  Israel, 69–70, 76, 78–79, 81
  Mexico, 162
  Sweden, 102, 114–115
  United States, 130
Division of Services of the Elderly of the
    Histadrut (Israel), 76
Dong Fang Hardware Manufacturing
    (China), 183
Dunken, H., 122

Economic issues, 226–227
  Brazil, 152–153
  Canada, 17–18
  China, 178, 180–182
  Germany, 40
  Japan, 97–98
  Mexico, 168–169
  Uganda, 203–204
  United States, 133–135
Edebalk, P. G., 112–114
Educational Leave of Absence Act (Sweden),
    106
El Colegio de Mexico, 163
Elder care defined, 5–6
Eldercare Locator (U.S.), 125

Eliasson Lappalainen, R., 116
Elmér, Å., 108, 113–115
Emlen, A. C., 5, 121
Employee assistance programs
  Brazil, 148–149
  Canada, 16
  United States, 123, 127–128
Employee Benefit Research Institute, 132
Employees' Pension Insurance (Japan), 92,
    98
Employment Ministry (Mexico), 163
Employment trends, 211
Employment-based welfare (China),
    179–182
England, S., 124
Enterprise Law (China), 180
Erdwins, C. J., 72
Espring-Andersen, G., 110
Eternod, M., 163
Ethnic issues, 212–213
  Brazil, 143
  Canada, 22–23
  Germany, 31
  Great Britain, 52, 60, 64
  Israel, 69–70
  Japan, 95
  Mexico, 166
  Sweden, 110, 116
  United States, 121, 125, 129, 132–133
European Commission, 63
European Union, 63, 107, 212, 222
Evandrou, M., 48
Excelsior, 171

Factor, H., 76, 78
Families and Work Institute (U.S.), 120
Family and Medical Leave Act (U.S.),
    122–123, 128, 131, 133–134
Family Expenditure Study (Great Britain),
    55
Family Law Act (Canada), 23
Family leave, 215–216
  Canada, 16, 19, 21
  China, 184, 187
  Germany, 32, 37–38
  Great Britain, 50–51, 58
  Israel, 73–74
  Japan, 88–89, 92, 96, 99
  Sweden, 105, 109, 111
  Uganda, 199–200
  United States, 121–128, 131, 133–134
Family patterns, 222–223
  China, 177–178, 190–191
  Germany, 40
  Great Britain, 54, 64

Japan, 86–87, 94–99
Mexico, 169–170
Uganda, 195, 197–198, 204–206
United States, 130–131
Fancey, P., 20
Female Employment Management Basic
    Survey (Japan), 92
Feuerbach, E. J., 72
Fields, V., 120
Filial piety (China), 190–191, 222
First Nations (Canada), 22–23
Fishlow, A., 228
Flextime, 217, 222
    Brazil, 148–149
    Canada, 15–16, 19–21
    China, 184–185, 187
    Germany, 32, 34, 37–38, 42
    Great Britain, 50–51, 56, 58, 62
    Israel, 74
    Japan, 89, 92
    Sweden, 106, 109
    Uganda, 199–200
    United States, 123, 125–128, 136
Foner, P., 132
Food and Agriculture Organization of the
    United Nations, 196
Ford, A. B., 6
Foundation for Promotion of Silver Services
    (Japan), 93
Fraboni, M., 13
Frail elderly defined, 5–6
Friedland, R., 124–125, 129
Friedman, D., 120, 126
Friss, L., 121
Furåker, B., 102, 104
Fure Telephone Service (Japan), 89–90
Future trends, 220–223
    Brazil, 156–157
    Canada, 21–23
    China, 191–192
    Germany, 43–44
    Great Britain, 62–65
    Israel, 80–81
    Japan, 98–99
    Mexico, 171–172
    Sweden, 115–116
    Uganda, 208–209
    United States, 135–136

Gaetz, C.G.R., 20
Galatin Glassworks (U.S.), 132
Galinsky, E., 120, 126
Gans, H., 131
García, B., 162–163
Garrison, A., 130

Gaunt, D., 114–115
Gelfand, D., 125
Gender differences, 212
    Brazil, 144, 146, 155–157
    Canada, 13–14
    China, 178
    Germany, 30, 41
    Great Britain, 47–49, 54–55
    Israel, 70–71
    Japan, 85–86, 92, 98–99
    Mexico, 161–162, 169–170
    Sweden, 103, 106, 111
    Uganda, 196–198, 207–208
    United States, 120–121, 132–133
General Accounting Office (U.S.), 127, 134
General Federation of Labor (Israel), 73–75
General Household Survey (Great Britain),
    47–48, 53
General Law of the Social Security (Mexico),
    164
General Social Survey of Canada, 12–13
Gerling, V., 31
German Basic Law, 41
Germany, 29–46, 212–219, 224, 227–228
    aging trends, 3, 39
    East/West differences, 31–32
    ethnic issues, 31
    future policy factors, 38–41
    future trends, 43–44
    per capita income, 3–5
    policies and programs, 32–38
    population size, 3–4
    recommendations 41–43
    social indicators, 4–5
    strengths and weaknesses, 38
    women in the workforce, 1–3
    work/family concerns, 29–32
Ghana, 162
Gignac, M.M.A., 14–15, 24
Gilhooly, M., 49–50, 56–58, 61, 63
Ginn, J., 13, 48
Glendinning, C., 48
Glossop, 23
Gold Plan (Japan), 84–85, 88–89, 93, 96–97
Gonyea, J., 131
Gonzalez, C. P., 169
Gooch, R., 50
Goodstein, J., 225
Gorey, K., 120
Gornick, M., 125
Gottlieb, B. H., 12–14, 24
Government policies/programs, 216,
    218–221, 228
    Brazil, 148–151, 156–157
    Canada, 15–17

Government policies/programs (*continued*)
China, 179–182
Germany, 35–38, 43
Great Britain, 51–53, 57–59
Israel, 73–76
Japan, 88–91
Mexico, 163–165, 167
Sweden, 103–104, 106–109, 111
Uganda, 200–202
United States, 122–125, 133–134
Grafström, M., 103
Graveling, M., 49
Great Britain, 47–67, 208, 211–219, 222,
224, 227–228
aging trends, 3, 54
future trends, 62–65
per capita income, 3–5
policies/programs, 49–54
population size, 3–4
social indicators, 4–5
strengths and weaknesses, 59–62
support factors, 54–59
women in the workforce, 1–3
work/family concerns, 47–49
Greek immigrants (Germany), 31, 212
Grundy, E., 48
Guangdong Province, China, 182
Guangzhou Lamp Factory (China), 183
Guangzhou, China, 178, 182–184, 192
Guaranteed Income Supplement (Canada),
16
Guberman, N., 24
"Guest workers" (Germany), 31, 212
Gupta, C., 121
Gustav Vasa, King of Sweden, 112

Habib, J., 69, 71, 76, 78
Haghenbeck, A., 165
Hallman, B. C., 17, 22, 24
HALSA (Sweden), 103
Halsig, N., 41
Ham, C. R., 161
Hanley, P., 77
Haron, T., 77
Harris, K. M., 77
Hart, K., 162
Havens, B., 11, 17
Heald, M., 132
Health and Medical Services Act (Sweden),
109
Health Insurance for the Aged (Japan), 89,
91
Health Law for the Aged (Japan), 93
Health maintenance organizations (U.S.),
125

Health Ministry (Brazil), 150–156
Hedborg, A., 110
Hedin, B., 106
Help the Aged (Great Britain), 48–49, 53,
59, 61
Herlitz, C., 102
Hernandez, C., 126
Hispanic Americans, 121
Histadrut (Israel), 73–76
Historical issues
Brazil, 155–156
Japan, 96
Mexico, 168–169
Sweden, 110, 112–115
Uganda, 194–195
United States, 132–133
Hofemann, K., 38
Home care services, 220
Brazil, 148, 150–151
Canada, 16, 19–20
China, 186–187
Germany 36–37
Great Britain, 51, 53, 57, 64
Israel, 74, 76–78
Japan, 85, 89, 93–94, 96
Sweden, 107, 109, 111–112, 114–115
Uganda, 200–202
United States, 123, 129
Hooyman, N., 131
Hosokawa, Prime Minister (Japan), 90
Hua Nan Stationary Factory (China), 183
Hunt, G., 121, 126

IBM (Germany), 32
IBM (U.S.), 126
IG Metall (Germany), 34
Immigrants
Germany, 31, 212
Great Britain, 60
Israel, 69, 71
Income security policies (Canada), 18
Indians
Brazilian, 143
Canadian, 22
Israeli, 69
Mexican, 166
Informal care, 202, 221
Brazil, 146–147
Canada, 12–13, 18
China, 177–179
Germany, 31–33
Great Britain, 49, 53, 60
Israel, 71–72
Japan, 85, 96
Mexico, 164

Sweden, 102–106
Uganda, 197, 201
United States, 130, 135–136
Infratest Sozialfurschung (Germany), 29–31
Ingersoll-Dayton, B., 5., 121, 126
Institute of Development Studies, 162
Institute of Gerontology (Germany), 29–30
Institute of Manpower Studies (Great
    Britain), 60
Institute of Social Security and Services for
    Civil Servants, 164, 166
Institutional care, 218
  Brazil, 154
  China, 188
  Germany, 30
  Great Britain, 58
  Israel, 76
  Japan, 85, 93, 96
  Sweden, 102, 106–109, 112–115
  United States, 124
Instituto Brasileiro De Georgrafia e
    Estatística, 143–144, 149–150, 155
Instituto de Estadistica Geografía e
    Informatica (Mexico), 169
Instrumental care, 12
International Labour Office, 2, 102, 130,
    155, 161, 196
International Monetary Fund, 221
Inuit Canadians, 22
Invalid Care Allowance (Great Britain), 48
Iraqi Israelis, 69
Irwin, S. H., 22
Ishii-Kuntz, M., 87–88, 94–96
Ishikawa, K., 84
Israel, 68–83, 212–213, 215–216, 218–219,
    222, 224, 227–228
  aging trends, 3, 73–74
  demographics, 69–70
  future trends, 80–81
  per capita income, 3–5
  policies/programs, 73–80
  population size, 3–4
  social indicators, 4–5
  women in the workforce, 1–3
  work/family issues, 69–73
Israeli Alzheimer's Association, 74
Italian immigrants (Germany), 31, 212

Janigan, M., 17
Japan Labor Institute, 88
Japan, 84–100, 212–214, 216–219, 221–
    228
  aging trends, 3, 94–95, 97–98
  demographics, 94–95
  future trends, 98–99

per capita income, 3–5
population size, 3–4
social indicators, 4–5
support factors, 94–98
supports, 88–94
women in the workforce, 1–3
work/family concerns, 85–88
Japanese Brazilians, 143
Japanese National and Social Health
    Insurance Schemes, 94
Japanese Trade Union Confederation, 91
Jelin, M., 130
Jette, A., 129
Job sharing
  Canada, 15, 20–21
  Germany, 37
  Great Britain, 50–51
  Sweden, 109
  Uganda, 200
  United States, 123
Johansson, L., 102, 104, 106, 115
Johnson, K. L., 19, 23
Johnston, 136
Jones, D., 52
Joseph, A. E., 17, 21, 24
Joshi, H., 47, 55
Junta de Asistencia Privada (Mexico), 165
Jusidman, C., 162–163

Kahn, A., 130
Kalache, A., 145–146, 156
Kamerman, S. B., 20, 130, 132
Kampala, 207
Kaplan, E., 75
Karsch, U., 145–146, 156
Katz, S., 6
Kaufmann, F., 32
Keefe, J. M., 24, 15, 19–20, 23
Keigher, S., 124
Keller, W., 154
Kelloway, E. K., 13, 14, 21, 24
Kenya, 194, 196
King, Y., 71, 76, 79
Kinsella, K., 69, 71, 145, 157
Klauder, W., 49
Kleiman, E., 74
Knesset (Israel), 77
Korazim, M., 78, 80
Korean Japanese, 95
Korpi, W., 110
Krenz, C., 121
Krouze, M., 130
Kuratorium Deutsche Altershilfe
    (Germany), 39
Kuznets, S., 223, 226

Laaksonen, 179
Labor insurance (China), 179, 185, 187–188
Labor reforms (China), 180–182
Labor unions, 216–217, 222
 Brazil, 148–149, 154–155
 Canada, 16
 China, 185–186
 Germany, 34–35, 37, 42
 Great Britain, 51–52, 58–59
 Israel, 73–75
 Japan, 89, 91–92
 Mexico, 167, 170
 Sweden, 110, 116
 Uganda, 200
 United States, 123, 128–129, 132–133,
 135
Labour Bureau of the Guangzhou Municipal
 (China), 183
Lake Victoria, 194
Lam, 179
Lang, F., 41
Language barriers (Canada), 22, 212
Law for the Welfare of Employees Engaged
 in the Care of a Family Member
 (Japan), 88
Law on Protection of the Rights and
 Interests of the Elderly (China), 191
Lawton, D., 55
Lawton, M., 6
Lazcko, F., 56
Lechner, V., 5, 121, 126, 128–129, 131–132,
 134
Lero, D. S., 19, 22–23
Leung, J.C.B., 177, 179–180, 185, 191
Levins, C. L., 24
Lewis, J., 55, 57, 59, 62
Lewis, S., 57, 59, 62
Liberal Democratic Party (Japan), 91
Liebig, P., 133
Life expectancies
 Brazil, 145, 157
 Germany, 39
 Israel, 69
 Uganda, 195
 United States, 130
Lifshitz, C., 72
Liljeström, R., 111
Linsk, N., 124, 130, 135–136
Listhaug, O., 110
Livingstone, S. R., 22
LOCATEL (Mexico), 166
Lodge, G. C., 96, 131
Logue, J., 111
Long-Term Care Insurance
 Germany, 32–33, 35–38, 41, 44

 Japan, 89–91, 97
 United States, 123, 126
Long-Term Care Leave (Japan), 88–97, 99
Long-term care services, 218–220
Lutheran Church (Sweden), 112

MacBride-King, J. L., 15
MacDonald, G., 21
Maddison, A., 149, 151–153, 155, 165, 170
Madeiros, M., 146
Mahovich, P., 126
Maia, R., 152
Makino, K., 84
Managed care programs (U.S.), 125
Management and Coordination Agency,
 Statistical Bureau (Japan), 84, 86, 91,
 93
Manager training, 217
 Canada, 16, 20–21
 Germany, 42
 Great Britain, 52
 United States, 122–124, 126–127
Manitoba, 11
Mann, K., 56
Manzochi, L., 146
Marcovina, S., 121
Marklund, S., 110
Marriage Law (China), 177
Marshal, V. W., 24
Martin, A., 116
Martin, J., 48
Martinez, 126
Martinez-Lara, J., 154
Martin-Matthews, A., 12–15, 19, 22, 24
Matthews, S. H., 13
McCaffrey, D., 77
McDaniel, S. A., 14–15, 18, 20
McDermott, S., 129
McLaughlin, E., 48
McMaster University, 24
McPherson, B. D., 12, 22–23
Meals-on-wheels
 China, 186–187
 Israel, 78
 Sweden, 107
Means, R., 58
Media influence (Brazil), 153–154, 156
Medicaid (U.S.), 123–125
Medical leave
 Canada, 16
 China, 184, 187
 Germany, 37
 Great Britain, 51
 Israel, 74
 Japan, 89, 92

Uganda, 200
Medicare (U.S.), 16, 123–125, 131
Medina Lima, I., 165
Meidner, R., 110
Meiji Restoration (Japan), 96
Mercedes Benz (Germany), 32
Metcalf, H., 60
Métis Canadians, 22
Metropolitan Life Insurance Company
    (U.S.), 121
Mexican Association of Malta (Mexico), 165
Mexican Institute of Social Security,
    163–164, 166, 168
Mexico City, 165–166
Mexico, 160–173, 212–214, 216, 218–224,
    226–227
  aging trends, 3, 161
  demographics, 171
  future trends, 171–172
  per capita income, 3–5
  population size, 3–4
  social indicators, 4–5
  strengths and weaknesses, 166–168
  support factors, 168–171
  supports, 163–166
  women in the workforce, 1–3
  work/family concerns, 160–163
Migration, 214, 222, 229
  Brazil, 145
  Germany, 40
  Mexico, 168–169
  Uganda, 195, 205–206
Ministério da Previdência e Assistência
    Social (Brazil), 149
Ministerio da Saúde (Brazil), 150
Ministry of Education (China), 182
Ministry of Family and Senior Citizens
    (Germany), 29
Ministry of Finance (Japan), 93
Ministry of Health (Israel), 74–76, 81
Ministry of Health and Welfare (Japan),
    84–85, 90, 93–94, 96
Ministry of Home Affairs (Japan), 93
Ministry of Labor (Japan), 86–88, 90, 92
Ministry of Labor and Social Affairs (Israel),
    74–76, 78
Moen, P., 120
Monitor, The, 208
Montes de Oca, Z. V., 160, 163
Moody, K., 132, 135
Moore, C., 23
Moore, E., 12, 23
Morgan, P., 57–58
Morginstin, B., 77–78
Moroccan Israelis, 69

Moscovice, I., 77
Moskowitz, R. W., 6
Moss, P., 54
Mossberg, A.-B., 102, 104
Mukono, Uganda, 202, 205, 209
Mulira, R., 197–198, 205
Municipal Labour Bureau (China), 182, 185
Muñoz, H., 163
Museveni, President (Uganda), 195, 203,
    208–209
Muslim Israelis, 70
Mutual Aid Pensions (Japan), 98
Myers, R., 124

Naegele, G., 29, 31–32, 35, 38–41
Nakasero Market (Uganda), 198
Namuwongo Market (Uganda), 208
Nann, R. C., 185, 191
Naon, D., 71–72, 76–78
National Association of AAAs (U.S.), 125
National Basic Pension Law (Sweden), 114
National Board of Health and Welfare
    (Sweden), 105, 108, 115
National Caregivers Survey (Great Britain),
    49, 61
National Carers Strategy (Great Britain), 59
National Council on Aging (Canada), 18
National Health Insurance (Japan), 89, 91
National Health Insurance Bill (Israel),
    74–76
National Health Service (Great Britain), 51,
    52, 58
National Health Survey (Mexico), 165
National Institute for Adult Education
    (Mexico), 165
National Institute for the Aged (Mexico),
    165
National Institute on Aging (U.S.), 2
National Insurance Institute (Israel), 75–77
National Pension (Japan), 89, 91, 98
National Policy on Care for the Elderly
    (Canada), 217
National Politics of the Elderly (Brazil),
    149–150, 154
National Security and Assistance System
    (Brazil), 149
National Social Insurance Board (Sweden),
    105
National Social Security Fund (Uganda), 201
National System of Integral Development of
    the Family (Mexico), 165
National Union of Retired Persons (Israel),
    74
National University (Mexico), 163
National Welfare Tax Bill (Japan), 90–91

National Work-Force Surveys (Mexico), 161
Neal, M., 5–6, 120, 126, 130, 132, 135–136
Neri, A., 155
New Eldercare System (Japan), 98
New Gold Plan (Japan), 93, 95, 97–98
New York City
  Labor Council, 128
  Office on the Aging, 129
Nile River, 194
Nilsson Motevasel, I., 116
Nippes, J., 126
Nkoyoyo, Archbishop, 198, 202
Noam, G., 71
Noden, S., 56
Non-Governmental Organization
  Committee on Aging (Uganda), 204
Norland, J., 22
North American Free Trade Agreement, 169
Northwest Territories, Canada, 12
Nova Scotia Home Life Support Program, 19
Nursing homes
  Brazil, 148, 150, 157
  Canada, 16
  China, 187, 220
  Germany, 37
  Great Britain, 50, 53, 58
  Israel, 74
  Japan, 93
  Mexico, 165–167
  Sweden, 107–109, 112–115
  Uganda, 200–203, 209
  United States, 123–124, 129
Nursing Leave (Japan), 97

Ochanomizu University (Japan), 84
Ochi, T., 87
Odén, B., 110, 113–114
Office of Population, Census and Surveys
  (Great Britain), 54
Ohmae, K., 229
Ohshima, C., 96
Ojulu, E., 206, 209
Okamoto, T., 85, 93, 98
Old Age Campaign Center (Uganda),
  201–202
Old Age Insurance Committee (Sweden),
  113
Old Age Pension Scheme (Sweden), 113
Old Age Security (Canada), 16, 18
Older Americans Act (U.S.), 125, 129
Oliveira, O., 163
Oliver, C., 225
One-child policy (China), 191–192
Ontario Court of Appeal, 23

Ontario Ministry of Community and Social
  Services, 13, 19
Ontario Women's Directorate, 13, 19
Opportunity 2000 (Great Britain), 62
Orloff, A., 133
Orthodox Jews, 70
ÖTV (Germany), 34
Oxfordshire County Council (Great Britain),
  49, 58
Oyakoko Loan (Japan), 91

Pacheco, E., 162–163
Packer, 136
Paid Caregiver Program (Sweden), 103–104
Pan-American Health Organization, 156
Panamerican University, 166
Parental Leave of Absence Act (Sweden),
  106
Paris, H., 20
Parker, G., 48, 55
Parker, M. G., 116
Parker, S., 162
Parsons, D., 32
Partido Revolucionario Institucional
  (Mexico), 170
Part-time work, 221
  Brazil, 149
  Canada, 19–20
  Germany, 32, 35, 37
  Great Britain, 50, 55, 58, 62
  Japan, 86, 89–90, 92
  Sweden, 106, 109, 111
  Uganda, 199–201
  United States, 123, 125–126
Peer Counseling Training Program (U.S.),
  128
Penhale, B., 59
Pensions, 214–215, 218–219
  Brazil, 149–150, 153
  Canada, 16
  China, 181, 185
  Germany, 36
  Japan, 89, 89, 91, 98
  Mexico, 164, 167, 170
  Sweden, 112–114
  Uganda, 200–201
  United States, 124–125, 132
Perkins, S., 54
Persson, I., 106, 111
Petty, D., 121
Pflegeversicherungsgesetz, 32
Phillips, J., 49–50, 53, 56–57, 59–61
Pickard, J., 56
Pierson, P., 107

Plan to Integrate Government Actions (Brazil), 150
Political issues
 Brazil, 152–153
 Germany, 41
 Japan, 96–97
 Mexico, 170
 Uganda, 203–204
 United States, 133–135
Poor Relief Ordinance (Sweden), 112
Portuguese Brazilians, 143
Poverty, 214, 218, 226–227
 Brazil, 143–144, 151–153
 Mexico, 162–163, 170
 Uganda, 195, 197–198, 202–204
 United States, 124–125
Powell, W., 225
Presse- und Informationsamt der Bundesregierung (Germany), 38
Princess Royal Trust for Carers (Great Britain), 56–57, 62
Pringle, K., 64
Privatization of government-owned businesses, 221
Privatization of social welfare programs, 220–221
 Canada, 17–18
 Germany, 41
 Great Britain, 53, 58
 Japan, 98–99
 Mexico, 165, 168
 Sweden, 115–116
 United States, 124
Program for Retired Teachers (Mexico), 165
Project Light (Mexico), 166
Project of the Social Assistance and Security Ministry (Brazil), 153
Public Insurance Scheme for Long-Term Care (Japan), 90–91, 93–95, 98
Public/private partnerships, 228–229
 United States, 129–130
Putnam, R., 110

Rake, A., 194, 203
Ramos, L., 146
Ramsey, D., 49
Rank Xerox (Great Britain), 50
Reading, P., 59
Recommendations, 228–231
 Germany, 41–43
Redpath, C., 49–50, 56–58, 61, 63
Regional Women's Association (Japan), 93
Reichert, M., 29, 35, 38, 42
Rengo, 91

Respite care, 220
 Germany, 35–37
 Great Britain, 51, 53, 57
 Israel, 79–81
 Japan, 89, 92–93
 Sweden, 105–106
 Uganda, 201–202
 United States, 124, 126
Revista Veja, 144
Rice, R., 120
Rio de Janeiro, Brazil, 143, 150
Roberts, C., 48
Robison, J., 120
Rosa, T., 146
Rosenberg, M., 12
Rosenbloom, J., 125
Rosenkranz, D., 39
Rosenthal, C. J., 13, 15, 18, 23–24
Rossi, I., 52, 56–57, 61–62
Rothgang, H., 35
Royal Bank of Scotland, 50
Royal Commission on Long Term Care (Great Britain), 59
Rückert, W., 39
Rural/urban differences, 213–214, 218
 Brazil, 144–145, 150, 157
 Canada, 22
 China, 178–179, 181
 Mexico, 161, 170
 Uganda, 195, 198–199, 205–206
Rürup, B., 40
Rwanda, 194
Rwenzori Mountains, 194

Sakamoto, S., 93
San Vincent Foundation (Mexico), 165
Sansom, S., 122–124
Santos, C. A., 146
São Paulo, 143, 146, 150, 152
Saskatchewan, 11
Scanlan, J., 121
Scharlach, A., 121–124
Schellenberg, G., 18, 21
Schemo, D. J., 221
Schneekloth, U., 34
Schneider, N., 39
Schulte, B., 35
Schütze, Y., 39, 41
Schwartz, 121
Secretaria da Assistência Social (Brazil), 149
Select Committee on Aging (U.S.), 120, 130
Senior Care Service (Great Britain), 53
Senior recreational centers (Japan), 89, 91, 93

Seniorcare Surveys (Great Britain), 61
Sepúlveda, J., 161–162, 165, 168
Serial caregiving, 12
SFS (Sweden), 101
Sha, J. C., 178
Shalev, 73, 75
Shanghai, 192
Shapiro, E., 17, 21
Sheltered housing
  Israel, 74, 79–80
  Sweden, 107–109, 114–115
  United States, 136
Shinshinto Party (Japan), 91
Shtarkshall, M., 79
Sick Fund (Israel), 73–76, 81
Siemens (Germany), 32
Silver Service (Japan), 89, 93
Simon-Rusinowitz, L., 124
Simson, S., 126
Single-parent households
  Germany, 40
  Great Britain, 54
  United States, 130
Sistema Único de Saúde (Brazil), 148,
    150–152
Skocpol, T., 133–134
Smith, K., 129
Smith, P., 20
Smith, R., 58
Snell, J. G., 23
Sobol, E., 71, 81
Social changes, 225–226
  Brazil, 152–153
  China, 178, 226–227
  Germany, 39–40
  Japan, 95–96
  Uganda, 197–198
  United States, 130–131
Social Democratic Party (Sweden), 109–111,
    114–116
Social Health Insurance (Japan), 92
Social Insurance Program (Sweden), 107,
    113
Social Security Trustee's Report (U.S.), 124
Social Security, 218
  Brazil, 148–149, 153, 156
  China, 179, 181, 187
  Great Britain, 48
  Israel, 74, 77
  Japan, 96–97
  Mexico, 161, 163–167
  Sweden, 109
  Uganda, 201
  United States 121, 123–124, 126, 150

Social Services Act (Sweden), 101, 104, 109,
    116
Social Welfare System (Sweden), 108–111
  goals, 110–111
Socialstyrelsen, 107–108
Sodei, T., 84–87, 95–96, 98
Sommer, B., 39
Soviet Israelis, 69, 71
Spanish immigrants (Germany), 31, 212
Spicker, P., 157
Spouse's/Widowed Spouse's Allowance
    (Canada), 16
Stanger, J., 122–124
State Units on Aging (U.S.), 125
Statistics Canada, 13
Statistics Sweden, 102, 110
Stevens, B., 131–135
Stevenson, O., 62
Stiglitz, J., 227, 229
Stolz-Willig, B., 32, 34, 43
Stone, L. O., 13, 15, 20
Strain, L. A., 18
Strosberg, N., 71, 76
Sudan, 194
Sundström, G., 102–104
Supports for eldercare, 23, 215–220
  Brazil, 147–151
  Canada, 15–18, 23
  China, 183–189
  Germany, 32–38
  Great Britain, 49–54
  Israel, 73–80
  Japan, 88–94
  Mexico, 160–163
  Sweden, 103–108
  Uganda, 199–202
  United States, 122–130
Survey on Life and Care in Old Age (Japan),
    86
Sussex University (England), 162
Sweden, 101–119, 124, 211–213, 215–216,
    218–219, 224–225, 227–228
  aging trends, 3, 102, 108
  demographics, 102
  future trends, 115–116
  per capita income, 3–5
  population size, 3–4
  social indicators, 4–5
  support factors, 108–115
  supports for caregivers, 103–107
  supports for older persons, 107–108
  women in the workforce, 1–3
  work/family issues, 102–103
Swedish Eurobarometer, 108

Swedish Parliament, 103, 112–115
Swedish Poor Relief Alliance, 113
Szebehely, M., 102

Taeuber, C. M., 3, 69, 70, 145, 157
Taft Hartley Act (U.S.), 133
Tamir, Y., 69
Tanzania, 194
Tax issues
  Canada, 18, 20
  Germany, 37, 43
  Israel, 74–77
  Japan, 89, 91–92
  Mexico, 163
  Sweden, 107, 111, 113
  United States, 122–124, 128, 131, 136
Taylor, K., 57
Tecnológico de Monterrey, 165
Telecommuting, 215–217
  Canada, 15, 19–20
  Great Britain, 50–51
  Japan, 88, 90
  United States, 125–126, 136
Third Age (Mexico), 166
Thorslund, M., 103, 116
Tianjin, 177
Tindale, J. A., 22
Tinker, A., 48
Toner, R., 135
Totta, J. M., 20
Tracy, M. B., 168
Trade Union Council (Great Britain), 52
Turkish immigrants (Germany), 31, 212
Turner, M., 54
Twigg, J., 48, 52–53, 55, 60

U.S. Bureau of the Census, 2, 102, 122,
    128–130, 132, 135, 160, 181, 197–198
U.S. Congress, 128, 133
U.S. Constitution, 133
U.S. Department of Commerce, 122, 128,
    130, 132, 135, 160, 177, 181, 197–198
U.S. Department of Labor, 127–129,
    227–228
U.S. Social Security Administration, 163,
    165, 199, 201
U.S. Women's Bureau, 124
Uganda AIDS Commission, 207
Uganda Council of Women, 208
Uganda, 194–210, 214–216, 218–224,
    226–227
  aging trends, 3, 196–197
  demographics, 196
  future trends, 208–209

per capita income, 3–5
population size, 3–4
social indicators, 4–5
strengths and weaknesses, 202–203
support factors, 203–208
supports, 199–202
women in the workforce, 1–3
work/family concerns, 196–199
Uganda: A Country Study, 194, 196, 207
Ujimoto, K. V., 24
Underwood, N., 18
Unemployment insurance (U.S.), 126
Unique Health System (Brazil), 150
United Nations Development Program, 169,
    195–196, 198–199, 204
United Nations Economics Commission,
    144, 151–152, 155
United Nations Educational, Scientific, and
    Cultural Organization, 4, 204
United Nations Global Program on AIDS,
    207
United Nations Year of Older Persons, 226
United Nations, 146, 153, 196
United States, 120–139, 195, 199, 211–213,
    215–219, 222, 224, 227–228
  aging trends, 3, 120, 136
  demographics, 130–131
  future trends, 135–136
  per capita income, 3–5
  population size, 3–4
  social indicators, 4–5
  support factors, 130–135
  supports, 122–130
  women in the workforce, 1–3
  work/family concerns, 120–122
Universidad Iberoamericana (Mexico), 166
Université de Québec à Montréal (Canada),
    24
Université de Québec (Canada), 24
University of Guelph (Canada), 24
University of Toronto (Canada), 24
University of Western Ontario (Canada), 24

Van Buren, L., 203–204
Veras, R., 145
Vitaliano, P., 121
Vogel, E. F., 96, 131

Wagner, D. L., 6, 120, 126
Walder, 179
Walker, A., 107
Wang, M., 178
Ward, C., 55
Waterson, J., 53

Watkins, 169
Weihl, H., 77
Weir, M., 133
Welfare Law for the Aged (Japan), 93, 96
Welfare Pension Fure (Japan), 89
Western, B., 132–135
Whatmore, K., 47, 57
Widow's Pension Act (Canada), 16
Wiener, J. M., 77
Wilensky, H., 226–228
Williamson, J., 124
Wilson, L., 126
Winter of Discontent, (Great Britain), 52
Winter, D., 48
Wister, A., 23
Women
  Brazilian workforce, 155–156
  British workforce, 48–49, 54–55, 57–58
  changing roles in Japan, 86–87, 95
  changing roles in Uganda, 204–205
  Chinese workforce, 178
  family relations in China, 190–191
  German trade unions, 34
  German workforce, 39–41
  Israeli workforce, 70–71
  Japanese workforce, 85, 92, 94–95, 97–99
  Mexican workforce, 161, 171
  predominant caregivers, 13
  Swedish workforce, 102, 110–111
  U.S. workforce, 120, 130–131, 136
  working outside the home, 1–3
Women's Employment Survey (Great
  Britain), 48
Work and Eldercare Research Group
  (Canada), 11–13, 24
Work culture
  Great Britain, 52, 55–57

  Japan, 95–96
  United States, 123
Work/family concerns
  Brazil, 144–147
  China, 177–178
  Germany, 29–32
  Great Britain, 47–49
  Israel, 69–73
  Japan, 85–88
  Mexico, 160–163
  Sweden, 102–103
  Uganda, 196–199
  United States, 120–122
Working Hours Act (Sweden), 106
World Bank, 2, 4, 145, 152, 170, 195, 197,
  205, 214, 219, 221, 224, 229
World Development Report 1997, 224
World Health Organization, 154, 156,
  194–195, 205
World War II, 96, 132, 143

Xia, C. L., 178
Xu, Q., 190

Yemenite Israelis, 69
Young and Elderly in Society (Uganda),
  202
Yuan, F., 177
Yugoslavian immigrants (Germany), 31, 212
Yukon, Canada, 12

Zaire, 194
Zhu Jiang Shirt Factory (China), 183
Zhu, C. Y., 190
Zipkin, A., 78